Case Formulation in Cognitiv Behaviour Therapy

Case formulation is the core skill of every practitioner carrying out psychological therapies at an advanced level. It is essential in providing an idiosyncratic understanding of individual clients and their clinical problems.

In this volume, Nicholas Tarrier brings together contributions that cover many of the clinical issues that will challenge practitioners in their practice of cognitive behaviour therapy. Each chapter serves as a practical guide to overcoming a particular clinical challenge and is grounded solidly in research evidence. Experts in each individual field discuss how case formulation aids clinical practice in their chosen area and demonstrate how detailed understanding of the clinical case leads to improved therapeutic outcome. Subjects covered include:

- A biopsychosocial and evolutionary approach to formulation with a special focus on shame.
- Case conceptualisation in complex PTSD.
- Cognitive behavioural case formulation in complex eating disorders.

This indispensable guide to formulating clinical cases will be welcomed by clinical psychologists, psychiatrists, psychiatric nurses, counsellors, social workers and students.

Nicholas Tarrier is Professor of Clinical Psychology at the University of Manchester. He has pioneered the development and evaluation of cognitive behaviour therapies for schizophrenia and other psychological disorders.

Wm 425.5 TAR   £24.99

Case Formulation in Cognitive Behaviour Therapy

The treatment of challenging and complex cases

Edited by Nicholas Tarrier

Routledge
Taylor & Francis Group

LONDON AND NEW YORK

First published 2006
by Routledge
27 Church Road, Hove, East Sussex BN3 2FA

Simultaneously published in the USA and Canada
by Routledge
270 Madison Avenue, New York, NY 10016

Reprinted 2007 (twice)

Routledge is an imprint of the Taylor & Francis Group, an informa business

Typeset in Times by
RefineCatch Limited, Bungay, Suffolk
Printed and bound in Great Britain by
TJ International Ltd, Padstow, Cornwall
Paperback cover design by Sandra Heath

British Library Cataloguing in Publication Data
A catalogue record for this book is available from the British Library

Library of Congress Cataloging-in-Publication Data
Case formulation in cognitive behaviour therapy : the treatment of
   challenging and complex cases / edited by Nicholas Tarrier.
      p. cm.
   Includes biographical references and index.
   ISBN 1-58391-840-X (alk. paper) — ISBN 1-58391-841-8 (pbk. :
   alk. paper)
1. Cognitive therapy. 2. Cognitive therapy—Case studies. I. Tarrier,
Nicholas.
RC489.C63.C33 2006
616.89'142—dc22   2005043532

ISBN: 978-1-58391-840-1 (hbk)
ISBN: 978-1-58391-841-8 (pbk)

Contents

List of tables and figures

Tables

Figures

Notes on contributors

Peter V. Armstrong is an experienced cognitive therapist, trainer and supervisor. He has particular interests in interpersonal process in therapy and provides supervision to experienced cognitive therapists who are developing specific therapeutic approaches for a range of problems. He is Deputy Course Director for the Newcastle Postgraduate Diploma in Cognitive Therapy. Over the last three years he has developed a supervisory practice to support supervisors, especially those starting supervision for the Newcastle diploma course.

Ivy M. Blackburn was Director of the Diploma in Cognitive Therapy course at the Newcastle Cognitive and Behavioural Therapies Centre from 1993 to 2000. Before coming to Newcastle, she was Senior Lecturer in Clinical Psychology in the Department of Psychiatry, Edinburgh University. She is currently Emeritus Professor of Cognitive Therapy at the University of Northumbria in Newcastle.

Jake Bowley is a clinical psychologist who has worked with refugee and asylum seekers for the last five years. He currently works with Children and Family Services in Rochdale as part of a 'Haven' project funded by the charity Action for Children in Conflict (http://www.actionchildren.org). Working with local schools and teachers, this provides direct psychological interventions to children and families, as well as giving consultation and supervision to teachers and other health professionals in their work with asylum seekers. Prior to this, Jake worked in Salford, where he provided cognitive therapy and other psychological interventions to adult asylum seekers in a primary care setting, and was involved in developing the mainstreaming of the local Primary Care Services' provision to adult asylum seekers.

Richard J. Brown received a PhD in psychology from University College London in 1999. He then spent three years conducting post-doctoral research on medically unexplained symptoms at the Institute of Neurology and National Hospital for Neurology and Neurosurgery, London. He completed his clinical psychology training at the University of Manchester in 2004 and has since worked as a lecturer in clinical psychology and as a clinical psychologist in Manchester. He has published several theoretical and empirical papers on medically unexplained symptoms and continues to conduct research and clinical work with this client group.

Helen Combes is Clinical Lecturer on the Shropshire and Staffordshire Clinical Psychology Training course. She currently works as a clinical psychologist in the child specialty for North Staffordshire Combined Healthcare NHS Trust. She has completed research in applied behaviour analysis and stimulus equivalence and has published various articles on working with people with learning disabilities. She is particularly interested in the philosophy of science and applied behaviour analysis.

Chris Cullen is Professor of Clinical Psychology at the University of Keele, and Clinical Director for Psychological Services with North Staffordshire Combined Healthcare NHS Trust. He has research interests in many areas, including sexual abuse, staff training, deinstitutionalisation, challenging behaviour and therapeutic interventions for children with autism. For many years he has been engaged in applying radical behaviourism in clinical practice.

Kate M. Davidson has worked in the National Health Service since qualifying in clinical psychology in 1981 from the University of Edinburgh. She is founding Director of the Glasgow Institute of Psychosocial Intervention, a joint NHS/university venture with the purpose of providing training and supervision to staff in psychosocial interventions and carrying out research in psychosocial therapies.

Alyson Flitcroft recently obtained her doctorate in clinical psychology at the Department of Clinical Psychology, University of Newcastle, and is currently working in Adult Services in Gateshead, UK.

Mark H. Freeston is an experienced researcher and trainer in CBT approaches to anxiety disorders. After spending the earlier part of his career in Canada, he moved to the UK five years ago. He is Professor of Clinical Psychology at the University of Newcastle and Director of Training and Research at the Newcastle Cognitive and Behavioural Therapies Centre, where he is Course Director of the Newcastle Postgraduate Diploma in Cognitive Therapy.

Paul Gilbert has a long-term interest in mood disorders related to shame. In recent years he has been developing compassion-focused training for people who come from traumatic backgrounds and find self-compassion difficult. This work has emerged from the complexities of treating intense shame-based difficulties.

Allison G. Harvey is a member of the Clinical Psychology faculty at the Department of Psychology, University of California at Berkeley. She has spent the past six years working at the Department of Experimental Psychology and Psychiatry at the University of Oxford, UK, where she directed and worked as a therapist on a study testing the efficacy of a new cognitive therapy treatment for chronic insomnia. The focus of her current work is to understand better the mechanisms that lead to comorbidity between sleep disturbance and psychological disorders and to develop better treatments for patients who suffer from sleep disturbance across disorders.

Ian A. James is Consultant Clinical Psychologist at the Centre for Health of the Elderly, Newcastle upon Tyne, and Research Tutor at the University of Newcastle.

Steven Jones is Reader in Clinical Psychology at the University of Manchester. He also holds the post of Honorary Consultant Clinical Psychologist with the Pennine Care Trust. He has a longstanding interest in the development of psychological approaches to the treatment of severe mental illness and in particular bipolar disorder. He has also been engaged in the development and evaluation of psychological models of bipolar disorder.

Willem Kuyken is a clinical psychologist specialising in recurrent depression. His clinical work, research and training with people with mood disorders spans more than a decade. After completing his PhD and qualifying as a clinical psychologist, he worked as a postdoctoral fellow at the Centre for Cognitive Therapy, University of Pennsylvania, for two years. He is currently Co-Director of the Mood Disorders Centre, a research, clinical and training centre in Exeter, UK.

Anna Lavender is a clinical psychologist within the Eating Disorders Service at the Maudsley Hospital, London, and Honorary Tutor at the Institute of Psychiatry, London. She qualified in clinical psychology and trained in cognitive behavioural therapy at the Institute of Psychiatry. Her clinical and research interests include obsessive-compulsive cognitions in eating disorders, rumination in eating disorders and mindfulness-based cognitive therapy.

Deborah Lee is a consultant clinical psychologist, who has specialised in working with traumatised people for 12 years. She is an honorary lecturer in clinical psychology at University College London. She currently works in the Oxford Cognitive Therapy Trauma Service and the Clinical Psychology Department at the Warneford Hospital, Oxford. She also works at the Traumatic Stress Clinic, London, where she offers supervision and training. She has extensive experience in the field of trauma and PTSD as a clinician and has contributed to the dissemination of her clinical knowledge through her writing and workshops. Her clinical and research inter-

xiv   Notes on contributors

ests lie in working with complex cases, shame and developing compassion in cognitive therapy.

Ulrike Schmidt is Reader in Eating Disorders at the Institute of Psychiatry, London, and Honorary Consultant Psychiatrist at the Maudsley Hospital, London. She qualified at Düsseldorf University, Germany, and trained in psychiatry at the Maudsley Hospital, London. Her research interests include the aetiology and management of eating disorders, in particular brief psychological treatments.

Gary L. Sidley is a consultant clinical psychologist with Bolton, Salford and Trafford Mental Health NHS Trust. His clinical work is with adults with severe and/or complex mental health problems within a secondary mental health service. His research interests concern the psychological processes that underpin suicidal behaviour, and he achieved a PhD from the University of Manchester in 2001. He is also a manager of an Early Intervention Service for people suffering first episode psychosis.

Nicholas Tarrier has been Professor of Clinical Psychology at the University of Manchester since 1991. He has pioneered the development and evaluation of cognitive behaviour therapies for schizophrenia and other psychological disorders, such as PTSD. He has an interest in the process and development of cognitive behaviour therapy and how research and clinical practice interact and inform each other.

Adrian Wells' research interests include cognitive factors in the cause and maintenance of emotional disorders, cognitive theory and cognitive therapy of anxiety disorders, including social phobia, generalised anxiety, obsessive-compulsive disorder and PTSD. He is the pioneer of metacognitive theory and therapy based on information processing approaches to emotion.

Preface

This book came about due to the increasing interest in and adoption of the case formulation approach to cognitive-behavioural treatments for a range of psychological and behavioural disorders. Many years of teaching case formulation to first-year trainee clinical psychologists with my colleague, Dr Rachel Calam, at the University of Manchester, and prior to that at the University of Sydney and before that even in providing clinical supervision in the National Health Service in Salford, has provided me with the opportunity for much thought and reflection about the nature and process of case formulation. I cannot honestly say that I always succeeded in doing this with the utmost clarity. But it did kindle a desire to attempt to produce a book in which a number of experts put their thoughts and opinions down on how case formulation aided their clinical practice in their chosen area. When I started teaching case formulation the term was rarely heard: now its use is widespread. Some professions, such as clinical psychology, and many schools and practitioners of cognitive behaviour therapy view case formulation as central and essential to their clinical treatments. This represents both a desire to understand patients from a psychological perspective and a recognition of the complexity and heterogeneity of the clinical presentations and problems of clients and patients. It also represents a feeling that strictly adhered to and rigidly prescribed 'one size fits all' treatment protocols are not suitable for many clinical problems and patients, and do not capture either the complexity of applied psychology or the depth and expertise of clinicians' skills and knowledge. The devil is in the detail. Individualised formulations which drive individualised treatment strategies would appear, on an *a priori* basis at least, to be most likely to be effective, ethical, inclusive and acceptable. The alternative to a rigid protocol is an empirically based and scientifically established procedure of case formulation leading to individualised and appropriate treatments. We may not be in a position to say that all the questions have yet been identified, let alone answered satisfactorily, but hopefully this book will move knowledge slightly further on. This volume attempts to put the argument for a case formulation approach by combining an impressive array of contributors, experts in their field, to provide guidelines to the case formulation of a series of topics which I trust will be of interest to practitioners and researchers. As with all edited books I am confident that some interesting areas will have been omitted or someone's pet topic over-looked. An editor is always constrained by length and the availability of authors. My hope is that within these pages there is something to interest and stimulate almost anybody who is interested in cognitive behaviour therapy and psychological treatments, so that those who are disappointed by omission do not judge me too harshly. I am indebted to the authors who have given their time and experience and worked so hard and diligently in producing their excellent contributions.

Nicholas Tarrier
Manchester, UK

Chapter 1

An introduction to case formulation and its challenges

Nicholas Tarrier

In introducing this volume on case formulation I thought it worthwhile to look briefly at some of the stages in the development of case formulation and some of the issues that have been raised. As with all aspects of clinical practice, the process of case formulation – working towards a psychological explanation of a patient's problem that has treatment utility – is not static. There remain numerous challenges and no doubt further challenges will arise in the future. To stop and reflect on these issues and the challenges they impose is helpful both to the individual clinician and to the clinical researcher.

The Boulder model of training in clinical psychology enshrined the concept of the scientific practitioner in training and practice in psychological treatment. The historical importance of this cannot be over-estimated. This represented a new paradigm in psychological practice in general and psychological treatment in particular. The scientific practitioner established the idea that psychological knowledge can be applied to clinical problems and that this should be done in a manner in accordance with scientific methodology and convention. This has many implications, but two are important here. First, psychological treatments are evaluated and adopted based upon the results of empirical evaluation. This has now been subsumed into the wider paradigm of evidence-based practice or evidence-based health care (see, for example, Sackett 1998). The second implication is that a psychological understanding of clinical problems is adopted to underpin psychological intervention. A seminal paper published in 1965 by Kanfer and Saslow further advanced this endeavour by proposing a psychological alternative, behavioural analysis, to the then-dominant medical conceptualisation of mental health problems.

Kanfer and Saslow's (1965) paper can really be thought of as the natural precursor to case formulation and represented a second paradigm shift. It is interesting to look in a little more detail at what Kanfer and Saslow proposed. They dismiss psychiatric diagnosis as being limited by issues of precision, consistency, reliability and validity to 'a crude and tentative approximation to a taxonomy of effective individual behaviours' (1965: 529). Some may well argue that this situation has not radically altered over the past 40 years. Kanfer and Saslow also outlined the criticisms, current at the time, of the medical model in psychiatry with which the contemporary reader will no doubt be familiar. Their main point remains pertinent: given the wide range of variability in an individual's circumstances and condition and the largely unknown aetiology of most psychiatric disorders, does a reduction to a crude taxonomic classification help or hinder treatment? They progressed to outline an alternative model of understanding clinical problems based upon learning theory in the form of a functional behavioural-analytic approach. This is encapsulated by:

> It [functional analysis] implies that additional information about the circumstances of the patient's life pattern, relationships among his behaviours, and controlling stimuli in his social milieu and his private experience is obtained continuously until it proves sufficient to effect a noticeable change in the patient's behaviour, thus resolving 'the problem'.
>
> (Kanfer and Saslow 1965: 533)

Interestingly, although their model is couched in learning theory terms they anticipated the cognitive revolution that was to follow by including the necessity to assess subjective experience. They suggested that the clinician should collect and organise information from a number of areas: analysis of a problem situation, classification of the problem situation, motivational analysis (reinforcers), developmental analysis (including 'biological equipment' and 'socio-cultural experience'), analysis of self-control, analysis of social relationships and analysis of the social–cultural–physical environment. The formulation, and Kanfer and Saslow used this term, is 'action oriented' (535) in that the problem is defined in operational terms so as to specify a feasible treatment option. Although written over 40 years ago there is much within this paper, both in terms of the inadequacies of psychiatric diagnosis and alternative conceptualisation of clinical problems, that modern-day cognitive behaviour therapists and clinical psychologists would find very familiar.

One of the problems that this new individualised approach unveiled was how to know whether an individualised formulation of a particular person's problem is correct and parsimonious: that is, is it true in a broad sense of the word and does it have functional value – is it clinically useful? That a formulation can be incorrect would also imply that there would be ways, potentially identifiable, by which a formulation could go wrong or deviate from accuracy. However, it may be difficult to discriminate a 'right' from a 'wrong' answer when the formulation pertains only to one individual. The nature and types of error that may contaminate clinical decision-making may include availability heuristic, representative heuristic, anchoring heuristic, biased search strategies, overconfidence and hindsight bias (Nezu and Nezu 1989a). By this Nezu and Nezu meant that a clinician may be subject to a number of sources of bias such as being overly influenced by recent clinical experience, being too quick to categorise or reach a conclusion on insufficient information and without the flexibility to adjust or modify those conclusions, selectively attending to types or aspects of information and further searching for information based upon a confirmatory bias, and being unable to react to new information in a way that increases accuracy and precision rather than confirms initial impressions. There is a tendency to look back retrospectively on a case with a confirmatory zeal. Unfortunately, although perhaps not surprisingly, clinicians and therapists appear to be subject to all the information processing distortions that they try to assess and rectify in their patients. The area of clinical judgement and decision-making is clearly one that requires further research and clinicians would benefit from reflection upon it. A consideration of alternative explanations, a wider viewpoint and a further appraisal of possible options would perhaps benefit clinical practice.

A related difficulty identified by Nezu and Nezu (1989a: 29) is how and when to select the appropriate treatment techniques from the array available. This problem is also pivotal to the work of other writers on case formulation (for example, Bruch 1998; Persons 1991; Turkat 1985) and in my experience it is often the issue that trainees and students find one of the most difficult. Nezu and Nezu (1989a) rightly say that because individual formulations take into account a large array of unique characteristics across a variety of person and environmental variables it is very difficult to know how to select the most effective treatment strategy. Nezu and Nezu (1989b: 57) advocate a problem-solving approach to clinical decision-making which consists of problem orientation, problem definition and formulation, generation of alternatives, decision-making, and solution implementation and verification. They also make the useful distinction between treatment strategy, tactics and methods. Treatment strategies are linked to each identified problem and provide a general approach to how that problem will be resolved, such as decreasing negative cognitive biases and self-defeating thoughts in someone with a depressed mood. Each treatment strategy should have a list of specific treatment tactics which indicate how the strategy will be achieved. For example, in the strategic example given the tactics might include monitoring automatic thoughts, investigation of the cognitive processes and identification of bias, examination of supporting evidence, generation of alternative interpretations of events, behavioural experiments to test out various expectations and so on. Nezu and Nezu (1989b) also introduce the idea of different treatment methods: they mean different ways in which tactical treatment techniques might be implemented. For example, a behavioural experiment to test out a biased interpretation of events may well be applied differently if the patient is a depressed adolescent male of 14, rather than a depressed middle-aged woman with a family, or a 28-year-old man with a psychotic illness who is also depressed.

The overall approach is that the formulation is a way of generating testable hypotheses about the clinical case; these hypotheses are tested through the application of treatment, and whether the formulation is functional or not will depend on the consequences – whether the problem is resolved. Case formulation is thus the translation of theory into therapy, but it is the function of all theories to be disproved if possible. The clinician should create explanatory structures or heuristics for understanding the patient's problems but proceed with caution not to muster evidence selectively only in their support but to examine critically why their heuristic and hypotheses may be incorrect and can be shown to be so. It is this refinement of testable hypotheses upon which treatment strategies are based that prevents cognitive behaviour therapy from becoming a mere cookbook of clinical techniques.

Although Kanfer and Saslow (1965) anticipated the importance of personal and subjective experience, the expansion of legitimate clinical information into the patient's private and subjective world that followed the 'cognitive revolution' introduced further challenges. The greater interest in unobservable cognitive products and processes rather than observable behaviour undoubtedly increased the availability of clinically powerful techniques but it also increased the possibility of biases in formulation, as described by Nezu and Nezu (1989a, 1989b). In some ways the concept of disease, rejected along with the psychiatric medical model, was in danger of being replaced by explanatory concepts such as dysfunctional assumptions, schema and similar that could be equally diffuse (Tarrier and Calam 2002). It is important, therefore, that clinicians and researchers do not uncritically accept unproven associations as causality.

Persons (1989) usefully made the distinction between 'overt difficulties', which were the patient's 'real life' difficulties, and the 'underlying psychological mechanisms', which were the putative psychological dysfunctions which underpin the patient's overt difficulties. The overt difficulties could be described at the macro or micro levels. These distinctions not only referred to quantifiable levels of analysis, where the macro level was an overall description and the micro level was a much more detailed description of the problem, but also referred at the macro level to how the problems 'might be described in the patient's own terms' (Persons 1989: 2). The micro level includes a breakdown into the three components of cognition, behaviour and moods (emotion or affect), and includes concepts such as synchrony – the positive correlation between these three components (or lack of it as in desynchrony) – and interdependence, where a change in one component will bring about a change in the others. So not only do the macro and micro levels involve a difference in level of description and detail; they also imply a difference in explanation. The patient's subjective description and most probably explanation or representation is characterised by the overall descriptor at the macro level, for example being depressed, anxious, having relationship problems and so on. The psychologist's or clinician's view is characterised by the more detailed micro level. A number of implications arise from this: to be effective the process of case formulation should be collaborative and not imposed, and it needs to take into account and accommodate the patient's views and beliefs about their problem. In health psychology this is known as illness representation, which is a set of complex beliefs about the origin, nature, severity, course and progress, prognosis and potential, appropriate and acceptable treatments of the patient's condition (see, for example, Leventhal *et al.* 1997). It seems safe to assume that anyone seeking the services of a cognitive behaviour therapist or psychologist will have similar representations or beliefs about their condition. These beliefs may be well worked out or rudimentary, and they may be held with strong conviction or be more tentative, but they do need to be assessed so the patient collaborates in the process of arriving at a case formulation. This is encapsulated in a quote from Persons (1989: 24): '[A] failure to agree on the problem list dooms the treatment'. Persons gives an excellent example of this. She describes a patient, after six months of unsuccessful treatment, declaring that she did not really consider that an inability to leave the house was her major problem, which instead she construed as the fact that 'she was fragile and delicate and that she needed to stay home and rest' (63–65). It would appear that the patient's definition of her problem was different from the therapist's and her cognitive (illness) representation and beliefs were also contrary. Part of the case formulation should be a thorough understanding of the patient's beliefs, understanding and expectations about his/her condition and what has lead them to consultation and treatment and into the health care system.

Persons' 1989 book, *Cognitive Therapy in Practice: A Case Formulation Approach*, provided one of the first guidebooks on case formulation and had an immense impact in terms of formalising the procedure and in particular incorporating psychological and cognitive mechanisms. It became the natural successor to Kanfer and Saslow's (1965) paper on behaviour analysis. Persons described the process of case formulation as having six parts: (a) creating the problem list; (b) describing the proposed underlying mechanisms; (c) accounting for the way in which the proposed mechanisms produce the problems on the problem list; (d) identifying the precipitants of current problems; (e) identifying the origins of the mechanism in the patient's early life; and (f) predicting obstacles to treatment based on the formulation. Central to Persons' process of case formulation is describing and understanding the underlying psychological mechanisms; these are in the main cognitive and information-processing factors although due attention is paid to the antecedents and consequences of any problem. Persons addresses the problem that these mechanisms are not frequently open to observation and run the potential risk of becoming causal fictions by suggesting a number of tests to which the hypothesised underlying mechanism can be subjected. The first test relates to how well the mechanisms account for the identified problems. This is a good criterion because a logical, comprehensive and above all parsimonious explanation has very clear advantages. Further, the formulation should easily be able to accommodate and be in accord with aspects of the patient's report, such as events associated with the onset of the problem or episode. The formulation, as an explanation, should generate specific hypotheses which when tested will support or refute the explanation. The sign of a robust formulation is that it can survive the rigours of such tests. Furthermore, the outcome of treatment based upon the formulation can also be viewed as hypothesis testing and thus there is a pragmatic test of the formulation which, if correct, should result in a good response to treatment. Persons also includes the patient's reaction to the formulation as a final test; if the formulation makes sense to the patient then it has at least some validity. The formulation, in common with any hypothesis put to an experimental test, can be refined, modified or even abandoned. All advocates of case formulation agree that the testable nature of the formulation is an essential characteristic (for example, Bruch and Bond 1998; Persons 1989; Tarrier and Calam 2002), and that this should be embarked upon in a collaborative manner. There are also ethical reasons why the formulation should be shared with the patient, in that they have the right to know how the therapist has formulated their problem and intends to treat it (Turkat 1990: 12). It is very difficult to understand how without this shared information and collaborative approach the patient could give informed consent to be assessed and treated.

It is the collaborative nature of this activity that should help forge engagement. However, whether this is so is an empirical question and there is some evidence to suggest that, in some patient groups, it might not always be the case. Chadwick *et al.* (2003), in a study of case formulation as part of cognitive behaviour therapy in the treatment of psychosis, found that although the formulation strengthened the therapeutic alliance as perceived by the therapist it did not have the same effect from the patient's viewpoint. Although a good proportion viewed the case formulation as helpful and beneficial, nearly half of what was admittedly a small sample also made negative comments. These related to a concern about the magnitude and longstanding nature of their problems which seemed to elicit a sense of pessimism. It is worth noting that four of the six patients who made negative comments also made positive comments. This effect may have been specific to patients with chronic psychotic disorders but it may also indicate that an excessive concentration on the childhood origins of problems, which the patients indicated had occurred, is neither parsimonious nor functional.

This raises a further point about the function of case formulation: it must be a precise account of the patient's problems which is accurate, parsimonious, comprehensive, logical and functional but also must provide to the patient a meaningful account of their problems. That is, it must have both clinical utility and subjective utility. Interestingly, AuBuchon and Malatesta (1998) describe ways in which the therapeutic relationship can be incorporated into the case formulation so that it can be utilised in the therapeutic process.

More recently Tarrier and Calam (2002) have suggested three further additions to traditional case formulation: (a) the conceptualisation of the dysfunctional system, especially relating to maintenance factors; (b) the historical background in terms of vulnerability and epidemiological factors; and (c) the important role of interpersonal and social behaviour and context.

The dysfunctional system consists of a systemic and circular relationship between the problem, in its micro level form, and antecedent and consequential events. This attempts to capture the intimate relationship between cognition, behaviour and mood in which, for example, a problem cognition could become an antecedent for another problem or be a consequence of a third (this is represented diagrammatically in Figure 1.1). The point of entry to the system is the problem as defined by the patient – the macro level. This systemic analysis has advantages over a purely linear account as it better accommodates the complex interactions of different factors and how they maintain the problem.

It is hypothesised that in any person's life there are stresses and strains, both internal and external, but a natural homeostatic process regulates activity to return to a normal level of functioning. A dysfunctional system arises from a failure of this corrective feedback or homeostasis. In spite of the most atrocious experiences, many people do not go on to develop psychological disorders. Thus some type of resilience must be operating which buffers against this adversity. This may be a characteristic of the person, such as personality or coping mechanisms, or an aspect of their environment, such as social support or low stress levels. Even when destabilisation occurs, restitution and a return to a regulated and normal mental state occurs

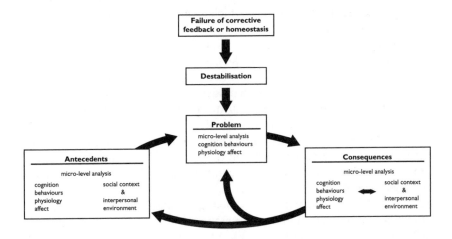

DYSFUNCTIONAL SYSTEM

Figure 1.1 The dysfunctional system approach to case formulation.

naturally and relatively quickly in many people. In others there is a tendency for feedback to destabilise and so amplify or maintain feedback processes which mitigate against self-correction; a dysfunctional system becomes established. Response patterns, cognitive, emotional and behavioural, often become entrenched and cyclical, and take on numerous secondary functions. So, because the chain of events often becomes circular rather than linear, it is easier to think of a dysfunctional system being activated in which the various components have interacting relationships which are strengthened through activation of the feedback system.

To avoid some of the tautological reasoning identified by Nezu and Nezu (1989a) in identifying historical events as causal in current problems, Tarrier and Calam (2002) proposed a probabilistic model in which individual characteristics of the patient's life and experience were matched to known vulnerability and risk factors drawn from the research literature to suggest possible pathways to the origins of the current problem. Thus historical aspects of case formulation need to be founded on epidemiological data on risk factors associated with the development of any subsequent disorder. The occurrence of a clinical problem or psychological disorder is postulated to be the product of vulnerability and stress. That some common characteristics render individuals more at risk to develop a specific disorder is seen as evidence of vulnerability. Increased vulnerability results in increased risk but does not inevitably result in the occurrence of disorder; some further destabilisation or stress is required to precipitate the disorder and also trigger help seeking (this is represented in Figure 1.2). Vulnerability may well be acquired through exposure to specific environments but such contentions should be supported by the research literature. This reiterates the place of case formulation within the scientific practitioner model, in which formulation and treatment have an empirical foundation.

One consequence of the development of cognitive models of psychological disorders and their strong influence on case formulation has been the potential decrease in importance being placed upon environmental (including social) factors. The focus on internal cognitive processes has distanced the analysis from the patient's social context. Meaningful social interactions and the interpersonal environment are central to human behaviour and clinical problems, and therefore their analysis needs to take centre stage in case formulation. There is good reason to do this: human beings have evolved into complex social animals with very complex social behaviours and goals. Socialisation and all that it entails is highly influential in our lives. It is also highly probable that mechanisms to elicit, maintain and regulate social interactions have also evolved and are operational in every aspect of a person's functioning. Aspects of problems seen in the clinic may well have their origins in this social evolution (Gilbert 2001). To emphasise the importance of social context Baumeister and Leary (1995), in their review of the need for meaningful social interactions, concluded that: (a) people naturally seek and form

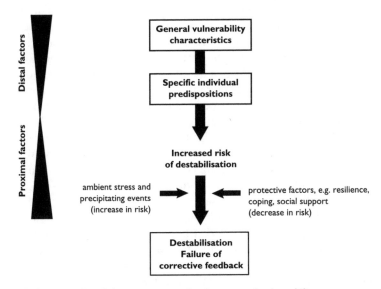

Figure 1.2 Systemic destabilisation as a result of stress and vulnerability.

relationships with others; (b) efforts to dissolve relationships are strongly resisted; (c) information about meaningful relationships and relationship partners are more thoroughly processed than information about other people; (d) the quality and intensity of relationships are directly associated with mood; and (e) intermittent or superficial social bonds do not result in the same mental health benefits as meaningful bonds.

There is evidence that good social support has a positive effect and can impact on mental health in two ways – by buffering against stress (Cohen and McKay 1984) or through social cognition (Cohen and Willis 1985; Rhodes and Lakey 1999). In the former, perceived social support may impact on the appraisal of stress by providing the individual with the belief that additional resources, in the form of others, are available. In the latter the positive role of social support may be in providing access to others who can provide information about positive health-related behaviour and positive beliefs and con-ceptualisation of situations and self-perceptions (Penn *et al.* 2004). There is also ample evidence for the negative effect of interpersonal relationships on the course and outcome of psychological and psychiatric disorders (for example, Butzlaff and Hooley 1998; Wearden *et al.* 2000), further emphasis-ing the importance of incorporating aspects of social context into case formulation and treatment. Lastly, incorporating social context into case formulation increases the treatment options available to the clinician in a range of different situations (for example, Henggeler *et al.* 1993; Keller *et al.* 2000; Tarrier and Humphreys 2003).

The advantages of the case formulation approach are that it allows a flexible and idiosyncratic understanding of each patient's individual problems irrespective of their diagnostic classification. It is collaborative, treats the patient with true regard and takes into account the importance of their beliefs and expectations. It is sufficiently flexible to be accommodated into clinical research and is based upon an empirical foundation generated from research. It can include epidemiological information on vulnerability and risk, a systemic approach to problem maintenance and the patient's interpersonal and social context. It is further advantageous in that individualised treatment strategies, tactics and methods can be produced from the formulation that are specific to the needs of that individual. Case formulation is particularly advantageous in treating complex cases that do not conform to standard classification and pigeon-holing (Tarrier *et al.* 1998). Although widely adopted, the research on case formulation is not extensive, although it is increasing as indicated by the following chapters within this volume. There are, however, many challenges which I hope the readers of this and the subsequent chapters will be stimulated to take up both in their clinical practice and also as active clinical researchers. There is a strong mutually dependent relationship between clinical research and clinical practice, and it is through this relationship, in which both the clinician and researcher identify problem areas and unanswered questions, that the practice and understanding of case formulation will expand and flourish.

REFERENCES

AuBuchon, P. G. and Malatesta, V. J. (1998). Managing the therapeutic relationship in behaviour therapy: The need for a case formulation. In M. Bruch and F. W. Bond (eds) *Beyond Diagnosis: Case Formulation Approaches to CBT*. Chichester, UK: Wiley.

Baumeister, R. F. and Leary, M. R. (1995). The need to belong: Desire for interpersonal attachments as a fundamental human motivation. *Psychological Bulletin* 117: 497–529.

Bruch, M. (1998). The UCL case formulation approaches. In M. Bruch and F. W. Bond (eds) *Beyond Diagnosis: Case Formulation Approaches to CBT*. Chichester, UK: Wiley.

Bruch, M. and Bond, F. W. (eds) (1998). *Beyond Diagnosis: Case Formulation Approaches to CBT*. Chichester, UK: Wiley.

Butzlaff, R. L. and Hooley, J. M. (1998). Expressed emotion and psychiatric relapse: A meta-analysis. *Archives of General Psychiatry* 5: 547–52.

Chadwick, P. *et al.* (2003). Impact of case formulation in cognitive behaviour therapy for psychosis. *Behaviour Research and Therapy* 41: 671–80.

Cohen, S. and McKay, G. (1984). Social support, stress and the buffering hypothesis: A theoretical analysis. In A. Baum *et al.* (eds) *Handbook of Psychology and Health*. Hillsdale, NJ: Lawrence Erlbaum.

Cohen, S. and Willis, T. A. (1985) Stress, social support and the buffering hypothesis. *Psychological Bulletin* 98: 310–57.

Gilbert, P. (2001). Evolutionary approaches to psychopathology: The role of natural defences. *Australian and New Zealand Journal of Psychiatry* 35: 17–27.

Henggeler, S. W. *et al.* (1992). Family preservation using multisystemic therapy: An effective alternative to incarcerating serious juvenile offenders. *Journal of Consulting and Clinical Psychology* 60: 953–61.

Kanfer, F. H. and Saslow, G. (1965). Behavioral analysis: An alternative to diagnostic classification. *Archives of General Psychiatry* 12: 529–38.

Keller, M. B. *et al.* (2000). A comparison of nefazodone, the cognitive behavioral-analysis system of psychotherapy, and their combination for the treatment of chronic depression. *New England Journal of Medicine* 342: 1462–70.

Leventhal, H. *et al.* (1997). Illness representations: Theoretical foundations. In K. J. Petrie and J. A. Weinman (eds) *Perceptions of Health and Illness*. Amsterdam: Harwood Academic Publishers.

Nezu A. M. and Nezu, C. M. (1989a). Clinical predictions. Judgment and decision making: An overview. In A. M. Nezu and C. M. Nezu (eds) *Clinical Decision Making in Behaviour Therapy: A Problem Solving Perspective*. Champaign, IL: Research Press.

Nezu A. M. and Nezu, C. M. (1989b). Clinical decision making in behaviour therapy. In A. M. Nezu and C. M. Nezu (eds) *Clinical Decision Making in Behaviour Therapy: A Problem Solving Perspective*. Champaign, IL: Research Press.

Penn, D. L. *et al.* (2004). Supportive therapy for schizophrenia: A closer look at the evidence. *Schizophrenia Bulletin* 30: 101–12.

Persons, J. B. (1989). *Cognitive Therapy in Practice: A Case Formulation Approach*. New York: Norton.

Rhodes, G. L. and Lakey, B. (1999). Social support and psychological disorder: Insights from social psychology. In R. M. Kowalski and M. R. Leary (eds) *The Social Psychology of Emotional and Behavioural Problems: Interfaces of Social and Clinical Psychology*. Washington, DC: American Psychological Association.

Sackett, D. L. (1998). *Evidence-Based Medicine: How to Practice and Teach EBM*. Edinburgh: Churchill Livingstone.

Tarrier, N. and Calam, R. (2002). New developments in cognitive-behavioural case formulation. Epidemiological, systemic and social context: An integrative approach. *Cognitive and Behavioural Psychotherapy* 30: 311–28.

Tarrier, N. and Humphreys, A.-L. (2003). PTSD and the social support of the interpersonal environment: Its influence and implications for treatment. *Journal of Cognitive Therapy* 17: 187–98.

Tarrier, N. *et al.* (eds) (1998). *Cognitive Behaviour Therapy for Complex Cases: An Advanced Guidebook for the Practitioner*. Chichester, UK: Wiley.

Turkat, I. D. (1985). *Behavioral Case Formulation*. New York: Plenum.

Turkat, I. D. (1990). *The Personality Disorders: A Psychological Approach to Clinical Management*. New York: Pergamon.

Wearden, A. *et al.* (2000) A review of expressed emotion research in health care. *Clinical Psychology Review* 20: 633–66.

Chapter 2

Evidence-based case formulation

Is the emperor clothed?

Willem Kuyken

From its inception cognitive-behavioural therapy (CBT) has aspired to be evidence-based (Beck 1976). That is to say, it utilises practice principles derived from consensus among CBT practitioners, is based on empirically supported cognitive theories of emotional disorders and has been subjected to rigorous efficacy and effectiveness outcome research. As a result CBT is generally regarded as an evidence-based therapeutic approach for a broad range of emotional disorders. Case formulation is a cornerstone of evidence-based CBT practice. For any particular case of CBT practice, formulation is the bridge between practice, theory and research. It is the crucible where the individual particularities of a given case, relevant theory and research synthesise into an understanding of the person's presenting issues in CBT terms which then informs the intervention.

The Hans Christian Anderson story *The Emperor's New Clothes* is a salutary fable. In it two dishonest tailors claim to make up a set of 'magnificent' new robes for the vain emperor. In reality there are no new robes, and the deceit involves the tailors convincing the emperor and his entourage that they have created a magnificent new set of robes. The emperor's courtiers and the people of the town all go along with the charade. During a procession through the town the emperor wears his 'new robes.' It takes a small child to say to her father, 'But the emperor doesn't have anything on,' for the sham to be exposed. The emperor's pride forces him to continue with the procession as if he were clothed in magnificent new robes.

CBT developed without much explicit reference to case formulation (Beck 1976). It is only more recently that various commentators have 'robed' CBT case formulation with mantles such as 'the heart of evidence-based practice' (Bieling and Kuyken 2003: 53), 'the lynch pin that holds theory and practice together' (Butler 1998) and a principle underpinning cognitive therapy (Beck 1995). Without carefully examining the conceptual and empirical foundations of CBT formulation it risks becoming the emperor's magnificent new robes.

This chapter sets out to examine CBT case formulation through the 'child's eyes' of empirical enquiry. The chapter proposes criteria whereby the evidence base for case formulation can be judged. These criteria form the platform for a suggested research programme that can empirically examine case formulation's evidence base. The chapter concludes with some general practice-oriented, evidence-based guidelines for CBT practitioners. However, it begins with the view from the emperor's entourage, setting out a definition of case formulation and the rationale for case formulation that has driven its rise to imperious status.

THE DEFINITION AND FUNCTION OF CASE FORMULATION: THE VIEW FROM THE EMPEROR'S ENTOURAGE

Case formulation aims to describe a person's presenting problems and use theory to make explanatory inferences about causes and maintaining factors that can inform interventions.[1] This definition has several key elements. First, there is a top-down process of cognitive-behavioural theory providing clinically useful descriptive frameworks. Second, the formulation enables practitioners and clients to make explanatory inferences about what caused and maintains the presenting issues. Third, case formulation explicitly and centrally informs intervention. Most case formulation schemes have several core elements: a description of the presenting issues; predisposing factors (more recent factors that acted as precipitants and more distal factors that acted to increase diathesis); perpetuating factors that maintain the presenting issues; protective factors that act as personal and social resources; and explicit guides for intervention. The purpose of case formulation is to provide a coherent set of explanatory inferences based in theory that describe and explain why the person has this problem at this time that can usefully inform intervention (Figure 2.1).

A CRITICAL PERSPECTIVE ON THE EVIDENCE BASE OF CASE FORMULATION: THE CHILD'S VIEW OF THE EMPEROR

A fairly typical definition of evidence-based practice is 'the conscientious, explicit and judicious use of current best evidence in making decisions about the care of individual patients. This practice means integrating individual clinical experience with the best available external clinical evidence from systematic research' (Sackett *et al.* 1996: 72–73). Evidence-based practice aspires to improve the quality of clinical care, improve clinical outcomes, improve cost-effectiveness and command the respect of service users and professionals (Addis 2002). Many CBT practitioners would readily claim that CBT formulation has almost identical aspirations. This chapter examines whether case

CBT formulation improves CBT practice by:

- Linking theory, research and practice

- Normalising problems and increasing empathy

- Organising large amounts of complex information

- Enabling high quality supervision

CBT formulation informs intervention by:

- Selecting, focussing and sequencing interventions

- Suggesting a person's preferred way of changing

- Suggesting likely 'therapy-interfering behaviours'

- Enabling the simplest and most cost-efficient interventions

Figure 2.1 Rationale for CBT case formulation.

formulation involves the conscientious, explicit and judicious use of best evidence in generating intervention plans with clients.[2]

WHAT IS EVIDENCE-BASED CASE FORMULATION?

To be able to claim that CBT based on individualised case formulations represents evidence-based practice, the criteria for evidence-based case formulation must be agreed upon and then subjected to systematic empirical enquiry. In an earlier paper 'Is Cognitive Case Formulation Science or Science Fiction?' Peter Bieling and I set out some criteria which are reproduced and extended here (Figure 2.2).

These criteria fall into two broad categories: top-down and bottom-up. The top-down criterion asks a simple question: Is the theory that underpins a formulation substantiated by empirical research? The CBT practitioner constantly draws on cognitive theories of emotional disorders to describe and explain clients' presenting problems. Elsewhere in this book we see a range of contemporary cognitive theories used to understand and work with clients with a range of presentations. Bottom-up criteria are concerned with the process, impact and utility of CBT case formulation. Is the process of describing and explaining clients' presenting issues reliable, does case formulation meaningfully relate to clients' experience and presenting issues and can it be cross-validated to other measures of clients' functioning? Finally, does it improve outcomes, lead to more cost-effective care and command the respect of practitioners and clients? These criteria will be considered in turn.

Top-down criterion

• Is the theory on which the formulation is founded evidence-based?

Bottom-up criteria

• Is the formulation reliable?

  – Is the formulation based on reliable inferences?

  – Can clinicians agree on the formulation?

• Is the formulation valid: Does it triangulate with the client's experience, any standardised measures, the therapist's clinical impressions and the clinical supervisor's impressions?

• Does the formulation improve the intervention and the therapy outcomes?

• Is the formulation acceptable and useful?

Figure 2.2 Criteria for evidence-based formulation.

IS THE THEORY ON WHICH THE FORMULATION IS FOUNDED EVIDENCE-BASED?

If evidence-based practice involves 'the conscientious, explicit and judicious use of current best evidence' (Sackett *et al.* 1996), then when CBT practitioners explicitly draw on cognitive-behavioural theories they should be able to argue that those theories are based on current best evidence. It is beyond the scope of this chapter to review the research literature concerned with the many cognitive-behavioural theories of emotional disorders. There are excellent reviews elsewhere of cognitive theories (e.g., Beck 1996). For example, 25 years of research into Beck's cognitive theory of depression (Clark *et al.* 1999) suggests that reformulated CBT theories provide a credible basis for practitioners to draw on in formulating the cases of clients presenting with depression. In their review of the literature relating to depression, anxiety disorders and personality disorders, Bieling and Kuyken conclude:

> Taken together, our review suggests that at a nomothetic level, cognitive theory of depression, anxiety disorders, and personality disorders is supported in many of its descriptive hypotheses, and cognitive models are understudied in their more difficult to operationalize explanatory hypotheses. Thus in the transfer to the idiographic level, which defines case formulation, it follows that descriptive statements are justifiable, but explanatory statements should be stated as exploratory hypotheses at best.
>
> (2003: 59)

This large body of research provides a credible basis for working with clients to develop formulations. The outstanding challenge for clinical researchers is to examine the explanatory elements of cognitive theories of mood, anxiety and personality disorders. The further challenges are for researchers to address more recent cognitive-behavioural theories of bipolar disorder (Newman *et al.* 2002), eating disorders (Fairburn *et al.* 2003), substance misuse (Thase 1997) and psychosis (Chadwick *et al.* 1996). In the interim these theories are provisional at best, and a conscientious approach would be to formulate understandings of clients' presenting issues with an explicit acknowledgement of the provisional status of the corresponding theory. Perhaps because of their origins in careful observation from clinical practice, most cognitive theories are good descriptive accounts of emotional distress. However, a good description does not necessarily provide any explanatory insights; neither does it necessarily provide guides for intervention.

IS CBT FORMULATION RELIABLE?

The first bottom-up criterion asks whether the process of generating a formulation is reliable, and the second asks whether CBT practitioners can agree with one another in the case formulations that emerge from the formulation process (Westmeyer 2003). These two criteria are related but different. That is to say, the process of describing and explaining presenting issues (the formulation process) leads to the generation of a working formulation, but is not the same as a working formulation. Just because one part of the judgment process is problematic, it does not necessarily follow that the output judgment is problematic. For example, a practitioner can draw a causal conclusion from two loosely associated phenomena but still produce a generally coherent working formulation.

Is the formulation process reliable?

Formulation involves attending to large amounts of complex information, making clinical judgments and progressively hypothesising as new information becomes available. There is now extensive evidence that people rely on a limited number of heuristic principles when making decisions under conditions of uncertainty (Kahneman 2003). Consider the following pieces of information about a case, allowing yourself to begin to formulate as you learn more about the case.

1   *Nigel presented with symptoms of PTSD (flashbacks with associated hyper-arousal).* Typically, CBT practitioners will ascribe Nigel's presentation to the category of people diagnosed with PTSD. They might see Nigel's presentation as representative of the category of people

presenting with PTSD and begin to consider how CBT theories of PTSD might help describe and understand Nigel's current concerns. Consequently a great deal of hypothesis generation is initiated from some abbreviated diagnostic impressions.

2 *Nigel enjoyed cross-dressing.* It is not immediately obvious how this information is consistent with the earlier information. It tends to draw on a range of attitudes and values that practitioners hold about cross-dressing (e.g., this is a free choice; Nigel should feel comfortable with his preference). In short, rather than immediately closing down a hypothesis it opens up a wide range of hypotheses and brings to bear value-based judgments. It creates dissonance because the inferential process of narrowing down hypotheses is interrupted, and instead there is a need to broaden the judgment process. This creates fertile ground for heuristic processes to simplify the task: 'People who are confronted with a difficult question sometimes answer an easier one instead' (Kahneman 2003: 707).

3 *Nigel was under the supervision of probation services following a series of incidents in which he had masturbated in view of neighbours, while dressed in women's underwear. He had been brutally victimised over the last three years by a group of youths on the housing estate following his antisocial behaviour.* This information reinstates dissonance, because Nigel's cross-dressing behaviour has antisocial elements and brings to bear another set of attitudes and values. Again, the dissonance provides fertile ground for heuristic reasoning as practitioners search to resolve the dissonance and create a coherent set of hypotheses about Nigel's presenting problems.

When presented with incomplete and ambiguous information, it is adaptive to use decision-making heuristics to make inferences. Heuristic decision-making is essentially simplifying reasoning by taking 'cognitive short-cuts' and confers survival value because 'good enough' simplified solutions confer advantages over optimal solutions derived from complex models of the world (Tversky and Kahneman 1974). That is to say, the extra costs of optimal solutions often do not outweigh the benefits of 'good enough' options. This is the basic premise for the increased fitness that heuristics confer.

CBT practitioners are no different in this regard and probably use judgment heuristics in each phase of the assessment and formulation process. The CBT assessment and formulation process comprises the initial assessment, summarising the assessment, making inferential hypotheses (i.e., formulation) and revising these hypotheses on the basis of new evidence throughout the clinical work (i.e., reformulation). Information will to some extent always be ambiguous and incomplete. Many professional training programmes would argue that they aim to ensure a systematic deductive and evidence-based approach to clinical problem-solving that minimises the use of problematic decision-making heuristics. In a seminal paper 'Why I Don't Attend Case Conferences,' Paul Meehl argued that clinical decision-making is routinely hampered by reasoning errors in every aspect of clinical work that are closer to inductive than deductive processes (Meehl 1973). That is to say, heuristics are used to create 'good enough' judgments rather than 'optimal' judgments. Estimating risk of suicide is greatly enhanced through the use of actuarial approaches yet case conferences, argues Meehl, gravitate towards simplistic explanations that amount to playing 'Russian roulette with patients' lives' (1973: 257). Evidence-based case formulation, I argue, makes judicious use of the best available evidence, provides an understanding of behaviour and has predictive value in managing risk and selecting interventions – an altogether more complex and difficult task.

Several broad categories of heuristics affect reasoning processes: representativeness, availability and anchoring/adjustment (Kahneman 2003; Tversky and Kahneman 1974). These will be reviewed and considered in the light of clinical judgment generally and CBT formulation specifically.

The representativeness bias refers to the tendency to see presenting issues (A) as representative of another set of issues (B), enabling what we know about B to be applied to A. In the case of Nigel above, we bring to bear what we know about PTSD to our understanding of Nigel's presenting issues. This process can become problematic when certain short-cuts are made. Knowledge of base rates of B are essential to making a judgment of representativeness and will determine how likely A is to be a member of B. Illusions of validity around categories make representativeness biases more likely. The most classic empirical demonstration of this effect was the seminal Rosenhan study in which he and his confederates presented to psychiatrists as normally functioning people reporting only one symptom (a voice saying 'dull,' 'thud' and 'empty'). The psychiatrists misapplied the representativeness heuristic and admitted the researchers to psychiatric hospital, often with a diagnosis of schizophrenia, where the patients on the ward applied alternative heuristics and correctly identified the researchers as imposters (Rosenhan 1973). In an analogue study of judgment processes, practitioners were given identical information about a person's functioning and relationships, but in one condition they were told he was a job applicant and in the other that he was a patient (Davis 1979). The 'patient' label led practitioners to make more maladjustment inferences than the 'job applicant' label. These studies illustrate how the representativeness heuristic can lead practitioners to ascribe qualities associated with a particular category (e.g., schizophrenia or patient) to the presenting case, sometimes taking unwarranted cognitive short-cuts. In the case of Nigel, practitioners who hold base rates of PTSD and the heterogeneity of PTSD presentations in mind are more likely to generate evidence-based formulations.

The availability bias refers to the tendency to make use of more readily available information in decision-making. That is to say, information that comes more readily to mind is more likely to be regarded as salient and used. Availability is determined by frequency, recency, vividness and effectiveness of search set. Several empirical studies have found evidence of the availability bias and suggest that it is particularly powerful because practitioners are largely unaware of its effects. A series of experiments using the draw-a-person projective test demonstrated that participants persisted in drawing illusory correlations between drawing characteristics and traits for which no evidence was presented in the study (Chapman and Chapman 1967, 1969). In relation to Nigel, a practitioner who has recently attended a compelling continuing professional development workshop on sexual trauma in sexual offenders may be more likely to generate a hypothesis that Nigel was the victim of sexual trauma and has learned maladaptive beliefs about intimacy and sexuality.

The anchoring and adjustment biases refer to the tendency to organise judgments around either an initial hypothesis or an otherwise over-riding attributional bias. This tendency to organise progressive hypothesising around a core idea has a long lineage in social psychology. For example, the fundamental attribution error refers to a basic tendency to attribute people's behaviour to dispositional qualities rather than their situation (Jones and Nisbett 1971). In the case of Nigel, a dispositional bias might lead to an over-emphasis on personalised hypotheses about his sexuality rather than an emphasis on his social roles or social context. An extension to this research suggests that professional training may engender greater confidence in clinical decision-making, and thereby increase proneness to anchoring effects (Friedlander and Phillips 1984). More recently, a correlational study has replicated the tendency for practitioners who are more confident in their judgments to make use of more dispositional inferential styles (Smith and Dumont 2002). These studies cannot enlighten us about the validity of practitioners' judgments – they tell us merely that they tend to be dispositional, an effect that is exacerbated when practitioners feel more confident in their judgments.

Representativeness, availability and anchoring biases occur in context. The task and the practitioner will interact to affect the extent to which these biases come into play. In relation to the task, a more highly affectively charged task and a task with a high information loading may both tilt towards greater reliance on heuristics (Kahneman 2003). In relation to the practitioner, there is some evidence that practitioners who use higher levels of complexity in their thinking style are less prone to heuristic biases (Spengler and Strohmer 1994).

Summarising the decision-making research literature needs to be done with several caveats. First, heuristics have adaptive value, and a measured reading of the literature suggests that there is a counter literature demonstrating that heuristics often lead to good solutions. Remarkably, studies showing a bias are cited significantly more often than studies failing to show biases

(Christensenszalanski and Beach 1984). Second, decision-making is determined by multiple intrinsic (e.g., values, cognitive complexity) and extrinsic (e.g., task complexity) factors that are constantly changing. To date there is a paucity of empirical research investigating the extent to which CBT practitioners are prone to these heuristic biases, although the weight of evidence from other areas of psychology and from the clinical decision-making literature suggests that it is likely that CBT practitioners routinely make use of heuristics to solve the dilemma of 'good enough' versus optimal formulations. Under conditions of uncertainty and high load it would be reasonable to conclude that sometimes systematic biases are used in processing information to arrive at formulations.

Reviewing several decades of decision-making research, Kahneman (2003) has suggested that two relatively independent but related cognitive systems underpin decision-making: intuitive and rational systems (see Figure 2.3). The intuitive system is fast, automatic, effortless, associative, implicit (not so available to introspection), automatic (difficult to directly control or modify), and may be emotionally charged. The rational system is slower, serial, effortful, consciously monitored and deliberately controlled. The rational system

	System 1: Effortless intuition	System 2: Deliberate reasoning
Process	Fast; automatic; effortless; associative; implicit; may be emotionally charged; difficult to control or modify	Rule-governed; slower; serial; effortful; consciously monitored; deliberately controlled; monitors intuitive outputs
Output	Impressionistic (e.g., metaphors and images); not readily available to introspection	Reasoned (e.g., verbal or diagrammatic); readily available to justification

Figure 2.3 Clinical (heuristic) decision-making: process and output in two systems (after Kahneman 2003).

monitors the outputs from the intuitive system, providing a check and balance on output judgments. A hypothesis or formulation can come forward when an intuitive judgment is initiated and then either endorsed or adjusted by the rational system. Alternatively, the intuitive system may be unable to generate a hypothesis and in this case the rational system takes over and generates the hypothesis. This model explicitly suggests that the intuitive system has primacy, and wherever possible a person will make judgments intuitively. The coordinating and balancing functions of the rational system are enhanced by intelligence, need for cognition and exposure to statistical thinking. They are impaired by time pressure, demands of concurrent tasks and mood state (Kahneman 2003).

It is easy to see how these two cognitive systems might operate in CBT formulation. Novice therapists may well spend long periods of time preparing for their client sessions, deliberating rationally about the best approaches. Well-trained, highly experienced and clinically effective CBT practitioners may well operate intuitively in much of their practice and when asked why they chose a treatment strategy will need to pause to unpick the intuitively generated rationale. As long as clinical work proceeds smoothly the intuitive system operates unchecked. However, therapeutic ruptures and unexpected poor outcomes may require the rational system to kick in and ask the question: How can my formulation make sense of this? Then a more rational approach is taken to formulate and choose a way forward.

In summary, the decision-making and clinical judgment literature suggests that heuristics are likely to play a central role in CBT formulation processes, and that these are problematic in circumstances of high uncertainty, time pressure and other forms of stressors. Recent models of decision-making (Kahneman 2003) provide a useful framework for understanding how intuitive and rational decision-making relate to one another.

Can clinicians agree?

The second aspect of reliability is the output of the formulation process: namely, the stated hypothesis or formulation practitioners hold at any given time. Competent CBT practitioners would normally have a set of hypotheses, a diagram or a written formulation as part of their case and supervision notes, which guides their intervention (Beck 1995). Given that case formulation aims to draw on appropriate CBT theory to make inferences about a particular case using a systematic approach, it is reasonable to suppose that two practitioners asked to make inferences about the same case using the same theory and same case formulation framework should construct similar formulations. On the other hand, given the complexity of this task and the intrinsic role of heuristics in formulation it may be too much to expect any level of consistency.

Perhaps the most comprehensive consideration of clinician agreement comes from psychodynamic research, where case formulation using the core conflictual relationship theme (CCRT) method of formulation has been examined in eight studies, and agreement in the moderate to good range (kappa range .6–.8) has been found (Luborsky and Diguer 1998). Reliability was better for some aspects of the CCRT method than others and more skilled and systematic judges tended to show higher rates of agreement with each other.

Less CBT formulation research on clinician agreement has been done, but a handful of studies have yielded some consensus findings as well as some areas of divergence. Jacqueline Persons *et al.* (1995) asked 46 practitioners to listen to audiotapes of initial interviews with two clients and identify the presenting problems and underlying core beliefs. The results suggested generally good agreement among judges in identifying the presenting problems, but poor agreement in identifying the hypothesised underlying cognitive mechanisms. In a second study, Persons and Bertagnolli (1999) attempted to increase reliability by supplying practitioners with a specific set of problem domains (psychiatric symptoms as well as interpersonal, work, financial, health, housing and recreational problems) and more formalised assessment of schemas (using anchor points and specific definitions of a variety of schemas). Again, however, inter-judge reliabilities in assessing schemas were adequate, but only across multiple judges (averaging .72 for five randomly selected judges; Persons and Bertagnolli 1999). Refinements in methodology across these two studies did not lead to improvements in reliability on the key inferences about underlying cognitive mechanisms. More recently the reliability of cognitive formulation was examined using a range of cognitive-behavioural interpersonal scenarios drawn from four cases (Mumma and Smith 2001). The results show that reliability of the mean ratings was good for all 15 dimensions (.83) when aggregated across the 10 clinical raters. However, as with earlier studies, the reliability of a single practitioner's ratings was acceptable for the descriptive elements but relatively low (from .33 to .63) for the inferential elements. Attempting to improve on design and ecological validity, a recent study trained 115 mental health professionals in a systematic case formulation method (the J. Beck Case Conceptualisation Diagram; Beck 1995), and asked them to formulate using information from a comprehensive CBT assessment of a single case (Kuyken *et al.* 2005). Rates of agreement were high for the descriptive aspects of the formulation (deriving the important developmental experiences), moderate for the more readily interpretable inferential aspects (core beliefs and compensatory strategies) and poor for the more difficult to infer dysfunctional assumptions.

In summary, these studies suggest that CBT practitioners can agree on the descriptive aspects of a formulation but agreement on the inferential aspects tends to be moderate in optimal conditions and poor more generally. This may be due either to problems with study methodology or to real difficulties in the formulation process. In terms of methodological issues, the nature of the case material presented for review is important. Studies have struggled to balance the need to use the data available to 'real world' practitioners – a comprehensive intake interview, standardised assessment instruments, prototypical examples of situation–thought–emotion–behaviour cycles, the downward arrow technique and clients' emotional shifts in session (Beck *et al.* 1979; Beck 1995) – with the need to maintain deign rigour (Heverly *et al.* 1984). Moreover, studies to date have used samples of convenience, rather than sampling a range of cognitive therapists from novice to expert.

However, it is also possible that poor agreement on cognitive case formulations is due to heuristic decision-making biases. If this is the case, it would follow that more systematic and objective case formulation systems should be less prone to these inferential biases and 'true' rates of agreement between practitioners should be observable. At least one study provides preliminary evidence that systematic frameworks such as the J. Beck Case Conceptualisation Diagram enhance the reliability of practitioners' formulations on the more readily interpretable cognitive and behavioural mechanisms (Kuyken *et al.* 2005).

IS THE FORMULATION VALID: DOES IT TRIANGULATE WITH THE CLIENT'S EXPERIENCE, ANY STANDARDISED MEASURES, PROFESSIONAL/ EXPERT/PANEL CONSENSUS AND CLINICAL SUPERVISOR'S IMPRESSIONS?

This simple question has been subjected to almost no research. There is no evidence of whether practitioner, client and supervisor formulations converge. Several of the reliability studies report that rates of agreement tend to be best across larger panels of judges, suggesting that panel consensus is achievable (Mumma and Smith 2001; Persons and Bertagnolli 1999; Persons *et al.* 1995). One recent study compared the formulations of a client diagnosed with depression and personality disorder derived by 115 mental health practitioners following a workshop on the J. Beck Case Conceptualisation Diagram with the prototype formulation derived by J. Beck of the same case. Agreement with the prototype formulation was high for the descriptive information, moderate for the easier to infer inferential information (core beliefs and compensatory strategies) and poor for the more difficult inferential beliefs (dysfunctional assumptions; Kuyken *et al.* 2005). This study also approached the issue from a different perspective, developing a measure of the quality of case formulations (defined as parsimonious, coherent and meaningful accounts). A minority of formulations were judged to be 'good enough' in quality. Importantly, the quality of formulations was significantly higher among practitioners with more clinical experience and among practitioners who were accredited as cognitive therapists.

Cognitive-analytic therapy (CAT) uses case formulation overtly to build a shared understanding of the presenting issues, develop the therapeutic relationship and inform intervention (Ryle and Kerr 2003). The underpinning theory is a mixture of psychodynamic and cognitive-behavioural concepts. In an innovative study, a client's CAT formulation was cross-validated to well standardised measures of underlying core conflictual relationship themes and interpersonal styles (Bennett and Parry 1998). The comparison supported the validity of the recurrent relationship patterns identified in the case formulation across triangulated sources of information.

In summary, the paucity of evidence is the most striking feature of the research examining the validity of CBT formulations. Preliminary work suggests that CBT formulations may prove to be valid on the more readily interpretable elements, and among more experienced CBT practitioners.

DOES THE FORMULATION IMPROVE INTERVENTION AND THERAPY OUTCOMES?

A primary criterion whereby case formulation stands or falls is whether it directly or indirectly improves the process or outcome of CBT. There is limited evidence linking case formulation with outcome. Behaviour therapy and to a lesser extent CBT has addressed this criterion in a series of fascinating studies. In behavioural therapy a functional analysis of the presenting issue is normally considered essential to the development of a behavioural intervention plan (Haynes and Williams 2003). Similarly more recent CBT approaches use formulation as a 'first principle' in intervention planning (Freeston et al. 2001; Morrison 2002).

An early study of behaviour therapy for couples who were distressed compared manualised with individualised therapy formats. The research rationale was that the individualised approach should outperform the manualised approach because each therapy was tailored to the needs of the particular couple. However, therapy outcomes for both conditions were comparable at termination, although individualised treatment led to somewhat improved maintenance of gains at six-month follow-up (Jacobson et al. 1989). In a seminal study of 120 clients diagnosed with phobias, clients were randomised to one of three conditions: manualised (exposure), individualised and a yoked control (i.e., clients received treatment based on a different client's individualised formulation!; Schulte et al. 1992). Contrary to the researchers' hypotheses, the manualised condition out-performed the other two conditions. An extended range of post-hoc analyses explored possible explanations for this finding, and although they found that therapists tailor manuals to individuals even if instructed not to, this did not explain away the findings (Schulte et al. 1992). An essential replication of this finding was reported by Emmelkamp and colleagues for clients diagnosed with obsessive-compulsive presentations (Emmelkamp *et al.* 1994). These studies of behaviour therapy fail to show any supremacy of individualised over manualised approaches, and indeed suggest that manualised approaches are associated with better outcomes.

No comparable CBT studies exist, although three single case series address the question. An early single case series of CBT for depression treated nine women with major depression with one of three treatments: multi-modal CBT (including three main components of CBT: behavioural activation, thought challenging and interpersonal focus), individualised CBT (modules matched to clients' particular presentations) and mismatched CBT (modules mismatched to clients' presentations; Nelson-Gray *et al.* 1989). While the numbers in each condition were very small, the data suggested that the multi-modal interventions produced more consistent clinically significant long-term gains than either the matched or mismatched interventions. Interestingly the matched interventions did not differentially impact on the corresponding area of function (e.g., cognitive structuring and change in negative beliefs).

As already mentioned, cognitive-analytic therapy (Ryle *et al.* 1997) involves the therapist and client in writing a joint formulation letter to increase clients' understanding of their presenting issues, enhance the therapeutic relationship and enable change. Research using a multiple baseline design with four difficult-to-help clients found no support for the hypothesis that the formulation letter would lead to improvements in the therapeutic alliance or to improvements in symptoms (Evans and Parry 1996). Two linked studies have used a similar single case series design to establish the effect of CBT case formulation on the therapeutic relationship, beliefs and symptoms among people with delusions (Chadwick *et al.* 2003). Interestingly, cognitive case formulation did not discernibly affect patients' ratings of the alliance, but did positively influence therapists' ratings of the alliance. Furthermore, case formulation, as an intervention in its own right, did not directly impact beliefs or symptoms, even though the evidence suggested that successful subsequent restructuring of beliefs led to symptom improvements.

In summary, these studies fail to demonstrate the direct impact of cognitive case formulation on improved CBT outcomes or on measured therapy processes. They do, however, raise important conceptual questions. First, these studies share in common the assumption that the formulation should be explicitly shared with the client, which is not necessarily a feature of cognitive therapy. Second, the earlier review suggests that a large proportion of practitioners' case formulation processes take place intuitively. These studies have not found a way of addressing how intuitive case formulation processes might impact on the process and outcomes of therapy. Third, studies have made the problematic assumption that case formulation might impact outcome directly rather than indirectly. A number of indirect pathways are possible, including the selection of more appropriate interventions throughout the therapy, anticipating problems in therapy, enabling high quality supervision, enhanced therapist confidence, encouraging accountability in the formulation process or some combination of these factors.

IS FORMULATION ACCEPTABLE AND USEFUL?

This criterion asks whether case formulation commands the respect of CBT clients, and is widely regarded as useful by practitioners, trainers and clinical researchers. Two studies have asked clients of CAT (Evans and Parry 1996) and CBT (Chadwick *et al.* 2003) about their experiences of case formulation. Clients reported reactions that were both positive (better understanding, therapist listened, way forward for therapy) and negative (overwhelming, frightening, involving 'material I had been trying to blank out,' problems seeming more complex and longstanding). This work is salutary as rationales for case formulation tend to focus on the positive and rarely consider possible negative impacts on clients.

In terms of clinical practice, it is increasingly accepted as a dictum among cognitive therapy trainers that a high quality case formulation is needed to work successfully with a person in distress, especially when the presenting problems are complex (Beck 1995; Needleman 1999). Indeed, a great deal of time and expense is devoted to the training and supervision of novice cognitive therapists in the 'art' of case formulation. Workshops on cognitive formulation are increasingly common and case formulation increasingly appears in the table of contents and indices of cognitive therapy texts. Beyond any doubt, cognitive therapy case formulation shows the promise of meeting the criterion of pragmatic usefulness in clinical practice. In terms of research, a literature search of empirical papers on case formulation in the last decade yields very few citations, suggesting that case formulation has found a place in practice well ahead of any evidence base for its purported advantages.

In isolation, the criterion of acceptability and usefulness is neither necessary nor sufficient to endorse the use of case formulation, as the psychological therapies arena is littered with examples of highly fertile but ultimately unsubstantiated ideas. However, using an evolutionary analogy, the 'fitness' of an idea will determine its advance. In this sense, the systematic evaluation of the case formulation approach can only contribute to its fitness with respect to a fuller understanding of its explanatory power, clinical application and acceptability to cognitive therapy providers and consumers.

RECOMMENDATIONS FOR RESEARCH AND CLINICAL PRACTICE

Recommendations for future research

Research to date suggests that cognitive theories of emotional disorders are at minimum good descriptive theories with high face validity. They provide a psychological description of emotional distress in cognitive and behavioural terms with clear practice implications. Empirical examination of cognitive theories is ongoing and enables practitioners to draw on best available research. For example, the original cognitive theory of depression has been reformulated to take into account conflicting research on the original theory and has since yielded further reformulations to address particular forms of depression, such as those marked by hopelessness (Abramson et al. 1989) or by frequent recurrence (Segal et al. 1996). These innovations are key to informing treatment innovations (Segal et al. 2002). An optimistic view would be that the challenge of an empirically supported theory and intervention for emotional disorders will in time be met (at least in part).

The main outstanding research challenges relate to the bottom-up criteria for case formulation. In brief, can the many claimed benefits of CBT case formulation (Figure 2.1) be subject to empirical enquiry? The fact that brief psychodynamic psychotherapy has benefited considerably from research into the CCRT (Luborsky and Crits-Christoph 1998) attests to the feasibility and utility of such a research programme.

How do cognitive therapists formulate in the 'real world'?

This simple question goes almost unanswered. One exploratory study asked CBT and psychodynamic therapists along the dimension novice–expert to formulate from some case descriptions and then answer some questions about the case, their formulations and their intervention recommendations (Eells and Lombart 2003). This study suggested that practitioners are reasonably consensual about what information is important (in decreasing order: symptoms/problems, precipitating stressors, coping style and childhood history) and are confident to begin to formulate from relatively limited amounts of case information, and that greater experience/expertise leads to longer intervention recommendations. A series of exploratory studies could usefully ask CBT practitioners what formulation means to them in practice. What form does it take, how much is it developed and elaborated collaboratively with clients, how does it relate to the intervention, at what stage is a formulation relatively coherent and complete and so on. Much is assumed about 'best case formulation practice' but there are no empirical data to substantiate that this is borne out in practice. This work could take the form of interviewing CBT practitioners and clients regarding the claimed benefits of case formulation and studying tapes of CBT sessions to examine the process of formulations being developed and explored.

What affects the quality of heuristic decision-making? What parameters on decision-making can yield 'good enough' working formulations?

The research to date suggests that rates of agreement on inferential aspects of CBT formulation tend to be low, especially when the process is less structured or arguably when the practitioners are less experienced. Examining clinical decision-making among CBT practitioners using extant decision-making theory and methodology will illuminate how a range of individual and situational factors affect formulation: the practitioner's values, cognitive complexity and preferred decision-making style, and the situation's inherent complexity, risk and emotiveness (cf. Kahneman 2003).

Do cognitive case formulations relate meaningfully to people's problems and the factors underlying these problems?

The question of whether CBT formulations are valid in a range of ways goes almost unanswered and a creative CAT study (Bennett and Parry 1998) provides one potential line of further research. Studies comparing case formulations with a benchmark standard and looking at the coherence of formulations (Kuyken *et al.* 2005) provide another possible line of further enquiry.

Does the quality of decision-making and/or working formulation affect the process and outcome of therapy?

Intriguing early studies into the relationship of formulation to therapy processes and outcome have raised more questions than they have answered. Studies that show indirect impacts on outcome through alternative pathways are urgently required. Formulation-adherent interpretations in brief psychodynamic psychotherapy do produce more symptom change than formulation non-adherent interpretations, as found in a seminal study that requires extension to CBT (Crits-Christoph *et al.* 1988).

In summary, CBT formulation is a cornerstone of CBT practice in urgent need of systematic research. For a therapeutic modality in its early stages of development, this is as it should be. The research agenda outlined above will move us closer to an evidence-based approach to cognitive formulation.

Implications for CBT training and practice

This review suggests several specific clinical implications for practitioners using case formulation in their work. The decision-making literature in particular suggests a number of helpful implications for practice (Figure 2.4 and see Arkes 1981, 1991; Kahneman 2003).

The basic CBT principle of collaborative empiricism is an excellent approach to balancing the natural tendency to use intuitive heuristic processes in clinical judgments with rational decision-making acting as a check and balance. An explicit stance of generating only provisional hypotheses, holding alternative hypotheses in mind and providing adequate tests of these hypotheses enables the rational system to counter-balance and correct any problematic biases. The work on the reliability of case formulations suggests that practitioners should stay closer to the descriptive levels of formulation because the further they move from description to inference the more likely they are to form idiosyncratic understandings. Moreover, these studies suggest that rates of agreement improve when more judges are involved, indicating the importance of supervision groups. Triangulation in assessment, formulation and evaluation is more likely to converge towards a valid formulation. If formulation functions to identify a core mechanism for therapeutic focus (Butler 1998), this triangulation towards a valid formulation becomes absolutely key.

Decision-making is known to be affected by a range of factors such as

---

Evidence-based guidelines for generating 'good enough' CBT formulations

1. Generate provisional formulations

2. Hold alternative formulations in mind

3. Provide adequate tests for formulations (e.g., behavioural experiments)

4. Triangulate by testing out hypotheses with client, individuals in client's network, supervisor and standardised assessments

5. Be sensitive to the impact of factors known to affect judgment (e.g., task complexity, practitioner competence and time pressures)

6. Justify formulations through case notes and/or supervision

7. Follow manualised approaches

8. Follow contemporary practice guidelines

9. Formulate using best available CBT theory and research

Figure 2.4 Evidence-based guidelines for generating 'good enough' CBT formulations.

problem complexity, therapist experience and time pressures. An awareness of how formulation may be adversely affected by these factors can enable practitioners to work towards systems and processes that enable high quality formulation. There is some evidence that training and experience are pre-requisites for high quality formulations; increased attention to formulation in professional training and continuing professional education is indicated. The argument has already been made that the rational system provides a check and balance to the dominant intuitive system in decision-making. Case notes and supervision should involve making explicit (and thereby testing) formulations.

The final implications for clinical practice emerge from the failure to date to demonstrate that case formulation affects outcomes and processes in therapy as would be hypothesised. At the same time, extensive work is invested in the development of practice guidelines about what therapies to use for whom which are based on the synthesis of large bodies of best available evidence (e.g., Hollon and Shelton 2001). The emerging use of case formulation approaches rather than manualised approaches or practice based on 'best understanding' requires a clear demonstration of the supremacy of case formulation approaches in terms of description, understanding and, crucially, outcomes. To date this has not been compellingly demonstrated. A natural conclusion is: when in doubt follow the evidence base and treatment guidelines. Reasons and rationales for alternative approaches need to be explicit and defensible using appropriate, valid and weighted evidence.

The research suggests a careful consideration of clients' positive and negative experiences of developing shared formulations. To use an analogy, a navigator who shares the whole road map with the driver may hinder rather than help the driver keep on track because the driver is given information not directly relevant to the current task and the amount of information may be overwhelming. Collaboratively and gradually developing shared understandings and responding to feedback is an important method in CBT for ensuring understanding is developed constructively.

In summary, these clinical implications are about generating formulations with attention to valid and weighted evidence (to minimise availability biases) with humility (to avoid dispositional biases that can occur with over-confidence) and with openness to any change required by new data (to avoid anchoring biases). Although in practice formulation is not a rational and systematic process, the balanced synthesis of the intuitive and rational cognitive systems can probably enable 'good enough' formulation that does not deviate too far on the continuum from optimal to frankly dangerous formulations. The guidelines in Figure 2.4 are intended to enable this balanced synthesis.

SUMMARY

At the outset of this chapter I asked whether CBT case formulation is evidence-based: is the emperor clothed? It is important that case formulation in CBT should be evidence-based because it is increasingly being advocated as an important determinant of intervention rationales and choices (e.g., Butler 1998; Needleman 1999). The findings of 25 years of increasingly sophisticated outcome research suggest that CBT is effective to a clinically significant degree for a majority of patients with a variety of presenting problems in a range of populations and settings. An evidence-based conclusion is that cognitive therapy is a treatment of choice for people diagnosed with depression, generalised anxiety, panic, bulimia nervosa, psychosis and a range of somatoform disorders. More recently, preliminary outcome studies suggest that cognitive therapy is a promising intervention for people diagnosed with personality disorders and substance misuse, but further research is indicated. Even though CBT theory has been extensively researched and CBT practice is the treatment of choice for many emotional disorders, CBT does not claim a complete theoretical explanation or an unfailing therapeutic approach. CBT is undoubtedly evidence-based: the 'CBT emperor' is clothed, albeit not imperiously.

This review set out some criteria against which to judge the evidence base for CBT formulation. It has shown that, for the most part, the evidence base for CBT formulation's haughty claims is limited and what evidence exists is weak. The evidence for the reliability of case formulation is supportive of descriptive but not inferential hypotheses and the evidence for the validity of case formulation is very limited but promising. There is no compelling evidence that CBT formulation enhances therapy processes or outcomes. The evidence for the acceptability and usefulness of formulation is mixed. In summary, CBT formulation practice has extended significantly beyond the evidence base. To conclude that cognitive case formulation is not an evidence-based element of CBT and should not be used would be premature; absence of evidence is not the same as evidence of absence. The 'CBT case formulation emperor' is only very sparsely clothed. Clearly there is a need for a systematic research agenda that will provide an invaluable augmentation of evidence-based CBT practice and this chapter has outlined a possible research programme. In the interim, the chapter set out some recommendations for practitioners that will enable the conscientious, explicit and judicious use of CBT case formulations.

ACKNOWLEDGMENTS

I am grateful to my collaborators Peter J. Bieling, Paul Chadwick and Rob Dudley in developing the ideas in this chapter and for their comments on an earlier draft.

NOTES

1   This chapter refers to case formulation and a person's presenting problems for the sake of consistency. However, a case formulation can equally be of the presenting issues of a couple, family, group or organisation.
2   A common critique I have faced from colleagues and students in considering this question has been: Is the question answerable? My response has been to point to the work of Lester Luborsky and colleagues over a quarter of century examining the Core Conflictual Relationship Theme (CCRT) case formulation method (Luborsky and Crits-Christoph 1998). The CCRT is a psychodynamic framework that enables practitioners and researchers to listen to clients describe their relationship problems and infer core conflicts from psychodynamic theory (wishes towards the self, wishes towards others, response from others and responses from the self). This research programme has elegantly demonstrated that the CCRT can be used reliably, corresponds with related measures of defensive functioning and, when used skilfully by therapists, improves clinical outcomes (Crits-Christoph *et al.* 1988). In short, the CCRT is an exemplar of an evidence-based approach to case formulation in psychodynamic psychotherapy.

RECOMMENDED READING

Bieling, P. J. and Kuyken, W. (2003). Is cognitive case formulation science or science fiction? *Clinical Psychology – Science and Practice* 10: 52–69.

Garb, H. N. (1998). *Studying the Clinician: Judgment Research and Psychological Assessment*. Washington, DC: American Psychological Association.

Needleman, L. D. (1999). *Cognitive Case Conceptualisation: A Guidebook for Practitioners*. Mahwah, NJ: Lawrence Erlbaum.

REFERENCES

Abramson, L. Y. *et al.* (1989). Hopelessness depression: A theory- based subtype of depression. *Psychological Review* 90: 372.

Addis, M. E. (2002). Methods of disseminating research product and increasing evidence-based practice: Promises, obstacles and future directions. *Clinical Psychology: Science and Practice* 9: 367–78.

Arkes, H. R. (1981). Impediments to accurate clinical judgment and possible ways to minimize their impact. *Journal of Consulting and Clinical Psychology* 49: 323–30.

Arkes, H. R. (1991). Costs and benefits of judgment errors – implications for debiasing. *Psychological Bulletin* 110: 486–98.

Beck, A. T. (1976). *Cognitive therapy and emotional disorders*. New York: Meridian.

Beck, A. T. (1996). Beyond belief: A theory of modes, personality and psychopathology. In P. M. Salkovskis (ed) *Frontiers of Cognitive Therapy*. New York: Guilford Press.

Beck, A. T. *et al.* (1979). *Cognitive Therapy of Depression*. New York: Guilford Press.

Beck, J. S. (1995). *Cognitive Therapy: Basics and Beyond*. New York: Guilford Press.

Bennett, D. and Parry, G. (1998). The accuracy of reformulation in cognitive analytic therapy: A validation study. *Psychotherapy Research* 5: 54–103.

Bieling, P. J. and Kuyken, W. (2003). Is cognitive case formulation science or science fiction? *Clinical Psychology: Science and Practice* 10: 52–69.

Butler, G. (1998). Clinical formulation. In A. S. Bellack and M. Hersen (eds) *Comprehensive Clinical Psychology*. New York: Pergammon Press.

Chadwick, P. *et al.* (1996). *Cognitive Therapy for Delusions, Voices and Paranoia*. New York: Wiley.

Chadwick, P. *et al.* (2003). Impact of case formulation in cognitive behaviour therapy for psychosis. *Behaviour Research and Therapy* 41: 671–80.

Chapman, L. J. and Chapman, J. P. (1967). Genesis of popular but erroneous psychodiagnostic observations. *Journal of Abnormal Psychology* 72: 193–204.

Chapman, L. J. and Chapman, J. P. (1969). Illusory correlation as an obstacle to the use of valid psychodiagnostic signs. *Journal of Abnormal Psychology* 74: 271–80.

Christensenszalanski, J. J. J. and Beach, L. R. (1984). The citation bias: Fad and fashion in the judgment and decision literature. *American Psychologist* 39: 75–8.

Clark, D. A. *et al.* (1999). *Scientific Foundations of Cognitive Theory and Therapy of Depression*. New York: Wiley.

Crits-Christoph, P. *et al.* (1988). The accuracy of therapists' interpretations and the outcome of dynamic psychotherapy. *Journal of Consulting and Clinical Psychology* 56: 490–5.

Davis, D. A. (1979). What's in a name? A Bayesian rethinking of attributional biases in clinical judgment. *Journal of Consulting and Clinical Psychology* 47: 1109–14.

Eells, T. D. and Lombart, K. G. (2003). Case formulation and treatment concepts among novice, experienced, and expert cognitive-behavioral and psychodynamic therapists. *Psychotherapy Research* 13: 187–204.

Emmelkamp, P. M. G. *et al.* (1994). Individualized versus standardized therapy: A comparative evaluation with obsessive-compulsive patients. *Clinical Psychology and Psychotherapy* 1: 95–100.

Evans, J. and Parry, G. (1996). The impact of reformulation in cognitive-analytic therapy with difficult-to-help clients. *Clinical Psychology and Psychotherapy* 3: 109–17.

Fairburn, C. G. *et al.* (2003). Cognitive behaviour therapy for eating disorders: A 'transdiagnostic' theory and treatment. *Behaviour Research and Therapy* 41: 509–28.

Freeston, M. H. *et al.* (2001). Cognitive therapy of obsessive thoughts. *Cognitive and Behavioral Practice* 8: 61–78.

Friedlander, M. L. and Phillips, S. D. (1984). Preventing anchoring errors in clinical judgment. *Journal of Consulting and Clinical Psychology* 52: 366–71.

Haynes, S. N. and Williams, A. E. (2003). Case formulation and design of behavioral treatment programs: Matching treatment mechanisms to causal variables for behavior problems. *European Journal of Psychological Assessment* 19: 164–74.

Heverly, M. A. *et al.* (1984). Constructing case vignettes for evaluating clinical judgment: An empirical model. *Evaluation and Program Planning* 7: 45–55.

Hollon, S. D. and Shelton, R. C. (2001). Treatment guidelines for major depressive disorder. *Behavior Therapy* 32: 235–58.

Jacobson, N. S. *et al.* (1989). Research-structured vs clinically flexible versions of social learning-based marital therapy. *Behaviour Research and Therapy* 27: 173–80.

Jones, E. E. and Nisbett, R. E. (1971). *The Actor and the Observer: Divergent Perceptions of the Causes of Behaviour*. Morristown, NJ: General Learning Press.

Kahneman, D. (2003). A perspective on judgment and choice: Mapping bounded rationality. *American Psychologist* 58: 697–720.

Kuyken, W. *et al.* (2005). The reliability and quality of cognitive case formulation. *Behaviour Research and Therapy* 43: 1187–201.

Luborsky, L. and Crits-Christoph, P. (1998). *Understanding Transference: The Core Conflictual Relationship Theme Method* (2nd edn). New York: Basic Books.

Luborsky, L. and Diguer, L. (1998). The reliability of the CCRT measure: Results from eight samples. In L. Luborsky and P. Crits-Crisroph (eds) *Understanding Transference: The Core Conflictual Relationship Theme Method* (2nd edn). New York: Basic Books.

Meehl, P. E. (1973). Why I do not attend case conferences. In P. E. Meehl (ed) *Psychodiagnosis: Selected Papers*. New York: Norton.

Morrison, A. (2002). *A Casebook of Therapy for Psychosis*. New York: Brunner-Routledge.

Mumma, G. H. and Smith, J. L. (2001). Cognitive-behavioral-interpersonal scenarios: Interformulator reliability and convergent validity. *Journal of Psychopathology and Behavioral Assessment* 23: 203–21.

Needleman, L. D. (1999). *Cognitive Case Conceptualisation: A Guidebook for Practitioners*. Mahwah, NJ: Lawrence Erlbaum.

Nelson-Gray, R. O. *et al.* (1989). Effectiveness of matched, mismatched, and package treatments of depression. *Journal of Behavior Therapy and Experimental Psychiatry* 20: 281–94.

Newman, C. F. *et al.* (2002). *Bipolar Disorder: A Cognitive Therapy Approach*. Washington, DC: American Psychological Association.

Persons, J. B. and Bertagnolli, A. (1999). Inter-rater reliability of cognitive-behavioral case formulations of depression: A replication. *Cognitive Therapy and Research* 23: 271–83.

Persons, J. B. *et al.* (1995). Interrater reliability of cognitive-behavioral case formulations. *Cognitive Therapy and Research* 19: 21–34.

Rosenhan, D. L. (1973). On being sane in insane places. *Science* 179: 250–8.

Ryle, A. and Kerr, I. (2003). *Introducing Cognitive Analytic Therapy*. Chichester, UK: Wiley.

Ryle, A. *et al.* (1997). *Cognitive Analytic Therapy and Borderline Personality Disorder: The Model and the Method*. London: John Wiley and Sons.

Sackett, D. L. *et al.* (1996). Evidence based medicine: What it is and what it isn't – It's about integrating individual clinical expertise and the best external evidence. *British Medical Journal* 312: 71–2.

Schulte, D. *et al.* (1992). Tailor-made versus standardized therapy of phobic patients. *Advances in Behaviour Research and Therapy* 14: 67–92.

Segal, Z. V. *et al.* (1996). A cognitive science perspective on kindling and episode sensitization in recurrent affective disorder. *Psychological Medicine* 26: 371–80.

Segal, Z. V. *et al.* (2002). *Mindfulness-Based Cognitive Therapy for Depression: A New Approach to Preventing Relapse*. New York: Guilford Press.

Smith, J. D. and Dumont, F. (2002). Confidence in psychodiagnosis: What makes us so sure? *Clinical Psychology and Psychotherapy* 9: 298.

Spengler, M. and Strohmer, D. C. (1994). Clinical judgment biases: The moderating roles of counselor cognitive complexity and counselor client preferences. *Journal of Counseling Psychology* 1: 8–17.

Thase, M. (1997). Cognitive-behavioural therapy for substance abuse disorders. In M. B. R. Dickstein and J. M. Oldham (eds) *American Psychiatric Association Review of Psychiatry*. Washington, DC: American Psychiatric Press.

Tversky, A. and Kahneman, D. (1974). Judgment under uncertainty: Heuristics and biases. *Science* 185: 1124–31.

Westmeyer, H. (2003). On the structure of case formulations. *European Journal of Psychological Assessment* 19: 210–6.

Chapter 3

Formulation from the perspective of contextualism

Chris Cullen and Helen Combes

SOME OLD HISTORY

Much of the behavioural approach is said to have its roots in early operant and classical conditioning work with non-human animals, notably rats and pigeons. It is from this pioneering work that the importance of setting events and consequences came to be understood. In clinical work arising from behavioural approaches, consequences, in particular reinforcement, have assumed a massive significance. Behavioural clinicians have been caricatured as always looking for reinforcers – notwithstanding the fact that reinforcement is a relation, and not a thing (cf. Catania 1992), but that's another story. Consider then, the following (somewhat hypothetical) scenario.

You are taken as a visitor to an operant laboratory – some time ago, since such experiments would rarely be carried out today – and you are shown a pigeon in an experimental chamber. All the usual paraphernalia are present, and the pigeon pecks at an illuminated key on the wall of the chamber. Nothing else happens, even though you wait for quite some time. What you notice especially is that there is no reinforcer delivered. You are then invited to explain why the pigeon is pecking in the absence of a reinforcing consequence.

This is an exercise we have used many times with trainee clinicians. If the point of the exercise is not immediately obvious, consider how many clients appear to engage in behaviour which seems to be pointless, or even dangerous, in the apparent absence of any positive pay-off.

Answers often given to the conundrum include: the pigeon is expecting food since the response was shaped up initially in the standard operant paradigm; the pigeon is bored; the pigeon has developed an obsessive-compulsive disorder (now we're getting closer to real-world clinical phenomena); and so on.

Eventually someone may hit upon the possibility that something unpleasant might happen if the pigeon doesn't peck. This is the correct answer. The pigeon's behaviour is on an avoidance schedule, and failure to peck results in some noxious event, usually electric shock. Because nothing appears to be happening, the person looking at the behaviour in the here and now, with no information about how the behaviour came to be established, will be at a loss to know how to explain it.

Early avoidance experiments used a discrete trial training approach, with each presentation of the shock preceded by a brief warning stimulus. Early theorists, puzzled by the absence of any obvious reinforcers for successful avoidance, talked of a reduction in the likelihood of expected shock, with concomitant reductions in fear and anxiety, which 'did the trick' (cf. Dinsmoor 2001a). Thus, the hapless pigeon was said to have become anxious as a result of its history of receiving shock, and when a brief warning stimulus sounded it would spring into action to prevent the shock which would follow. Because the bird was successful at preventing shocks its anxiety would decrease, an obvious (albeit unseen) reinforcer. We can imagine apparent parallels in real-world clinical situations – for instance, the client who escapes at the first signs of someone getting close to her because intimate relationships have failed in the past, with concomitant heartache.

Even more challenging to explain, however, is avoidance behaviour when there is no warning stimulus (Sidman 1953). In this paradigm, brief shocks are presented at pre-determined intervals unless the animal responds. Responding postpones the shock. Some theorists have postulated that tactile and proprio-ceptive stimuli generated by ineffective or non-avoidance behaviour would become aversive to the animal, and hence the animal would behave in order to escape from these. Continuing with the example above, perhaps the person would learn to avoid any situation which might conceivably lead to the possibility of a relationship.

Whatever is the 'correct' theory need not concern us here. There is continu-ing debate on this matter in the behaviour analytic literature (cf. Baron and Perone 2001; Baum 2001; Bersh 2001; Branch 2001; Dinsmoor 2001a, 2001b; Hineline 2001; Michael and Clark 2001; Sidman 2001; Williams 2001). Although this may seem remote from the concerns of clinicians, there is relevance to the problem of formulation from a behavioural standpoint. Our contention is that much clinical formulation requires not only a careful and thorough assessment of client behaviour now, and its relation to current environmental events, but also an understanding of the person's behavioural history. Unfortunately this will rarely be clear or obvious to us, or indeed to the client. We should also point out that we are not claiming any direct analogy between real-world situations for humans and the relatively simple experimental manipulations researchers have conducted with non-humans. These may point the way to an understanding of basic processes, but simple schedules rarely explain human behaviour (cf. Cullen 1981; Poppen 1982).

BASIC BEHAVIOURAL FORMULATION

Traditionally, formulation from a behavioural perspective involves a detailed description of current behaviour(s) and attempts to identify the relatively immediate antecedents and consequences which appear to be related to the behaviour. For example, a client gets upset and tearful when challenged which leads to people not challenging. So, being upset and tearful becomes a prominent part of the person's repertoire when they face difficult and challenging circumstances.

It has typically been in services for people with intellectual disabilities that simple formulation in terms of antecedents (A)-behaviour (B)-consequences (C) has survived. In some cases these simple formulations prove to be very helpful, especially to staff with little experience. For example, a client presents with self-injurious behaviour, which consists of hitting himself on the side of his head. Over several days care staff are asked to note each time he hits himself; what was going on at the time; what happened immediately after he hit himself; who was present; and so on. An examination of the records shows that this tends to happen during morning and afternoon occupational therapy sessions, when he is expected to participate in various tasks. Once he starts hitting himself he is removed to another room and 'diverted' by a dedicated member of staff.

It becomes clear that his hitting has an escape function, and has positive consequences. Formulating the problem in this way allows questions to be asked about the value (to the client) of the tasks he is expected to do, and why he experiences one-to-one contact as so desirable – so much so that he is willing to hurt himself in order to get it. Perhaps the task can be altered so that he doesn't want to escape from the situation, maybe by providing powerful consequences for participating. Perhaps the consequences can involve giving him dedicated one-to-one contact while productively engaged.

The utility of such relatively simple formulations should not be undervalued, since they can lead to significant changes. In recent years, for example, a methodology has evolved which enables the clinician/researcher to manipulate aspects of the environment to determine whether a behaviour is maintained by a consequence, or is an escape response, or an avoidance response, or is happening because the person effectively has nothing else to do. This 'analogue assessment' is very useful in determining relatively simple behavioural functions (cf. Sturmey 1995).

However, it is often the case – as in the avoidance paradigms we discussed at the beginning of this chapter – that more is needed. Consider the infamous historical behavioural 'experiment' to condition 'emotional reactions' in an 11-month-old child, Albert B. (Watson and Rayner 1920). Albert was made to fear a white rat which he had previously played with, by having a loud noise paired with presentations of the rodent. His fear generalised to other stimuli, such as a rabbit, a dog, a fur coat and a Santa Claus mask. They had planned to reverse the fear, but Albert's mother removed him from the institution before re-conditioning could begin. Watson and Rayner (1920) considered the difficulty future clinicians might have in formulating an analysis of Albert's fear, and they mischievously contributed to the battle between behaviourists and psychoanalysts which was raging at the time:

> The Freudians twenty years from now, unless their hypotheses change, when they come to analyse Albert's fear of a seal skin coat – assuming that he comes to analysis at the age – will probably tease from him the recital of a dream which upon their analysis will show that Albert at three years of age attempted to play with the pubic hair of the mother and was scolded violently for it. (We are by no means denying that this might in some other case condition it). If the analyst has sufficiently prepared Albert to accept such a dream when found as an explanation of his avoiding tendencies, and if the analyst has the authority and personality to put it over, Albert may be fully convinced that the dream was a true revealer of the factors which brought about the fear.
>
> (Watson and Rayner 1920: 14)

The problem the therapist has is that s/he does not have direct access to the classical or operant conditioning processes which were involved in establishing the behaviour. All they can access is the present, which includes the clients' views on what parts of their history are relevant to their current problems. This is not a difficulty faced only by behavioural clinicians, of course.

THE CONSTRUCTIONAL APPROACH

The process of formulation involves the structured gathering of data, a point made throughout this book. An early attempt to devise an assessment protocol which would allow a more sophisticated behavioural formulation was that of Israel Goldiamond (Goldiamond 1974; Schwartz and Goldiamond 1975). This arose from Goldiamond's observations that many clinicians adopted pathological approaches, in the sense that they tended to focus

> on the alleviation or elimination of distress through a variety of means which can include chemotherapy, psychotherapy, or behaviour therapy. . . . Such approaches often consider the problem in terms of a pathology which – regardless of how it was established, or developed or is maintained – is to be eliminated.
>
> (Goldiamond 1974: 14)

His claim here is that such pathological approaches ignore formulation. He believed that it would be better to be constructional, wherein the 'solution to problems is the construction of repertoires . . . rather than the elimination of repertoires' (Goldiamond 1974: 14).

In order to adopt a constructional approach, client and therapist would have to agree on: (a) what outcomes are desired; (b) what the client already does which is relevant to these outcomes; (c) therapeutic techniques to enable the client to move from the present position to the desired future; and (d) what in the client's life and environment is likely to maintain the new ways of thinking, feeling and behaving. Goldiamond devised an information gathering protocol – the Constructional Questionnaire – which helps not only in identifying outcomes and current behaviour, but also leads to a rudimentary formulation. After all, if we don't know what is maintaining the current problems, the new outcomes may not be maintainable. By preference the new outcomes ought to become linked to similar contingencies to those which are implicated in the current difficulties. So, for example, if attention from one's spouse is currently involved in maintaining a range of dependent behaviours, and if the desired outcomes are a range of more independent behaviours, some way has to be negotiated of having spousal attention contingent on independence rather than dependence.

The Constructional Questionnaire guides the clinician through a data-gathering exercise which asks about outcomes; what areas of the person's life would be unchanged and what might change as a by-product of achieving the outcomes; what attempts the client has made in the past; what strengths and skills the client has; and what consequences result from, or are avoided or evaded, by the current problems.

The process is iterative, and takes time to achieve, but the outcome is a behavioural formulation, linked to outcomes the client would like to achieve.

CONTEXTUALISM

Modern behavioural formulations are contextualist (Pepper 1942). This is both a philosophy of science and a world view, although the wider ramifications of contextualism need not concern us here. The essence for a clinical formulation is to understand that all behaviour must be considered in context. This is why the doyen of behavioural formulation, B. F. Skinner, emphasised that it was not the response which is the fundamental behavioural unit, but the operant – that is, the antecedent–behaviour–consequence relationship. Behaviour cannot be understood outside its immediate and historical context.

Hayes (2004: 8) puts it thus: Contextualists are supremely interested in function over form, because formal events literally have no meaning. An event disconnected from its history and current situational context is, in some sense, not an 'event' at all.

Consider the person walking down a street, heard talking to themselves. Possibly evidence of some form of psychosis, or an actor on her way to an audition? The only way we could know would be to have more information, either from the person herself or from some other reliable source. How should we interpret a client's score of 25 on the Beck Depression Inventory (Richard and Haynes 2002)? Without relevant historical and present contextual information such a score tells us only that the person has a clinical level of depression. But if we knew the client's scores over previous sessions this would tell us whether there has been significant improvement or worsening, which is more useful in formulation than the labelling we can do by having only the score at a single point in time.

The essence of all behavioural formulations is to be able to identify and understand enough of the context to inform appropriate intervention. This is not a call for trying to identify all possible contextual influences, in some kind of ever-widening circle. Contextualists hold a pragmatic view of truth, with the main criterion being successful working. Steven Hayes, writing recently on the relevance of contextualism, quotes from a 30-year-old Skinner text:

> It is true that we could trace human behaviour not only to the physical conditions which shape and maintain it but also to the causes of those conditions, and the causes of those causes, almost ad infinitum but we need take analysis only to the point at which 'effective action can be taken' (Skinner, 1974, p. 210). . . . That stance on truth, built into behaviour analysis, has a big impact on treatments that take a functional analytic approach.
>
> (Hayes 2004: 8)

Modern contextualist approaches include dialectical behaviour therapy (Linehan 1993), acceptance and commitment therapy (Hayes *et al.* 1999), functional analytic psychotherapy (Kohlenberg and Tsai 1991) and mindfulness-based cognitive therapy for depression (Segal *et al.* 2002). As well as adopting a broadly contextualist approach, each of these therapies have other elements in common, such as Zen-inspired approaches to acceptance. The various proponents of these therapies have together produced work which identifies commonalities (cf. Hayes *et al.* 2004)

CLINICALLY RELEVANT BEHAVIOURS

Clients do not seek therapy because they have difficulties in the therapist's office. They have problems at home, at work, and with spouses, friends and neighbours. Often the problems they describe do not occur in the presence of the therapist, and this gives a special and peculiar difficulty to the behavioural clinician. Usually we would be expecting to analyse the person's behaviour in terms of its antecedents (proximal and distal), and the consequences produced. But we have little access to any of these. One of Skinner's close collaborators, Charles Ferster, put it thus:

> The application of behavioural psychology to one-to-one office therapy is . . . complicated because the most important reinforcers supporting the patient's life occur out of the office, inaccessible to the therapist. The most available reinforcers are those involved in the interpersonal actions and reactions between patient and therapist. . . . The main avenue open to the therapist to bring the patient into contact with natural reinforcers in daily life is learning about his own repertoires, including his private processes, his reaction to others, and his observations of the functional connection between his behaviour and that of others, by learning to discover his interaction with the therapist.
>
> (Ferster 1974: 156–7)

The emphasis here is on how the relationship between client and therapist – the therapeutic relationship – can serve as a vehicle for helping the client to deal with problems that occur outside the therapy setting. Kohlenberg and Tsai (1991) invoke the concept of clinically relevant behaviour (CRBs) which are:

- Client problems that occur in the sessions (CRB 1)
- Client improvements that occur in the session (CRB 2)
- Client verbalisations which describe behaviour and what causes it, both during therapy and in their normal environment (CRB 3).

For example, the client who makes little eye contact with the therapist, and who seems very difficult to engage, may behave in the same way with others (CRB 1), which leads to them having few friends.

The client who comes to trust the therapist, and becomes more open in describing their feelings (CRB 2), may be able to start doing this with their spouse. The client who starts to recognise the way in which he interacts with his family and friends, and who can describe what is happening outside the therapy situation (CRB 3), is gaining insight, which will be useful outside therapy.

Understanding and utilising the concept of CRBs is fundamental to formulation from a functional analytic psychotherapy perspective and is, we would argue, very helpful in all behavioural formulation. We do not have space here to discuss this in detail, but comprehensive descriptions, with clinical examples, can be found in Kohlenberg and Tsai (1991) and Kohlenberg *et al.* (2004).

CASE STUDY

At this point it is timely to consider a case study and consider how it might be formulated from a contextual viewpoint. This requires us to think about what is going on in that moment, although we also need to understand past events which may impact upon that moment. The formulation has to evolve throughout the period of the therapeutic process. We will also need to understand how verbal descriptions might influence how people (including the therapist) respond to events. Our behavioural formulation assumes that the therapeutic relationship will, in itself, provide the context in which clinically relevant behaviours (CRBs) will be evoked (Kohlenberg and Tsai 1991). A contextual model also assumes that there will be a transfer of function – behaviours that emerge in the therapeutic context will be equivalent to those seen in other significant relationships. We have identified clinically relevant behaviours in this case study – client problems and improvements that occur in the session. Clinically relevant behaviours would (at least in the first instance) be held as hypotheses to be explored, rather than assuming any truth to our observations. To reiterate, Kohlenberg and Tsai described three classes of clinically relevant behaviours which the therapist should watch for during sessions. The first are client problems that occur in the session (CRB1). These behaviours are usually under the control of aversive stimuli, and are based on avoidance repertoires. For example, someone who finds it hard to build relationships may arrive late for appointments and never disclose any personal information about themselves. The second behaviours to observe are client improvements that occur in the session (CRB2). These are usually of low strength at the beginning of therapy. Using the above example, one therapeutic goal might be to increase the level of trust between the client and therapist. One strategy might be for the therapist to ensure that appointments are held where agreed and at the time specified. This increased trust might then lead to a more open relationship where the client is able to share personal information. Finally, the therapist should watch and listen for how their clients reason about and interpret their own behaviour. Sometimes these descriptions in sessions will be equivalent to examples from the person's life and can help with the change process. Sometimes, however, the client's description of their problem may not be equivalent to the actual experience. These verbal descriptions can mislead the therapist: the therapist (and consequently the client) may fail to see both client improvements and client problems as they occur during the session.

Context of the referral

The referral was made by a general practitioner to the community mental health team. The GP was asking for psychological support because of the client's increased panic attacks, which he related to previous armed combat. An initial care programme assessment had been initiated by the therapist's (HC) supervisor. This had indicated that Mr Smith's panic attacks had started 12 months earlier. It was assumed that anxiety management and help around panic attacks would be the most useful intervention as there were no apparent symptoms of post-trauma, such as flashbacks.

The initial assessment

Mr Smith was offered an initial appointment which was to be held at the GP practice. He arrived late, having waited outside for a while before coming in (CRB1). He said that he had had to work himself up to coming in (CRB3). Mr Smith said that he would like to feel less anxious and more relaxed when coming to therapy and that eventually he would like to be able to return to work. Mr Smith lived at home with his wife and two sons. One son was about to move away from the family home.

At the time of his first appointment Mr Smith was signed off from work, but had a job working in a factory. He described having had a number of 'attacks' while at his workplace. He depicted a loud and noisy work environment, with a lot of machinery. He was constantly in fear of losing his job through sickness – and indeed had to have many meetings about when he would return to work. Mr Smith had financial problems and was finding it difficult to pay his rent. He said that he had tried blowing into a paper bag to control his panic attacks, but that often the attacks happened without warning and he was unable to control them in that way (CRB3). His GP had prescribed anxiolytics, but they had made little difference to his life.

In his early sessions Mr Smith described his experience of being in the army. He had been in armed combat and was on board a battleship when it was attacked. He could remember helping the injured and knew that his two close friends had died. He described his recollection of that period as being fragmented. He remembered being constantly on the go and had been told that he had been unable to speak for several days afterwards. On returning to England he drank heavily and was consequently discharged from the army without a war pension.

Initial formulation

It appeared that some of Mr Smith's difficulties may have been related to experiential avoidance – that is, his behaviour appeared to be under the control of aversive stimuli. This is reflected in the following observations.

During the initial assessment period Mr Smith was very uneasy. He would jump when doors opened and closed and when he arrived for his appointment he was perspiring (CRB1). It was difficult for him to talk about events around the trauma (CRB1). We agreed to try some relaxation techniques at the beginning and end of each session to see if it helped Mr Smith to feel calmer and more able to reflect upon his previous experiences.

The initial assessment highlighted the possibility of experiential avoidance occurring outside the sessions. Mr Smith was no longer going to work and had withdrawn from other aspects of his life.

However, although Mr Smith had found it hard to come into the session, he had made it (CRB2). If Mr Smith was experiencing experiential avoidance it is possible to see that his coming into the session was an example of him achieving one of his goals. The therapist being present and providing a calm and quiet environment for him to talk naturally reinforced Mr Smith's attendance (CRB2). The aim of using relaxation techniques was to help to promote feelings of calm during the sessions – a desired longer-term outcome for Mr Smith (CRB2).

Reformulation

At this point in the therapeutic process Mr Smith stated that although he had experienced 'flashbacks' in the past, he had not had any for two years, nor had he experienced any nightmares (CRB3). However, his wife had informed the GP that Mr Smith frequently woke up screaming. To challenge him on this might have been counterproductive, since one therapeutic aim was to keep Mr Smith engaged in therapy, and it was important to nurture rather than jeopardise the therapeutic relationship.

Mr Smith would describe the 'hurry up and wait' attitude of the army. His adoption of this repertoire was apparent in early sessions. Mr Smith would rush in perspiring and anxious (CRB1). As the session progressed he became visibly calmer and more relaxed (CRB2). This was discussed with Mr Smith as an in-session clinically relevant behaviour. He also described his need to 'fight' his panic attacks. This is an example of tracking (Hayes *et al.* 1999) and another example of a CRB3. How some people attempt to deal with anxiety actually serves to maintain it and may make the client and therapist insensitive to change. A metaphor was introduced to help Mr Smith to understand the difficulties associated with 'fighting' anxiety.

Therapist: Imagine that you are in a tug of war with a monster. It is big, ugly and immensely strong. Between you and the monster is a pit and it is bottomless. If you lose this tug of war you will fall and be destroyed. So you pull and pull, but the more you pull the harder the monster pulls. The hardest thing is not to win. What should you do?

Mr S: Well you should drop the rope, but I've always been taught to fight things . . . all my life . . . [CRB3].

Mr Smith went on to relate that he was now becoming anxious and fearful when driving, and also when visiting supermarkets. When this happened he would return home. It seemed that he was participating in fewer lifestyle activities as the therapy progressed. However, Mr Smith was not able to describe a 'trigger' that led to him becoming anxious. Mr Smith knew that fighting was not helping him to get rid of his anxiety and fears, but at this stage in therapy was unable to find an alternative way out.

During later sessions Mr Smith described his recent working environment. There were often periods of frenetic activity, followed by calm. Mr Smith was asked whether his working life had always been thus, or were there times when things were different. He said that his working life had always been like that, and that in the army there were long periods of doing nothing, and then suddenly everything was expected of you. The therapist wondered whether work now reflected his life in the army. Mr Smith agreed that, although life was different now, there was an unnerving similarity in the pattern of 'hurry up and wait'.

Mr Smith was asked to monitor the circumstances under which he became anxious. He took the monitoring forms away, but the following week had not completed any, despite being able to talk within sessions about a number of occasions when he had had an attack. One was when he was in a super-market. Mr Smith said that for no apparent reason he had become 'child-like' and felt helpless (CRB3) – shrinking onto the floor, unable to move. On another occasion he was driving home late at night and a car had flashed its headlights. He panicked and had to pull over. Since then he had not felt able to return to work because he was fearful of driving home during the winter months. He described an image of events on the battleship suddenly coming into his awareness. He did not feel that he had any control over when this happened and had to 'lay low' for a number of days afterwards.

At this point it started to become apparent that Mr Smith's anxiety attacks were often associated with loud noises and lights. He had experienced such attacks at work, in the supermarket and during the dark evenings when car headlights were on full beam. He said that he remembered that it was very noisy on the ship just prior to it being hit by a bomb. He said he could recall the noise as the bomb hit the ship, but little else. He had friends on the ship but did not know what had happened to them. He had a photograph of the commemorative service; they were presumed dead.

It seemed that Mr Smith was in some way re-experiencing this event when-ever he was in a noisy, unpredictable environment. The therapist asked whether Mr Smith wished to revisit this time in his life. He said he would like to but that there were parts he just could not remember. He revealed that he had started to keep a book of the war, hoping that this would help him to piece the events together. He regretted how little was documented in the press at that time, because it meant that there were still portions missing to him. Mr Smith described being restless at night, experiencing images of the war and having a constant headache. He said he had 'lost information' about people who were important to him and that he had a numbness in his head all of the time. At this point he became tearful. The therapist reflected on how much more Mr Smith was able to talk about the war than when they had first met. It also seemed that Mr Smith was beginning to remember more of this battle experience.

Supervision

The therapist and her clinical supervisor discussed whether there were techniques that might help Mr Smith to remember events more clearly. The supervisor agreed to meet with him during the next session and explore the possibility of carrying out eye movement desensitization and cognitive reprocessing (EMDR; cf. Shapiro and Maxfield 2002) to help Mr Smith to assimilate the trauma. Mr Smith said that he would be willing to try if there was a possibility that it might help him.

From a contextual perspective EMDR requires the reporting of an event. This description is in itself related to the original condition, and can have an equivalent function. Exposure to the story can help survivors to increase their self-knowledge and change how they interact with the world.

During the session Mr Smith was asked to talk about the last thing he remembered. He talked about the explosion and the ship rocking violently. He was then asked to describe what had happened just prior to the explosion. He described a flash of light and other significant parts of the event, which he had previously been unable to talk about. He could remember trying to help his friends, but finding them dead. He cried and shook, but was able to talk through the sequence of events from the bomb hitting the ship, including trying to find and help his friends. He remembered that prior to the noise of the explosion there had been a sudden flash of light in front of him. It seemed that this was the stimulus that Mr Smith continued to respond to – headlights and supermarket lights had become equivalent to the bombing of the ship and created feelings of fear, anxiety and frenetic activity, followed by a long period of exhaustion.

Mr Smith had carried on in active service after the bombing. He said that once the conflict ended he had felt euphoric, and was glad to be alive. He continued in active service throughout the war and came home to a hero's welcome. He was, however, discharged from the army some six months after the conflict because he was drinking heavily.

Mr Smith left that session saying that he felt elated, promising to return the following week. However, at this point the therapeutic relationship changed. Mr Smith telephoned the therapist to say that he had found the supervisor to be rather 'officer-like' and would prefer not to meet with him (CRB1). After discussion between the supervisor and therapist it was agreed that the therapist would meet with Mr Smith on her own. The important point was to keep Mr Smith engaged in the therapeutic process (CRB2); otherwise there was a risk of earlier patterns of withdrawal being reinforced.

Mr Smith arrived drunk at the next session. He said that after the EMDR session he had felt so good he had gone drinking and had been in the pub regularly since. The therapist wondered about ending the session, but was mindful that this would be confirming the pattern of avoidance (numbing through alcohol, non-compliance and finally leaving the army) that he had experienced in the past. The therapist was also aware of how much the current experiencing of the event, followed by a brief period of elation, relief and drinking, mirrored Mr Smith's description of events when he was on active service. It was important not to mirror the subsequent hypothesised feelings of abandonment. Therefore, the session lasted the usual hour and they talked about Mr Smith's initial meeting with the supervisor. He said he had met him in the past for an initial visit and that he had found that difficult. He had not wanted to tell him about the flashbacks because he looked like an officer. This fear of connecting with someone Mr Smith saw as 'officer-like' highlights again the equivalence relationship between past events and the current context. Experience of the supervisor, rather than avoidance, might ultimately have helped Mr Smith to have a different experience. It was agreed that at this stage the supervisor did not need to come to sessions, but Mr Smith was asked to think about how they might make that relationship easier in the future. This was an attempt to give Mr Smith more explicit control over the situation now, in a way which he may not have experienced in the past.

Mr Smith agreed to meet the following week, but then rang to say that he could not go outside without drinking and did not want to go to the doctor's surgery. However, he was still engaging in the therapy relationship. The therapist was concerned that seeing him at home might encourage Mr Smith's avoidance of contact with the world outside his home, but she was aware that it was the 15-year anniversary of the conflict and that there had been a lot of television coverage of events, so agreed to a home visit.

The home context

Mr Smith, together with his wife, met the therapist at home. For the visit he produced all of his photograph albums. There were photographs of his friends and of the places in which he had served, as well as of the ship that he had been on. On the wall there was a map of the conflict area. He had photographs of his return home and talked about how proud people had been of him. He felt that now only a few people were remembered. He felt that his own experiences had been forgotten. It was clear that a significant part of Mr Smith's identity was associated with this. He was not avoiding talking and thinking about the conflict – he was still living it. They discussed this interpretation and Mr Smith described how hurt he was that the army had abandoned him. He had no pension and no emotional support. Friends had been lost and he had no way of contacting them. At that time the army would not disclose addresses to 'civvies'; Mr Smith was one now. He was also upset that the hero's welcome he had received on coming home was now forgotten and that he was effectively unemployed and his experiences devalued.

They carried on meeting at home for all sessions, but the goal was now more related to his world outside the therapeutic session. Mr Smith wanted to try to reconnect with the army. The therapist obtained contact details for the Royal British Legion (among other army charities) and Mr Smith contacted them himself (CRB2). He tried to find out where friends were and managed to get one old address (CRB2), but his colleague had moved. Together, the therapist and Mr Smith contacted a charitable organisation that worked with ex-servicemen (CRB2). The army agreed to reassess Mr Smith. If the army felt that he was experiencing post-trauma then he would be eligible for a pension and would be able to attend reunions, make contact with other servicemen and participate in other events. They visited him at home. He was pleased, but anxious about meeting officers again. The army agreed that he could attend their rehabilitation centre. Mr Smith cancelled the first scheduled visit; he had travelled to the centre (CRB2) but could not walk up the drive (CRB1). During the next few sessions the therapist and Mr Smith talked about the difficulties he had experienced. Together they broke the journey into manageable steps making up the task of rearranging the visit (CRB2) – telephoning the centre (CRB2), walking up the drive (CRB2) and going into the building to meet people (CRB2). Mr Smith called the centre and agreed that the next time he would visit with his wife. They were sympathetic. Mr Smith revisited the centre two months later (CRB2).

CONCLUSION

There are many methods of formulation, and it becomes clear that apparently diverse models have huge overlap in their methods of formulation. Behavioural approaches have moved on in recent years. We are not tied to considerations of the here and now, or the overtly observable – but then we never were (cf. Skinner 1945). The important elements of formulation from a radical behavioural or contextualist stance are the scientific method, and eschewing apparently explanatory constructs which have no psychological reality. Ultimately, contextual formulation takes a scientifically pragmatic approach: What is the most effective way of helping the client?

'So far as I am concerned, science does not establish truth or falsity; it seeks the most effective way of dealing with subject matters' (Skinner 1988: 241).

REFERENCES

Baron, A. and Perone, M. (2001). Explaining avoidance: Two factors are still better than one. *Journal of the Experimental Analysis of Behaviour* 75: 357–61.

Baum, W. M. (2001). Moler vs molecular as a paradigm clash. *Journal of the Experimental Analysis of Behaviour* 75: 338–41.

Bersh, P. J. (2001). The molarity of molecular theory and the molecularity of moler theory. *Journal of the Experimental Analysis of Behaviour* 75: 348–50.

Branch, M. N. (2001). Are responses in avoidance procedures 'safety' signals? *Journal of the Experimental Analysis of Behaviour* 75: 351–4.

Catania, A. C. (1992). *Learning* (3rd edn). Englewood Cliffs, NJ: Prentice Hall International Inc.

Cullen, C. (1981). The flight to the laboratory. *The Behavior Analyst* 4: 81–3.

Dinsmoor, J. A. (2001a). Stimuli inevitably generated by behaviour that avoids electric shock are inherently reinforcing. *Journal of the Experimental Analysis of Behaviour* 75: 311–33.

Dinsmoor, J. A. (2001b). Still no evidence for temporally extended shock – frequency reduction as a reinforcer. *Journal of the Experimental Analysis of Behaviour* 75: 367–78.

Ferster, C. B. (1974). The difference between behavioural and conventional psychology. *Journal of Nervous and Mental Disease* 159: 153–7.

Goldiamond, I. (1974). Toward a constructional approach to social problems. *Behaviourism* 2: 1–84.

Hayes, S. C. (2004). Acceptance and commitment therapy and the new behaviour therapies: Mindfulness, acceptance, and relationship. In S. C. Hayes *et al.* (eds) *Mindfulness and Acceptance: Expanding the Cognitive-Behavioural Tradition*. New York: The Guilford Press.

Hayes, S. C. *et al.* (1999). *Acceptance and Commitment Therapy: An Experimental Approach to Behaviour Change*. New York: The Guilford Press.

Hayes, S. C. *et al.* (eds) (2004). *Mindfulness and Acceptance: Expanding the Cognitive-Behavioural Tradition*. New York: The Guildford Press.

Hineline, B. N. (2001). Beyond the moler–molecular distinction: We need multi-scaled analyses. *Journal of the Experimental Analysis of Behaviour* 75: 342–7.

Kohlenberg, R. J. and Tsai, M. (1991). *Functional Analytic Psychotherapy: Creating Intense and Curative Therapeutic Relationships*. New York: Plenum Press.

Kohlenberg, R. J. *et al.* (2004). Functional analytic psychotherapy, cognitive therapy, and acceptance. In S. C. Hayes *et al.* (eds) *Mindfulness and Acceptance: Expanding the Cognitive-Behavioural Tradition*. New York: The Guildford Press.

Linehan, N. M. (1993). *Cognitive-Behavioural Treatment of Borderline Personality Disorder*. New York: The Guilford Press.

Michael, J. and Clark, J. W. (2001). A few minor suggestions. *Journal of the Experimental Analysis of Behaviour* 75: 354–7.

Pepper, S. C. (1942). *World Hypotheses: A Study in Evidence*. Berkeley, CA: University of California Press.

Poppen, R. (1982). The fixed-interval scallop in human affairs. *The Behavior Analyst* 5: 127–36.

Richard, D. C. S. and Haynes, S. N. (2002). Behavioural assessment. In M. Hersen and W. Sledge (eds) *Encyclopaedia of Psychotherapy*. London: Academic Press.

Schwartz, A. and Goldiamond, I. (1975). *Social Casework: A Behavioural Approach.* New York: Columbia University Press.

Segal, Z. V. *et al.* (2001). *Mindfulness-Based Cognitive Therapies for Depression: A New Approach to Preventing Relapse*. New York: The Guilford Press.

Shapiro, F. and Maxfield, L. (2002). Eye movement desensitisation and re-processing. In M. Hersen and W. Sledge (eds) *Encyclopaedia of Psychotherapy*. London: Academic Press.

Sidman, M. (1953). Avoidance conditioning with brief shock and no exteroceptive warning signal. *Science* 118: 157–8.

Sidman, M. (2001). Safe periods both explain and need explaining. *Journal of the Experimental Analysis of Behaviour* 75: 335–65.

Skinner, B. F. (1945). The operational analysis of psychological terms. *Psychological Review* 52: 270–7, 291–4.

Skinner, B. F. (1988). Reaction to commentary on 'An operant analysis of problem solving'. In A. C. Catania and S Harnard (eds) *The Selection of Behaviour: The Operant Behaviourism of B. F. Skinner. Comments and Consequences*. Cambridge: Cambridge University Press.

Sturmey, P. (1995). Analogue baselines: A critical review of the methodology. *Research in Developmental Disabilities* 16: 269–84.

Watson, J. B. and Rayner, R. (1920). Conditioned emotional reactions. *Journal of Experimental Psychology* 3: 1–14.

Williams, B. A. (2001). Two-factor theory has strong empirical evidence of validity. *Journal of the Experimental Analysis of Behaviour* 75: 362–5.

Chapter 4

Cognitive therapy case formulation in anxiety disorders

Adrian Wells

Cognitive therapy is implemented on the basis of case formulations that aim to represent the predisposing, triggering, and maintenance factors involved in individual disorders. Such formulations have typically included a range of diverse components such as a problem list, dysfunctional beliefs, triggers, hypotheses concerning mechanisms of maintenance, and a treatment plan (e.g., Persons 1989). The case formulation should provide the therapist with a guide for what to do in therapy, and consequently the most useful approaches will be those that reveal the factors involved in the aetiology and maintenance of anxiety disorders. This chapter presents such an approach to case formulation based on empirically supported cognitive models.

Early cognitive therapy formulations were based on general schema theory (Beck 1976; Beck *et al.* 1985). A basic tenet of this approach, which has been carried over to recent models, is that underlying beliefs and assumptions concerning danger (danger schemas) constitute vulnerability to anxiety disorder. Such schemas shape interpretations of experience and when activated by precipitating events introduce distortions in processing that are manifest as negative automatic thoughts. Cognitive distortions and behavioural responses contribute to the maintenance of disorder since individuals are unable to reality-test their beliefs effectively. This approach gives rise to a model of disorder depicted in Figure 4.1. As we shall see in the remainder of this chapter, more recent work has focused on determining in detail the non-specific and unique psychological factors involved across different anxiety disorders.

This chapter has four aims: (a) to outline the features of different anxiety disorders to facilitate their identification; (b) to present the models of panic disorder, social phobia, obsessive-compulsive disorder, and generalized anxiety disorder on which formulation is based; (c) to describe methods for generating each cognitive therapy case formulation; and (d) to outline a generic algorithm for case formulations involving co-morbid presentations or those that do not fit a particular diagnosis.

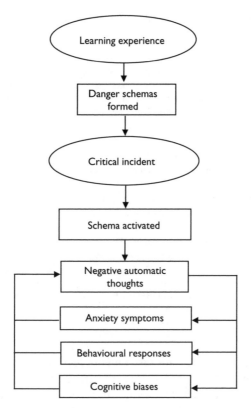

Figure 4.1 General schema model of anxiety disorders (reproduced from *Cognitive Therapy of Anxiety Disorders* by A. Wells, 1997 © Copyright John Wiley & Sons, Ltd.).

IDENTIFYING THE TARGET PROBLEM

Accurate identification of the presenting problem is a necessary prerequisite to valid case formulation. Diagnosis provides one means of identifying a presenting problem, and can be used as a basis for selecting an appropriate model. The diagnostic approach is augmented by identification of the primary or central cognitions in a presentation. There is a degree of content specificity in anxiety disorder cognitions, such that the predominant themes in negative thoughts can be used as indicators of the likely nature of the problem. Table 4.1 presents the key diagnostic features of each anxiety disorder and the typical cognitive themes.

The use of standardised diagnostic interviews such as the structured clinical interview for *DSM-IV* (American Psychiatric Association 1994), the Anxiety Disorders Interview Schedule for *DSM-IV* (ADIS; Brown *et al.*

Table 4.1 Key diagnostic features (DSM-IV) and cognitive themes in four anxiety disorders

Anxiety disorder	Key diagnostic features	Cognitive themes
Panic disorder	Recurrent, unexpected panic attacks followed by at least one month of persistent concern about having another attack	Concern about the consequences of panic; misinterpretation of anxious symptoms
Social phobia	Fear of social or performance situations in which embarrassment may occur	Concern about appearing anxious in front of others; concern about being embarrassed in public
Obsessive-compulsive disorder	Recurrent obsessions or compulsions that are time-consuming or cause marked distress or impairment	Concern about the consequences of obsessional thoughts and of not reducing distress by use of rituals
Generalized anxiety disorder	Excessive and uncontrollable worry about a number of events, and anxiety occurring more days than not for at least six months	Concern about the uncontrollability and dangers of worrying

1994), and self-report screening instruments (e.g., Zimmerman and Mattia 2001) are recommended as a first step towards accurately identifying target disorders. This is particularly useful when there are multiple presenting problems.

Differential diagnosis is aided by understanding the specificity of cognitive content. Panic disorder is usually associated with apprehension and fears about having panic attacks; the person with agoraphobia avoids situations because of fears that panic attacks will occur. Panic attacks may occur in the context of any anxiety disorder but this is unlikely to constitute a panic disorder if the focus is not primarily fear of having a panic attack. Social phobia is characterized by fear of humiliation and embarrassment when being the focus of attention. Avoidance occurs as a means of avoiding embarrassment and negative evaluation by others. In obsessive-compulsive disorder, fears centre on the occurrence and consequences of intrusive thoughts and urges, and on the need to perform rituals and behaviours in order to avoid negative outcomes. In OCD intrusions are interpreted as abhorrent, repugnant, and uncharacteristic of the self (i.e., they are ego-dystonic). This is not usually the case with the thoughts and worries of the patient with generalized anxiety disorder (GAD), and the intrusive thoughts about trauma in the patient with post-traumatic stress disorder (PTSD). GAD is characterized by worry about a range of topics and somatic symptoms, and a central negative cognition is the idea that worrying is uncontrollable and potentially harmful. PTSD involves intrusive recollections and thoughts about a trauma, coupled with avoidance and arousal symptoms. The focus of apprehension is typically on the possibility of future traumas and environmental threats to the self.

The assessment of anxiety presentations can be complicated by medical conditions that give rise to anxiety-like symptoms. Hyperthyroidism, mitral valve prolapse, cardiac arrhythmias, tumours, vestibule disturbances, and a range of other conditions can be the source of panic-like sensations and other anxiety-like symptoms such as dizziness, cardiac symptoms, blushing, loss of balance, and so on. An anxiety disorder is not diagnosed if the symptoms can be explained by medical conditions, or if the symptoms occur solely as a result of dependence on or withdrawal from substances such as caffeine or alcohol. Accurate and thorough assessment is required in order to formulate and plan an appropriate intervention.

EVIDENCE-BASED, DISORDER-SPECIFIC MODELS

In the remainder of this chapter I will describe the specific models that have been constructed and evaluated as a basis for formulating the psychological mechanisms underlying the development and persistence of anxiety disorders. These models are at various stages of empirical validation, but each one has either a substantial or significant amount of support from empirical studies. Following a brief presentation of each model, a method for generating a formulation in each case is presented.

PANIC DISORDER

Panic disorder is a good starting point for developing knowledge of formulation in anxiety because it is the least complex of the anxiety disorders. According to David M. Clark (1986), a particular sequence of events leads to a panic attack in panic disorder. This sequence involves the catastrophic misinterpretation of internal events, which are taken as a sign of an immediate catastrophe. The events misinterpreted are bodily sensations or mental experiences. These are often the effects of normal reactions such as those caused by postural changes in blood pressure, tiredness, excitement, or anxiety/stress. The first panic attack may not involve catastrophic misinterpretation but may be due to other biological factors. However, the persistence of panic attacks in the absence of biological or chemical causes is associated with catastrophic misinterpretations.

Misinterpretations are believable at their time of occurrence and involve themes such as dying, suffocating, having a heart attack or seizure, and fainting or collapsing. Other common themes include losing one's mind, going crazy, or losing control of behaviour. Once misinterpretations develop, coping behaviours and selective attention to internal events contribute to problem maintenance. Some coping behaviours inadvertently exacerbate symptoms (Wells 1997). For example, taking deep breaths due to fears of suffocating may lead to hyperventilation and associated symptoms. Coping behaviours can lead to the persistence of catastrophic beliefs in other ways. The non-occurrence of catastrophe is attributed to use of 'safety behaviours' (Salkovskis 1991), thereby preventing belief change. Selective attention to bodily events increases awareness of sensations, which can act as a further trigger for misinterpretation (Clark 1986; Wells 1997).

A revised version of Clark's (1986) diagrammatic model is presented in Figure 4.2. The model has been extended to include feedback loops involving safety behaviours and selective attention, and it drops the term 'apprehension' used in the original model in favour of 'anxiety'. This revised model (Wells 1997) offers a template for case formulations.

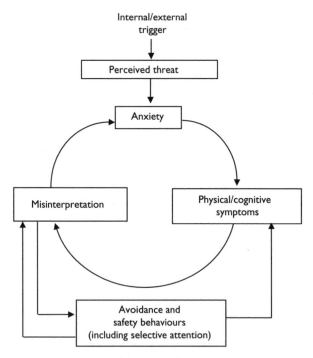

Figure 4.2 Cognitive model of panic (reproduced from *Cognitive Therapy of Anxiety Disorders* by A. Wells, 1997 © Copyright John Wiley & Sons, Ltd.).

Generating a panic formulation

In Clark's (1986) model the sequence of events leading to a panic attack involves thoughts–emotions–sensations–thoughts–emotions–sensations and so on. This sequence can begin at any point so it may run emotions–sensations–thoughts, or sensations–thoughts–emotions. This sequence is represented in the primary vicious cycle in Figure 4.2. A sequence of this kind implies that the therapist should attempt to track the sequence in a recent panic episode in order to generate a formulation.

In tracing the sequence the therapist asks the patient to recount slowly a very recent panic attack by responding to a sequence of questions. In generating an idiosyncratic version of Figure 4.1 the therapist should not begin to track the sequence longer than a few seconds before the panic attack occurred. If this does happen, the vicious cycle stem is likely to be long and much time wasted. In plotting the formulation the stem ends when anxiety is elicited in the sequence. This is the cue for the therapist to enter the vicious cycle and search for symptoms as a prerequisite to determining the catastrophic misinterpretation. Once misinterpretations are elicited the next step is to obtain a rating of how much it was believed at the time of panic. The cycle is then closed by linking back to anxiety. The next step is to determine the feedback cycles involving coping behaviours and selective attention. This is accomplished by asking about the strategies the patient used to avert the threat depicted in the catastrophic misinterpretation. The therapist also asks about the development of bodily hypervigilance. A recommended sequence of specific questions is presented in Box 4.1 for the purposes of generating the case formulation.

Box 4.1 Panic case formulation interview

Introduction: I'm going to ask you about a recent typical panic attack so that we may begin to map out what happened. When was your most recent panic attack?

1   Thinking about just before you panicked: what was the very first thing that you noticed that indicated that you might panic. Was it a thought, a sensation, or an emotion?
    Answer = thought, go to Q3, answer = sensation, go to Q2, answer = emotion, if anxiety go to Q4 and if other emotion ask: When you had that emotion what sensations did you have? Then proceed with Q2.
2   When you noticed that sensation what thought went through your mind?
3   When you noticed that thought how did that make you feel emotionally?

4 When you noticed that emotion what sensations did you have?
5 When you had those sensations what thought went through your mind?
6 How much did you believe [insert catastrophic misinterpretation] at that time?
7 What happened to your anxiety when you thought that?
8 Did you do anything to prevent [insert catastrophic misinterpretation]? What was that?
9 Did you do anything to lower anxiety? What was that?
10 Since you have developed panic do you focus attention on your body/thoughts? In what way?

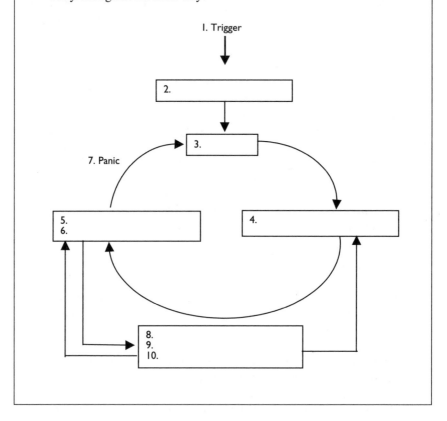

Illustrative dialogue

An illustration of the use of this dialogue is given below. Note that there is some use of probe questions building on the basic interview questions in Box 4.1 in order to clarify meaning. This line of questioning gives rise to the formulation in Figure 4.3.

Therapist:	Thinking about just before you panicked. What was the very first thing that you noticed that indicated that you might panic? Was it a thought, a sensation or an emotion?
Patient:	It was an emotion, frustration.
Therapist:	When you had that emotion what sensations did you have?
Patient:	I felt dizzy, vertigo I suppose you'd call it.
Therapist:	When you noticed that sensation what thought went through your mind?
Patient:	I thought it's going to bring it on.
Therapist:	When you had that thought how did that make you feel emotionally?
Patient:	I felt scared and anxious.
Therapist:	When you noticed that emotion what sensations did you have?
Patient:	I got the lot, dizziness, choking, chest tight, sweating, nausea.
Therapist:	When you had those sensations what thought went through your mind?
Patient:	I thought I was dying of a heart attack or something.
Therapist:	How much did you believe you were having a heart attack at that time on a scale of zero to 100%?
Patient:	I was convinced, 70%.
Therapist:	What happened to your anxiety when you thought that?
Patient:	I panicked very quickly.
Therapist:	Did you do anything to prevent a heart attack?
Patient:	Yes, I had a drink of alcohol and tried to calm down. I also took an aspirin.
Therapist:	How did you try to calm down?
Patient:	I took deep breaths and tried to slow my pulse down.
Therapist:	Since you developed panic do you focus more attention on your body/thoughts?
Patient:	I take my pulse and try to listen to my heart beating when I'm falling asleep.

SOCIAL PHOBIA

Social phobia is characterized by a persistent fear of social or performance situations in which the individual is exposed to scrutiny. The central fear is of acting in a way that is embarrassing or humiliating. This includes a fear of showing signs of anxiety or related symptoms such as trembling, blushing, babbling, or appearing odd. There may be a fear of performing ineptly by talking strangely or being unable to talk, or a concern about being boring or sounding stupid.

The Clark and Wells' (1995) cognitive model of social phobia is depicted in Figure 4.4. On entering a feared social situation, the person with social

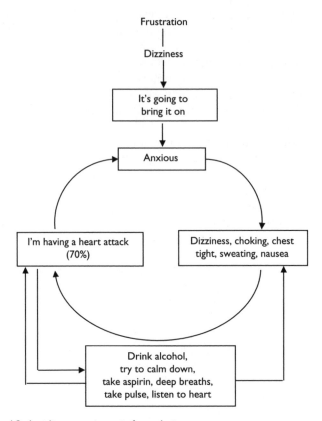

Figure 4.3 An idiosyncratic panic formulation.

phobia activates negative beliefs and/or assumptions about the self as a social object, and/or rigid rules for social performance. Examples of beliefs are: 'I'm stupid,' 'I'm boring,' and 'I'm abnormal.' Examples of assumptions are: 'If I blush everyone will stare at me,' and 'If I show signs of anxiety everyone will lose confidence in me.' Rigid rules include: 'I must always be calm and collected,' 'I must never show I'm anxious,' and 'I must always sound intelligent.' Once activated these beliefs lead to negative automatic thoughts about social performance and are associated with a shift in the direction of attention. Attention becomes self-focused on feelings and symptoms, and most centrally on an impression of how the person thinks they appear to others. This impression often occurs as a mental image from an observer perspective, so called because the person sees the self as if looking back on the self from another person's point of view. In this image the individual's anxious symptoms and failed performance are highly conspicuous. When self-processing does not occur as an image it is typically expressed as a 'felt sense' such as a feeling of being conspicuous or a feeling of looking peculiar. This image or

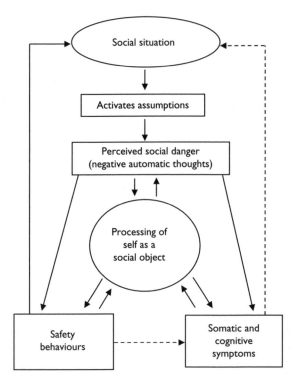

Figure 4.4 Cognitive model of social phobia (reproduced from *Cognitive Therapy of Anxiety Disorders* by A. Wells, 1997 © Copyright John Wiley & Sons, Ltd.).

the 'felt sense' is accepted as an accurate portrayal of appearance, but it typically represents an exaggeration of actual appearance. Negative automatic thoughts and the negative self-image contribute to heightened anxiety in social situations.

In order to avert the feared social outcomes represented in negative thoughts and the self-image, the individual engages in safety behaviours. For example, the person fearful of sweating wears extra layers of clothes, wears light colours, and does not show his/her armpits. The individual fearful of talking strangely will mentally rehearse sentences before speaking, plan what to say, and concentrate on talking fluently and clearly without pausing. There are four potential problems with safety behaviours that contribute to a persistence of the problem: (a) the non-occurrence of social catastrophe is attributed to use of the behaviour and so negative beliefs about failed performance or showing signs of anxiety persist; (b) some safety behaviours intensify or prolong unwanted symptoms (e.g., wearing extra clothing increases sweating); (c) some safety behaviours increase self-focused attention as the person focuses attention inward to monitor and gauge the effectiveness of those behaviours – the problem here is that self-attention amplifies awareness of symptoms, contributes to self-consciousness, and interferes with the task concentration required for effective social performance; and (d) safety behaviours can contaminate the social situation by making the person appear withdrawn, disinterested, or unfriendly. For example, avoiding eye contact and avoiding talking about the self can lead others to think that the person is disinterested in them. Contamination of the social situation can lead to a minimization of the positive social feedback that could normally provide opportunities for challenging negative thoughts and beliefs.

Generating a social phobia formulation

It is recommended as a starting point that the therapist identifies a recent situation in which the patient felt socially anxious. Questions are asked to determine the nature of the anxiety and the symptoms experienced. From here the therapist should proceed to establishing the content of negative automatic thoughts, the nature of safety behaviours, and finally the contents of the negative self-image. This sequence of questioning does not reflect the sequence of processes operating in a situation, as depicted by the model. However, clinical experience has shown that this is the simplest way of eliciting each of the components, with the aim of generating a formulation of the in-situation or maintenance factors. Underlying schemas can be explored at the initial formulation stage or included in the formulation later in treatment in order to simplify the model. Box 4.2 presents a basic interview schedule for generating a social phobia formulation.

Box 4.2 Social phobia case formulation interview

Introduction: I'm going to ask you about the last time you had problems with social anxiety in a situation. I have a series of questions to help to understand what happened.

1   Where were you the last time you felt anxious in a social situation?
2   How did you feel emotionally? (What physical symptoms did you have? What were the cognitive symptoms, e.g., poor memory/ concentration?)
3   When you had those symptoms what thoughts went through your mind? (Probe: Did you think anything bad could happen? Were you concerned what others might see or think or you?)
4   When you had those thoughts, did you do anything to prevent that feared outcome from happening. What did you do?
5   When you were in the situation were you self-conscious? (What impression did you have about how you appeared or how you performed? What could other people see?)

---

6   Did you do anything to make yourself look better or conceal anxiety? What did you do?

To explore schemas:

7   Do you have any negative beliefs about your ability to socialize?
8   Do you have any life rules, like it is bad to show anxiety, or that you must always present a favourable impression?
9   Do you ever believe you are boring or don't fit in? In what way?

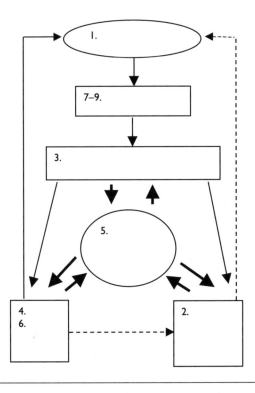

Illustrative dialogue

The following dialogue utilizes the questions in Box 4.2. Notice how the therapist augments some of the initial questions to obtain a sufficient level of information, which provides the basis for the case formulation in Figure 4.5.

Therapist: Where were you the last time you felt anxious in a social situation?
Patient: Walking on Booth Street.
Therapist: How did you feel emotionally?

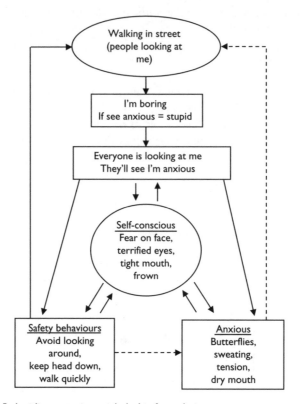

Figure 4.5 An idiosyncratic social phobia formulation.

Patient:	I felt uncomfortable, like everyone was looking at me.
Therapist:	What anxious symptoms did you have?
Patient:	I felt butterflies in my stomach, sweating, tension in my arms, and a dry mouth.
Therapist:	When you had those symptoms what thoughts went through your mind?
Patient:	I thought, everyone is looking at me and they'll see I'm anxious.
Therapist:	When you had that thought, did you do anything to prevent people seeing that?
Patient:	I avoided looking around, kept my head down, and walked quickly.
Therapist:	Anything else?
Patient:	I would normally try to keep my face muscles relaxed.
Therapist:	When you were in the situation what impression did you have about how you appeared? What could other people see?
Patient:	A look of fear on my face.
Therapist:	What does that look like? Can you describe it to me?

Patient: Terrified eyes, a tight mouth, and a frown.
Therapist: Did you do anything to make yourself look better or conceal anxiety?
Patient: I try to keep my face relaxed.
Therapist: Do you have any negative beliefs about your ability to socialize?
Patient: I'm concerned people will think I'm boring.
Therapist: In social situations do you believe that?
Patient: Yes.
Therapist: Do you have any beliefs about showing anxiety?
Patient: If people see I'm anxious they'll think I'm stupid.

OBSESSIVE-COMPULSIVE DISORDER (OCD)

The cognitive model of OCD (Wells 1997, 2000) introduces the realm of metacognition as an area to be formulated. Metacognition refers to the cognitive factors that appraise, monitor, and control thinking (e.g., Flavell 1979; Nelson and Narens 1990). Interest in this area from a cognitive therapy standpoint has emerged from the metacognitive analysis of emotional disorders (Wells 2000; Wells and Matthews 1994, 1996). The cognitive model of OCD described here is grounded in this metacognitive approach.

The metacognitive model is shown in Figure 4.6. In the model, intrusive internal experiences such as thoughts, doubts, and urges are considered normal events. However, in OCD they activate dysfunctional metacognitive beliefs about the danger, meaning, and significance of these events. As a result they are negatively appraised as having importance, being especially meaningful, and/or dangerous. Negative metacognitive beliefs about intrusions typically involve one or more of the following themes:

1   Thought event fusion (TEF): the belief that thoughts and feelings mean that something bad has happened or they will have the power to make bad things happen in the future. For example: 'Thinking of accidents will make it more likely to happen,' 'If I have an image of a murder it means I have committed it.'
2   Thought action fusion (TAF): the belief that having thoughts or urges will lead to the uncontrollable commission of an unwanted act. For example: 'Thinking of stabbing someone will make me do it,' 'If I think of hitting someone this means I really will hit them.'
3   Thought object fusion (TOF): the belief that thoughts, memories, or feelings can be transferred into objects and be spread by contact. For example: 'My bad thoughts can be transferred into my clothes,' 'I can contaminate objects with unpleasant feelings.'

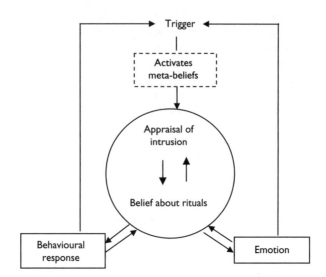

Figure 4.6 Meta-cognitive model of OCD (reproduced from *Cognitive Therapy of Anxiety Disorders* by A. Wells, 1997 © Copyright John Wiley & Sons, Ltd.).

Once the intrusion has been imbued with negative significance, the individual activates beliefs about rituals or strategies that can be used to reduce anxiety and reduce threat. In the model, negative appraisal of intrusions and beliefs about rituals interact in moderating the subsequent level of anxiety experienced. When the person is unable to reduce threat by completing behaviours, anxiety is elevated, but the successful commission of behaviours can lead to the temporary reduction of anxiety. However, there are several problems with the use of rituals, and neutralising and avoidance behaviours. Some behaviours have counterproductive effects and increase the likelihood of further intrusions. For example, thought suppression tends not to be ineffective and activates a thought monitoring plan that can maintain awareness of intrusions. Some behaviours require strict control over thinking in order to be successfully completed, and this level of control is often inconsistent, leading to negative appraisal of mental states and fluctuating anxiety levels. When behaviours are successfully implemented they prevent the individual discovering that negative outcomes would not occur as a result of the intrusion, and so negative metacognitive beliefs about intrusions persist.

A feature of the model, captured by the concept of beliefs about rituals, is the tendency of many patients to use inappropriate internal criteria for guiding neutralising behaviours and making judgements. For example, in response to an intrusive thought (e.g., 'Have I turned off the stove') a person may use the criterion of having a perfect mental image of the action or aim to achieve a specific feeling state to signal that it is safe to stop checking or repeating behaviour. Some individuals use an inverted reasoning process, such as looking for gaps in memory as evidence that an action has or has not been performed. For example, in response to an intrusive image about an accident a patient tried to recall his entire journey home, and conceded: 'I don't remember my whole journey home, therefore I probably caused an accident.' The use of inappropriate criteria of this kind means that the person with OCD does not process more adaptive sources of data that would lead to challenging beliefs about the importance of the intrusion.

Generating an OCD case formulation

The therapist should identify the occurrence of a recent obsessional intrusion that caused distress and culminated in neutralising responses. The sequence of questions presented in Box 4.3 offers a basic interview schedule for generating a formulation.

Box 4.3 OCD case formulation interview

Introduction: I'm going to ask you about the last time you were distressed by an obsessional thought and you felt compelled to respond to it.

1   What was the thought/image/impulse that triggered you?
2   When you had that thought how did you feel emotionally (e.g., anxious/scared)?
3   What did you think might happen as a result of having that thought? (What is the worst that could happen? What would happen if you did nothing to deal with the thought?)
4   Do you believe these thoughts mean something? What's the worst they could mean? How much did you believe that at the time?
5   Did you do anything to stop [insert negative belief about thought] from happening? Did you do anything to stop yourself doubting? Did you try to prevent feeling anxious? (What did you do?)
6   Do you believe that you must behave in certain ways in order to remain safe and stop bad things from happening? How much do you believe that? Do you have any special ways of doing things or special ways of thinking? What would happen if you no longer responded to your thoughts/doubts/feelings by doing these things?

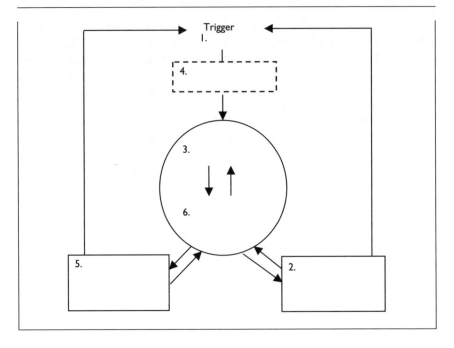

Illustrative dialogue

The following dialogue, based around the interview in Box 4.3, gives rise to the case formulation depicted in Figure 4.7.

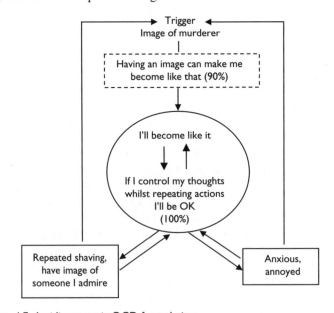

Figure 4.7 An idiosyncratic OCD formulation.

Therapist:	When was that?
Patient:	This morning when I was shaving.
Therapist:	What was the thought/image/impulse that triggered you?
Patient:	I had the mental picture of that child murderer.
Therapist:	When you had that thought how did you feel emotionally (e.g., anxious/scared)?
Patient:	I was freaked by it, I was anxious and annoyed that I'd have to shave again.
Therapist:	What did you think might happen as a result of having that thought?
Patient:	I might become like that.
Therapist:	Do you believe these thoughts mean something?
Patient:	If I think about it then they could make me take on those characteristics.
Therapist:	How much did you believe that at the time, from zero to 100%?
Patient:	I do believe it, 90%.
Therapist:	Did you do anything to stop that from happening?
Patient:	I washed and shaved all over again whilst keeping an image of someone I admire in mind.
Therapist:	Do you believe that you must behave in certain ways in order to remain safe and stop bad things from happening?
Patient:	I have to think good thoughts, and repeat any actions associated with bad thoughts by having good thoughts instead. If I control my thoughts I'll be OK.
Therapist:	How much do you believe that?
Patient:	100%.

GENERALISED ANXIETY DISORDER (GAD)

The key feature of GAD is the occurrence of uncontrollable worry (for at least six months) about a number of different topics, in combination with a selection of specific somatic and behavioural symptoms. The worries cannot be better explained by the presence of another anxiety disorder. The somatic and behavioural symptoms should include at least three of the following: restlessness, easily fatigued, difficulty concentrating, irritability, muscle tension, and sleep disturbance (*DSM-IV*; APA 1994).

The metacognitive model of GAD (Wells 1995, 1997) is presented in Figure 4.8. Worry episodes have a trigger, often in the form of a negative 'What if . . .?' question. This activates positive metacognitive beliefs about the use of worrying as a coping strategy. Positive beliefs include themes such as: 'Worrying means I'll be prepared,' 'If I worry I won't be taken by surprise,' and 'If I worry I'll be able to cope.' As a consequence the individual with GAD engages in Type 1 worrying, in which a range of negative outcomes are

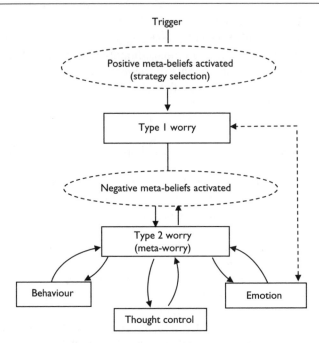

Figure 4.8 Meta-cognitive model of GAD (reproduced from *Cognitive Therapy of Anxiety Disorders* by A. Wells, 1997 © Copyright John Wiley & Sons, Ltd.).

contemplated and ways of coping considered. This activity continues until the person reaches a desired internal state that signals that the work of worry is complete. This state is often a 'feeling' that is interpreted as a sign that the person will be able to cope. However, in some cases it is a sense of being prepared, or knowing that most possibilities have been covered. The occurrence of Type 1 worrying has differential effects on anxiety. It can increase anxiety as the person contemplates a range of catastrophes, but subsequently anxiety decreases as the person reaches successful completion of the activity.

GAD develops when negative metacognitive beliefs about worrying are activated. There are two categories of negative belief that are important: (a) beliefs about the uncontrollability of worry; and (b) beliefs about the dangers of worrying for physical, psychological, and social functioning. Examples of these beliefs include: 'Worrying is uncontrollable,' 'Worrying will damage my body and cause a heart attack,' 'If I worry I could become schizophrenic or lose my mind,' and 'When people discover I worry they will reject me.' During the course of Type 1 worrying, negative beliefs are activated and lead to the negative interpretation of worrying and the symptoms associated with it. Negative interpretations (called Type 2 worry or meta-worry) lead to an intensification of anxiety and interfere with the person's ability to reach an internal state signalling that they can cope.

Two further processes contribute to problem maintenance. These are the behaviours that the person engages in, and the thought control strategies adopted. Behaviours such as avoidance of situations that may trigger worrying, seeking reassurance, and information search (such as surfing the internet) are used to try and stop worrying. However, these strategies have counterproductive effects. Some increase preoccupation with worry, some increase the range of triggers for worrying, and some pass the control of worry onto others. As a result, negative beliefs about the personal controllability of worry are not challenged.

Typically, thought control strategies are also unhelpful, and comprise two factors. The person with GAD will attempt not to think thoughts that may trigger worrying. Suppression of this kind is not consistently effective and may backfire, increasing intrusions and adding to fears of uncontrollability. Furthermore, patients seldom interrupt the Type 1 worry process once activated. This is because interrupting it would be equivalent to 'not coping,' or because the idea of interrupting it is inconsistent with the view that worrying is an inevitable part of the person's personality. As a result the person does not discover that worrying can be interrupted. Note, however, that interruption of the catastrophising worry process is different from suppression (i.e., attempts to remove entirely the content of a thought from consciousness).

Generating a GAD case formulation

The therapist begins by identifying a recent occasion on which the patient experienced a distressing and uncontrollable worry episode. Questioning aims to identify erroneous metacognitions, emotional responses, behaviours, and thought control strategies active in the episode. A particular sequence of questioning is recommended as an efficient means of eliciting components of the model. This sequence is presented as a case formulation interview in Box 4.4.

Box 4.4 GAD case formulation interview

Introduction: I'd like to focus on the last time you had a significant and uncontrollable worry episode and you were distressed by it. I'm going to ask you a series of questions about that experience.

1 What was the initial thought that triggered your worrying?
2 When you had that thought, what did you then worry about?
3 When you worried about those things how did that make you feel emotionally? (Probe: Did you feel anxious? What symptoms did you have?)

---

4   When you had those feelings and symptoms, did you think some-
    thing bad could happen as a result of worrying and feeling that way?
    (Probe: What is the worst that could happen if you continued to
    worry?)

5   a Do you believe that worrying is bad in any way? (Probe: Can
    worry be harmful?)
    b Worrying appears to be a problem, so why don't you stop
    worrying? (Probe: Do you believe worrying is uncontrollable?).

6   Apart from negative beliefs about worrying, do you think that
    worrying can be useful in any way? (Probes: Can worrying help you
    cope? Does it help you foresee problems and avoid them? Are there
    any advantages to worrying?)

7   When you start worrying do you do anything to try and stop it?
    (Probe: Do you avoid situations, ask for reassurance, try to find out
    if there is really something to worry about?)

8   a Do you use more direct strategies to try and control you thoughts,
    such as trying not to think about things that may trigger worrying?
    b Have you ever tried to interrupt a worry by deciding not to engage
    in it at the time?

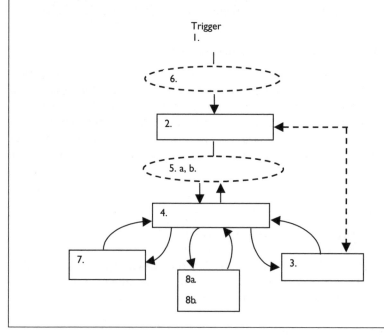

Illustrative dialogue

The following dialogue, based on the case formulation interview in Box 4.4, gives rise to the case formulation in Figure 4.9.

Therapist: What was the initial thought that triggered your worrying?
Patient: I had the thought of going to work and my supervisor being there.
Therapist: When you had that thought, what did you then worry about?
Patient: I was worried that I'd ordered the wrong equipment, and what if it was a wasted journey, it would be my fault, and they'd think I was incompetent.
Therapist: When you worried about those things how did that make you feel emotionally?
Patient: I felt anxious and wanted to cry.
Therapist: Any other symptoms?
Patient: I was tense and had butterflies in my stomach.
Therapist: When you had those feelings and symptoms, did you think something bad could happen as a result of worrying and feeling that way?

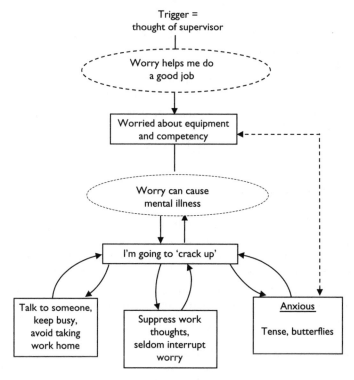

Figure 4.9 An idiosyncratic GAD formulation.

Patient: Not at first but later on I just lost it.
Therapist: What did you think was happening when you lost it?
Patient: I thought I was going to crack up.
Therapist: Do you believe that worrying is bad in any way?
Patient: I think it's bad for your physical and mental health.
Therapist: What's the worst that could happen if you worried a lot?
Patient: I think you could become mentally ill or something.
Therapist: Worrying appears to be a problem, so why don't you stop worrying?
Patient: I can't, it's uncontrollable.
Therapist: Apart from negative beliefs about worrying, do you think that worrying can be useful in any way?
Patient: I think it means I do a good job and I don't miss important things.
Therapist: When you start worrying, do you do to anything to try and stop it?
Patient: I try to talk to someone to find out if there is something I should worry about.
Therapist: Anything else?
Patient: I try to keep busy, but it doesn't work because I go back to the worry.
Therapist: Do you avoid things that might make you worry?
Patient: I try to avoid taking my work home.
Therapist: Do you use strategies to try and control your thoughts, such as trying not to think about things that may trigger worrying?
Patient: I try not to think about work.
Therapist: Have you ever tried to interrupt a worry by deciding not to engage in it at the time?
Patient: No, I feel there's not much I can do about it.

AN ALGORITHM FOR GENERIC CASE FORMULATION

Reviewing the disorder-specific models illustrates a number of recurring features in case formulation. These features are discrete cognitive and behavioural components and the dynamic processes that operate between them. The basic components are danger-related thoughts, danger-related beliefs, coping behaviours, and anxiety symptoms. The dynamic maintenance processes (or arrows in the different models above) are combinations of some of or all of the following:

1   Deleterious effects of coping behaviours
    a   Prevention of disconfirmation
    b   Paradoxical symptom effects

   c   Cognitive overload/interference
   d   Social contamination
   e   Confirmatory processing (e.g., attention to threat)

2   Dysfunctional internal processing
   a   Interpretation of symptoms as evidence of threat
   b   Use of internal data to evaluate status of self
   c   Use of feelings to guide behaviour

3   Effects of arousal on triggering stimuli
   a   Anxiety-associated changes in cognitive and autonomic activity (e.g., intensification of specific internal events).

Equipped with this taxonomy of components and processes, a generic procedural model or algorithm is possible as the basis for constructing a formulation. This may be useful when a presenting disorder does not fit a specific diagnosis, and in circumstances such as those involving mixed presentations that have multiple disorder features. It should be noted, however, that at this time there is no evidence to support this approach, but it may provide greater malleability than the disorder-specific models. The basic algorithm is depicted in Figure 4.10. Note that the maintenance processes are denoted by

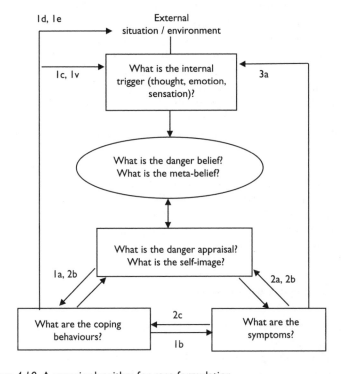

Figure 4.10 A generic algorithm for case formulation.

their respective alphanumeric code (e.g., 1a, 1b) as per the listing above. So, for instance, the code 1a in Figure 4.10 denotes that the arrow can represent deleterious effects of coping, in this case prevention of disconfirmation. It is not envisaged that every process will operate in each individual case, and the clinician has the task of elucidating those that are pertinent. By broadening the scope of the belief and appraisal factors beyond their danger content, this formulation may be extended to disorders other than anxiety disorders. However, it is possible that additional maintenance processes will be operating.

BEHAVIOURAL ASSESSMENT TESTS (BATs)

In some anxiety disorder cases, avoidance of feared situations is a significant feature of the presentation, and as a consequence it is difficult to identify a recent occasion involving anxiety around which to base formulation. A behavioural assessment test (BAT) involving exposure to an actual or ana-logue feared situation can be used to activate anxiety and provide the basis for the formulation interview. The therapist then configures questioning to exploring emotional, cognitive, and coping responses during the BAT. For example, a patient who was fearful of drinking in public went on a 'fact-finding mission' with the therapist during the first treatment session. This consisted of visiting a busy café nearby and drinking cups of tea. During this mission, the therapist monitored the patient's thoughts ('What are you thinking is the worst that could happen right now?'), emotions ('How do you feel emotionally?'), safety behaviours ('Are you doing anything to prevent bad things from happening?'), and self-image ('How do you think you appear right now?'). Visible changes in emotional state and the apparent use of safety behaviours/avoidance were useful markers of the points at which to ask these questions.

Aside from the use of BATS to inform formulation, self-report instruments are a valuable source of information concerning cognitions, behaviour, and symptoms. Instruments such as the Social Phobia Rating Scale, the Panic Rating Scale, and the Generalized Anxiety Disorder Scale (Wells 1997) contain items assessing most of the components required for generating formulations of these disorders.

OVERVIEW OF TREATMENTS

Because of the emphasis on different processes and domains of cognition provided by the models reviewed, treatment should be guided by personalised versions of the appropriate model. This gives rise to a different emphasis and focus of treatment for each disorder, although many of the strategies used for achieving cognitive-affective change are generic. However, specific change techniques have been devised for specific purposes in some disorders. For a detailed description of treatments and techniques for each disorder covered in this chapter the interested reader should consult Wells (1997, 2000). For case formulation and metacognitive treatment in PTSD two sources of reference are provided by Wells and Sembi (2004a, 2004b). In the remainder of this section I will provide a brief overview of the focus and nature of treatment for panic disorder, social phobia, OCD, and GAD.

In treating panic disorder, the therapist focuses on challenging beliefs in the catastrophic misinterpretation of symptoms. The goal of treatment is to reduce belief in the range of catastrophic misinterpretations to zero. Some of the most powerful strategies for achieving this consist of behavioural experiments in which panicogenic symptoms are induced and the patient is asked to engage in behaviours that provide evidence that catastrophe will not occur. For example, a person fearful of her legs collapsing during a panic might be asked to induce symptoms through exposure to feared situations or through hyperventilation, and then perform a disconfirmatory act such as standing on one leg to determine if collapse occurs. Verbal re-attribution strategies involving reviewing the evidence that anxiety is harmless and has a protective function are also used to challenge catastrophic beliefs. Verbal methods often consist of education, in which, for example, anxiety is re-framed as part of the individual's 'fight or flight' mechanism thereby representing an advantage to the individual rather than a threat.

In the treatment of social phobia a range of strategies have been developed to deal with the unhelpful effect of safety behaviours, self-focused attention, negative self-image, and negative thoughts about the consequences of failed performance. Treatment normally follows a sequence of modification. First, safety behaviours are reduced and the patient is encouraged to adopt an external focus of attention in social situations in order to potentiate disconfirmatory processing. Next, video feedback is used to challenge the distorted self-image. Video feedback is presented in a special way involving cognitive preparation in which the patient is guided in constructing a detailed mental image of the conspicuousness of symptoms present in the self-image. This is followed by observing the discrepancy that exists between the internal image and the image presented on the video. The procedure does not aim to show that symptoms are not visible, but aims to show the discrepancy that exists between the internal image and the objective self. Following this stage, treatment proceeds by interrogating the social environment. Here, exposure experiments are used in which the patient observes the reactions of others while deliberately showing signs of anxiety or failed performance. The final stage of treatment consists of challenging the negative underlying beliefs about the social self. For example, a patient who believed that he was boring was asked to describe the characteristics that render someone boring. Having done so he was then asked to rate himself on the extent to which he possessed each of the characteristics. He found that he possessed very few of them, and this was used as evidence to challenge his negative belief.

In the treatment of OCD, the therapist focuses on negative beliefs about the meaning and power of intrusive thoughts. To facilitate engagement it is often necessary to provide information that normalizes and de-stigmatizes the experience of intrusions, so that the patient feels that it is safe to disclose the content of intrusions. Following this, the therapist introduces the idea that it is not the occurrence of thoughts but negative interpretation of them that is the source of the problem. Metacognitive beliefs are challenged by introducing exposure and response prevention experiments that have a metacognitive rationale. This rationale emphasizes developing a de-centred relationship with intrusions, in which they are viewed as passing events in the mind, and beliefs about their meaning and power are challenged. For example, a patient who believed that having thoughts about causing accidents meant that he had caused one was asked to hold the thought in mind all of the time he was driving, and refrain from checking his journey. In this way he was able to discover that his thoughts did not represent accurate portrayals of events.

Verbal re-attribution techniques in OCD are used to question and challenge the mechanism by which patients believe that thoughts alone have special significance or power to affect outcomes. For example, one patient believed that having thoughts of stabbing her partner would lead her to commit the act. The therapist asked her what the mechanism was that would translate thoughts into actions. After some discussion she realized that thoughts become actions when there is a desire to act on them. The therapist asked if she had such a desire, which was clearly not the case given the ego-dystonic nature of the intrusions.

Turning to the treatment of GAD: negative beliefs about uncontrollability of worry are targeted first. The techniques used here include questioning the evidence that worrying is uncontrollable, questioning how it is that worrying stops if it is uncontrollable, and using a specially-devised 'worry postponement experiment' to challenge uncontrollability. The concept of loss of control is challenged further by experiments in which the patient is invited to try and deliberately lose control of worrying. Beliefs about the dangers of worrying are modified through education and experiments in which attempts are made to induce negative outcomes by worry alone.

Positive beliefs about worrying are modified by strategies such as 'worry modulation experiments' in which predicted improved outcomes due to worry can be tested by deliberately increasing and decreasing worry and observing the real-world effects of doing this. For example, a patient believed that she performed better at work when she worried about making mistakes. She was asked to complete a homework task in which she worried intensely on alternate working days, while worrying little on other days. She was able to discover that worrying had little or no effect on her performance, apart from the fact that she felt better on the days she worried little.

In each of these treatment approaches, therapeutic effort is devoted to reducing the overall use of unhelpful coping behaviours that lead to a failure to learn from experience, or exacerbate symptoms in other ways. Manipulation of behaviours such as avoidance, maladaptive self-control, reassurance seeking, information search, and safety behaviours is typically a component of behavioural experiments. Increasing some of these behaviours provides a means of demonstrating their deleterious effects. Abandoning these behaviours allows the patient to have experiences that can be the basis of learning that anxiety and feared situations are not dangerous.

CONCLUSION

In this chapter I have described in detail individual models of specific anxiety disorders. These models are supported by empirical findings, and provide a basis for idiosyncratic case formulations. They are generated through the use of specific combinations of questions. I have presented in the form of case formulation interviews basic questions and their sequences that I have found most effective in each case.

The formulations capture a recurring range of cognitive and behavioural factors that are interrelated in a dynamic web of maintenance processes. Extracting the central components and processes enables the construction of a generic model, which may be used when specific models cannot be implemented. However, in most instances of discrete disorders it is recommended that a specific model is used. Each formulation provides a schematic that can be shared with the patient in developing an understanding of the factors that maintain disorder. Furthermore, these formulations direct the focus of cognitive therapy towards modifying particular maintenance processes with a view to changing danger-related negative appraisals and associated dysfunctional beliefs.

REFERENCES

American Psychiatric Association (1994). *Diagnostic and Statistical Manual of Mental Disorders – Revised* (4th edn). Washington, DC: APA.

Beck, A. T. (1976). *Cognitive Therapy and the Emotional Disorders*. New York: International Universities Press.

Beck, A. T. *et al.* (1985). *Anxiety Disorders and Phobias: A Cognitive Perspective*. New York: Basic Books.

Brown, T. A. *et al.* (1994). *Anxiety Disorders Interview Schedule for DSM-IV, Adult Version*. New York: Graywind Publications.

Clark, D. M. (1986). A cognitive model of panic. *Behaviour Research and Therapy* 24: 461–70.

Clark, D. M. and Wells, A. (1995). A cognitive model of social phobia. In R. Heimberg *et al.* (eds) *Social Phobia: Diagnosis, Assessment and Treatment*. New York: Guilford Press.

Flavell, J. H. (1979). Metacognition and metacognitive monitoring: A new area of cognitive-developmental inquiry. *American Psychologist* 34: 906–11.

Nelson, T. O. and Narens, L. (1990). Metamemory: A theoretical framework and some new findings. In G. H. Bower (ed) *The Psychology of Learning and Motivation*. New York: Academic Press.

Persons, J. B. (1989). *Cognitive Therapy in Practice: A Case Formulation Approach*. New York: Norton.

Salkovskis, P. M. (1991). The importance of behaviour in the maintenance of anxiety and panic: A cognitive account. *Behavioural Psychotherapy* 19: 6–19.

Wells, A. (1995). Meta-cognition and worry: A cognitive model of generalised anxiety disorder. *Behavioural and Cognitive Psychotherapy* 23: 301–20.

Wells, A. (1997). *Cognitive Therapy of Anxiety Disorders: A Practice Manual and Conceptual Guide*. Chichester, UK: Wiley.

Wells, A. (2000). *Emotional Disorders and Metacognition: Innovative Cognitive Therapy*. Chichester, UK: Wiley.

Wells, A. and Matthews, G. (1994). *Attention and Emotion: A Clinical Perspective*. Hove, UK: Erlbaum.

Wells, A. and Matthews, G. (1996). Modelling cognition in emotional disorder: The S-REF model. *Behaviour Research and Therapy* 34: 881–8.

Wells, A. and Sembi, S. (2004a). Metacognitive therapy for PTSD: A preliminary investigation of a new brief treatment. *Journal of Behavior Therapy and Experimental Psychiatry* 35: 307–18.

Wells, A. and Sembi, S. (2004b). Metacognitive therapy for PTSD: A core treatment manual. *Cognitive and Behavioral Practice* 11: 365–77.

Zimmerman, M. and Mattia, J. I. (2001). The Psychiatric Diagnostic Screening Questionnaire: Development, reliability and validity. *Comprehensive Psychiatry* 42: 175–89.

Chapter 5

A biopsychosocial and evolutionary approach to formulation with a special focus on shame

Paul Gilbert

Formulation and diagnosis share overlapping features, but differ in important ways. Diagnosis addresses the question: What is the nature of a person's difficulties (Kendell 1975). It seeks to categorise a problem in terms of (say) a disorder (e.g., depression, anxiety or psychosis), a set of basic beliefs/schema, a problem list or biological dysfunction. Formulation in psychological therapies may address such questions but in addition: (a) considers onset/triggers, maintenance factors and their treatment implications; (b) seeks to develop a functional analysis of symptoms and presentations; and (c) is guided by a therapist's theories of disorders. Thus, a psychodynamic, systemic, behavioural or cognitive therapist might diagnose a disorder in similar ways (e.g., via a symptom checklist for depression or panic disorders), but would formulate the causes and treatment quite differently. Psychodynamic therapists might seek to identify unconscious motives and conflicts; systemic therapists might try to understand problems in the context of family interactions; behavioural therapists might focus on the functions of certain behaviours; and cognitive therapists might explore automatic thoughts and core beliefs. Although many schools of therapy acknowledge patient–therapist collaboration as key to therapeutic work, generally the patient is expected to collaborate in formulating and working with their difficulties in the way their particular therapist conceptualises difficulties. In a broader sociocultural context the very nature of a disorder, and the relationship between 'patient' and 'healer', are contextualised in cultural meaning systems that give rise to explanations for disorders (e.g., as soul loss or possession) and to healing rituals and processes (Csordas 2002). While some diagnoses can be relatively culture-free (one either has cancer, diabetes or heart disease or not), formulations, and especially psychological ones, are not.

When engaged in the process of formulation it is important to try to articulate what culturally informed meaning-making systems underpin such efforts. This chapter rests on two basic paradigms for understanding mental functioning. The first is that of evolutionary psychology (Buss 2003), and in particular social mentality theory (Gilbert 1989, 1995, 2000a, 2002a, 2005a).

The second is the biopyschosocial approach (Gilbert 1995; Kiesler 1999), which focuses on interactions between different domains.

The fact that we are evolved beings is important because it enables us to think about human *needs* (e.g., for love, care, respect, identity). We are not born as *tabula rasa*s but enter the world with a number of innate, social role seeking and forming mentalities that mature over time. Thus we can consider:

- Basic social motive systems for engaging in social roles: e.g., forming attachments to care-givers (Bowlby 1969), belonging to groups (Baumeister and Leary 1995) and seeking out sexual partners (Buss, 2003)
- Basic emotions: e.g., anger, fear, disgust and joy
- Basic behavioural displays and defences: e.g., courting, sharing, fight, flight, submission and freezing (Gilbert 2001; Marks 1987)
- Basic cognitive competencies: e.g., abilities relating to symbolic representation of self and other, to 'language' our thinking, theory of mind, meta-cognitions and meta-presentations (Suddendorf and Whitten 2001).

How a person comes to engage or avoid thinking, feeling and behaving in regard to social roles (e.g., forming intimate attachments or sexual relationships) emerges from innate dispositions shaped by social experiences. Different schools of psychotherapy give primacy in their formulation to different aspects of these (e.g., to motives, emotions, cognitions or behaviours). In fact, many clinicians including Freud (Ritvo 1990), Jung (1972; Knox 2003), interpersonal theorists (Leary 1957; Wagner *et al.* 1995), attachment therapists (Bowlby 1969, 1973, 1980), cognitive therapists (Beck 1987, 1996, 1999; Beck *et al.* 1985) and behaviourists (Timberlake 1994) include some notion of evolution in their thinking and model building.

The second paradigm to inform formulation is the biopsychosocial and ecological approach to mental functions. This approach directs attention to the emergence of patterns of interaction between different systems in the brain (e.g., motives, emotions, thoughts and behaviours) and how such patterns are choreographed and shaped through social relating and ecological conditions. For example, a child may be motivated to form an attachment to care-givers, but how a child's attachment system matures and expresses itself, how attachment security may come to regulate other motive systems (e.g., for power or status, or care for others), and how attachment experiences affect the development of beliefs and inner working models of self and other, all depend greatly on whether care-givers are loving or abusive (Mikulincer and Shaver 2004; Schore 1994), and cultural values (MacDonald 1992).

Although there is general agreement that many human social needs and motives (e.g., for attachment, sex and belonging), emotions (e.g., anger, fear and disgust) and competencies (e.g., theory of mind) are products of evolution (Baumesiter and Leary 1995; Bowlby 1969; Buss 2003; Gilbert

1989), there is considerable disagreement about how to conceptualise these processes and how they are shaped into different phenotypes via learning and experience (Beck 1996; Heyes 2003; Laland and Brown 2002; Li 2003; Lickliter and Honeycutt 2003; Smith 2000). For example, the finding that the human brain is far more malleable (a property termed 'neuroplasticity') than was thought even 10 years ago has focused attention on the power of learning and experiences to sculpt brain pathways (Knox 2003; Schwartz and Begley 2002). Geary and Huffman (2002) draw attention to the possibility that humans evolved small genetic changes that had considerable impact on how our neuronal systems interact and lay down complex networks of pathways.

Human neuroplasticity (the way the brain wires and re-wires itself via learning) is a double-edged sword because the maturing brain is highly sensitive to external influences (Hofer 1994). For example, unconditioned social signals (e.g., facial expressions, voice tone, holding, stroking) play a key role in infant–child brain maturation (Schore 1994; Trevarthen and Aitken 2001). Early abuse activates stress in the child's developing brain, and the neurophysiological effects of stress (e.g., high cortisol), combined with lack of affection and safeness, have a major impact on the maturation of brain pathways – which some have argued can result in forms of brain damage (Schore 2001; Teicher 2002). Thus, people who have been abused or who have grown up in stressful environments will have matured the neuro-architectures of their brains in certain ways. Formulation should be mindful of this; clinicians should be wary of beliefs that everyone's brain is basically the same and it is only the software (thoughts and beliefs) that needs addressing. Although we have common needs, people also vary in numerous ways (both in genetic make-up and brain-shaping life experiences). As Eisenberg (1986) noted some time ago, failure to appreciate the intricacies of the biopsychosocial approach has lead to mental health systems that are either 'mindless' (and drug dominated) or 'brainless,' and with little regard for social contexts.

In general it is now recognised that most psychological difficulties emerge from non-linear, complex interactions that involve genes, physiological systems and social relationships (Li 2003). We now know that relationships (e.g., secure and helpful versus exploitative or hostile) have powerful effects on physiological processes (Cacioppo et al. 2000) and can affect gene expression (Suomi 1997). Relationships shape and choreograph evolved cognitive competencies, such as theory of mind and meta-cognition (Heyes 2003). These cognitive competencies, when informed by social relationships, give rise to self–other schema and self-identities. These can then act as high-level regulators of behaviour and emotions (e.g., 'I am a person who does not do that, or does do this'). Beliefs, attitudes and meta-cognitions (that are often acquired in a social context) are also key recruiters and regulators of emotions, social behaviours and physiologies (Lambrie and Marcel 2002).

Consider also that social ecologies impact on health and are related to factors such as poverty, gendered role identities and living in a macho/

warlord society versus a free one. Local ecological conditions do much to shape identities and offer narratives for social relating (e.g., men should be tough and women submissive; Gilmore 1990). Exploitative versus affiliative styles of social relating within groups, and the self-identities formed within them, are highly influenced by cultural factors (Cohen 2001). A simple model that indicates a constant dynamic interplay of such processes is given in Figure 5.1.

WORKING WITH INDIVIDUALS

In an ideal world clinicians would be holistic in their case formulation and operate, with complex cases, as part of a multi-disciplinary team. For example, it is important to ensure that people are not suffering from some obvious physical disorder (e.g., hypothyroidism), and not ignore physical health needs (e.g., poor diet, lack of exercise) and ecologies (e.g., poverty, ability to gain meaningful work, social support systems). The quality of people's intimate relationships is also key to health (e.g., whether they are supportive and warm or hostile and rejecting); the way in which a person may themselves alienate others through being too defensive or needy, or is harmful to others, requires consideration. Psychological therapies involving working

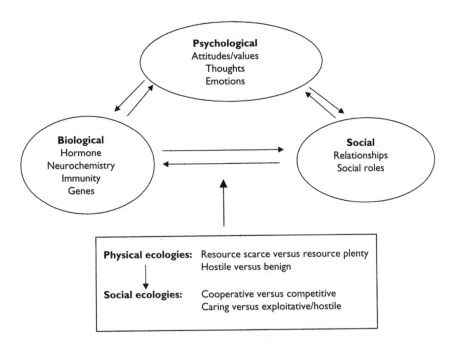

Figure 5.1 Biopsychosocial and ecological interactions.

directly with people's thoughts, feelings, behaviours and memories must be contextualised in lived experience, with recognition of how powerful these social and biological variables are with regard to brain physiologies and patterns of symptoms and distress.

THE NEED FOR AFFILIATION AND THE DAMAGE OF SHAME

A key social and psychological process that can influence disorders and their formulation across a range of disorders is shame. Thus the rest of this chapter will focus on the issue of shame in formulation using the evolutionary and biopsychosocial approach. Shame is not easy to define but, at its simplest, is the experience of 'self as flawed and undesirable in the eyes of others' (Gilbert 1998a, 2003; Tangney and Dearing 2002). However, shame is a multi-faceted experience, which has various aspects and components. These include:

1   A social or externally focused cognitive component: shame that is focused on what others think about the self (in contrast to what the self thinks about the self) has been called external shame (Gilbert 1998a). Shame is often elicited in social contexts and is associated with automatic thoughts that others see one as inferior, bad, inadequate and flawed; that is, others are looking down on the self with a condemning or contemptuous view. How one reacts to such experiences (e.g., with anger or fear) influences the full shame response – but shame experiences begin with an experience of an actual or imagined self in the mind of 'the other.'

2   An internal self-evaluative component: although we may be born with dispositions to become self-aware and self-conscious, and with varying degrees of shyness, we are not born ashamed. Nonetheless, for many theorists shame involves a global negative self-evaluation of oneself as bad, inadequate and flawed (Tangney and Dearing 2002). Shame is thus commonly associated with negative automatic thoughts about the self. Indeed, many self-critical and self-attacking thoughts (e.g., I am useless, worthless, ugly, no good, a bad person, a failure) are, in essence, self-devaluations and internally shaming thoughts.

3   An emotional component: the emotions and feelings recruited in shame are various but can include anxiety, anger, disgust and contempt.

4   A behavioural component: because shame is a threat to self it is often associated with specific defensive behaviours such as a strong urge not to be seen, to avoid exposure, to hide and/or run away (Tangney and Dearing 2002). Eye gaze is commonly averted and the individual may feel behaviourally inhibited. These responses have been linked to a rapid onset of submissive defensive behaviours (Gilbert and McGuire, 1998; Keltner and Harker 1998). However, when anger is the emotion elicited

in shaming encounters, the desire to retaliate or gain revenge against the one who is 'exposing' the self (as inferior, weak or bad) can be high, which may be inhibited or expressed (Retzinger 1998). When there is a focus on the other as bad for the shaming, this has been referred to as humiliation (Gilbert 1998a).

5   A physiological component: shame is related to a stress response, although the exact nature of it is unclear. In some cases it may involve heightened parasympathetic activity, especially when the behavioural profile is one of disengagement and inhibition (Schore 1994, 1998). Recently Dickerson and colleagues (e.g. Dickerson and Kemeny 2004) have explored stress responses associated with social evaluative threats. The combination of a social evaluative threat and uncontrollability (a typical shame experience) is associated with the largest cortisol and adrenocorticotropin hormone changes, with the longest recovery times. Although we know something of the neurophysiology of primary emotions, such as anger, anxiety and disgust (Panskepp 1998), we know much less about the neurophysiology of shame.

6   A cultural component: what is shaming and what is esteemed in social groups is related to cultural values (Leeming and Boyle 2004). Hearing voices may be seen as madness or linked to spirituality; expressing feelings can be genderised. In anthropological writings, shame is linked to narratives of (dis)honour (Lindisfarne 1998). Honour killings of wives and daughters, who are deemed to have brought shame to the family, are linked to the cultural values of 'male' honour. The ways in which different shame and honour systems work in different cultures, and their impact on sources of mental (ill) health and help seeking, are important for therapists to consider (Gilbert *et al.* 2004a).

A MODEL FOR SHAME

Human and animal social relationships can be marked by high levels of aggression, with one individual simply imposing his/her will or interests on another. In this domain it is either threaten or be threatened. However, many mammals and especially primates also rely on affiliation and are orientated to develop positive, sharing and caring relationships with each other (de Waal 1996). This is especially true of humans. From the moment of birth, the child emerges into a social world where the actions of others determine life and death and (as noted above) have a major impact on physiological and brain maturation (Schore 1994). From the earliest days of life, therefore, humans need others to engage positively with them, to invest, support and offer resources, and to be sources of comfort, soothing and care. Stated briefly, humans seek to stimulate positive emotions in the minds of others about the self. We seek to be valued, desired, wanted and esteemed (Barkow 1989;

Gilbert 1989). Indeed, if we think about all of our major relationships, including with our friends, lovers, bosses, patients and doctors, the underlying desire is to be valued and seen as a talented, deserving, desirable individual.

Our early experience of being valued and eliciting positive affect in the minds of others lays down emotional memories that build into self-referent systems of self (Gilbert 2003). To clarify this we can imagine a young child who proudly takes a drawing to her mother and holds it up for approval. The mother's response, 'Wow, did you do that?' accompanied with positive facial expressions of positive affect, stimulates a positive experience of self in the child. In other words, the child's positive emotions for self depend on experiences of positive affects that he/she can generate in another. Suppose, however, that the parent is dismissive, too busy or outright critical; clearly the child has not stimulated positive affect in the parent, but rather anger and rejection, and as a result will not experience positive affect in the self for their drawing (Gilbert 1998a). They may creep away in a state of shame and certainly be less keen to draw or share their drawing in the future. The degree to which non-verbal signals (e.g., facial expressions, voice tone and body posture) in the (m)other can automatically elicit an experience of shame means that shame affects are highly conditionable (Perry et al. 1995) and lay down 'feeling memories' that operate at implicit levels (Gilbert 2003).

Shame and shaming can also be a common experience of children growing up with peers, especially if they are bullied, and this can leave deep scars and fears in the self (Gibb et al. 2004; Hawker and Boulton 2000). Shaming and criticising (bullying) can be distressing throughout life, in work and adult family relationships. In contrast, accepted children and adults, who develop affiliative relationships and are given messages of being valued and supported, have a less threatened and more positive sense of self.

These two alternative strategies (aggression vs affiliation) for engaging social relationships are given in Table 5.1.

There is increasing evidence in support of this model, with findings that

Table 5.1 Strategies for gaining and maintaining rank status in relationships (from Gilbert and McGuire 1998)

	Aggression	Attractiveness
Tactics used	Coercive Threatening Authoritarian	Showing talent Showing competence Affiliative
Outcome desired	To be obeyed To be reckoned with To be submitted to	To be valued To be chosen To be freely given to
Purpose of strategy	To inhibit others To stimulate fear	To inspire and attract others To stimulate positive affect

beliefs that one has qualities others will value are linked to self-esteem (Santor and Walker 1999) and moderate the link between self-evaluations and depression (Thwaites and Dagnan 2004). Recent research has shown that priming people with pictures of approving or disapproving faces, presented fast and outside of consciousness, can have a major impact on self-evaluations and emotions (see Baldwin 2005; Baldwin and Fergusson 2001 for reviews). Hence, shame can be seen as a problem of the social positive affect system, where the self believes that he/she has not, or will not, be able to create a positive affect in the mind of the other about the self. Rather, the other will see the self as undesirable, bad or disgusting, or will attribute some other characteristic to the self that renders the self inferior, worthy of rejection or being ignored (not helped) or even persecuted. Although shame is related to socially orchestrated meta-cognitive beliefs about the self (i.e., is linked to self-focused judgements about what it means to feel certain things, have certain characteristics or behave in certain ways), the experience of shame is also often a rapidly activated affect that is linked to powerful early conditioning (as noted in the drawing example above). Shame is therefore a social emotion which involves a complex interaction between self-experience and 'self in the mind of the other' experience. This is an essential element of formulation, because it requires the therapist to spend time focusing on patients' experiences and beliefs of how they think other people see them (i.e., on interpersonal schemas; Baldwin 1992, 2005).

TYPES OF SHAME

Typical beliefs for shame-prone people focus on two key themes.

One is, 'Others see me as inadequate in some way.' This may be related to concepts of weakness or deficit (lacking certain qualities). These individuals fear they may not have enough positive qualities to be able to stimulate much interest in other people. They therefore worry about being abandoned, being passively avoided or passed over. They can feel that life is a competition to win other people's affection or a social place. A common belief here is: 'Unless I have certain qualities or achieve certain things, others will lose interest in me and prefer to relate to someone else – someone more interesting, talented, attractive and able.' This can be linked to early life experiences. The tragedy is that sometimes people try so hard to earn the tokens to buy into social relationships (e.g., be very ambitious and hardworking) that they neglect their intimate relationships – the very relationships that might give them some sense of security. In severe cases, people feel they have had so little impact on the minds of others that they feel they 'don't exist,' or are 'invisible.' In the formulation, therapist and patient can explore this very basic theme about the experience of self for other. Discussion can be focused on just how much of the patient's life is geared towards influencing how others think about the self and avoiding (what are experienced as) the catastrophes of abandonment, rejection and disgrace.

A second common theme is focused on being positively bad in some way. For example, in this context shame can be seen as closeness to the 'undesired self' (Ogilvie 1987). Lindsay-Hartz *et al.* found that:

> when ashamed, participants talked about being who they did *not* want to be. That is, they experienced themselves as embodying an anti-ideal, rather than simply not being who they wanted to be. The participants said things like, 'I am fat and ugly,' not 'I failed to be pretty,' or 'I am bad and evil,' not 'I am not as good as I want to be.' This difference in emphasis is not simply semantic. Participants insisted that the distinction was important.
>
> (1995: 277)

This kind of shame is not (just) about falling short of standards (in the eyes of self or others), but more about becoming something positively undesirable. Although self-blame can be part of shame it is not always so. For example, an abused person may recognise the fault is not his/hers but still feel 'spoiled and damaged.' Based on a review of the evidence and current theory, Gilbert suggested that it is:

> the inner experience of self as an unattractive social agent, under pressure to limit possible damage to self via escape or appeasement, that captures shame most closely. It does not matter if one is rendered unattractive by one's own or other people's actions; what matters is the sense of personal unattractiveness – being in the social world as an undesired self; a self one does not wish to be. Shame is an involuntary response to an awareness that one has lost status and is devalued.
>
> (1998a: 22)

As noted, then, whereas we may hope to elicit positive feelings (e.g., liking and desire to associate with the self) in the mind of others, when we feel shame there is a belief and experience that we have (or will have) stimulated negative feelings (contempt, ridicule, disgust or disinterest) in the minds of others and, as a consequence, this will lead them to not wish to form useful relationships with us, to disengage, actively reject the self or even attack the self. However, we should also note that other people's unwanted desires for self, which we cannot defend against and/or feel powerless to resist, can also result in shame (e.g., as a child being seen as a sexual object).

It is helpful to keep in mind the distinction between 'What I think others think about me' and 'What I think about myself,' especially during the formulation. Models of the other are key to the way in which an individual may experience therapy, the ease with which they feel safe or not, the degree of revelation, the fear of losing control (e.g., crying) in front of the therapist, being subordinated to the therapist, and the terror of being seen or revealed as bad or weak. One patient, for example, said, 'I want to be understood in therapy but I will then have to reveal myself and you will see the horrible person underneath.' The key here is to discuss these fears openly, normalise them and ask patients to tell you if and when they have a feeling that you are rejecting them or looking down on them. In some complex cases people may fear such revelation or believe that you won't tell them the truth. For example, one patient said, 'I am sure you will act nice but I doubt that's what you will be thinking.' This allows the therapist to focus on the issue of trusting a therapist, and to what degree, and what would be helpful given the patient's understandable difficulties in believing in surface appearances. If this is aired as part of the formulation, that the difficulties are likely to be encountered in the therapy, patients may make more effort to engage and collaborate.

Although shame can be experienced as a global sense of self it usually has a focus. Gilbert and McGuire (1998) drew attention to role-focused shame, where shame can be experienced during the co-construction of a role. For example, people might experience shame when they try to engage in (say) sexual relating or expressing needs for affection. Gilbert and McGuire (1998) coined the term 'role miss-match' to indicate common shame triggers – e.g., one seeks to express affection, sexuality or friendship but the other does not want to co-construct this role and turns away, withdraws or condemns the effort. Outside that role, shame may not be active and people believe they can perform and co-construct roles adequately. The role of 'patient' can be especially shame-prone because we will have to show our disabilities, our loss of functions, our diseases and infections that may smell or look 'disgusting.' In psychological therapy we will have to reveal areas where we are not coping, allow the therapist see our fear and vulnerabilities or reveal painful past events, hostile feelings or bizarre thoughts. In both cases we can feel ourselves to be unattractive and inadequate in the eyes of strangers on whom we may depend for help. As MacDonald and Morley (2001) found, disclosing shame or engaging with things that could result in shame can be more difficult for people than discussing other emotions.

Although people can have generalised beliefs about being undesirable to others, as Leeming and Boyle (2004) note, shame is commonly experienced via social episodes that illuminate role abilities (e.g., to assert oneself or be sexually competent) and specific domains. Andrews (1998) has noted how shame can be focused on aspects of one's character, behaviour and body. One can also feel shame about one's feelings, desires, thoughts, fantasies, memories or history. It is when a therapist and patient engage in the patient's personal shame domain that the experience of shame can be activated. These specificities (not just global beliefs of self as inadequate) can be key to formulation.

STIGMA

Stigma overlaps with shame but is also different. Stigma refers to a set of values or characteristics that a group has decided warrant rejection or condemnation (Gilbert 2002b). There are a number of evolutionary reasons why certain characteristics such as diseases, laziness, fatness or criminalities are stigmatised when they threaten group cohesion or are deemed unattractive attributes (Kurzban and Leary 2001). The fear of stigma is related to shame in the following way: people worry that they won't be evaluated for themselves but will be allocated to a stigmatised group. For example, Pinel (1999) coined the term 'stigma consciousness' to indicate the degree to which women are aware that they can be rejected (e.g., for status roles) because they have been allocated to a negative stereotype of female. They are not judged for what they can do as an individual, but because they are seen to belong to a certain group. The issue of stigma consciousness is very important in mental health. This is because people worry about being allocated to a stigmatised group (e.g., one of the mentally ill), which attracts all of the cultural stereotypes that are associated with that label. People feel that they won't be judged for themselves but dismissed as 'one of them' (e.g., a nutter, bonkers, a neurotic etc.) and excluded from social roles (e.g., jobs and other relationships) or sources of help and empathic understanding. Stigma consciousness is a form of external shame; one believes that in the mind of others one will be devalued simply because one has characteristics that link one to a stigmatised group.

DEFENCES AND SAFETY STRATEGIES

When individuals are exposed to rejecting or threatening social information, they will automatically attempt to defend themselves. These defences can be triggered very rapidly and can involve fight, flight, submission or avoidance, and can be associated with a range of emotions such as anger, anxiety and disgust. Indeed, individuals can find themselves experiencing these feelings and behaviours before being consciously aware of them and in these cases may find it difficult to 'pull back' from a defensive response once it gets going. People can feel threatened and start responding before they can consciously articulate what they feel threatened about (Baldwin and Fergusson 2001; Koole et al. 2001). If one's immediate response to a threat is anger then the anger will come not only with various action tendencies but also with dispositions for information processing that affect subsequent processing. Lerner and Keltner (2001) call this 'appraisal tendency' – appraisals that are guided by the aroused affect.

It is because the threat of rejection and social put-down can be so powerful to humans and rapidly trigger different types of defence (e.g., one person will counter-attack and another person may take flight) that therapists should explore this in the formulation. For example, the therapist can ask: 'If people are critical of you what are your typical feelings, thoughts and behaviours?' One would then discuss this in terms of a person's basic social defensive, protective or safety repertoire. Consider the example of Sam, who often gets angry if criticised.

Therapist: From what you have been saying, if someone criticises you, you experience an immediate flush of anger and want to get back at them.

Sam: Very much so. You can't let people get away with that sort of thing.

Therapist: So it sounds like letting people get away with things is a concern for you.

Sam: Yes, if they are critical.

Therapist: Would it be reasonable to say that showing your anger then is a way of defending your position or even yourself?

Sam: Absolutely. You can't let people get one over on you.

Therapist: Would it be fair to say then that one way to protect yourself from 'others getting one over on you' is to be ready with anger? In that sense your anger is protective and a safety behaviour for you?

In this short dialogue the therapist has focused on talking to Sam about defensive and safety behaviours and strategies, and has linked Sam's anger, and aggression, to sensitivity towards being criticised. The therapist might explore how this has helped Sam survive, but also note that anger might arise in the therapy. The belief that 'You can't let people get one over on you' would also be noted, with exploration of the fear of what would happen if they did. But it is formulating anger as a defensive safety response that is crucial in the first instance, for this enables an empathic appreciation of the threat Sam experiences.

Here is a submissive dialogue with someone we will call Jane.

Therapist: How do you respond if somebody is critical of you?

Jane: I have this immediate anxious feeling that goes through my body and my mind often goes blank.

Therapist: So what happens then?

Jane: Depends on who it is but mostly that makes me really anxious. I immediately worry about what I have done and focus on where I might have made a mistake.

Therapist: What do you actually want to do at that point?

Jane: I try to get away or apologise.

Therapist: Would it be fair to say then that when somebody criticises you, the anxiety you feel focuses you inwardly on yourself, 'What have

I done,' and triggers a strong desire to escape or apologise or appease? It is as if this is trying to protect you. It is like a set of safety behaviours?

Again the therapist might explore how this has helped Jane survive, but also note fear that anger might arise in the therapy. Submissive defences are common in people who have experienced cold, abusive or blaming parents or have been bullied. In these examples we see very different defences, associated with different beliefs, *to the same threat* – the threat of criticism, rejection and put-down. Sam, however, has an externalising, attacking defence, whereas Jane uses an internalising, submissive self-focused defence (for a further discussion see Gilbert and Irons 2005). If a therapist can see that the defences are one thing but the key is the underlying vulnerability, this can sometimes help to build a therapeutic relationship. This is because the therapist can connect with the intense sense of threat that can be felt, and does not shame it. How much a rapidly activated emotion drives a set of cognitions/beliefs is an open question (Lambrie and Marcel 2002; Lerner and Keltner 2001).

Following this way of thinking, medical classifications in terms of anger disorders and anxiety disorders risk ignoring similarities in underlying vulnerabilities. During the formulation the therapist is trying to de-shame the patient's automatic defences of shame-focused concerns, exploring how these have in the past been the best way the patient thought they could defend themselves, and then formulate the problems in terms of vulnerabilities and safety behaviours and strategies. One need not try to identify a 'pathology,' which can be shaming.

Nonverbal communication can be key to triggering shame. For example, I was working with a patient I will again call Jane. About 10 minutes into our therapy she went quiet, looking down and wringing her hands. The conversation went something like this.

Therapist: Jane you seem to have gone quiet.
Jane: [Pauses, looking away] Yes I feel quiet.
Therapist: Can we explore that? Were you feeling like that when you first came?
Jane: No I don't think so.
Therapist: So something has happened here?
Jane: Don't know.
Therapist: Hmm, what's going through your mind?
Jane: [Looking down and anxious] Oh it is probably me being silly but you seem distant today – like you are distracted.

Now my first feeling was one of mild irritation, with the automatic thought, 'I am trying hard with you and you are slowing down again.' This alerted me to a possible shame rupture – but whose was it? As I reflected I had to acknowledge that I *was* feeling very rushed that morning. My irritation was linked to my own shame about not been attentive and relaxed with her – trying to hurry her along in the therapy. It is important, then, for therapists to be mindful of their own shame triggers and be mindfully accepting of such feelings without defending the self or acting them out. A simple acknowledgement can help.

Therapist: You know you are right about that. I have felt rushed today. [Smiling] I am going to take a deep breath and slow down. [Pause] Did anything else come to mind?
Jane: Well it reminded me of my mother. She was always rushing and I had the feeling I was getting in the way.

My nonverbal behaviour had triggered an emotional memory for Jane. But there was more to her shame than this because we then focused on feelings of being a nuisance and getting in the way. Why the self-reference ('I'm being silly') and submissive self-blame and not anger? I asked her: 'I see, so my manner today has given you this feeling again. I wonder also if you might have been a touch annoyed that I came in here rushed?'

Jane again looked down and appeared to curl up in her chair – a typical shame marker – and then said that she knew I was a 'busy man' and that she was 'being silly' and 'too demanding'. Here we see again a self-referent, submissive explanation and denial of anger. I said to her: 'Well that is one view, but just for a moment let's imagine that you might have felt understandably annoyed with me. What would be your worst fear be of showing me that?'

Slowly Jane was able to speak of her fear that I would become angry and reject her. She was in conflict about actually feeling a nuisance and slow in therapy, and anger with me. Even if I 'acted nice' I would (secretly) want to reject her.

One empathises with that fear and conflict, ask if this is typical of her interactions with others, what might be helpful to giving voice to a more assertive way of expressing her feelings. The point of this example is to indicate how episodes within the therapeutic relationship can be useful for formulation, that shame ruptures can be common in psychotherapy interactions, and that formulation is an ongoing process.

When patients struggle with homework or engaging in therapeutic tasks, or even in contemplating change, one of the big blocks is fear of shame. Patients may fear that they will not do their homework right or, if they change, that things will turn out worse for them. A patient may fear telling the therapist that their efforts at change are not working, or that they are angry with the therapist, or that they desperately want the therapist to be there for them all the time or have even fallen in love with him/her. In such cases there is major concern with what the therapist thinks about them.

Some patients fear being controlled by or dependent on a therapist. For example, Sally was a 50-year-old, unmarried, chronically depressed person with a long history of eating disorder and severe agoraphobia; the latter had been helped with behaviour therapy.

Sally was very distant in therapy, rarely making eye contact, going through the motions and doing homeworks agreed but not really getting anywhere. She prided herself on the fact that she did not really need other people to help her and had coped alone. She had a very abusive mother. Using an evolutionary formulation I noted that attachment-seeking was part of most children's early needs: children seek out others to care for them, love them and approve of them. However, if this seeking out of others for protection, love and approval results in rejection, over-control and/or abuse, this 'seeking system' is, in a way, poisoned and becomes toxic. Self-reliance becomes the best way to survive. She noted, 'It is safer not to look to others – for they will either let you down or hurt you.' The problem was, however, that Sally also felt desperately alone and 'empty' and was intensely envious of others who had happy relationships and lives. She often had thoughts like, 'If I kill myself nobody will care.'

This became part of the formation and over some months we discussed how we might gradually detoxify this care-seeking system, so that she could ask others for help and not see dependency needs as shameful and dangerous or as completely undermining her pride in her self-reliance. How might she begin to develop more sharing relationships with others? Over time she gradually began to speak of her fear of becoming dependent on me and her fear that her needs for love would be insatiable. In this formulation we did not try to identify maladaptive beliefs as such, but focused on her whole self-protection system (and set of safety behaviours and thoughts) and the closing down of a basic human motive system – seeking help, love and support from others. In addition we worked with her terror of 'crying and falling apart' – of being sent home in a 'terrible state' and being so ashamed that she could not 'pull herself together'.

Shame-focused therapies seek to de-shame needs, feelings, thoughts, behaviours and memories, enabling people to acknowledge and become mindful and capable of tolerating their thoughts and feelings without fear of them. In these contexts the therapeutic relationship can be crucial, for it is the therapist who acts, in the first instance, as a de-shaming other – a person who provides sufficient safeness and validation for such explorations of the patient's inner world (Leahy 2005).

Although we have explored shame as a basic response to a specific trigger, the full shame response is rather more complex. Frijda (1993) pointed out that appraisals can relate to emotion in a number of ways. They can be part of the emotional experience itself, neither antecedent to it nor its consequence. Second, appraisals can follow the early instigation of emotions – we start to realise that we will need to cope with an emotion as it is being aroused. Third, we can appraise our own reactions to things sometime later ('I should not have felt or acted like that . . .'). Fourth, there are pre-existing beliefs (e.g., 'I am not lovable') that predispose to both the affect and evaluation of situations. Shame-based information processing can operate at each level.

Within the formulation the following elements can be kept in mind.

- the domains of shame and role enactments
- the triggers and nature of the fast shame (defensive) emotions that alert us to an emotion arising in us
- the immediate coping – such as getting angry, or wanting to cover up, go silent or use humour to deflect attention
- the secondary coping, how one might try to conceal the anger or anxiety – or, with therapy, learning to be mindful of shame feelings without acting on them
- the meaning placed on past events – looking back and feeling ashamed by (or from) past events
- shame-focused ruminations
- plans to avoid areas and role engagements when shame is a risk
- the social contexts for shaming (e.g., living or working in abusive relationships).

Different therapeutic interventions can be formulated for each of each of these aspects, such that we learn to tolerate (become mindful of) our feelings, change our immediate coping behaviours, change the meanings we place on events, change our ruminations, and focus on ways to engage with rather than avoid that which we find shaming. This latter aspect obviously involves moral considerations.

INTERNAL SHAME

Internal shame relates to our own self-focused evaluations and feelings. Internalisation occurs via conditioning (as in the example of drawing above (p. 87), or as a result of repeated abuse or rejection of efforts to connect with others). This can lead to automaticity of feelings about the self in response to triggers (especially nonverbal cues). People can also internalise the meta-cognitive labels of others (e.g., 'Mother said I was an ugly child so I am ugly'). When shame is internalised individuals may have very negative evaluations of parts of themselves, and certain aspects of the self activate feelings of self-directed anger, contempt or hatred rather than feelings of acceptance and pleasure.

Buchbinder and Eisikovits (2003) explored battered women's experience of shame using qualitative interviews. They found that inner shame can act as a trap that stops the women from seeking help, changing or moving away. They live in an environment where to rebel (or leave) brings counter-attack or stigma from others, but where not to rebel only demonstrates one's weakness.

The sense that there really is something bad about themselves haunts them and undermines assertive efforts or beliefs that they deserve any better.

Our own research has taken yet another avenue to the 'process' of inner shame. This has enabled us to consider some important distinctions in the experience of inner shame (for a review see Gilbert and Irons 2005). The first is that internal shame can be thought of as a form of self-to-self relating experience (Gilbert 2000b). That is, one part of the self is critical and another part of the self experiences the criticism and responds (e.g., with feelings of anxiety and defeat). One can therefore take a dialogic approach to internal shame – focusing on the experience of self talk, or 'What I tell/say myself.' Here we make clear there is a teller and a listener/receiver part to the self. It then becomes possible to ask people what the critical part of them feels and thinks about them, what their self-critical part wants them to do.

A second issue is that the concept of being flawed needs to be significantly developed in order to offer therapists a method of working with internalised shame dialogues. For example, our own research has suggested that internal shame is associated with various forms of self-attacking. We have identified two functions (Gilbert *et al.* 2004b): one we call self-correcting/improvement, and the other is self-persecution. Here it can be useful for the therapist to focus on the patient's typical feelings and thoughts and even ask directly, 'Are you a self-critical person?' and then subsequently, 'When you are self-critical what kind of thoughts and feelings go through your mind?' In the formulation you would also ask: 'When did you first start to think of yourself like that?' 'What was happening at the time?' 'What feelings come to mind when you recall that?' 'Who else was with you?' 'What was their attitude to you?' It is often possible to show that we are not born with self-criticism but pick it up along the way. Core beliefs can be maintained because they seem too dangerous to risk changing.

It is important to look at the functions of this style of thinking and feeling about the self. Generally, self-improving/self-attacking is intended to spur the person on, stop them making mistakes and help them 'get on' in life. In mild forms many people might use this and get cross with themselves if they make mistakes (e.g., sports people). These are momentary and pass. However, for distressed people these inner dialogues can have severe warnings attached: 'If you don't try harder nobody will love you, you'll be an unlovable failure.' These individuals may be very reluctant to give up their self-attacking because it has been with them a long time and they have invested it with a lot of hope – that if they do do the right things then they will be safe and find a way to co-construct desired roles.

Self-persecution/self-attacking, however, is rather different. This is significantly linked to self-hatred and here the desire is not to improve but to punish, get rid of or destroy parts of the self. Individuals may engage in self-harming in an effort to cleanse themselves. For example, one patient said, 'When I cut myself I think my blood will be black and all the badness will

flow out.' Self-harm is a complex behaviour, however, which has many functions, but the desire to control and get rid of inner feelings of badness is one
of them. Self-persecution is often based on self-hatred. If past or current
abuse seems key to self-hating during formulation, the therapist can explore
the way in which the abuse has somehow come to be internalised, to be
something that the person hates within themselves. For example, the therapist
can ask: 'Before these abusive experiences do you think you might have been
self-hating?' 'What do you think it was about these experiences that might
have lead you to be self-hating?' Through the use of guided discovery patients
can sometimes recognise that some of their hatred is for their abuser and
some of it is for feeling powerless at the time or even having sexual feelings.
As part of the formulation, then, one can focus very specifically on self-
hatred as a key theme to work on. One way to do this is to share the idea that
developing compassion for the self might be helpful (Gilbert and Irons 2005).

OVERVIEW AND MODEL

A formulation of shame in a biopsychosocial model is given in Figure 5.2.
Our propensity for shame arises from being social animals with needs for
attachment and group belonging/attachment; that is to exist positively in the
minds of others. Because humans have complex cognitive abilities to evaluate
how they exist in the minds of others and also to self-evaluate, thwarting
these needs can lead to a sense of self as undesirable. It is this experience of
undesirability that is at the root of shame. At the next level, what becomes a
focus of shame arises from the cultural dynamics of groups and the way in
which individuals can be stigmatised, chosen or rejected because they occupy
certain positions in society or have certain traits. Societal values are transmit-
ted through specific groups that elevate some and stigmatise others (e. g., as
for body weight in young women). At this level, people are in actual contact
with other social agents who relate to them in certain ways (e.g., with acceptance or exclusion/bullying). At the more intimate level, families can be
intensely shaming through processes of criticism, high expressed emotions
and abuse. Some shaming–shame interactions can be related to problems
parents experience in processing their own shame. This leads to intergenera-
tional shaming sequences (e.g., abuse).

The central component of this model, therefore, is external shame: one has
experienced oneself in the mind of the other as undesirable or bad in some
way and vulnerable or experiencing rejection, exclusion or social harm.
Now arise the defences to such harm. These experiences can lead on to
internal shame, whereby some people become self-focused and self-protection
is primarily submissive and self-blaming. In contrast, others might use a
different defence – externalising and being ready with anger. In this context
we generally talk more about the experience of humiliation (e.g., we speak of

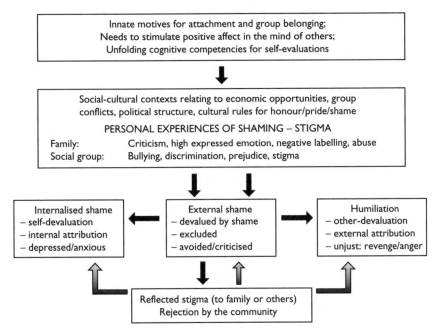

Figure 5.2 An evolutionary and biopsychosocial model for shame (adapted for Gilbert 2002b).

the humiliation of torture, not the shame of torture). People who have difficulties with or fear their own submissive anxious responses, and who believe that submissive behaviour would have catastrophic consequences, especially for self-identity, are particularly prone to feeling humiliation in response to put-downs and rejections.

It is also clear from cultural studies that there can be an intense concern with reflected shame. Hence, even if one does not experience personal shame for an attribute or activity, there can be a fear of bringing shame to others. In our work with Asian women (Gilbert *et al.* 2004) a number of younger women noted that they would personally be happy to marry out of caste or race but would be very anxious about how this would 'shame' their family, and how their community and families would react. At times reflected shame can relate to guilt.

In the model shame is highly interpersonal, based on the human need to create positive affect in the mind of the other and the activation of evolved defensive behaviours when the opposite (negative affect in the mind of the other) may arise. Shame cannot therefore be thought of only as an individual process – and this is why the therapeutic relationship becomes so important for people who are chronically burdened by shame.

COMPASSION FOR SELF

People can change by evaluating evidence and testing out in homeworks (Beck *et al.* 1985), changing meta-cognitions (Wells 2000) or developing mindful acceptance of their various feelings and thoughts. Many clinical trials suggest that all these can be helpful (Roth and Fonagy 1996). In general, because shame has self-protective functions, trying to help people explore and believe in evidence against a negative self-focused belief can be difficult and the patient may engage in a lot of 'yes buts' – basically they feel they cannot risk change or dropping their defences. It is preferable then to focus on building reasons for and experiences of the benefits of engaging and believing in alternatives.

However, many therapists working with complex and chronic problems have noted that although people can develop insight, learn to re-focus their attention, generate alternative thoughts and practise alternative coping behaviours, these efforts may not feel very reassuring. There is, as Lee (2005) argues, a head–heart discordance. There are many possible reasons for this difficulty, related to fear of change, fear of a new identity and lack of experience of the benefits or changing, that will not be explored here. However, one reason is related to the way in which people's positive emotional systems work.

Work in neuroscience and evolutionary psychology suggests that we have different types of positive affect (Panksepp 1998). Stated briefly, we have a positive affect system that is alerting and orientates us to positive rewards and achievements. These positive affects are energising and may operate with dopamine as the key neurotransmitter system. However, there is another positive affect system that may use opiates and neurohormones like oxytocin. This system is soothing and is highly responsive to social affiliation and feeling safe and comforted by others (Depue and Morrone-Strupinsky 2005). The soothing system is especially sensitive to gentle touch and affectional displays and has a major impact on brain maturation. Although at risk of over-simplification these three systems – defensive, incentive and soothing – are shown in Figure 5.3.

These systems are in constant interaction and it is the patterns of their interaction that give rise to feeling textures for self and others.

Developing inner warmth

When some people with complex problems try to alter their thinking and de-shame themselves they are often unable to do this with any warmth. Their alternatives are often delivered in a rather cool logical manner, or even with hostility ('Come on, you don't need to think like this, look at the evidence – stupid!'). If they try new coping behaviours they may bully themselves into them ('Come on, stop being weak and get on with it!'). It is clear that if people are to experience their alternative thoughts and de-shaming efforts as

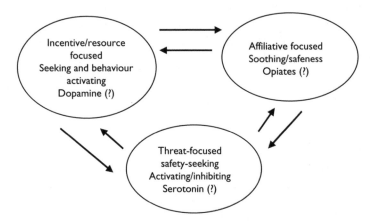

Figure 5.3 Types of affect-regulating systems (from Gilbert 2005a).

supportive and encouraging then they need to *feel* them to be supportive and encouraging. When I first started to try to build warmth and feelings of support into alternative thinking, I was surprised by how often I drew a blank. Patients said things like, 'I don't know what that would feel like,' or 'I have never done that' (Gilbert and Irons 2004). For some patients it felt frightening and it made others want to cry – which frightened them. They had thoughts like, 'I will lose control if I cry and fall apart.' Not only may people have many negative beliefs about why warmth and compassion for self is a bad idea (e.g., it is weak, lets self off the hook, is dangerous – lets one's guard down, is overwhelming, too emotional, will change my whole identity and sense of who I am), they may also rarely have experienced it (Gilbert and Irons 2004).

Many of my more complex patients had suffered severe emotional neglect and abuse. They could not self-soothe because (it seemed to me) this soothing-warmth system, the basis for social affiliation (Depue and Morrone-Strupinsky 2005), had hardly ever been stimulated. All they knew were attacks, rejections and how to try to avoid them. Feelings of warmth from others, experiencing others as having genuine interest in their well-being and being empathic to their distress, were alien. They were often attracted to people who also had problems expressing warmth. So how could people develop and learn to be empathic, understanding, kind and supporting of themselves if this system was toned down? It seemed this could be one reason why people could do the logical and evidence part of cognitive therapy, but not feel the effects.

Behaviourists have long focused on the importance of de-sensitising people to negative emotion via exposure, where one must elicit/feel the emotion. Similarly, in re-activating or re-sensitising positive affect (especially in depression through doing and achieving) there must be an experience of positive affect. However, less attention has been given to re-sensitising or activating positive affect based on affiliation, warmth and inner soothing. Indeed, until recently behaviourists made no distinction between affiliative rewards and 'achieving/doing' rewards. However, they are quite different. Hence, in regard to formulation it is useful to investigate the possibility that the warmth-soothing affect systems, the ability to feel reassured by others, or soothed by looking at things in a new way, or to be self-supportive and compassionate when trying new behaviours, is not much engaged.

Engaging warmth

Affiliation signals, which are attuned to signals of kindness, support and care from another, are calming (not behavioural activating as in 'doing and achiev-ing'; Panksepp 1998). They create feelings of safeness (Gilbert 1989) and involve the opiate system (Depue and Morrone-Strupinsky 2005). These are the most crucial signals early in life that help a child regulate his/her emotions ('Mother makes safe') and facilitate the sharing of positive affect between mother and child. This creates feelings of safeness and connectedness (Gilbert 2005b). Via the soothing behaviour of the mother there is a stimulation of inner warmth that later builds into capacities for self-soothing and self-liking (for reviews see Cassidy and Shaver 1999; Gilbert 2005a; Mikulincer and Shaver 2004).

Inability to engage with feelings of inner warmth and care for the self may become part of the formulation. Patients may acknowledge that they have never had feelings of warmth or care for the self – or from others. One way to formulate this with patients, and offer understanding of what one might try to achieve in therapy, is to take a simple neurophysiological approach. We might introduce the idea of the value of developing inner warmth by suggesting:

> When we attack ourselves we stimulate certain pathways in our brain, but when we learn to be compassionate and supportive of our efforts we stimulate different pathways. Sometimes we are so well practised in stimulating inner attacks that our ability to stimulate inner support and warmth is rather under-developed. Hence, now that we have seen how we can generate alternatives to our self-attacking thoughts, we can explore ways to help them have more emotional impact.
>
> (Gilbert and Irons 2005: 298)

The therapist might then discuss what this might entail and offer it as an 'experiment' to see if it helps. The most straightforward way to start to bring warmth into people's alternative thoughts is first to help a patient generate some alternative thoughts to whatever negative thoughts one has captured. Then one can ask the patient to imagine what a warm and compassionate other may look and sound like. Because an evolutionary approach focuses on signals it is important to try to capture these (often sensory) signals (Lee 2005). The therapist may spend time exploring these signals (e.g., really focusing on a kind face or the sound of a soothing voice). Next, the patient may read through their alternative thoughts slowly, but this time let the logic be in the background and instead focus on the feelings of warmth and compassion: 'Attend to your thoughts with the soothing voice.' Spend time really trying to offer an experience of warmth in the alternative. It is not, in this example, a question of how much one believes alternative thoughts but how much warmth one can put into them. Moreover, it is quite common for people to note that the more warmth they put into their alternatives the more they believe them.

When working on homeworks of new behaviours one might explore how they could engage with support and encouragement: 'What would a compassionate self-practice or task be to help you?' 'What warm supportive feelings could you bring to your coping thoughts as you try to do this activity?'

We call this approach 'compassionate mind training' (Gilbert 2000b; Gilbert and Irons 2005) because it really is about training people to generate new emotions using specific qualities of their minds. There are of course a variety of complex difficulties in working this way and it should be stressed that this is not an alternative therapy or a new school of therapy, but is firmly embedded in basic cognitive behavioural skills. When people have obtained some experience of using non-judgmental warmth, it can then be easier to work with more painful material because one can come back to the image of a warm-soothing other. This is not an alternative to avoid working with people's anger or facing anxieties. It adds a doorway to help people begin to feel safe and tap into alternative affect systems that can have an impact on the re-organisation of self–other schema. As we have noted above, shame can be one of the major experiences that turn people towards self-protection and away from inner warmth.

SOCIAL IMPLICATIONS

Many of our self-evaluative processing systems are designed for social behaviour (Baldwin 1992, 2005). Failure to appreciate this can lead to a notion of autonomous individuals moving around in the world with autonomous internal self-schema, negating the impact of the (social) environment on patterns of thinking and strategies. The way various psychotherapies tend to pathologise individuals, rather than environments, has drawn strong criticism from some quarters (e.g., Smail 2001). Indeed, there is increasing evidence that competitive and materialist environments have higher rates of crime and ill health than supportive environments (Arrindell *et al.* 2003; Kasser 2002). There is a long history of linkage between various indices of physical/mental ill health and the social stratification of society and poverty (Melzer *et al.*

2004). As noted elsewhere (Gilbert 1989), competitive environments can also push competitive behaviour to extremes (e.g., to stay thin, stay 'beautiful' or possess qualifications). Competitive groups can create a sense of self as a 'marketable object', where one is focused on appearance and having to prove oneself worthy of acceptance, but one's place is never secure (Lasch 1979).

The implications of this way of thinking about formulation rest on the degree to which we conceptualise an individual's difficulties in terms of their temperament, history, current social contexts and cultural values. If we are to address the changing rates of disorders in communities – and the World Health Organisation has indicated a rapidly increasing rate of certain disorders such as depression (especially in younger women) – then individual-focused models of psychopathology will be limited. Clearly, the nature and value of our formulation depends on the purpose to which it is put. However, it also raises other questions such as the degree to which we engage with discussing and 'getting to know' a person in their historical and social contexts, and the kind of discussions we have with people, especially those that seek to de-shame problems.

THERAPEUTIC IMPLICATIONS OF DE-SHAMING

Evolutionary approaches can help to de-stigmatise mental health issues for people with complex problems (i.e, we focus on people's threat–defensive repertoires, feelings, memories, blocked desires and maturational opportunities; Gilbert 1993). For example, people who are labelled as having a personality disorder, because they are (say) impulsive and perhaps poor at developing affiliative bonds or self-soothing, may be following strategies that evolved as their best means of coping with socially hostile environments. Evolution has no interest in whether people are happy or not, only in the best survival and reproductive strategies for local conditions. When we try to help such people (e.g., to become more emotionally regulated and affiliative) we are often trying to teach them to 'turn off', 'tone down' or switch strategies (coded in brain pathways) that have become psychobiologically organised over a long time, we may try to help them 'turn on' other strategies (e.g., for trust, affiliation and affect regulation). The inputs needed, and the ease and rapidity with which one can achieve this re-organisation in the psycho-physiological processes underpinning strategies, is subject to much debate.

Looked at this way, the whole focus of a therapy moves away from trying to identify so-called maladaptive schema or distorted cognitions, and towards openly discussing with people their coping as being their best efforts in their environments. This focus seeks to de-shame people's problems, share insights from evolutionary psychology, and engage in functional analysis of behaviour, feelings and cognition. As people come to understand that they can feel driven by feelings and thoughts that are routed in various automatic defensive strategies, and they are not bad, mad, weak or just distorted thinkers, there is a new framework for developing collaborative approaches to change (Gilbert and Irons 2005). Thus, from an evolutionary approach it is useful to help people link 'distorted thinking' to (for example) a 'better safe than sorry' strategy that can operate automatically (Gilbert 1998b).

Hence, for example, depression may be discussed as a natural response when stressors seem overwhelming and escape impossible. Self-blame may be safer than being angry with others. Having a desire to escape and run away is not evidence of weakness but can be a natural response to some circumstances, even if we judge it to be weak or it makes us feel guilty (Gilbert *et al.* 2004c). Wanting to cut the body can be a natural desire to try to get rid of bad feelings and memories, just as we may wish to vomit out/expel noxious substances or cut out infectious tissue (Gilbert and Irons 2005). Impulsiveness may be useful when environments are uncertain and hostile and one has no time to ponder actions. Many of us may become (a little) impulsive when under stress, when there are multiple demands on us or we are over-stimulated – all factors that some believe are in high abundance for children in modern societies, with impacts on brain maturation (Restak 2003). Aggression can be a natural way to deal with threats to the self, and gives one courage and protects the self. Vengeance is a natural response to being hurt. We can learn to be mindful of these responses and understand their source without feeling ashamed of them.

In some complex cases people can have so much shame around their natural defences (and at times fear of them; e.g., fear of the strength of their anger and rage, or fear of their needs for love and support) that the therapist may need to work hard (and empathise with their functions) to de-shame them. This does not mean that human depressions (or other difficulties, such as panic or rage) are adaptive or desirable today – mostly they are not – but that the mechanisms that are recruited into a depression or other problems might be linked to underlying protective or resource-seeking processes that evolved a long time ago to fit a different environment and to be regulated by that (older) environment (Smith 2002). Our love of sweet and fatty foods is fine when these are controlled by environmental scarcity, but not with modern food production. Self-regulation is difficult because it was the environment (society) that usually regulated how much we ate. Many adaptive defences (even vomiting or high temperature) and desires can become maladaptive if they are too easily triggered, too frequent, last too long or are too intense. Genes, associative learning and cognitive processes play a part in shifting adaptive defensive and seeking strategies into maladaptive ranges. What is adaptive and what is maladaptive depends on the person–environment fit. Being gentle and trusting (which most therapists like to see themselves as!) might be quite maladaptive in (say) a prison or a harsh social context. De-shaming, however, is only a stage in a process of change: helping people change so that they don't feel so threatened, lose control over their defences or act out their defences is the salient therapeutic endeavour.

Not only can natural defences or desires be undesirable, they also tend to generate their own styles of reasoning. Sometimes they are positively endorsed and amplified via cultural discourse. For example, while retaliation strategies have had their uses over evolution, human cycles of vengeance and the desire to terrorise others are deeply disturbing. However, individuals, groups and whole societies can get caught up in them, spinning out their own logic for their maintenance. Change may come via opportunities to create social justice or opportunities for reconciliation. Reconciliation in the public domain is a way of having stories heard, offering validation and beginning a process for forgiveness. Trying to change people's thinking without these social processes in place may not be successful. These social dynamics also impinge on therapy, for as resource constraints in health care systems apply pressure to 'get people better quickly' the context is set for mutual feelings of failure and shame – especially for those with complex problems.

Maturation

Shame can be a special problem if therapists working with complex difficulties fail to recognise that sometimes people don't just need to learn new cognitive-behavioural or emotion regulation skills, but may require help in a maturational process that will go through stages. For example, mentalities for sexuality begin in earnest around puberty, and run in parallel with physical maturation and maturation of certain types of cognitive competencies that enable understanding of the meaning of such relating, and socially shared values. Cognitive abilities and moral thinking, salient for many forms of social relating, also go through stages. Understanding where people are in their maturation process can be important for therapeutic work (Kagan 1984; Mahoney 1990). Having rapid access to a therapist to act as a soothing other can be important for some people to help attachment systems mature and provide needed inputs for internal self-regulating soothing processes (Linehan 1993).

As competencies such as affect regulation (which matures with the frontal cortex – an area of the brain affected by abuse), theory of mind, perspective taking and concern for others mature, these can be used in a range of different social roles (Heyes 2003). People who have problems with affect regulation, theory of mind or taking the perspective of others can be handicapped in a variety of social roles, from child-care to sexuality and pair bonding. Thus one cannot approach complex difficulties as if they are located in isolated schema or core beliefs. The mind works in terms of patterns of activity, and as one competence changes or matures this can ripple though the system, producing re-organisation (Hayes and Strauss 1998). As a person de-shames and becomes able to self-soothe, and accept aspects of themselves that have been problematic for a long time, the whole pattern of emotions and sense of self may change. It is an issue of the person they can become, not just the problems they have.

CONCLUSIONS

The way in which therapists think about psychological problems influences greatly how a formulation with a patient will unfold. If therapists hold to only one model of therapy then that is the formulation the patient will experience. However, formulation can also be informed by approaches that suggest that our experiences of self and others are emergent from complex biopsychosocial interactions shaped by evolved dispositions. Into this process we can place shame and the avoidance of shame with its feared implications of being de-valued, demeaned and rejected. Shame is not just an individual issue but speaks to complex cultural and socialisation processes. We are not born ashamed but learn what to feel shame about.

A sense of the intricacies of shame can therefore texture the process of formulation as we recognise that for many people, problems of aggression, anxiety, appeasement, competitiveness, concealment, fear of intimacy, drug use and avoidance can in fact be solutions – solutions to threats on the very essence of self. Formulation in these terms focuses first and foremost on people's efforts at self-protection, empathically validating them as understandable (if undesirable and problematic) while at the same time exploring options to go beyond them and re-construct a sense of self and engage with self and others in warmer and more compassionate ways.

REFERENCES

Andrews, B. (1998). Shame and childhood abuse. In P. Gilbert and B. Andrews (eds) *Shame: Interpersonal Behavior, Psychopathology and Culture*. New York: Oxford University Press.

Arrindell, W. A. *et al.* (2003). Higher levels of depression in masculine than in feminine nations. *Behaviour Research and Therapy* 41: 809–17.

Baldwin, M. W. (1992). Relational schemas and the processing of social information. *Psychological Bulletin* 112: 461–84.

Baldwin, M. W. (ed.) (2005). *Interpersonal Cognition*. New York: Guilford Press.

Baldwin, M. W. and Fergusson, P. (2001). Relational schemas: The activation of interpersonal knowledge structures in social anxiety. In W. R. Crozier and L. E. Alden (eds) *International Handbook of Social Anxiety: Concepts, Research and Interventions to the Self and Shyness*. Chichester, UK: J. Wiley.

Barkow, J. H. (1989). *Darwin, Sex and Status*. Toronto: Toronto University Press.

Baumeister, R. F. and Leary, M. R. (1995). The need to belong: Desire for interpersonal attachments as a fundamental human motivation. *Psychological Bulletin* 117: 497–529.

Beck, A. T. (1987). Cognitive models of depression. *Journal of Cognitive Psychotherapy: An International Quarterly* 1: 5–38.

Beck, A. T. (1996). Beyond belief: A theory of modes, personality and psychopathology. In P. Salkovskis (ed) *Frontiers of Cognitive Therapy*. New York: Oxford University Press.

Beck, A. T. (1999). Cognitive aspects of personality disorders and their relation to syndromal disorders: A psycho-evolutionary approach. In C. R. Cloninger (ed) *Personality and Psychopathology*. Washington, DC: American Psychiatric Association.

Beck, A. T. *et al.* (1985). *Anxiety Disorders and Phobias: A Cognitive Approach*. New York: Basic Books.

Bowlby, J. (1969). *Attachment: Attachment and Loss, Vol. 1*. London: Hogarth Press.

Bowlby, J. (1973). *Separation, Anxiety and Anger: Attachment and Loss, Vol. 2*. London: Hogarth Press.

Bowlby, J. (1980). *Loss: Sadness and Depression: Attachment and Loss, Vol. 3*. London: Hogarth Press.

Buchbinder, E. and Eisikovits, Z. (2003). Battered women's entrapment in shame: A phenomenological study. *American Journal of Orthopsychiatry* 73: 355–66.

Buss D. M. (2003). *Evolutionary Psychology: The New Science of Mind* (2nd edn). Boston: Allyn and Bacon.

Cacioppo, J. T. *et al.* (2000). Multilevel integrative analysis of human behavior: Social neuroscience and the complementing nature of social and biological approaches. *Psychological Bulletin* 126: 829–43.

Cassidy, J. and Shaver, P. R. (eds) (1999). *Handbook of Attachment: Theory, Research and Clinical Applications*. New York: Guilford Press.

Cohen, D. (2001). Cultural variation: Considerations and implications. *Psychological Bulletin* 127: 451–71.

Csordas. T. J. (2002). *Body/Meaning/Healing*. New York: Palgrave MacMillan.

Depue, R. A. and Morrone-Strupinsky, J. V. (2005). A neurobehavioral model of affiliative bonding. *Behavioral and Brain Sciences* 28: 313–95.

Dickerson, S. S. and Kemeny, M. E. (2004). Acute stresses and cortisol responses: A theoretical integration and synthesis of laboratory research. *Psychological Bulletin* 130: 355–91.

Eisenberg, L. (1986). Mindlessness and brainlessness in psychiatry. *British Journal of Psychiatry* 148: 497–508.

Frijda, N. H. (1993). The place of appraisal in emotion. *Cognition and Emotion* (special issue: *Appraisal and Beyond: The Issue of Cognitive Determinants of Emotion*) 7: 357–87.

Geary, D. C. and Huffman, K. J. (2002). Brain and cognitive evolution: Forms of modularity and functions of the mind. *Psychological Bulletin* 128: 667–98.

Gibb B. E. *et al.* (2004). Emotional maltreatment from parent, verbal peer victimization, and cognitive vulnerability to depression. *Cognitive Therapy and Research* 28: 1–21.

Gilbert, P. (1989). *Human Nature and Suffering*. Hove, UK: Lawrence Erlbaum Associates.

Gilbert, P. (1993). Defence and safety: Their function in social behaviour and psychopathology. *British Journal of Clinical Psychology* 32: 131–53.

Gilbert, P. (1995). Biopsychosocial approaches and evolutionary theory as aids to integration in clinical psychology and psychotherapy. *Clinical Psychology and Psychotherapy* 2: 135–56.

Gilbert, P. (1998a). What is shame? Some core issues and controversies. In P. Gilbert and B. Andrews (eds) *Shame: Interpersonal Behavior, Psychopathology and Culture.* New York: Oxford University Press.

Gilbert, P. (1998b). The evolved basis and adaptive functions of cognitive distortions. *British Journal of Medical Psychology* 71: 447–63.

Gilbert, P. (2000a). Social mentalities: Internal 'social' conflicts and the role of inner warmth and compassion in cognitive therapy. In P. Gilbert and K. G. Bailey (eds) *Genes on the Couch: Explorations in Evolutionary Psychotherapy.* Hove, UK: Brunner-Routledge.

Gilbert, P. (2000b). Varieties of submissive behaviour: Their evolution and role in depression. In L. Sloman and P. Gilbert (eds) *Subordination and Defeat: An Evolutionary Approach to Mood Disorders.* Hillsadale, NJ: Lawrence Erlbaum.

Gilbert, P. (2001). Evolutionary approaches to psychopathology: The role of natural defences. *Australian and New Zealand Journal of Psychiatry* 35: 17–27.

Gilbert, P. (2002a). Evolutionary approaches to psychopathology and cognitive therapy. In P. Gilbert (ed) *Cognitive Psychotherapy: An International Quarterly* (special edition: *Evolutionary Psychology and Cognitive Therapy*) 16: 263–94.

Gilbert, P. (2002b). Body shame: A biopsychosocial conceptualisation and overview, with treatment implications. In P. Gilbert and J. N. V. Miles (eds) *Body Shame: Conceptualisation, Research and Treatment.* London: Brunner-Routledge.

Gilbert, P. (2003). Evolution, social roles and the differences in shame and guilt. *Social Research* 70: 401–26.

Gilbert, P. (2005a). Compassion and cruelty: A biopsychosocial approach. In P. Gilbert (ed) *Compassion: Conceptualisations, Research and Use in Psychotherapy.* London: Routledge.

Gilbert P. (2005b). Social mentalities: A biopsychosocial and evolutionary reflection on social relationships. In M. Baldwin (ed) *Interpersonal Cognition.* New York: Guilford Press.

Gilbert P. and Irons, C. (2004). A pilot exploration of the use of compassionate images in a group of self-critical people. *Memory* 12: 507–16.

Gilbert, P. and Irons, C. (2005). Focused therapies for shame and self-attacking, using cognitive, behavioural, emotional, imagery and compassionate mind training In P. Gilbert (ed) *Compassion: Conceptualisations, Research and Use in Psychotherapy.* London: Routledge.

Gilbert, P. and McGuire, M. (1998). Shame, social roles and status: The psychobiological continuum from monkey to human. In P. Gilbert and B. Andrews (eds) *Shame: Interpersonal Behavior, Psychopathology and Culture.* New York: Oxford University Press.

Gilbert, P. *et al.* (2004a). A focus group exploration of the impact of izzat, shame, subordination and entrapment on mental health and service use in South Asian women living in Derby. *Mental Health, Religion and Culture* 7: 109–30.

Gilbert, P. *et al.* (2004b). Criticizing and reassuring oneself: An exploration of forms and reasons in female students. *British Journal of Clinical Psychology* 43: 31–50.

Gilbert, P. *et al.* (2004c). Life events, entrapments and arrested anger in depression. *Journal of Affective Disorders* 79: 149–60.

Gilmore, D. D. (1990). *Manhood in the Making: Cultural Concepts of Masculinity*. New Haven, CT: Yale University Press.

Hawker, D. S. and Boulton, M. J. (2000). Twenty years' research on peer victimisation and psychosocial maltreatment: A meta-analytic review of cross sectional studies. *Journal of Child Psychology and Psychiatry and Allied Disciplines* 41: 441–55.

Hayes, A. M. and Strauss, J. L. (1998). Dynamic systems theory as a paradigm for the study of change in psychotherapy: An application to cognitive therapy for depression. *Journal of Consulting and Clinical Psychology* 66: 939–47.

Heyes, C. (2003). Four routes of cognitive evolution. *Psychological Review* 110: 713–27.

Hofer, M. A. (1994). Early relationships as regulators of infant physiology and behavior. *Acta Paediatiricia Supplement* 397: 9–18.

Jung, C. G. (1972). *Four Archetypes*. London: Routledge and Kegan Paul.

Kagan, J. (1984). *The Nature of the Child*. New York: Basic Books.

Kasser, T. (2002). *The High Price of Materialism*. Boston, MA: MIT Press.

Keltner, D. and Harker, L. A. (1998). The forms and functions of the nonverbal signal of shame. In P. Gilbert and B. Andrews (eds) *Shame: Interpersonal Behavior, Psychopathology and Culture*. New York: Oxford University Press.

Kendell, R. E. (1975). *The Role of Diagnosis in Psychiatry*. London: Blackwell Scientific Publications.

Kiesler, D. J. (1999). *Beyond the Disease Model of Mental Disorders*. New York: Praeger.

Knox, J. (2003). *Archetype, Attachment, Analysis: Jungian Psychology and the Emergence of Mind*. London: Brunner-Routledge.

Koole, S. L. *et al.* (2001). What's in a name: Implicit self-esteem and the automatic self. *Journal of Personality and Social Psychology* 80: 669–85.

Kurzban, R. and Leary, M. (2001). Evolutionary origins of stigmatisation: The functions of social exclusion. *Psychological Bulletin* 127: 187–208.

Laland, K. N. and Brown, G. R. (2002). *Sense and Nonsense: Evolutionary Perspectives on Human Psychology*. Oxford: Oxford University Press.

Lambrie, J. A. and Marcel, A. J. (2002). Consciousness and the varieties of emotion experience: A theoretical framework. *Psychological Review* 109: 219–59.

Lasch C. (1979). *The Culture of Narcissism: American Life in an Age of Diminishing Expectations*. New York: Norton.

Leahy, R. L. (2005). A social-cognitive model of validation. In P. Gilbert (ed) *Compassion: Conceptualisations, Research and Use in Psychotherapy*. London: Brunner-Routledge.

Leary, T. (1957). *The Interpersonal Diagnosis of Personality*. New York: Ronald Press.

Lee, D. (2005). The perfect nurturer: A model to develop a compassionate mind within the context of cognitive therapy. In P. Gilbert (ed) *Compassion: Conceptualisations, Research and Use in Psychotherapy*. London: Brunner-Routledge.

Leeming, D. and Boyle, M. (2004). Shame as a social phenomenon: A critical analysis of the concept of dispositional shame. *Psychology and Psychotherapy* 77: 375–96.

Lerner, J. S. and Keltner, D. (2001). Fear, anger and risk. *Journal of Personality and Social Psychology* 81: 146–59.

Li, S. C. (2003). Biocultural orchestration of developmental plasticity across levels: The impact of biology and culture in shaping the mind and behavior across the life span. *Psychological Bulletin* 129: 171–94.

Lickliter, R. and Honeycutt, H. (2003). Developmental dynamics: Toward a biologic-
    ally plausible evolutionary psychology. *Psychological Bulletin* 129: 819–35.
Lindisfarne, N. (1998). Gender, shame, and culture: An anthropological perspective.
    In P. Gilbert and B. Andrews (eds) *Shame: Interpersonal Behavior, Psychopathology
    and Culture*. New York: Oxford University Press.
Lindsay-Hartz, J. *et al.* (1995). Differentiating guilt and shame and their effects on
    motivations. In J. P. Tangney and K. W. Fischer (eds) *Self-Conscious Emotions: The
    Psychology of Shame, Guilt, Embarrassment and Pride*. New York: Guilford Press.
Linehan, M. (1993). *Cognitive Behavioral Treatment of Borderline Personality Disorder*.
    New York: Guilford Press.
MacDonald, J. and Morley, I. (2001). Shame and non-disclosure: A study of the
    emotional isolation of people referred for psychotherapy. *British Journal of Medical
    Psychology* 74: 1–21.
MacDonald, K. (1992). Warmth as a developmental construct: An evolutionary
    analysis. *Child Development* 63: 753–73.
Mahoney, J. (1991). *Human Change Process*. New York: Basic Books.
Marks, I. M. (1987). *Fears, Phobias and Rituals: Panic, Anxiety and their Disorders*.
    Oxford: Oxford University Press.
Melzer, D. *et al.* (2004). *Social Inequalities and the Distribution of the Common Mental
    Disorders* (Maudsley Monographs). Hove, UK: Psychology Press.
Mikulincer, M. and Shaver, P. R. (2004). Security-based self-representations in
    adulthood: Contents and processes. In W. S. Rholes and J. A. Simpson (eds) *Adult
    Attachment: Theory, Research and Clinical Implications*. New York: Guilford Press.
Ogilive, D. M. (1987). The undesired self: A neglected variable in personality research.
    Journal of Personality and Social Psychology 52: 379–88.
Panksepp, J. (1998). *Affective Neuroscience*. New York: Oxford University Press.
Perry, B. D. *et al.* (1995). Childhood trauma, the neurobiology of adaptation and
    'use–dependent' development of the brain: How 'states' become 'traits'. *Infant
    Mental Health Journal* 16: 271–91.
Pinel, E. C. (1999). Stigma consciousness: The psychological legacy of social stereo-
    types. *Journal of Personality and Social Psychology* 76: 114–28.
Restak, R. (2003). *The New Brain: How the Modern Age is Re-Wiring Your Mind*. New
    York: Rodale.
Retzinger, S. (1998). Shame in the therapeutic relationship. In P. Gilbert and
    B. Andrews (eds) *Shame: Interpersonal Behavior, Psychopathology and Culture*.
    New York: Oxford University Press.
Ritvo, L. B. (1990). *Darwin's Influence of Freud: A Tale of Two Sciences*. New Haven,
    CT: Yale University Press.
Roth, A. and Fonagy, P. (1996). *What Works for Whom: A Critical Review of Psycho-
    therapy Research*. New York: Guilford Press.
Santor, D. and Walker, J. (1999). Garnering the interests of others: Mediating the
    effects among physical attractiveness, self-worth and dominance. *British Journal of
    Social Psychology* 38: 461–77.
Schore, A. N. (1994). *Affect Regulation and the Origin of the Self: The Neurobiology of
    Emotional Development*. Hillsdale, NJ: Lawrence Erlbaum.
Schore, A. N. (1998). Early shame experiences and infant brain development. In
    P. Gilbert and B. Andrews (eds) *Shame: Interpersonal Behavior, Psychopathology
    and Culture*. New York: Oxford University Press.

Schore, A. N. (2001). The effects of early relational trauma on right brain development, affect regulation, and infant mental health. *Infant Mental Health Journal* 22: 201–69.

Schwartz, J. M. and Begley, S. (2002). *The Mind and the Brain: Neuroplasticity and the Power of Mental Force*. New York: Regan Books.

Smail, D. (2001). *The Nature of Unhappiness*. New York: Random House.

Smith, E. A. (2000). Three styles in the evolutionary analysis of human behavior. In L. Cook *et al.* (eds) *Adaptation and Human Behavior: An Anthropological Perspective*. New York: Aldine De Gruyter.

Smith, E. O. (2002). *When Culture and Biology Collide: Why we are Stressed, Depressed and Self-Obsessed*. New Jersey: Rutgers University Press.

Suddendorf, T. and Whitten, A. (2001). Mental evolutions and development: Evidence for secondary representation in children, great apes and other animals. *Psychological Bulletin* 127: 629–50.

Suomi, S. J. (1997). Early determinants of behavior: Evidence from primate studies. *British Medical Bulletin* 53: 170–84.

Tangney, J. P. and Dearing, R. L. (2002). *Shame and Guilt*. New York: Guilford Press.

Teicher, M. H. (2002). Scars that won't heal: The neurobiology of the abused child. *Scientific American* 286(3): 54–61.

Thwaites, R. and Dagnan, D. (2004). Moderating variables in the relationship between social comparison and depression: An evolutionary view. *Psychology and Psychotherapy* 77: 309–24.

Timberlake, W. (1994). Behavior systems, associationism, and Pavlovian conditioning. *Psychonomic Bulletin and Review* 1: 405–20.

Trevarthen, C. and Aitken, K. (2001). Infant intersubjectivity: Research, theory, and clinical applications. *Journal of Child Psychology and Psychiatry* 42: 3–48.

de Waal, F. B. M. (1996). *Good Natured: The Origins of Right and Wrong in Humans and Other Animals*. London: Harvard University Press.

Wagner, C. C. *et al.* (1995). Assessing the interpersonal transaction cycle: Convergence of action and the reaction interpersonal circumplex measures. *Journal of Personality and Social Psychology* 69: 938–49.

Wells, A. (2000). *Emotional Disorders and Metacognition: Innovative Cognitive Therapy*. Chichester, UK: Wiley.

Chapter 6

Case formulation in depression

Ivy M. Blackburn, Ian A. James and Alyson Flitcroft

Depressive illness was the first area of research in cognitive therapy (CT; Beck 1963, 1964, 1967) and remains to this day the psychological disorder where the most evidence has been accumulated, theoretically, empirically and clinically. In this chapter, we describe briefly the cognitive theory of depression and review the clinical evidence for the efficacy of CT in depression. We then describe the structure and process of formulation, using case examples. Some preliminary data relating to a research project on the formulation process in depression will also be presented. We use the terms 'formulation' and 'conceptualisation' interchangeably, as is usually the case in CT. An equivalent term used in behaviour therapy is 'functional analysis' (Kanfer and Phillips 1970).

THEORETICAL BACKGROUND

Clinical case formulation is always theoretically driven, whatever type of therapy is being delivered. A cognitive therapist and a psychodynamic psychotherapist, for example, presented with the same clinical data – that is, the history, presenting problems and symptoms of an individual patient – will reach a different understanding of the case, propose totally different formulations and employ different therapeutic methods, because they are guided by different theories. It follows that, for a cognitive therapist, a good understanding of cognitive theories is necessary if a theoretically valid cognitive formulation is to be reached.

The basic cognitive theory of depression (Beck 1967, 1976) described the development and maintenance of depression from careful clinical observation. All the symptoms of depression, including the so-called biological indicators such as retardation, agitation, sleep disturbance, loss of libido and disturbed appetite, could be understood as deriving from the negative content of thought relating to the self, the world and the future. This negative cognitive triad is maintained by a number of negatively biased cognitive distortions: selective abstraction, arbitrary inference, overgeneralisation, magnification of the negative, minimisation of the positive and personalisation of negative outcomes.

These observable cognitive events – that is, the negative content of thought seen in habitual automatic thoughts and images, with intrinsic biased cognitive style – are explained by the hypothetical construct of schemata, also called basic attitudes, beliefs or premises. These are well-known constructs in the psychological literature (Bartlett 1932; Piaget 1952), comprising stable cognitive structures that represent all an individual's past learning and knowledge. They are made up of beliefs and theories about oneself, other people and the world in general. They will, therefore, affect what aspects of a situation we attend to and encode in our memory, our interpretations and expectations. They will determine the processing short-cuts or heuristics in our thinking, the biases in our thinking and, finally, the content of our automatic thoughts. In depression, the schemata are negatively toned, whether referring to self or others, because of early negative experiences with meaningful adults or peers, and they often reflect a theme of loss. The basic schemata lead to specific assumptions, rules of behaviour and compensatory or dysfunctional behaviours. In depressive illness, the depressogenic schemata could be dormant for long periods but could be reactivated by particular critical events, such as perceived or real loss, which would trigger the cycle leading to a depressive episode. This vulnerability framework is known as the diathesis-stress perspective. The model is represented in Figure 6.1.

Beck's early theoretical model has been refined and improved over the years, through the contribution of basic cognitive science and a plethora of experimental and theoretical work (Clark *et al.* 1999). The importance of real negative events, as opposed to distorted thinking, was emphasised by Coyne and Gotlib (1983). Kahneman *et al.* (1982) pointed out that the cognitive distortions described by Beck were normal in non-depressed individuals, the difference between depressed and non-depressed thinking being in the direction of the bias, which is negative in the former and positive in the latter (Alloy and Abramson 1979; Schwartz 1986). The effect of negative cognitions on mood was perhaps overemphasised in Beck's earlier work and he clarified the situation later (Beck 1987). Negative thinking is part and parcel of the depressive syndrome. It is a symptom of depression and may be seen as an important and accessible entry point into the depressive system for therapeutic interventions. Similarly, the unidirectional effect of cognition on mood is now seen as a reciprocal relationship between mood and cognition (Bower 1981; Teasdale 1983). The theory has also been criticised for overemphasising conscious thoughts at the expense of unconscious thoughts, in contrast to the general meaning of cognition in cognitive psychology, where it is assumed that the majority of cognitive processing is below awareness or automatic (Teasdale 1983).

Empirical studies have supported many aspects of the cognitive theory of depression, while others remain more elusive. For detailed reviews, see Haaga

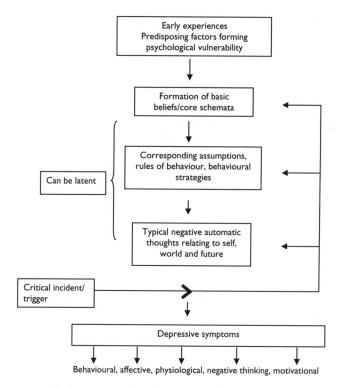

Figure 6.1 Cognitive model of depression.

et al. (1991), Clark *et al.* (1999), Blackburn *et al.* (1996) and Coyne and Gotlib (1983). Briefly, at a descriptive level, the negative content of thought differentiates depressed groups from non-depressed groups, but it is not clear whether the three elements of the negative cognition triad are equally predominant in the syndrome of depression (Nekanda-Trepka *et al.* 1983). Negative self-referent thoughts appear to be the most important (Blackburn and Eunson 1989), but the three elements of the triad overlap and are not easily discriminated. In information processing style, a memory bias has been well established in depression (for example, Blaney 1986; Teasdale and Barnard 1993; Williams *et al.* 1988). On the other hand, the stability of negative schemata has not been demonstrated (for example, Simons *et al.* 1984) and the specificity of depressogenic schemata has not been investigated to our knowledge. If the activation of specific schemata is seen as central in the causation and maintenance of depression (see Figure 6.1), then it is intriguing how cognitive therapy can be effective, both in acute treatment and the prevention of relapse, without the application of schema modification methods or methods to modify the impact of the schema (Gortner *et al.* 1998; Jacobson *et al.* 1996).

Beck and colleagues (Beck *et al.* 1983) have also proposed two stable personality traits as being important in the theoretical understanding of depression: sociotropy and autonomy. Sociotropy relates to concerns about disapproval, about attachment/separation and about pleasing others. Autonomy relates to individualistic achievement, freedom from control by others and preference for solitude. These two constructs indicate different vulnerabilities: vulnerability to interpersonal events in the case of sociotropy and vulnerability to loss of status or of freedom in the case of autonomy. In general, sociotropy has been shown to be the more reliable and valid construct (Hammen *et al.* 1989; Moore and Blackburn 1996). Autonomy has been shown to be only minimally related to level of depression (Clark and Beck 1991), poorly correlated to other measures of independence and not consistently related to negative achievement events in producing depression (Hammen *et al.* 1989).

Conclusion

Several components of the cognitive theory of depression have been demonstrated as valid in research studies. However, the theory, like all good theories, will certainly continue to evolve in the light of empirical research and the rapidly developing area of cognitive science (Teasdale 1996; Teasdale and Barnard 1993).

EMPIRICAL BASIS FOR COGNITIVE THERAPY

There have been a number of comprehensive reviews of controlled trials of CT in depression, both for acute treatment and in the prevention of relapse, which cannot be described in detail here (Blackburn and Moorhead 2000; Blackburn *et al.* 1996; Williams 1992). Instead, the main conclusions of meta-analytical studies and some more recent studies will be reviewed.

Since the seminal randomised controlled trial of Rush *et al.* (1977), there have been over 80 studies comparing CT with antidepressant medication and/or other types of psychotherapies. Dobson (1989), in the first meta-analysis of 28 studies, concluded that CT in depression was superior to waiting-list control, antidepressant medication, behaviour therapy and miscellaneous therapies. Gaffan *et al.* (1995) extended Dobson's study by taking Dobson's 28 studies published between 1976 and 1987 and adding 37 further studies published between 1987 and 1994. This meta-analysis, therefore, includes two important recent studies (Elkin *et al.* 1989; Hollon *et al.* 1992). Gaffan *et al.* (1995) used a different methodology from Dobson (1989), but nonetheless confirmed his conclusions from the earlier studies, although smaller effect sizes were obtained and the only significant differences were in comparisons of CT with waiting-list and attention control groups. In agreement with Robinson *et al.* (1990), they found that superior effect sizes were obtained when the therapists rated themselves as having higher allegiance to CT. In the analysis of the 37 later studies, Gaffan *et al.* again found CT to be significantly superior to waiting-list, attention control and psychotherapy; it was non-significantly superior to antidepressant medication, but behaviour therapy (few studies) was non-significantly superior to CT. In general, in these later studies effect sizes were smaller and the allegiance effect was not significant. One possible reason for the results is that, with time, researchers in CT may have become less effective. They certainly do not appear to show the strong allegiance of the early pioneers. More plausible reasons for the smaller effect sizes are: clinical trial methodology has improved over time; more complex cases may now be included in studies; other therapies, including pharmacotherapy, are now better developed; or earlier studies could have reflected selective publication – studies with less positive effect for CT not being submitted for publication, or journal editors turning down research papers with negative results.

The latest meta-analytic study (Gloaguen *et al.* 1998) reviewed 78 outcome trials, of which 30 were rejected because of poor methodology. The results indicated that CT was significantly superior to waiting-list, placebo control, antidepressant medication and miscellaneous psychotherapies, but equal to behaviour therapy. The equivalence with behaviour therapy was considered not surprising, in view of the fact that CT uses a large number of behavioural techniques and behaviour therapy uses cognitive methods, such as 'disputing non-constructive self talks' (Lewinsohn *et al.* 1990).

Some recent studies, not included in the last meta-analytic study reviewed above, need to be mentioned. These studies refer to specific groups of depressed patients: namely, patients with residual symptoms of depression after adequate treatment with medication and patients with recurrent depression (i.e., with at least one previous episode of depression).

Fava and his colleagues (1994) examined the efficacy of CT in 43 patients with residual or prodromal symptoms of depression after 3–5 months of treatment with antidepressants. Patients were randomly allocated to continuation medication with CT or continuation medication with clinical management. Medication was gradually withdrawn and treatment (CT or clinical management) was minimal, consisting of 10 sessions of 40 minutes every fortnight. At the end of the study period, patients receiving CT showed a highly significant decrease in residual symptoms, while those receiving clinical management showed no significant change. A follow-up two years later showed that 15% of the CT group and 35% of the clinical management had suffered a relapse. In a second study, Fava and colleagues (1998) followed the same methodology in a two-year follow-up of 40 patients with recurrent major depression (more than three episodes of depression). No medication was used during the follow-up period, unless a relapse or recurrence of depression occurred. In patients who received CT, the relapse rate was

20%, while in patients who received clinical management, the relapse rate was 80%.

Blackburn and Moore (1997), in a controlled acute and follow-up trial, compared CT and antidepressant medication in 75 patients suffering from recurrent major depression (mean of three episodes). One group received medication for 16 weeks of acute treatment and were maintained on medication for two years. A second group received CT during the acute phase of treatment and were maintained on CT for two years. The third group were switched from medication for acute treatment to CT maintenance for follow-up. After acute treatment, all three groups improved significantly, with no difference in level of improvement or in pattern of response over time. Similarly, during the follow-up period, patients in all three groups continued to improve over time, with no significant difference between groups. Three main conclusions were drawn from this study. First, in this group of recurrent depressed patients, CT was as effective as medication during acute treatment. Second, maintenance CT (three times in the first month, twice in the second month and once a month thereafter) was as effective as maintenance medication. Third, for patients who are reluctant to take medication long-term, it is feasible and effective to switch to CT during the follow-up period.

Moore and Blackburn (1997) examined how patients who had not responded fully to medication during the acute phase of treatment fared during follow-up on maintenance medication ($n = 7$) or on maintenance CT (those patients who were switched over from medication to CT maintenance). Those who had switched to CT improved significantly more on two measures of depression. These results support those of Fava and colleagues (1998). On the other hand, Stewart and colleagues (1993) found that in 17 depressed patients who had not responded to CT, a follow-up of six weeks on antidepressants or placebo showed that patients assigned to medication had a clear-cut response and those assigned to placebo did not. These last two studies indicate that medication and CT may be effective for different groups of patients. No study has yet delineated what these differentiating characteristics may be, although some psychological variables (for example, level of perfectionism; Blatt *et al.* 1996) and some biological variables (for example, abnormal EEG sleep profile; Thase *et al.* 1996) have been implicated.

Scott and colleagues (2000) examined the effectiveness of CT in depressed patients with residual symptoms after adequate antidepressant medication. All 158 patients received adequate levels of medication with clinical management during a 20-week acute treatment phase and a one-year follow-up phase. Patients were randomly allocated to receive clinical management alone or clinical management with CT, which consisted of 16 sessions during acute treatment and two booster sessions during follow-up. During acute treatment, 26% of patients receiving CT experienced full remission, as compared to 12% of those receiving clinical management alone. At the end of the one-year follow-up, 30% of patients in the CT group had relapsed as compared with 49% in the clinical management alone group.

Summary and conclusions

This brief review indicates that CT has been shown in a large number of studies to be effective in the acute treatment of depressive illness and in the prevention of relapse. Most studies to date relate to out-patients suffering from major depression or dysthymia. A few studies have examined the effectiveness of CT with specific groups, for example patients with recurrent depression or chronic depression, or non-responders to antidepressant medication.

CT follows closely the cognitive model of depression, but we cannot deduce that the therapy works because the theory is right or right in its entirety. Which aspects of CT are sufficient and necessary for the therapy to work and the role played by non-specific factors (for example, therapist variables and patient characteristics) are currently unclear. From a theoretical point of view, as indicated in the first section of this chapter, a cognitive formulation or conceptualisation of cases is considered essential for effective therapy. In the following sections, we will describe the role of individual case formulations, discuss some research findings, and elucidate how formulations are derived and what role they play in treatment.

CASE FORMULATION IN DEPRESSION

Definition of formulations and research findings

There have been several publications relating to case formulation or case conceptualisation in cognitive therapy (Bruch and Bond 1998; Butler 1999; Eells 1997; Freeman 1992; Henry and Williams 1997; Persons 1989, 1993). In this section we draw up a schedule detailing step by step the process of conceptualisation; this is derived from our own clinical experience, the cognitive theory of depression and suggestions from the relevant literature.

'Case formulation is not a treatment procedure, it is a method for understanding the patient and their problems that allows for the selection and design of treatment procedures, based on the knowledge of their case' (Adams 1996: 78). Thus, as Butler (1998) specifies, a formulation is the tool used by clinicians to relate theory to practice. In depression, case formulation is based on Beck's diathesis-stress model of the emotional disorders, as described in the first section of this chapter. It emphasises the specification and measurement of overt problems; functional hypotheses regarding the nature of triggers are made – for example the depression may be due to loss of achievement factors (autonomy) or of social factors (sociotropy); and structural mechanisms are hypothesised – for example, the activation of dysfunctional schemata acquired in early childhood.

Case formulation has sometimes been described as a 'road map' (Butler 1998), a 'guiding framework' (Henry and Williams 1997), a 'clinical theory' (Bruch 1998: 20) and the 'therapist's hypothesis' (Persons 1993: 33), and most writers on the subject accept that an individual case formulation is necessary to make sense of the patient's problems, to plan therapy, to ensure that appropriate methods of treatment are used, to help keep to the short-term format of CT, to prevent relapse and to anticipate difficulties which may arise in the course of therapy.

These convictions come from clinical experience and from a theoretical stand-point, but are not, to date, strongly supported by research findings (Beiling and Kuyken 2003). Some authors (for example, Hayes *et al.* 1987) suggest that the accuracy of the formulation is not at issue, but that its treatment utility should concern us: that is, does it improve treatment? Some recent research has begun to address this question (Persons and Bertagnolli 1999).

Despite the debate over the importance of the accuracy of formulations, there is growing evidence that case formulation is an under-taught skill in psychotherapy training (Sperry *et al.* 1992). Eells *et al.* (1998) found that most formulations did little more than describe information, with no hypothesis or underlying mechanisms inferred. Similarly, Henry and Williams (1997) suggested that CT trainees find case conceptualisation a difficult skill to master and consequently widely differing hypotheses are produced for individual cases. Persons *et al.* (1995) also found low reliability between clinicians' formulations for the same case.

While these findings do not necessarily imply poor outcome in therapy, they do imply an assumption that certain case formulations will be more or less helpful than others. At present, there is a clear lack of consensus over what should be included in a good formulation (Eells *et al.* 1998) and it is evident that, in teaching this skill, there is a need for improved, reliable clinical tools (Henry and Williams 1997). This is becoming increasingly relevant as more work is being done on taking an integrative approach to CT formulations, to account for wider influences such as the systemic context (Tarrier and Callam 2002) and social power (Hagan and Donnison 1999). Because of this, for practitioners the job of formulating a case becomes an increasingly complex process.

Individuals working with a cognitive model of depression may follow their own ideas about how to construct a formulation. However, recent research, using Q-sort methodology, examined the degree of consensus among experienced clinicians regarding the contents of a good formulation (Flitcroft 2004). Ten experts in the field of cognitive therapy generated statements relating to the function of formulations. The resulting 75 statements were then analysed by 23 experienced CT clinicians. The Q-sort, which has similarities to factor analytic techniques, revealed a three-factor model. The first factor accounted for almost a third of the variance and was labelled 'here-and-now aspects' of illness. It was related to the situational-level formulation described by Persons and Tomkins (1997). The second factor emphasised historical and interpersonal aspects. The final factor was related to process issues and the rationale shared with the patient. The top five features defining each factor are listed below. The lists describe the overall features defined as essential for each factor, not the distinguishing items defining a factor. Hence there is some overlap of items in each factor.

Factor 1: Here-and-now situational factor

1   The formulation explains how problems are maintained; it displays the causal and maintaining mechanisms underlying the patient's current difficulties.
2   It demonstrates a matching of thoughts, emotions etc. There is a synchrony or interdependence between the components of the patient's problems (i.e., a change in one produces a change in another).
3   It explains at an individual level a personal experience of depression. It takes a set of symptoms or diagnosis and puts it in a personalised context.
4   It identifies typical negative automatic thoughts relating to the self that recur in the here and now. These can also take the form of images and dreams (for example, 'I'll never get this work done').
5   It helps to makes sense of the apparently senseless for the patient.

Factor 2: Historical and interpersonal factor

1   The formulation shows a logical consistency from early experiences through to maintenance; the past fits with the present.
2   It identifies core beliefs since childhood. These are the beliefs about oneself, the world and the future, whether conscious or pre-conscious, that develop in later life. They may be verbally based or emotionally based (for example, 'Others are not trustworthy').
3   It identifies early experiences. These are the events or situations that influenced the development of both unconditional and conditional beliefs about the self, world and future (for example, neglected by mother, feeling the 'odd one out' at school).
4   It predicts potential reactions to interventions and allows the therapist to predict possible outcomes to any intervention.
5   It identifies interpersonal style. This represents the patterns of behaviour that are repeated throughout the patient's life (for example, needing a partner to feel secure, unable to trust anyone).

Factor 3: Process and function factor

1   The formulation informs on possible ways to intervene (the how rather than the where). It provides a shared rationale for the use of specific behavioural and cognitive interventions.
2   It is acceptable to the patient and others.
3   It explains how problems are maintained; it displays the causal and maintaining mechanisms underlying the patient's current difficulties.
4   It helps to makes sense of the apparently senseless for the patient.
5   It acts to facilitate the therapeutic alliance. It is a shared process and heavily dependent on feedback from the patient; it provides a shared understanding of the patient's difficulties.

It is important to note that these factors capture the opinions of a relatively small number of clinicians. However, the research is useful in defining what clinicians expect to achieve from carrying out a formulation for depression. There is clearly some overlap between factors regarding what the purpose of the formulation should be. Factor 1 accounts for most of the variance, suggesting this is what the majority of clinicians see as most essential. However, the existence of two other factors does imply that clinicians differ in their opinions about what the purpose of a formulation of depression is. This may in part begin to explain the difficulty clinicians have in agreeing on formulations in clinical cases.

How individual case formulations are derived

Having outlined some research findings relating to content and process issues of formulations in general, the following practical steps are proposed for conducting idiographic formulations in clinical settings:

1   The referral letter, if available, provides useful information and will give some idea of the patient's personal details, history and presenting problems.
2   The first encounter with the patient can be a rich source of information: for example, posture, eye contact, self-confidence, facial expression and dress code.
3   Identification information needs to be complete. We emphasise this because, too often, we find that trainee therapists gather the scantiest of information, which causes problems later on in therapy. The information would typically include: sex, age, marital status, children, education level, occupation, posts held over the years, whether the parents are alive, their occupation, the sibship, place in the sibship, network of friends and leisure activities.
4   The first two or three interviews will cover:

a   A diagnostic assessment: a diagnosis is not sufficient for a formulation, as it is purely descriptive and specific symptoms may belong to two or more categories (for example, social avoidance may be a symptom of social anxiety or of loss of interest in social activities due to depression, or it may be part of a schizophrenic delusional syndrome). Diagnosis does not explain the onset of the problems, how they developed or how they are maintained. A diagnosis alone does not help us to understand the complexity of an individual's problems. When multiple diagnoses are involved, the relationships between or among these diagnoses are not explained. However, we believe that, apart from providing a short-cut for communication between colleagues, a diagnosis is necessary for a formulation, as it will direct the therapist towards generic models of disorders and thus give pointers for an idiographic formulation. If a diagnostic assessment is conducted correctly, a large amount of information is incidentally collected relating to non-symptomatic issues. For example, the patient may talk about certain individuals in their lives, about specific events and about their life conditions. The therapist will then be able to help the patient elaborate on these points at a later stage of the assessment process.

b   It is helpful to use valid measures of severity early on in the assessment stage for obtaining a base-line against which the progress of therapy can be measured. In depressive illness, the usual measures will include the Hamilton Rating Scale for Depression (HRSD; Hamilton 1960), the Beck Depression Inventory (BDI; Beck *et al.* 1961) and the Hopelessness Scale (HS; Beck *et al.* 1974). Specific cognitive measures may also be useful, for example the Automatic Thoughts Questionnaire (ATQ; Hollon and Kendall 1980) and the Dysfunctional Attitudes Questionnaire (DAS; Weissman and Beck 1978). A personality inventory which taps the two dimensions of sociotropy and autonomy, as described earlier in this chapter, will also contribute to the case formulation (the Sociotropy–Autonomy Scale or SAS; Beck *et al.* 1983).

5   A list of presenting problems is then drawn. This list needs to be concrete, specific and exhaustive. Typically, it will consist of: the main symptoms which may be altered by cognitive-behavioural methods (for example, inactivity, loss of pleasure, avoidant behaviours); interpersonal problems; occupational problems, career problems; financial problems; family problems; and self-related problems such as loss of self-confidence, loss of self-esteem, guilt and shame (all with concrete examples).

6   During these assessment interviews the therapist needs to pay attention to and note the typical automatic thoughts expressed by the patient. In

depression, these can be classified as self-, world- and future-related (the negative cognitive triad).

7   Similarly, typical emotions are noted. Apart from low mood, anxiety is likely to be present in depression. As anger and hostility are generally less commonly spontaneously expressed, the therapist may need to ask specific questions to elicit these.

8   Typical behaviours are useful in the formulation to indicate which are the usual coping strategies of the patient. Some strategies may have been helpful in the past but are no longer functional, or the patient may have a restricted range of coping strategies.

9   The patient may spontaneously voice rules of behaviour regarding themselves or others which will help in the formulation. From rules, a simple question may lead the therapist to uncover the underlying assumptions which may give a clue to the patient's core beliefs. For example, if the patient says, 'I should have been able to cope,' the therapist may ask, 'If you consider that you did not cope in this situation, does that say something about you?'

10   Precipitating events or triggers of the current episode of depression, of lowering of mood, and of previous episodes of depression in the case of recurrent depression are an essential aspect of formulation (see Figure 6.1). They may have much in common and thus give an insight into the individual's areas of vulnerability.

11   Some time is spent on the developmental history of the patient: relationship with parents and siblings, key experiences at school and during higher education, patterns of friendships, past negative events, past positive events and current social/occupational functioning.

12   The therapist is now ready to arrive at a working hypothesis or a preliminary formulation. This can be presented diagrammatically (Figure 6.1) and shared with the patient by the fourth or fifth session. This formulation attempts to account for all the problems on the problem list, includes functional hypotheses ('It seems that when you have perceived rejection by others, you have tended to get depressed?') and includes the area of the core self-referent belief (something to do with how loveable or likeable you are?; something to do with your self-worth?; something to do with your normality or social acceptability?; something to do with your appearance or looks?).

13   Based on the assessment material being gathered, it is helpful for the therapist to anticipate what would be the most suitable CT formulation framework to employ with the patient. For example, the therapist may think a schema-focused approach (for example, Young 1994) is suitable for patient X but not for patient Y. In this case, the two patients would be socialised to different treatment models, the delivery of each model differing in terms of pace and scope. A concrete example of this feature is

provided in Case 2, where the patient is socialised to a model highlighting her positive core beliefs.

The overall model of formulation described above has sometimes been called 'case level formulation'. In contrast, 'situation level formulation' is what therapist and patient work on during therapy when a particular problematic situation arises, for example worsening of mood. A hypothesis about the mechanisms underpinning and explaining that situation is discussed with the patient. These 'mini-formulations' are part of the testing out of the validity of the more comprehensive case level formulation.

CASE EXAMPLES

Aspects of the previous discussion are now illustrated via two case studies. The first case is a rather standard presentation in which a diathesis-stress model is used to formulate the patient's difficulties. In the second case, a less standard scenario is described in which the diathesis-stress model is less clear. The latter formulation illustrates the multidimensional nature of depression, and demonstrates how patients' coping strategies can sometimes play a key role in exacerbating their distress.

Each case is introduced with a summary of the referral letter received from the psychiatrist. The conceptual model is then presented and subsequently reflected upon.

Case I

Referral from consultant psychiatrist

The referral read as follows:

> I saw Mrs Ann Smith, aged 39, in my clinic today. She met criteria for depression, with a five-month history of low mood. This was triggered by an argument with her husband during the Christmas period. Despite receiving a lot of support from her husband, Ann continues to experience 'black spells', which can go on for five days per episode. In March she expressed some suicidal thoughts, which precipitated her referral to psychiatric services.
>
> At interview Ann was well presented, clear and articulate. However, both her eye contact and concentration were poor, and she reported having lost 10lbs in weight. This is the first time she has been referred to psychiatric services, but has been prescribed antidepressant medication on three previous occasions by her GP. She states that she has experienced low times throughout her life.

She is the middle child of three and stated that she missed a lot of schooling due to the combination of having chronic asthma and an overprotective mother. She left school without qualifications, feeling she had not realised her potential in any area. She married Michael 14 years ago. Owing to his job as a vicar, they entertain frequently. She finds the entertaining difficult. I would welcome your assessment of this case, with a view of taking her on for therapy.

Formulation

The psychiatrist's letter presents a picture consistent with a diathesis-stress model of depression. This model suggests that owing to difficulties in her past, she developed a vulnerability to depression. Ann seemed cognisant of the issues underpinning her problems, and up until this point in her life had not suffered from a severe depressive episode, minor episodes being successfully treated by her GP. Administration of the BDI, HS and DAS, in conjunction with assessment work, highlighted the key issues further (Table 6.1). The initial conceptual framework is presented in Figure 6.2.

The argument, which the referring letter had identified as a trigger to the current episode, when assessed factually consisted of her husband letting out his frustration at his wife's performance during a game of bridge. He said, 'Now that was a bl**dy stupid thing to do. . . . You are so stupid!' She took this badly, particularly as a number of the other players ribbed her about the incident. Ann was unable to settle for the rest of the evening, and so made an excuse to leave early. Subsequently, she refused to attend all the other social functions arranged over Christmas. When asked about this incident via a Socratic questioning technique, Ann thought that this incident had publicly exposed her inadequacies. She said it had opened the pandora's box containing all her beliefs about being stupid, a fraud and intellectually inadequate.

When these issues were explored historically and across different settings in the present, it was evident that there was a self-referent belief around the issue of being stupid that was fuelling her distress. Ann had left school at 16 without qualifications, while her two brothers had done well and had often teased her about her school grades. She remembered her grandmother saying, 'Poor Ann is not very good at school work, but she is a nice girl.' Thus, Ann had been aware of this issue for most of her life, and had consequently avoided testing herself in many domains (job interviews, driving tests, pub quizzes) because of a fear that she would be exposed. She said that she found socialising with her husband's friends particularly difficult because they all had university degrees. However, she also said that she had learnt to deal with these graduates by rarely expressing an opinion, and by perfecting the role of the interested listener. In addition to these strategies, she prepared herself prior to social evenings. For example, she would read *The Telegraph*, a daily broadsheet newspaper, and listen to Radio 4 on the BBC for a few days before

Table 6.1 Ann's personal details and problem list

Key areas	Details
Family of origin	Middle child of three, and only daughter; father was a labourer who died when Ann was 13; mother has a history of anxiety, worked in grocer's shop after death of father
Marital status/family	Married to Michael for 14 years; he is a vicar; no children
Education	Missed lots of schooling; unable to make good relationships with classmates due to absence
Social network	Socialised with husband's colleagues and parishioners; few friends entirely of own making
Career	She has never worked, although role of vicar's wife often involves administrative duties
Relevant medical details	Chronic asthmatic; minor episodes of depression over past 16 years
Interests/hobbies	Reading non-fiction, playing bridge
Baseline questionnaires:	
BDI	24 (non-depressed score 9 or less)
DAS	162 (normal population score 113 or less)
HS	19 (normal population score 3 or less)
Medication	Initially imipramine, then citalopram
Problem list	1 Depressed 2 Suicidal ideation 3 Views herself as stupid 4 Thinks her husband will decide to leave her 5 Avoiding people 6 Avoiding speaking to her husband about her problem 7 Angry feelings and thoughts towards her mother 8 Neglect of self (dress and make-up) 9 Lethargy

an event. She noted that these compensation strategies, although giving her only a veneer of intelligence, had proven most effective up until this point.

Reflections

Consistent with the framework outlined in Figure 6.1, Ann's core belief was forged in childhood. This belief had always been central to the way she saw herself, and hence it was indisputable in her mind. In order to navigate life's

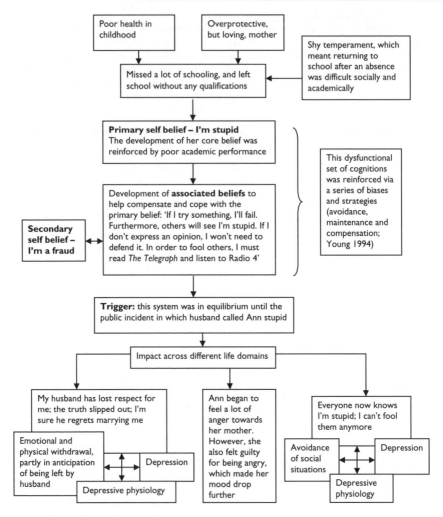

Figure 6.2 Ann's initial conceptualisation.

trials and tribulations with such a negative sense of self, she developed a number of assumptions, life rules and behavioural strategies to help her cope (for example, 'Don't test yourself,' 'Never express an opinion'). These avoidant strategies served to maintain the belief. Her negatively biased cognitions (minimisation of the positive, and personalisation of negative outcomes) and her use of compensatory strategies (for example, reading *The Telegraph*, listening to Radio 4) meant that any potential challenges to her belief were either belittled or attributed to the employment of a fraudulent strategy. In many ways, in the past, she had attempted to shield herself from the rest of the world. Unfortunately, her husband's comments, spoken in public in a moment of pique, triggered her worst fear. Now, perceiving herself as being publicly exposed, she withdrew. In her eyes, her negative sense of worth had been confirmed, and thus she was now helpless in an unkind world and with few prospects for a brighter future. Furthermore, owing to the maelstrom of emotions she was experiencing, she was unable to think rationally. She was extremely confused, sometimes experiencing extreme levels of depression, anger and guilt in the space of a few minutes.

Treatment plan

In attempting to help Ann, four broad strategies were used early on. Initially, a risk assessment was undertaken regarding her intentions regarding suicide. Her withdrawal from her support systems, including her husband and mother, and her high level of hopelessness, were major concerns. Thus, working on her wish to be dead and thoughts of hopelessness (Beck *et al.* 1979) was a priority. Behavioural reactivation was also an early goal, and this was facilitated through the use of mastery and pleasure charts. Third, she was gently socialised to the CT model. This needed to be done slowly and concretely owing to her reduced information processing capacity and executive deficits resulting from the depression. Fourth, in the fifth session the therapy focused on developing Ann's case level formulation collaboratively. This became the road map for targeting subsequent interventions. It was evident that the engine room for much of her distress was the core belief 'I am stupid,' and thus either it had to be modified or its impact coped with better. In discussions with Ann, she thought that the belief was too much a part of her to be changed, and so she chose to make it more flexible (less unconditional and more conditional; James *et al.* 2004). Over a period of 10 further sessions, she was able to move towards self-referent statements such as: 'I do stupid things sometimes,' 'My stupidity is relative,' 'When I think "stupid", I usually mean I'm forgetful, daft, or uncertain,' 'There are many things I can do well,' and 'Lack of education is not equivalent to stupidity.' Other useful statements were: 'My husband often upsets people by saying stupid things,' and 'I can't change the past.' In order to develop and give credence to these alternative cognitions, Ann needed a lot of support. The support helped her develop an ability to re-frame scenarios, using the facts of the situation rather than her biases. The work involved using many behavioural (demonstration, role-play, provocation tasks) and cognitive (continua, imagery) methodologies.

Case 2

The following case differs from the former because the manner in which the depression has been conceptualised suggests that it did not result from the re-emergence of a dysfunctional belief. Rather it was a product of a number of interacting issues, such as: (a) the lack of reinforcement within a life domain that had previously enhanced her self-esteem; and (b) the patient having a limited and inflexible set of coping strategies. The issue of inflexibility was particularly important in the present case, as adaptability is vital in helping one to navigate one's way through life. In most circumstances, when therapists address the issue of rigidity and inflexibility, they examine beliefs. However, in this case it was the inflexibility in the person's range of coping strategies that played a significant part with respect to her depression.

Referral from consultant psychiatrist

The referral read as follows:

> Megan, aged 61, was referred by her GP for treatment of an unresolved grief reaction; she lost her husband 20 months ago. Despite the depression clearly being linked to the bereavement, the association is not direct because her mood lifted temporarily four months ago for a period of two months. She has no prior history of mental health difficulties.
>
> Megan was happily married for 38 years. She has one daughter with whom she has a close relationship; they maintain regular contact by phone. Her daughter is married and lives in the neighbouring town.
>
> Megan was popular at school, both with her fellow pupils and the teachers. Her upbringing was happy, and she enjoyed good relationships with parents and her younger brother. She left school at 15, and went to work for a firm of local butchers. Teachers informed her parents that she had the ability to go to university. However, the family were neither willing nor able to support her through higher education. She met her future husband in the butcher's shop. She married Jon when she was 21 years of age. After the birth of her daughter she gave up work, and quickly became a sort of spokesperson for the local community. She had always perceived herself to be strong, with few self-doubts. In the past she seems to have dealt with her problems in a balanced and appropriate manner. Indeed, the current episode of depression represents the first time that she has felt overwhelmed by a problem.
>
> The trigger to the current episode is unclear, but it is evident that she is feeling guilty about some episode from her past. She was initially seen for grief therapy (Worden model) by the counsellor at the GP's practice, but stopped attending when her mood deteriorated further. I have changed her antidepressant medication, and would appreciate an assessment for a course of cognitive therapy.

This helpful letter from the psychiatrist informs us of a number of important things about Megan's depression: (a) the current episode may not be linked directly to the loss of her husband, but may have been mediated by a happening that occurred two months ago; (b) the latter event seems to have triggered feelings of guilt; (c) the nature of the depression is possibly inconsistent with a diathesis-stress model; and (d) for whatever reason, the counselling was unsuccessful.

Formulation

As part of the assessment, Megan was asked to complete the BDI and DAS. She was asked to complete the DAS in terms of former and current self in order to determine recent changes in her self-beliefs (Table 6.2). During the

Table 6.2 Megan's personal details and problem list

Key areas	Details
Family of origin	One of six children from RC family; second eldest, and eldest daughter; mother had a weak heart, and Megan was involved in lot of child-rearing duties; father a miner, seldom at home
Marital status/family	Married to Jon for 38 years; he died February 2002; one daughter, Jane, who is in regular contact mainly by phone
Education	Left school 15 but according to teachers could have gone to university; liked school and socialised well with other pupils
Social network	Many friends within local community; she enjoys socialising
Career	She has never worked, but pillar of local working-class community
Relevant medical details	Lump removed from breast aged 55, coped with this well
Interests/hobbies	'Too busy for hobbies' (quote)
Baseline questionnaires: BDI DAS pre-morbid	19 (normal population score 9 or less) Self-predicted score of 100 (normal population score 113 or less)
DAS now	180
Medication	Imipramine
Problem list	1 Depressed 2 Views herself as being weak 3 Socially isolated, withdrawn from friends 4 Embarrassed by inability to control her crying 5 Wants to stay in bed, and not looking forward to day 6 Waking early in the morning 7 Lethargic

assessment phase, it became evident that she was surprised that she was actually still depressed. She stated that prior to this episode, she had always been able to 'beat the blues, by sheer determination and through hard work.' Indeed, one of the things that upset her most was her inability to conquer her difficulty. She was particularly upset by her tearfulness, and lack of control with respect to crying. Table 6.2 presents relevant background information, psychometric data and a problem list.

Megan explained that her husband's death, although a blow, had been anticipated. She thought that they had been given sufficient time to prepare together for its occurrence – 'as much as any couple can prepare.' She also noted that six months previously her mood had started to lift and she had begun to reinvest in friendships and her social network. Then two months ago her mood dropped again. The precipitant to this relapse was a phone call from a long-lost male friend she had dated prior to meeting her husband. Megan informed me that she had lost her virginity to this man, something she had never told her husband. The phone call had caused her to ruminate on this issue. She particularly regretted the fact that she had not told her husband, something she had actually meant to do throughout her married life. In truth she had never felt guilty about the affair until recently, but had always deeply regretted not speaking to her husband about the matter.

She responded to the ruminations by throwing herself into work and activities. She was pretty sure that this coping strategy was going to work because it had always worked in the past. In many respects this strategy was similar to a mindfulness methodology (Segal *et al.* 2002), because she described the approach as focusing on the tasks at hand and trying to become totally absorbed in whatever she was doing. She was confident of a positive outcome due to the fact that she saw herself as a strong person, someone who could deal with anything. For the first time in her life the strategy failed, and after a few weeks this coping strategy became counterproductive as she began to get more tired. Unfortunately, unlike many other people, who out of necessity have developed an arsenal of coping strategies, she did not have any other well-rehearsed strategies to draw upon. When queried about her limited range of strategies, she said that hard work had always got her through in the past. Following a visit to her GP, she was advised to see the practice counsellor. This acceptance that she needed external help served to lay the foundations for self-beliefs regarding weakness. These beliefs were further reinforced following her experiences with the counsellor, who encouraged her to speak to her friends about her difficulties. Without proper forethought and preparation, this strategy backfired because her social network was composed of people only accustomed to receiving advice from Megan; they had never had to give her advice before. Most of her friends were uneasy at this reversal in expectations and roles. Problems also occurred because Megan was not well practised in self-disclosing personal difficulties. In retrospect, she probably went into too much detail about the circumstances of the affair, possibly inviting unwanted judgements. The resultant interactions led to the development of an additional dimension of shame. She was particularly upset when one of her closest friends said to her, 'I'd always thought you and Jon had no secrets from each other. . . . I'd always looked to you as an example of a wonderful marriage. . . . and at least I'd saved myself until I'd met my husband.'

With her declining mood, Megan began to withdraw and dropped out of counselling. The physiological symptoms also began to take their toll, as she stopped eating and her sleep pattern became disrupted. One of her biggest problems was her tendency to cry in public at the merest provocation. This reinforced her sense of shame, and she began to withdraw further. Over a period of weeks her self-beliefs underwent a radical change. With a perceived loss of respect from her friends, lack of contact with them, and the loss of support from her deceased husband, her previous positive self-belief faded – she began to question her previous belief of being strong. In contrast, her inability to conquer her problem, together with her new sense of shame, resulted in the emergence of a self-belief about being weak. Over time the relationship between her mood, physiology, behaviour and thoughts produced the vicious cycle that commonly characterises depression. Once established, the attitudinal and memory biases helped to maintain the depression.

In a depressed state, she started to review her life and reassessed her roles and motivations. For example, previously she had seen herself as unconventional and a free spirit; this view was now becoming corrupted. Indeed, she was now beginning to see her previously relaxed attitude towards sex as sluttish behaviour.

Reflections

The conceptualisation was developed jointly (Table 6.3). As one can see it is a multi-dimensional framework. Indeed, the therapist could have looked at many different facets of her experiences. For example, the therapist could examine the regret and the ruminations, the bereavement or the shame. However, Megan was very clear that her biggest difficulty was the emergence of a sense of being weak. Hence, this was the focus for the subsequent therapy. This weakness belief undermined her sense of power and control, and hence she felt more anxious and vulnerable. It also related to her sense of shame. As the sense of shame grew it began to generalise into other areas, as well as into her past. Once again, she began to reassess decisions she had made previously (for example, 'Was I too firm then, or was I just being pig-headed?'). Her confidence in her decision-making ability became undermined.

It is relevant to note that the particular formulation developed was only one of a number of theoretically driven CT frameworks that could have been produced to account for Megan's distress. Indeed, one could have even conceptualised her difficulties within a diathesis-stress model, with her belief

Table 6.3 Megan's longitudinal conceptualisation

	Event	Emotion(s)	Associated thoughts and comments
1	Prior to depression	Contentment and happiness	Husband, Jon, had been suffering from a chronic condition. Both Megan and Jon had accepted the situation and were trying to make the best of the time they had available. At this stage Megan saw herself as a strong person: 'I can deal with anything life throws my way.'
2	Death of husband	Deep sadness and loneliness	Megan missed Jon greatly, but she kept herself busy: 'I've dealt with his death as well as anyone could. I just need to keep busy and I'll get through this.'
3	16 months post bereavement	Sadness, but increasing motivation to do things	Decided to visit family and friends abroad: 'It's time to start doing things again. I can feel my strength coming back.' It is relevant to note that although she felt better, the loss of her husband meant the loss of an important positive reinforcer with respect to her positive sense of self. He used to praise her daily and she used to draw strength from this.
4	Telephone call from ex-friend	Surprise and regret	Initial shock gave way to a sense of regret that she had never told her husband about the relationship. 'This is the only important thing I ever kept from him.' 'Why didn't I say something, he really wouldn't have minded.' At this stage there were no feelings of guilt.
5	Ruminating on the regret	Regret	According to Landman (1993) regret is the mechanism by which the self attempts to re-visit past decisions to ascertain whether any undoing or modification of their effects is possible. Owing to the demise of her husband, clearly Megan was stuck in a insoluble 'regret loop'.
6	Employment of the ubiquitous coping strategy	Initial optimism, giving way to a drop in mood	Megan was cognisant that the ruminations were unhelpful, and so she threw herself into activities in an attempt to regain control of her thoughts. Unfortunately, this strategy did not work and over time she became exhausted: 'What's happening to me, I don't seem to be able to shake these damn thoughts off . . . and I'm feeling so tired.'
7	Visit to GP and counsellor	Acceptance, yet shame	Admitting defeat undermined her self-belief about being strong: 'I used to think I could cope with anything. Now look at me . . . I am so weak and pathetic.'

8	Discussions with friends	Embarrassment and shame	Her friends seemed at a loss about how to react to both the disclosure and Megan's distress: 'I didn't know what to say to them, and they didn't know what to say to me . . . I've just made a show of myself.'
9	Impact of friends' comments	Humiliation and depression	In the past her friends had helped reinforce Megan's positive self-perception. She had always been their confidante, decision-maker and problem-solver. The sudden role shift turned her social network from a worth-enhancing resource into a worth-detracting area.
10	Increasing avoidance and isolation	Guilt	The increasing isolation and increasing depressogenic thinking led to self-questioning – both in terms of present and past events. For the first time she started to doubt her decision-making ability. She also began to doubt the value base of the decisions she had made in the past. 'I'd always thought I was just lively and headstrong, but probably I was just a slut?' 'I wish I kept myself for my husband.'
11	Self neglect and withdrawal	Severe depression	The full-blown development of the dysfunctional core beliefs: 'I'm weak, and the future is hopeless.'

about being strong seen as a compensatory strategy for an underlying core belief of weakness. Employing such a hypothesis would have involved socialising Megan to a slightly different perspective (for example, Young's early maladaptive schema; Young 1994), and one that placed more emphasis on dysfunctional beliefs. Despite being cognisant of the different formulation frameworks available, the therapist chose to emphasise the more functional aspects of her belief system. This was done for two reasons. First, it provided Megan with a greater sense of hope. Second, it conceptualised the current depression as a transient feature. This is in contrast to the diathesis-stress perspective, which may have caused her to review many aspects of her life afresh, subsequently seeing her actions as being governed and directed by fear and/or a low sense of worth. For example, Megan may have started to reassess occasions when she had helped people merely as attempts to get people to like her. Previously, 'helping out' was something she had taken great pride and enjoyment in. It is noteworthy that this negative life-reviewing process had started to occur anyway due to her depression and the impact of the negative memory biases.

The presentation of the conceptualisation in tabular form is rather non-standard. This method is often used to illustrate the dynamic nature of events, emotions and thoughts. In this manner it reflects the diary structure frequently employed in homework assignments, and thus aids in the teaching of how to complete diaries. As already outlined, Megan's situation could have been formulated within a number of different frameworks. However, conceptualising her problems in this manner helped Megan to see how her belief about being strong had gradually given way to her current notion of weakness. Tracking the interplay between events, emotions and thoughts, using classical thought restructuring methods (for example, the dysfunctional thoughts record), also provided some ideas on how to reverse the process and guidance on how to avoid falling into similar traps in the future. This method is also particularly helpful in highlighting the presence of positive beliefs, and avoids the problems of focusing in an unbalanced way on the dysfunctional ones (see above). After all, for most of her 61 years Megan had held a very positive self-affirming view of herself, and had functioned well in the different areas of her life.

Treatment plan

In the course of treatment, the initial task was to reduce her self-induced isolation by engaging her in an activity that was not action based. In the past Megan had taught yoga, and so mindfulness techniques (Segal *et al.* 2002) were used initially. This was a useful methodology to employ while the formulation was being developed, because one does not require a case level formulation to use mindfulness. Once the formulation had been collaboratively established in the fourth session, the focus on mindfulness was reduced and Megan started to use some helpful breathing exercises from her yoga meditation. Furthermore, the formulation (Table 6.3) now provided a useful guiding framework for setting specific treatment goals. Key goals were to try to re-nourish her previous positive sense of self (worth-enhancing beliefs; James *et al.* 1999), and help her develop a larger and more flexible range of coping strategies. As one might expect with such an autonomous individual, the conceptual overview had a powerful impact on her mood. She described her previous situation, when using her activity-based coping strategy, as like being stuck in a spider's web: 'the more I struggled the more entangled I became.' Megan truly used the formulation as a form of road map ('my A–Z to recovery'). She was particularly energised by the fact that the formulation highlighted that she had held a positive view of herself for many years. Indeed, only a few months ago she had been planning trips abroad.

As her confidence grew, she decided that she needed to broaden her social network. She wanted to establish new friendships, ones which would be more reciprocal in relation to emotional support. When she reflected on this, she acknowledged that a review of her social network would had to have happened anyway following the death of her husband.

Towards the end of therapy, some time was spent with Megan examining the key roles and goals in her life (Champion and Power 1995), as it was evident that, in addition to the inflexible coping strategies she employed, she had also demonstrated over-investment in the role of being the 'strong one'. Such an over-investment in one area was likely to leave her vulnerable to depression in the future (James *et al.* 1999). Thus, the latter part of treatment examined other potential areas of her life from which she could obtain a sense of worth. It was noted, however, that she had started doing some of this work already with her decision to achieve more fulfilling and reciprocal relationships within her expanded social network.

RECOMMENDED READING

Blackburn, I. M. *et al.* (1996). *Cognitive Therapy in Action.* London: Souvenir Press.

Bruch, M. and Bond, F. W. (1998). *Beyond Diagnosis. Case Formulation Approaches in CBT.* Chichester, UK: John Wiley and Sons.

Butler, G. (1998). Clinical formulation. In A. S. Bellack and M. Hersen (eds) *Comprehensive Clinical Psychology* Vol. 6 (special ed, P. Salkovskis). Oxford, UK: Elsevier Science Pergamon Press.

Clark, D. and Beck, A. T. (1999). *Scientific Foundations of Cognitive Theory and Therapy.* New York: John Wiley and Sons.

Persons, J. B. (1993). Case conceptualisation in cognitive behaviour therapy. In K. T. Kuelhwein and H. Rosen (eds) *Cognitive Therapy in Action.* San Francisco: Jossey-Bass Publishers.

REFERENCES

Adams, H. E. (1996). Further clarification on case formulation. *The Behaviour Therapist* 19: 78.

Alloy, L. B. and Abramson, L. Y. (1979). Judgement of contingency in depressed and non-depressed students: Sadder but wiser? *Journal of Experimental Psychology* 108: 441–85.

Bartlett, F. J. (1932). *Remembering.* Cambridge: Cambridge University Press.

Beck, A. T. (1963). Thinking and depression. I. Idiosyncratic content and cognitive disorders. *Archives of General Psychiatry* 9: 324–33.

Beck, A. T. (1964). Thinking and depression. II. Theory and therapy. *Archives of General Psychiatry* 10: 561–71.

Beck, A. T. (1967). *Depression: Clinical, experimental and theoretical aspects.* New York: Harper and Row.

Beck, A. T. (1976). *Cognitive Therapy and the Emotional Disorders.* New York: International Universities Press.

Beck, A. T. (1987). Cognitive models of depression. *Journal of Cognitive Psychotherapy* 1: 5–37.

Beck, A. T. *et al.* (1961). An inventory for measuring depression. *Archive of General Psychiatry* 4: 561–71.

Beck, A. T. *et al.* (1974). The measurement of pessimism: The Hopelessness Scale. *Journal of Consulting and Clinical Psychology* 42: 861–5.

Beck, A. T. *et al.* (1979). *Cognitive therapy of depression*. New York: Guilford Press.

Beck, A. T. *et al.* (1983). Cognitions, attitudes and personality dimensions in depression. *British Journal of Cognitive Psychotherapy* 1: 1–16.

Beiling, P. J. and Kuyken, W. (2003). Is cognitive case formulation science or science fiction? *Clinical Psychology: Science and Practice* 10: 52–69.

Blackburn, I. M. and Eunson, K. M. (1989). A content analysis of thoughts and emotions elicited from depressed patients during cognitive therapy. *British Journal of Medical Psychology* 62: 23–33.

Blackburn, I. M. and Moore, R. M. (1997). Controlled acute and follow-up trial of cognitive therapy and pharmacotherapy in out-patients with recurrent depression. *British Journal of Psychiatry* 171: 328–34.

Blackburn, I. M. and Moorhead, S. (2000). Update in cognitive therapy for depression. *Journal of Cognitive Psychotherapy* 14: 305–36.

Blackburn, I. M. *et al.* (1996). *Cognitive therapy in action*. London: Souvenir Press.

Blaney, P. H. (1986). Affect and memory: A review. *Psychological Bulletin* 99: 229–46.

Blatt, S. J. *et al.* (1996). Interpersonal factors in brief treatment of depression: Further analysis of the National Institute of Mental Health Treatment of Depression Collaborative Research Program. *Journal of Consulting and Clinical Psychology* 64: 162–71.

Bower, G. H. (1981). Mood and memory. *American Psychologist* 36: 129–48.

Bruch, M. (1998). The UCL case formulation model: Clinical applications and procedures. In M. Bruch and F. W. Bond (eds) *Beyond Diagnosis. Case Formulation Approaches in CBT*. Chichester, UK: John Wiley.

Bruch, M. and Bond, F. W. (1998). *Beyond Diagnosis: Case Formulation Approaches in CBT*. Chichester, UK: John Wiley and Sons.

Butler, G. (1998). Clinical formulation. In A. S. Bellack and M. Hersen (eds) *Comprehensive Clinical Psychology* Vol 6 (special ed, P. Salkovskis) Oxford, UK: Elsevier Science Pergamon Press.

Champion, L. A. and Power, M. (1995). Social and cognitive approaches to depression: Towards a new synthesis. *British Journal of Clinical Psychology* 34: 485–503.

Clark, D. A. and Beck, A. T. (1991). Personality factors in dysphoria: A psychometric refinement of Beck's Sociotropy–Autonomy Scale. *Journal of Psychopathology and Behavioural Assessment* 13: 369–88.

Clark, D. A. *et al.* (1999). *Scientific Foundations of Cognitive Theory and Therapy of Depression*. New York: John Wiley and Sons Inc.

Coyne, J. and Gotlib, I. (1983). The role of cognition in depression. *Psychological Bulletin* 94: 472–505.

Dobson, K. (1989). A meta-analysis of the efficacy of cognitive therapy for depression. *Journal of Consulting and Clinical Psychology* 57: 414–9.

Eells, T. *et al.* (1998). What's in a case formulation: Development and use of a content coding manual. *Journal of Psychotherapy Practice and Research* 7: 144–53.

Eels, T. D. (1997). *Handbook of Psychotherapy Case Formulation*. New York: Guilford Press.

Elkin, I. *et al.* (1989). National Institute of Mental Health Treatment of Depression Collaborative Research Program. *Archives of General Psychiatry* 46: 971–82.

Fava, G. A. *et al.* (1994). Cognitive behavioural treatment of residual symptoms in primary major depressive disorders. *American Journal of Psychiatry* 151: 1295–9.

Fava, G. A. *et al.* (1998). Prevention of recurrent depression with cognitive behaviour therapy. *Archives of General Psychiatry* 55: 816–20.

Flitcroft, A. (2004). *Defining a Quality Cognitive-Behavioural Formulation?* Doctoral dissertation, University of Newcastle upon Tyne, UK.

Freeman, A. (1992). The development of treatment conceptualizations in cognitive therapy. In A. Freeman and F. M. Dattilo (eds) *Comprehensive Casebook of Cognitive Therapy*. New York: Plenum Press.

Gaffan, E. A. *et al.* (1995). Researcher allegiance and meta-analysis: The case of cognitive therapy for depression. *Journal of Consulting and Clinical Psychology* 63: 966–80.

Gloaguen, V. *et al.* (1998). A meta-analysis of the effects of cognitive therapy in depressed patients. *Journal of Affective Disorders* 49: 59–72.

Gortner, E. T. *et al.* (1998). Cognitive-behavioural treatment for depression: Relapse prevention. *Journal of Consulting and Clinical Psychology* 66: 377–84.

Haaga, D. A. *et al.* (1991). Empirical status of cognitive therapy of depression. *Psychological Bulletin* 110: 215–36.

Hagan, T. and Donnison, J. (1999). Social power: Some implications for theory and practice of cognitive behaviour therapy. *Journal of Community Applied Social Psychology* 9: 119–35.

Hamilton, M. (1960). A rating scale for depression. *Journal of Neurology, Neurosurgery and Psychiatry* 23: 56–61.

Hammen, C. *et al.* (1989). Sociotropy/autonomy and vulnerability to specific life events in patients with unipolar depression and bipolar disorders. *Journal of Abnormal Psychology* 98: 154–60.

Hayes, S. C. *et al.* (1987). The treatment utility of assessment: A functional approach to evaluating assessment quality. *American Psychologist* 42: 963–74.

Henry, L. A. and Williams, R. M. (1997). Problems in conceptualisation within cognitive therapy: An illustrative case study. *Clinical Psychology and Psychotherapy* 4: 201–13.

Hollon, S. D. and Kendall, P. C. (1980). Cognitive self-statements in depression: Development of an automatic thoughts questionnaire. *Cognitive Therapy and Research* 4: 383–95.

Hollon, S. D. *et al.* (1992). Cognitive therapy and pharmacotherapy for depression: Singly and in combination. *Archives of General Psychiatry* 49: 774–81.

Jacobson, N. S. *et al.* (1996). A component analysis of cognitive behavioural treatment for depression. *Journal of Consulting and Clinical Psychology* 64: 295–304.

James, I. A. *et al.* (1999). Conceptualizations of depression in older people: The interaction of positive and negative beliefs. *Behavioural and Cognitive Psychotherapy* 27: 285–90.

James, I. A. *et al.* (2004). Schema revisited. *Clinical Psychology and Psychotherapy* 11: 369–77.

Kahneman, D. *et al.* (eds) (1982). *Judgement Under Uncertainty: Heuristics and Biases*. Cambridge: Cambridge University Press.

Kanfer, F. H. and Phillips, J. S. (1970). *Learning Foundations of Behaviour Therapy*. New York: Wiley.

Landman, J. (1993). *Regret: The Persistence of the Possible.* New York: Oxford University Press.

Lewinsohn, P. M. *et al.* (1990). Cognitive behavioural treatment for depressed adolescents. *Behavior Therapy* 21: 385–401.

Moore, R. G. and Blackburn, I. M. (1996). The stability of sociotropy and autonomy in depressed patients undergoing treatment. *Cognitive Therapy and Research* 20: 69–80.

Moore, R. M. and Blackburn, I. M. (1997). Cognitive therapy in the treatment of non-responders to antidepressant medication: A controlled study. *Behavioural and Cognitive Psychotherapy* 25: 251–9.

Nekanda-Trepka, C. J. S. *et al.* (1983). Hopelessness and depression. *British Journal of Clinical Psychology* 22: 49–60.

Persons, J. B. (1989). *Cognitive Therapy in Practice: A Case Formulation Approach.* New York: W. W. Norton and Co.

Persons, J. B. (1993). Case conceptualization in cognitive behaviour therapy. In K. T. Kuehlwein and H. Rosen (eds) *Cognitive Therapies in Action.* San Francisco: Jossey-Bass Publishers.

Persons, J. B. and Bertagnolli, A. (1999). Inter-rater reliability of cognitive-behavioural formulations for depression: A replication. *Cognitive Therapy and Research* 23: 271–84.

Persons, J. and Tomkins, M. (1997). Cognitive-behavioural case formulation. In T. Eells (ed) *Handbook of Psychotherapy Case Formulation.* New York: Guilford Press.

Persons, J. *et al.* (1995). Interrater reliability of cognitive-behavioural case formulations. *Cognitive Therapy and Research* 19: 21–34.

Piaget, J. (1952). *The Origins of Intelligence in Children.* New York: International Universities Press.

Robinson, L. A. *et al.* (1990). Psychotherapy for the treatment of depression: A comprehensive review of controlled outcome research. *Psychological Bulletin* 108: 30–49.

Rush, J. A. *et al.* (1977). Comparative efficacy of cognitive therapy versus pharmacotherapy in out-patient depression. *Cognitive Therapy and Research* 1: 17–37.

Schwartz, R. M. (1986). The internal dialogue on asymmetry between positive and negative automatic thoughts. *Cognitive Therapy and Research* 6: 591–605.

Scott, J. *et al.* (2000). Effects of cognitive therapy on psychological symptoms and social functioning in residual depression. *British Journal of Psychiatry* 177: 440–6.

Segal, Z. *et al.* (2002). *Mindfulness-based Cognitive Therapy for Depression: A New Approach to Preventing Relapse.* New York: Guilford Press.

Simons, A. D. *et al.* (1984). The process of change in cognitive therapy and pharmacotherapy for depression: Changes in mood and cognition. *Archives of General Psychiatry* 41: 45–51.

Sperry, L. *et al.* (1992). *Psychiatric Case Formulations.* Washington, DC: American Psychiatric Press.

Stewart, J. W. *et al.* (1993). Imipramine is effective after unsuccessful cognitive therapy: Sequential use of cognitive therapy and imipramine in depressed out-patients. *Journal of Clinical Pharmacology* 13: 114–9.

Tarrier, N. and Calam, R. (2002). New developments in cognitive-behavioural case formulation. Epidemiological, systemic and social context: An integrative approach. *Behavioural and Cognitive Psychotherapy* 30: 311–28.

Teasdale, J. D. (1983). Negative thinking in depression: Cause–effect or reciprocal relationship? *Advances in Behavioural Research and Therapy* 5: 3–25.

Teasdale, J. D. (1996). Clinically relevant theory: Integrating clinical insight with cognitive science. In P. M. Salkovskis (ed) *Frontiers of Cognitive Therapy*. New York: Guilford Press.

Teasdale, J. D. and Barnard, P. J. (1993). *Affect Cognition and Change: Re-modelling Depressive Thought*. Hove, UK: Lawrence Erlbaum Associates Ltd.

Thase, M. E. *et al.* (1996). Abnormal electroencephalographic sleep profiles in major depression: Association with response to cognitive therapy. *Archives of General Psychiatry* 53: 99–108.

Weissman, A. N. and Beck, A. T. (1978). *Development and Validation of the Dysfunctional Attitude Scale*. Paper presented at the annual meeting of the Association for the Advancement of Behaviour Therapy, Chicago. (Reproduced in Blackburn, I. M. and Davidson, K. (1990). *Cognitive Therapy for Depression and Anxiety*. Oxford: Blackwell Scientific Publications.)

Williams, J. M. G. (1992). *The Psychological Treatment of Depression* (2nd edn). London: Routledge.

Williams, J. M. G. *et al.* (1988). *Cognitive Psychology and Emotional Disorders*. Chichester, UK: Wiley.

Young, J. E. (1994). *Cognitive Therapy for Personality Disorders: A Schema-Focused Approach* (rev. edn). Sarasota, FL: Professional Resource Press.

Chapter 7

Case conceptualisation in complex PTSD

Integrating theory with practice

Deborah Lee

INTRODUCTION

Case conceptualisation in complex posttraumatic stress disorder (PTSD) is the topic of this chapter. A case formulation is the 'lynch pin that holds theory and practice together' (Butler 1998). It can be viewed as a theoretically guided way of structuring information concerning a patient's presenting difficulties (Wolpe and Turkat 1985). It provides an explanatory system within which the material presented by the client can be understood and therein offers direction to apply an appropriate intervention in the light of a particular theory (Butler 1998). Thus it is essential that any discussions of case conceptualisation in complex PTSD emerge from an exploration of the theory. For the purposes of this chapter, complex PTSD is defined and a brief review of current theories is presented. Finally, illustrative casework is used to demonstrate how one can integrate current theoretical understandings of PTSD with clinical interventions.

POSTTRAUMATIC STRESS DISORDER

The characteristic feature PTSD is continual reliving of an event from the past, with the same emotional intensity as the original experience. PTSD has three symptom clusters: intrusions, avoidance and hyperarousal. It is the most common psychiatric disorder in those who have experienced traumatic events. Studies indicate a lifetime prevalence of 5–10% in the general population (Litz and Roemer 1996). Prevalence rates vary according to the event experienced, with the highest rates observed in those who have suffered interpersonal violence such as rape or torture (see Lee and Young's 2001 review paper). PTSD is not the only outcome after trauma. Conditions such as acute stress disorder, phobias, somatisation, depression, OCD, suicide, substance abuse, psychosis and head injury/neurological damage are common sequelae following trauma.

Since PTSD was first described in *DSM III* (APA 1980), a variety of theories have been proposed to account for the disorder, including information processing theories (e.g., Brewin *et al.* 1996; Chemtob *et al.* 1988; Dalgleish and Power 2004; Foa and Kozak 1986), behavioural theories (e.g., Keane *et al.* 1985a, 1985b; Mowrer 1960), socio-biological theories (Christopher 2004; van der Kolk *et al.* 1996; Yehuda 2001), socio-cognitive theories (Horowitz 1986; Janoff-Bulman 1992; Resick and Schnicke 1992, 1993) and, more recently, the cognitive model of PTSD (Ehlers and Clark 2000). All of these theories offer useful theoretical insights into the etiology and maintenance of PTSD, in the aftermath of a traumatic event. Furthermore, all of these theories (with the exception of Dalgleish and Power 2004) view the predominant emotional experience associated with trauma as fear. This view is supported in the current *DSM IV-TR* definition of a traumatic event (APA 2000). Indeed it is now a requisite for the diagnosis of PTSD to be met, for the trauma to have involved a subjective element of intense fear, helplessness and/or horror (APA 2000). The inclusion of a subjective response to a traumatic event in the diagnostic criteria implies that individuals consistently experience certain emotions during trauma.

Consequent to the notion that fear, helplessness and horror are key emotional experiences in the etiology of the disorder has been the development of therapeutic interventions aimed at alleviating fear. Typically treatments have drawn on exposure-based paradigms (as used in other disorders characterised by fear/anxiety), whereby exposure to traumatic memories (via imaginal exposure, *in vivo* exposure or reliving) has become central to any effective therapeutic treatment program for sufferers of PTSD (Blake and Sonnenberg 1998; Foa and Kozak 1986; Keane *et al.* 1985a; Marks *et al.* 1998; Richards *et al.* 1994; Shalev *et al.* 1996a). Indeed, so effective is the paradigm of exposure to traumatic memories in the recovery from PTSD that recent NICE (National Institute of Clinical Excellence) guidelines on the treatment of PTSD recommend trauma-focused CBT as the treatment of choice. Trauma-focused CBT involves directly eliciting the memories of trauma (e.g., via reliving or eye movement desensitisation reprocessing (EMDR), Shapiro 1997) and working on the associated emotions and meaning, using cognitive-behavioral therapy.

Simple and complex PTSD

Simple PTSD can be described as a fear-based PTSD (Lee *et al.* 2001) and a typical case scenario is as follows. A psychologically resilient individual experiences a simple Type I event (e.g., a train crash). The label of Type I trauma has been used to describe unanticipated single event(s) whereby the full details of what happened are often 'etched' in memory and relived with the full intensity of the peritraumatic emotions. Essentially, the experience 'stays alive' and is repeatedly 'relived' with clear recollection via intrusions, flashbacks and nightmares. During their ordeal they experience intense fear, helplessness and/or horror and subsequently, due to the novel and over-whelming nature of the event, and/or the intensity of their emotional response, they are unable to integrate the experience into their autobiograph-ical memory and develop intrusions/flashbacks relating to their experience. In contrast, Type II trauma refers to long-standing and repeated ordeals. It is often associated with experiences such as childhood sexual abuse or physical and emotional abuse (Terr 1991). Type II trauma will not be discussed in this chapter and readers should refer to the literature on childhood trauma for more information on this topic.

Case conceptualisation in complex PTSD is the focus of this chapter. Complex PTSD refers to cases in which there is a clear Type I experience(s) but there may be a number of factors that make the presentation more chal-lenging to formulate and work with clinically. These will be discussed in more detail later on in the chapter.

CONTEMPORARY THEORIES OF PTSD

For the purpose of case formulation in PTSD, three contemporary theories are discussed: emotional processing theory (Foa and Kozak 1986; Foa and Rothbaum 1998), the cognitive model of PTSD (Ehlers and Clark 2000) and dual representation theory (Brewin *et al.* 1996). Together these theories offer a comprehensive CBT framework for understanding and conceptualising PTSD. It is not possible to discuss these theories in depth given the param-eters of this chapter. However, the salient issues are presented below, with a particular emphasis on aspects of theory that: (a) help structure clinical case conceptualisations; and (b) provide the rationale for various therapeutic interventions. For those readers who would like to expand their knowledge of these theories see Holmes and Brewin's (2003) excellent review paper.

Emotional processing theory

This model proposes that the emotional experience (fear) generated by the traumatic event is presented in the memory as a fear structure, which is said to be a network of interconnected memories, emotions, behaviours and physiological responses (Foa and Kozak 1986; Foa and Rothbaum 1998). Hence the emotional experience is encoded in organised semantic networks that contain sensory information about the stimulus (sights, sounds, smells, texture), the behavioural, physiological and cognitive responses (heart pounding, sweating) and the meaning of the event (vulnerability, near death; Lang 1977, 1979). The model proposes that the fear network in trauma is coherent, stable and generalisable, which differentiates it from fear networks associated with phobias. As a result of higher order conditioning and stimu-lus generalisation, the fear network is readily activated and brought to the conscious mind (Foa and Kozak 1986). Thus, many other stimuli present at the time of the event and/or stimuli that resemble the traumatising stimuli take on the capacity to activate the fear response. For example, a neutral stimulus, like a car of the same colour or model as that involved in a road traffic accident, may provoke a fear response in the victim of a road traffic accident.

Given the size, complexity and easy accessibility of the fear network, activation alone does not lead to exposure (under optimum conditions), as not all aspects of the fear network are brought to the conscious mind. Thus the individual is repeatedly exposed to the traumatic material under poor exposure conditions (Rachman 1980), and this perpetuates the fear response by preventing habituation from taking place.

The model proposes that the fear network contains information about meaning. Foa and Kozak (1986) suggest that the meaning element of the fear network needs to be re-evaluated for emotional processing to be complete. They propose a treatment approach using prolonged exposure, which activates the fear structure in its entirety. This involves taking the individual through the traumatic event in great detail, allowing for exposure to all aspects of the trauma network (sensory, physiological, behavioural and cognitive). This technique is the basis and origins of what is now commonly known as reliving the trauma. While the trauma network is activated the therapist helps the individual to introduce and accommodate new incompatible information, which changes the meaning element of the network. For example, in the case of a serious assault during which the individual thought they might die, exposure to the feared stimuli (memories of the assault) no longer means near death but survival.

What is not clear from this theory is the answer to a rather perplexing question: why does the memory of a traumatic event give rise to such an intense experience of fear and belief that, as in the case above, one is in imminent danger of death, when in most cases the threat has been removed? Ehlers and Clark (2000) have noted this idiosyncrasy of PTSD (classified as an anxiety disorder in *DSM IV-TR*) when compared to other anxiety disorders. Central to the maintenance of other anxiety disorders are fears about things that might happen in the future (for instance fear of contamination in OCD or fear of illness in health anxiety), whereas in PTSD, sufferers report fear in relation to an event that has already happened and is clearly in the past.

Ehlers and Clark's cognitive model

This model offers a synthesis of ideas to explain the persistence of PSTD in the sub-group of individuals who experience persistent PTSD. They suggest that persistent PTSD occurs only if individuals process the traumatic event and/or its sequelae in way that produces a sense of serious current threat. They suggest that the threat may be to the physical self or to the psychological self.

As a consequence of the way in which the event is processed, the memories are: (a) experienced with the full force of peritraumatic emotions (as if it were happening again); (b) frozen in time; (c) not updated; (d) have no temporal context or meaning context; and (e) are involuntarily recalled. Thus, in the context of PTSD, traumatic memories are experienced by individuals as if they were literally experiencing the original event again.

Ehlers and Clark (2000) propose that two key processes lead to a sense of current threat: (a) individual differences in the appraisal of the trauma and/or its sequelae; and (b) individual differences in the nature of the memory of the event and its link to other autobiographical memories.

First, the model proposes that individuals with persistent PTSD are characterised by idiosyncratic negative appraisals of the traumatic event that have the common effect of creating a sense of current threat. This threat may be either external (e.g., the world is a more dangerous place) and/or internal, as in a threat to one's view of oneself as a capable/acceptable person (Ehlers and Clark 2000). Predominant emotional responses in persistent PTSD are dependent on the specific appraisals. For instance, an appraisal concerning one's own sense of responsibility for causing the event may lead to guilt, whereas appraisal concerning one's violation of internal standards may lead to shame.

The second tenet of Ehlers and Clark's model is the suggestion that implicit trauma memories are characteristically encoded via data-driven processing systems. They note the discrepancy between difficulties in intentional recall of the traumatic memory and easily triggered re-experiencing of the event, and propose that this can be accounted for by poor elaboration and inadequate integration of the trauma memory into its context in time, place, subsequent and previous memories and other autobiographical memories. This explains problematic intentional recall, no context in time and hence the perception of current threat, the absence of links to subsequent information and the easy triggering by physically similar cues. The model proposes that easy triggering of traumatic memories and/or emotional responses by associated stimuli can be explained because the stimulus–stimulus (S–S) and the stimulus–response (S–R) connections are particularly strong for traumatic material (Charney et al. 1983; Foa et al. 1989; Keane et al. 1985a). Thus triggering of such memories is more likely given the large number of associated stimuli present at the time of trauma (Ehlers and Clark 2000).

A number of possible treatment interventions arise from Ehlers and Clark's model. First, the sense of current threat – i.e., the meaning assigned at the time of trauma – requires updating and re-insertion into the trauma memory (as also suggested by Foa and Kozak 1986, who discuss the need to introduce new incompatible information to change the meaning of the fear network). Second, they emphasise the need to address pre-existing beliefs (which may give rise to different emotional states in the aftermath of trauma), as they may need to be adapted before a new meaning can be ascribed (Lee *et al.* 2001). Third, the model highlights the importance of assessing negative posttrauma appraisals and behaviours (such as avoidance), which play a role in maintenance strategies.

Although the cognitive model highlights the importance of interpreting current threat in PTSD, it does not elaborate substantially on how trauma memories may be processed to lead to a sense of current threat. This question, however, is more fully addressed by the third theory presented below.

Dual representation theory

Brewin *et al.* (1996) offer a synthesis of fear networks (Foa and Kozak 1986) and socio-cognitive theory by proposing that there are two parts to the fear structure in their model – an unconscious part that they refer to as situationally accessible memories (SAMs), and a more conscious part that they refer to as verbally accessible memories (VAMs). They postulate that part of the fear network generated by the traumatic event is not readily accessible to the conscious mind and is stored in SAMs. This storage is hypothesised to involve the amygdala. SAMs include information about the stimulus, its meaning and the person's state of consciousness at the time of trauma (Brewin *et al.* 1996). SAMs are encoded via non-conscious processes and cannot be deliberately accessed. Situationally accessible knowledge can only be retrieved when the person is in a context (internal or external) which is similar to the traumatic event. Furthermore, they propose that SAMs are associated with the conditioned emotional responses that were experienced at the time of the trauma (e.g., intense fear, anger). Hence, flashback memories with a dissociative quality or emotional arousal would be indicative of a SAM.

In contrast to SAMs, VAMs can be conceptualised as the person's conscious experience of the trauma – as a series of autobiographical memories encoded via conscious processes. These memories can be deliberately and progressively edited; are readily available for conscious inspection; and are central to the process of accommodating incongruous information received from the traumatic event, appraising meaning and understanding causality. The hippocampus is thought to be involved in these cognitive functions. Attribution and appraisal processes are associated in turn with secondary emotions such as guilt, remorse and shame.

Brewin *et al.* (1996) postulate that aspects of the trauma memories are stored in SAMs because, under extreme threat, the hypothalamus secretes glucocorticoid steroids, which inhibit processing of information via the cortex (where VAMs, appraisal, attributional and meta-cognitive process are ascribed to events). Thus, under extreme threat, the mind 'does not have time to think' but needs to process information about threat in order to maximise the chance of survival. This can be viewed as a primitive and rapid process but because these memories are not available for cognitive inspection, they remain de-contextualised and, most importantly, when accessed in the form of flashbacks have the same meaning that was ascribed at the time of the event. Automatic reactivation of SAMs may be prevented by incorporating new information about the meaning into the original fear network or SAM (Foa and Kozak 1986) or by creating new SAMs that block access to the original one (Brewin 1988).

Thus, in essence, this model proposes that trauma memories are stored in two parallel forms: (a) VAMs which are autobiographical, deliberately recalled, accessed and edited, and are thought to involve the hippocampus; and (b) SAMs which are encoded during trauma, fragmented and sensory, and can only be involuntarily recalled. Successful emotional processing of the traumatic experience occurs when sufficient VAMs are formed and accommodated into the individual's belief system, which, in turn, inhibits the reactivation of SAMs. The new VAMs need to contain all of the information stored in the SAM plus new novel information about meaning. This serves to make the new memories distinctive and more likely to be recalled under triggering circumstances. In order to achieve this, Brewin *et al.*'s (1996) theory proposes some key intervention routes. First, the activation of SAMs can be achieved via prolonged exposure or reliving and second, new meaning is introduced to update SAMs (which is essentially the paradigm suggested by both Foa and Kozak 1986 and Ehlers and Clark 2000). This can be done via a number of cognitive steps: (a) restructure meaning outside of reliving; (b) rehearse the new appraisal; and (c) relive the whole event and bring in 'new' (and rehearsed) information to modify the cognition/meaning – this can be achieved either verbally or through imagery work. For a more detailed description of this technique see Grey *et al.* (2002).

Case conceptualisation in fear-based PTSD

Drawing on the theories discussed above and returning to the fear-based scenario of the train crash presented before, one might hypothesise the development of an elaborate fear memory (see informational processing theory; Foa and Kozak 1986) which contained a vast amount of information about: (a) the actual train crash, including sights, sounds and smells; (b) the individual's behaviour during the event and emotional and physical responses; and (c) the meaning of the event ascribed at the time of the incident ('I am going to die'). Due the nature of the intense emotional experience, the memories were encoded via the amygdala's threat perception system as sensory-based experiences (SAMs). There may have been a number of peak moments of distress (also known as hotspots) associated with intense fear experienced during their ordeal. Typically flashbacks and intrusions contain memories that relate to peak moments of distress (Holmes *et al.* 2005). In this case these hotspots were represented in flashbacks that developed in the aftermath of the event. These flashbacks were not readily integrated in the 'here and now' autobiographical memories (VAMs; see Brewin *et al.*'s 1996 dual representation theory) as they conveyed a sense of imminent death (current threat; see Ehlers and Clark's 2000 cognitive model) and were associated with intensely overwhelming fear. Due to the size and non-specificity of the stimuli present at the time of the trauma and original encoding of the memory, a number of internal (physiological) or external (sound, smell, colour, sight) stimuli readily trigger the flashbacks, which are experienced by the individual as if the event were happening again. The intensely aversive experience of these flashbacks motivates them to engage in a number of elaborate avoidance behaviours (such as avoiding trains, watching TV, or engaging in conversations about their experiences) to reduce the likelihood of flashbacks being triggered.

Treatment implications

In simple, fear-based PTSD, the theories indicate that treatment should involve activation of the fear network in its entirety, via a reliving paradigm, whereby as much detail as possible about the original event is retrieved and, at the peak moments of distress, where salient meaning can be identified (Grey *et al.* 2002), the therapist encourages the client to reframe the meaning using Socratic dialogue. For instance, in the case above: first, the therapist and client identify all flashbacks and intrusions relating to the event and their associated meaning ('I am not going to get out alive,' 'I will be burnt to death'); second, they discuss the fact that, although at the time this was the meaning, in the aftermath of the trauma the client knows that they survived and were not burnt to death; third, the therapist uses the reliving paradigm to activate the fear network and flashbacks under controlled circumstances; and fourth, at previously identified peak moments of distress, the therapist asks the client, 'And what do you know now?' which allows the client to say, 'I survive this, I don't burn to death.' This technique, known as cognitive restructuring within reliving, facilitates the formation of a verbally accessible memory. This encodes the experience in the here and now, rather than as it was experienced at the time of the event (Ehlers and Clark 2000).

This type of presentation of fear-based PTSD is central to most theories of PTSD, which attempt to explain why the individual, in the aftermath of the trauma, remains in a heightened state of arousal and fear and continues to re-experience the event with the same intensity of emotions (Brewin *et al.* 1996; Ehlers and Clark 2000; Foa and Kozak 1986; Foa and Rothbaum 1998). A good working understanding of fear-based PTSD and its theoretical underpinning provides the 'first principles' to build upon when dealing with increasingly complex presentations of PTSD.

INTEGRATING THEORY WITH PRACTICE IN CASES OF COMPLEX PTSD

Before embarking on a case conceptualisation of PTSD it is important to remember that most people recover from traumatic events without developing persistent PTSD. The resilience of the human mind and its capacity to assimilate trauma and tragedy is evident in epidemiological studies of PTSD (Lee and Young 2001). Yet Horowitz, in his writings on the human stress response (1986), aptly notes that everyone has their breaking point. Thus, key to a working hypothesis about a case conceptualisation of PTSD are these questions: What is it about the trauma experience that presents such a challenge to the individual's view of the self, world and/or others that they cannot readily integrate it with their pre-existing beliefs? For instance, what (negative) conclusion did they draw about themselves as they appraised why they experienced the trauma and how they felt and behaved during that experience? What keeps the memories of this experience, highly emotionally charged, intruding into the conscious mind and unresolved? What is the meaning of this experience for this individual? To answer these questions we need to draw on our theoretical knowledge of how an individual creates meaning via the process of attribution and appraisal, how meaning gives rise to emotional responses and how the mind creates memories in the aftermath of trauma.

What makes PTSD more complex to work with?

Typically there is a fear-based trauma reaction in most complex case presentations of PTSD. However, a number of factors, either relating to the event itself or to the individual who experiences the event, affect the complexity of the presenting PTSD. It is worth bearing in mind that persistent and complex PTSD is not necessarily related to the extent of suffering or the perceived severity of the event. It is not uncommon to work with complex PTSD which has arisen in the aftermath of a seemingly minor road traffic accident and, conversely, to work with a seemingly complex array of psychological problems experienced in the aftermath of an horrific event and find that the individual makes a swift recovery. Hence, unpacking the meaning of the experience provides the route to understanding the psychological reaction.

The event characteristics

Often in PTSD individuals have experienced overwhelming, horrific, violating and/or shocking events characterised by profound human suffering and violation of the rights of humanity. These types of event present not only a psychological challenge to the client, but also to the therapist. Such events may include experiences of physical, sexual and psychological torture, rape, deliberate mutilation and mass catastrophes to name but a few. Therapists are often overwhelmed by the extent to which the client has suffered and may experience a sense of 'therapist paralysis' and incomprehension at how they will help the client deal with/overcome things that they themselves find so shocking and unbelievable. While it is essential to validate the extent of the client's suffering, in these cases it is helpful to remain knowledgeable about theory and focused on the task in hand, namely the exploration of the psychological mechanisms/factors that keep the client in a state of traumatisation, and which therapeutic interventions are appropriate to aid a return to psychological well-being.

Clients with complex PTSD often present with multiple traumatic events and/or prolonged/repeated exposure to traumatic events over a period of months or years. This may include combat experience, kidnapping, imprisonment, domestic violence and/or multiple events such as two or three road traffic accidents as well as histories of childhood sexual abuse. Suffering posttrauma consequences such as permanent physical scars, pain, physical disability and loss of job, status, mental wellbeing, loved ones and relationships are common as well.

In cases where there are multiple traumatic events and/or prolonged exposure, the therapist can draw on the same principles that apply to single event trauma. Namely, it is important to identify all peak moments of distress and the content of flashbacks. In a trauma that lasted several months, there may have been key experiences that are represented in flashbacks, and there may be themes to emotional responses and meaning that can be identified and worked with in cognitive therapy. For instance, a client who has been repeatedly subjected to incidents of domestic violence and rape may have six or seven flashbacks with differing content, but which convey the same meaning (e.g., 'I am worthless') and trigger the same emotional response (e.g., shame). This same principle can be applied to multiple traumatic events, including childhood trauma. It is common in complex PTSD to find the personal meaning assigned to adult Type I trauma intrinsically linked to key childhood experiences, such as abuse. There may or may not be intrusions and flashbacks to these childhood events, but there is invariably a link or congruence of meaning between childhood and adult experiences in complex PTSD. For instance a client who nearly died in childbirth assigned the meaning, 'I don't count, my life if not worth saving.' One can only understand her meaning for this event if one examines pretrauma factors. Her childhood was characterised by emotional neglect. She grew up believing that no-one cared for her. Consequently her interpretation of her near-death experience was not fear but shame.

The psychological experience

Complex emotional responses

It is common to identify a range of emotions experienced during and/or in the aftermath of the experience (Holmes *et al.* 2005). Not all clients with PTSD report feeling fearful. Recent research has shown that 45% of hotspot emotions (peak moments of distress) experienced during the trauma are not fear, helplessness or horror but include other cognitive themes such as revenge, self-criticism, feeling let down by others and confusion (Holmes *et al.* 2005). Shame and anger also have a major role in the disorder (Andrews *et al.* 2000). Yet shame and, to a lesser extent, anger are not adequately dealt with in theoretical conceptualisations of PTSD, empirical research and resultant treatment packages. This is in spite of the fact that shame and anger would appear to pose a barrier to effective exposure programs and to be associated with chronic presentations of PTSD (Brewin *et al.* 1996; Ehlers and Steil 1995; Foa *et al.* 1995; Riggs *et al.* 1992).

Given this, a case conceptualisation in complex PTSD needs to identify all of the emotional responses associated with the event. Typically in complex PTSD the therapist may identify several emotional states experienced during the trauma. These emotions may be associated with different parts and evidenced in the content of flashbacks and/or intrusive imagery. Exploration of the cognitions/appraisals assigned to these (emotional) experiences often allows access to the core meaning. In complex PTSD it important to identify the source of the emotional response. Does it come from pre-existing core belies and is it associated with a pervasive/global emotional experience? Does it come from an appraisal made at the time of the event (peritraumatic) and is it associated with a circumscribed emotional state? Or is the emotional response associated with an appraisal made about the aftermath of the experience (posttraumatic appraisals)? Or does the emotional response come from all three sources of cognition?

Different routes for therapeutic interventions will be required to alleviate pervasive shame (Lee 2005) as opposed to pervasive anger or circumscribed guilt based on hindsight (Chemtob *et al.* 1997; Kubany and Manke 1995). Pervasive pre-existing emotional states associated with negative core beliefs need to be addressed first in therapy before an update of SAMs can be successfully achieved (Lee *et al.* 2001). Thus, working on the meaning of the event is facilitated by identifying core emotional responses and associated cognitions.

Meaning

An individual's perception of a traumatic event(s) may confirm or indeed activate dormant core beliefs. For instance, a woman's experience of rape may confirm a salient, premorbid, cognitive theme that she is disgusting and not worth protecting (Lee *et al.* 2001). The experience may also challenge/ shatter core beliefs. For instance, the belief that we live in a just and fair world where good things happen to good people and bad things happen to bad people (Lerner and Miller 1978; Janoff-Bulman 1992) is frequently challenged in the aftermath of trauma. Janoff-Bulman and Frantz (1997) suggest that, 'trauma survivors see the world as it really is, stripped of the meaning and order we all too readily assume to exist.' Most people who experience ongoing trauma describe difficulties in ascribing a meaning to their experience either on an existential level and/or on a personal level. In the aftermath of trauma, there is typically an overwhelming need to ponder meaning-related concerns about comprehensibility ('Does this event make sense or fit my understanding of the world?') and personal significance ('Does this event challenge my own sense of value and worth?'). In complex PTSD, one often sees the client struggle with re-assigning meaning to their now meaningless world. Indeed, Janoff-Bulman and Frantz (1997) suggest that success in overcoming this existential crisis (meaningless world) is only achieved when individuals are able to shift their meaning concerns to a focus of significance and value in their own life. Thus, the task of therapy is to help the client to create a meaningful life when faced with living in a meaningless world. This task can be more difficult to achieve in complex PTSD, as the meaning of the event is rarely solely about threat to physical self (fear) but relates to psychological threat ('Why did this happen to me?' 'What does this event say about me?'). Hence being able to identify the exact nature of the threat to psychological integrity is a crucial process in conceptualising the experience of trauma in these cases.

Co-morbidity

Co-morbidity may also present quite a challenge to the clinician, as there are high levels of co-morbidity between PTSD and other psychiatric disorders such as depression (Blanchard *et al.* 1998), substance abuse, panic and somatisation (Deering *et al.* 1996). Indeed, somewhere in the region of 78% of traumatised refugees present with both depression and PTSD. Excessive use of alcohol and/or recreational drugs, as a means of avoiding painful recollections of traumatic experiences, are also common features of complex PTSD presentations. Other behaviours such as self-harm, binge eating and dissociation may form part of an individual's repertoire of avoidant behaviours.

In case conceptualisation, it is important to identify the nature, maintenance and function of the co-morbid disorder and to identify core themes across the disorders. For instance, it is not surprising that PTSD and depression have such a high co-morbidity, especially if one uses a cognitive model to explain both conditions. This is because persistent PTSD and depression can be explained, in some cases, by the activation of negative core beliefs (Beck 1963; Ehlers and Clark 2000). Also, emotions such as shame and guilt have been identified in both disorders (Andrews *et al.* 2000; Gilbert 1992). Sometimes other problems such as substance misuse or self-harm can be conceptualised as avoidance strategies and become part of important maintenance cycles. For instance, it is not uncommon for clients to use alcohol to 'numb' their emotional responses and 'switch off' their minds from intrusive images. In cases where shame is a problem, self-harm and dissociation are often included in the avoidance strategies and maintenance cycles. For instance, a client may have a tendency to dissociate when faced with overwhelming affect of shame, triggered by a flashback of rape. The client may have learned this strategy in childhood and/or may trigger dissociation by engaging in self-harm. It is important to conceptualise each of these strategies and identify unhelpful or negative beliefs that perpetuate the vicious cycles of maintenance. In a clinical setting, these behaviours may need to be targeted first using cognitive methods described elsewhere (Kennerley 1996) before work on trauma memories can begin.

CASE EXAMPLES

Two case studies are presented in this section – each with a different focus on complexity of the PTSD presentation. In order to aid discussion of these cases, the clinical material will be presented with reference to the diagrammatic formulation adapted from Ehlers and Clark's (2000) cognitive model of PTSD and shown in Figure 7.1. The original formulation diagram has been modified for the purpose of this chapter.

   In each of the cases, the role of pretrauma factors (box 1) will be discussed. They may include factors such as key childhood experiences, beliefs about the self and world, and state at the time of exposure to the traumatic event, and provide information about how the person functioned prior to the index trauma and, importantly, the influence of core beliefs in processing their experiences. In order to understand the nature of the trauma memory, peritrauma factors (box 2) – information about what the person experienced at the time including salient emotions – will be identified. In particular it is useful to examine all peak moments of distress and elucidate the emotional reaction associated with them and the meaning ascribed to them. Salient posttrauma factors (box 3), which affect both secondary emotional responses and perpetuate the manifest sense of current threat (box 4), will be discussed. Finally key maintenance processes will be addressed (box 5).

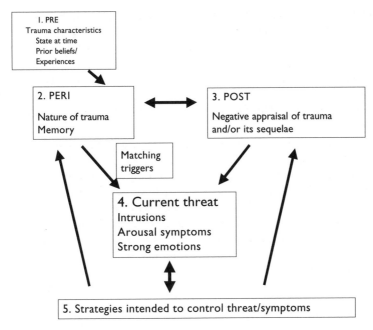

Figure 7.1 Persistent PTSD (adapted from Ehlers and Clark 2000).

Case I

This case is characterised by peritraumatic emotions other than fear and represented in SAMs with co-morbid features of depression and traumatic bereavement.

The index trauma

Jo presented with posttraumatic stress disorder, traumatic bereavement and depression, after experiencing an RTA five years previously. During this RTA, her father was driving, her mother was a passenger and her five-year-old brother died. Their car was hit by another car whose driver was drunk. Further investigation of the trauma experience revealed that, at the time of the accident, she and her family were on holiday in Spain and were driving back to their hotel after a day at the beach. Jo and her brother were sitting in the back, cuddling, holding hands and playing games. At the moment of impact, Jo reported that everything seemed to slow down and she recalled tightening her grip on her brother's hand. At some point she recalled letting go of his hand. Her next memory was of her father screaming and pacing up and down the road. She remembered getting out of the car and searching for her brother; she found him lying dead in the road, having suffered horrific head injuries. Her mother was unconscious at the scene. In the aftermath of the accident, her father persuaded Jo to tell her mother that her brother had died in hospital rather than at the scene, as he thought this would be easier for her mother to deal with. To this day her mother believes this is the story. Jo presented for treatment five years later. Her presentation for treatment coincided with her redundancy from her job in an investment bank. At assessment she described characteristic reliving of the accident via flashbacks and intrusive imagery. Her family never discussed the accident or mentioned her brother's name.

When discussing her reactions to the accident, Jo admitted feeling that she was responsible for her brother's death. She was plagued by images of letting go of his hand and tortured by thoughts that if only she had held on to him he would not have died. In order to cope with her overwhelming sense of responsibility for her brother's death, she had submerged herself in her work and kept herself very busy in order to avoid thinking about the accident or indeed allowing herself to grieve for her brother. Her elaborate avoidance strategy had been taken away when she was made redundant and she was assailed with the full onslaught of her traumatic experience and loss of her brother (box 5).

Salient premorbid features

As the older sibling to a much younger brother, Jo had shouldered a significant amount of responsibility for her brother. Her working mother was often absent and relied upon Jo to care for her younger sibling. Although she recalled a happy and uneventful childhood, she described the family motto as 'carry on regardless.'

Jo's case conceptualisation

In order to inform Jo's case conceptualisation one can draw predominantly on two theories: dual representation theory (Brewin *et al.* 1996) and Ehlers and Clark's (2000) cognitive model of PTSD. The predominant emotional experience associated with Jo's trauma was guilt. There was also intense fear but this was masked by her overwhelming sense of guilt about her brother's death. Jo's flashbacks and intrusive imagery were associated with guilt (peritraumatic experience), followed by an engagement in ruminating thought patterns about what she could have done to keep her brother alive (posttrauma appraisals).

The important factor in Jo's case conceptualisation is that she experienced a sense of guilt and fear at the time of the traumatic event. Thus her peritraumatic emotional experiences, encapsulated in SAMs, were fear and guilt (box 2). Re-experiences of these memories via flashbacks and intrusive thoughts led to a sense of current threat to Jo's psychological integrity ('I'm a bad person for letting my brother down') and to a lesser extent her physical integrity (fear of her own death), and were associated with guilt and fear (box 4). Furthermore, exploration of her pretrauma experiences highlights a consistent theme of responsibility – the belief that she was responsible for her brother's well-being (box 1). The implication of this is that her VAMs, which are subject to appraisal and attributional processes in the aftermath of the trauma experience (posttrauma appraisals), are also characterised by the guilt-ridden conclusion that Jo was responsible for her brother's death (box 3). For Jo, the meaning of her trauma experience was, 'I am responsible for my brother's death and therefore I am a bad person.' Both her pretrauma beliefs and her posttrauma appraisals formed part of the maintenance cycle. The feeling of guilt and the beliefs about responsibility perpetuated her PTSD, and so Jo's grief continued to be unresolved: she could not face her guilt about her brother's death (box 4). Hence, with an understanding of the core meaning, it is clearer to see why Jo had never been able to grieve properly for the loss of her brother – every time she thought of him she was overcome with a feeling of intense guilt that, to her, had no resolution. Jo's case conceptualisation is shown in Figure 7.2.

Treatment plan

Based on Jo's case conceptualisation there was a clear treatment plan. First, in order for her to begin to grieve for the loss of her brother, she needed to

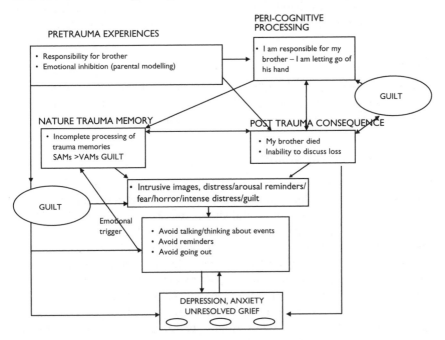

Figure 7.2 Jo's case conceptualisation (adapted from modified version of model of persistent PTSD (from Ehlers and Clark 2000)).

address her guilt about his death and the belief that she was responsible. This was done using standard cognitive therapy techniques and Socratic dialogue for trauma-related guilt (described elsewhere; Kubany and Manke 1995). After six sessions, Jo was able to access a more balanced belief – that although she had taken on a lot of responsibility for her brother when he was alive, she did not cause the accident, and whether or not she had been able to hold his hand was not the reason or cause of his death. By exploring all the factors involved in the accident Jo was able to see that she had grossly over-represented her role in his death and indeed her ability to change the outcome of the accident. Jo was now able to access a new belief: 'I did not cause my brother's death.' However, whenever she experienced a flashback, she felt intense guilt and was overwhelmed with the belief that she had caused it. In those moments of flashback, she could not access her new meaning or verbally accessible memory. Given this, when the therapist explained the rationale for reliving, Jo agreed to relive the accident and insert the new appraisal at the appropriate moment using the techniques described above (Foa and Kozak 1986; Grey *et al.* 2002). During the reliving and at the critical moment, Jo wanted to say, 'I can't stop this happening to you, I love you.' This provoked not only a release from the guilt she had felt for four years but the start of her profound grieving for the loss of her brother. Now she was able to focus on grieving for her loss of her brother, which became the focus of the next six sessions of therapy. At the end of treatment, Jo did not suffer from PTSD, and was in the process of grieving in a normal way for her brother.

Case 2

This case highlights a number of complex issues. It is characterised by the experience of an overwhelming and prolonged index event, complex peritraumatic emotional reactions, negative core beliefs, co-morbidity and chronicity.

Index trauma and aftermath

Amy's presenting problems included PTSD, depression, binge eating, panic attacks and chronic fatigue. At the age of 18 Amy was brutally raped by three men. They broke into her home and systematically attacked her. The details of her attack were horrific and shocking. Her ordeal lasted for eight hours and during that time she was repeatedly physically and sexually assaulted. She did not tell her family about the attack. In the aftermath of the attack, she tried to suppress its emotional impact by not talking about it and withdrawing from friends and family. She put on six stones in weight and developed a habit of binge eating. About 10 years after the event she began to develop chronic fatigue and eventually had to give up work because her condition had become so debilitating.

Since the attack Amy had suffered from flashbacks and fragmented images of the assault, which made her feel intense shame, humiliation and fear. She was highly avoidant of anything that brought back reminders of the attack and rarely went out as she feared being attacked again. Amy constantly ruminated about the attack and was plagued by thoughts such as: 'How could I let this happen to me, I feel so degraded, why didn't I fight them off? I feel so stupid, what is wrong with me that they would want to do this to me? It was my fault, I am no good, the way I looked caused me to be attacked.' She was also constantly assailed by a range of emotions, such as intense shame, rage, humiliation and fear, when she was reminded about the attack.

She sought treatment 22 years after the initial assault. She had tried to get help in the past, but had never discussed the details of the rape with her previous therapists.

Salient premorbid features

Until the attack, Amy had been functioning well in life. She was working hard at her job in the fashion industry and had plans to study fashion design at college. She described her childhood as idyllic. She was brought up in a small town in north Wales, where her family had settled in her early childhood. Although she enjoyed school she struggled with her schoolwork and in her late teens she was diagnosed with dyslexia. She reported suffering mild verbal bullying and some racial abuse, as she was one of two black children at her school. However, at the time Amy felt unaffected by these experiences, as her parents had brought her up to believe that she was different and special. She was also able to gain status at school by excelling at athletics and being striking in appearance. She had always been proud of her looks and the attention she received. Further investigation of her premorbid beliefs revealed that she was brought up to have a strong sense of justice and believed, 'You get what you deserve in life.' She had a sound belief in herself but, with hindsight, she wondered whether she had been too cocky and arrogant. When discussing her prior beliefs about rape, Amy said that she had been brought up to believe that men wanted to marry virgins, 'slutty' women got raped and raped women were 'damaged goods'.

Case conceptualisation

Central to understanding Amy's reaction to her assault was unpacking the meaning of the event and how this placed her psychological integrity as well as her physical integrity under threat (box 4). In order to access meaning, and as part of the assessment process, we identified the content of all Amy's flashbacks and intrusive images, the associated emotional responses and the core cognition ascribed to the image (peritraumatic appraisals, box 2). Although Amy's ordeal lasted some eight hours there were five key images that repeatedly caused her distress:

1   Seeing herself tied to the bed and being beaten: this flashback was associated with intense fear and the thought, 'I am going to die, why am I letting this happen to me?'
2   Being urinated on: this was associated with feelings of shame and humiliation and the thought, 'This is disgusting, I must be disgusting and worthless.'
3   Being raped: this was associated with feelings of shame and humiliation and the thought, 'They hate me, I am to blame for this.'
4   Hiding under the bed after the attackers had left: this was associated with a feeling of intense shame and the thought, 'I am disgusting and worthless.'
5   Seeing herself losing consciousness: this was associated with intense fear and the thought, 'I am going to die here.'

After identifying Amy's prior beliefs it became clear that her experience of rape had both confirmed and challenged pre-exisiting beliefs about herself (Lee *et al.* 2001). Amy's dormant beliefs about unworthiness and unacceptability had been activated and became the predominant mode of her thinking pattern (box 1). Interestingly, Amy's prior beliefs about being special and different served to maintain her sense of shame, as one of the meanings she assigned to the event was, 'I had my come-uppance.' Amy believed she was attacked because she was arrogant and because of the way she looked – thus it was her fault and this made her feel both shame and humiliation.

In the aftermath of the event her posttrauma appraisals of herself were congruent with her pretrauma beliefs about women who were raped – these men must have thought of her as a slut and deserving of her punishment (box 3). Furthermore, her dormant negative beliefs about herself as unworthy and unacceptable were incongruent with her dominant mode of thinking prior to the attack, yet because of her experience and her search to understand it based on her prior beliefs, she had concluded that she must be unworthy and unacceptable. In essence, the meaning of the trauma for Amy was that she deserved to be raped because of who she was – not special and different but unworthy and slutty.

As well as maintaining her PTSD, the activation of these fundamental core beliefs of unworthiness/unacceptability was also at the root of her depression (Beck 1967). Thus, in this case, a working hypothesis was that her PTSD and depression were maintained by core beliefs about unworthiness and the experience of intense shame. A functional analysis revealed that her binge eating was part of her avoidance of affect. However, this behaviour also made her feel ashamed and unworthy and was caught up in a vicious maintenance cycle (box 5). Her withdrawal from family, friends and work was maintained by her depression and her sense of shame but also served as a safety behaviour to avoid talking about reminders of the attack.

Amy's situationally accessible memories were encoded at the time of trauma with overwhelming emotions of shame, humiliation and fear. Her posttrauma appraisals (verbally accessible memories) were congruent with her peritraumatic appraisals, as, in the aftermath of the attack, dormant beliefs about herself as unworthy were activated and influenced her predominant thinking pattern about herself. Amy's case conceptualisation is shown in Figure 7.3.

Treatment plan

Amy's case highlights an important clinical issue relating to the question of when it is appropriate to do reliving. From the case conceptualisation, this technique would be indicated because Amy presented with fragmented situationally accessible memories (experienced as both flashbacks and intrusions) associated with overwhelming affect such as shame, fear and humiliation.

Yet Amy's case is characterised by activation of core beliefs (pretrauma factors). As these are now the predominant mode of thinking and linked to her depression, Amy would not be able to access a different or more balanced meaning for her hotspots, other than meaning that is congruent with her negative self-beliefs. Consequently, attempting the reliving of the trauma under these circumstances (when pervasive and global beliefs and affect are activated) could serve to perpetuate the disorder. Effectively, this could be considered re-traumatising if the individual is unable to assign

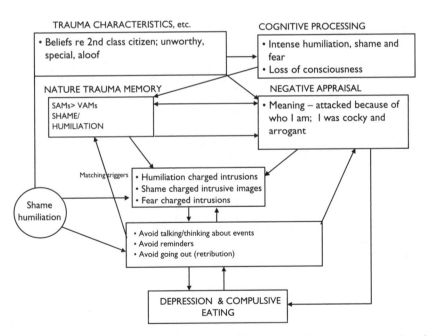

Figure 7.3 Amy's case conceptualisation (adapted from modified version of model of persistent PTSD (from Ehlers and Clark 2000)).

another meaning to the event. In Amy's case, therapy began with 18 months of schema-focused cognitive therapy using methods and techniques described by Padesky (1994). Once Amy was consistently rating her new beliefs at 60–70%, we returned to her experience of rape. Amy identified five key hotspots, which she experienced in flashbacks. For each one Amy came up with a new meaning that was congruent with her new beliefs. Having substantially rehearsed these new thoughts Amy agreed to relive the rape and, when cued by the therapist, inserted her new beliefs. For instance, at the point when she saw herself being raped, which had the previous meaning of 'I'm to blame for this, they hate me,' she inserted, 'This attack is about their badness and not about who I am.' The rest of Amy's hotspots and the new updates are outlined in Figure 7.4.

Amy was extremely surprised that she was not overwhelmed by shame when she relived the rape, and that she had been able to assign a new evaluation of meaning in the context of her new adaptive core beliefs. During the reliving, which took place over five sessions, there was an increase in Amy's compulsive eating behaviour; however, this returned to its usual levels at the end of the process. After 51 sessions, over a period of 20 months, Amy no longer suffered from flashbacks and intrusive imagery. Her mood was much improved. She did however still have problems with compulsive eating and she was referred to a specialist eating disorders unit.

CONCLUSIONS

This chapter has discussed case conceptualisation in complex PTSD. A number of factors have been highlighted that may make PTSD complex.

HOTSPOT UPDATE

SITUATION	THOUGHT	EMOTION(S)	RATING	UPDATE
1. Being beaten and tied up	Why am I letting this happen to me? I'm going to die	Fear	10/10	I survive I can't do anything to stop them, I tried to fight them
2. Being urinated on/defecation	This is disgusting, I must be disgusting and worthless	Humiliation, shame	10/10	I am worthy and I don't deserve this
3. Being raped	I am to blame, they hate me	Shame	10/10	This attack is about their badness and not about who I am
4. Hiding under bed	I am disgusting and worthless	Shame, guilt	10/10	I am worthy and loveable
5. Losing consciousness	I am going to die here	Intense fear	10/10	I survived this vicious attack because of my inner strength They did not defeat me, I defeated them

Figure 7.4 Amy's hotspot chart.

Contemporary theories have been drawn upon to provide a framework in which case conceptualisation can be understood. Routes to clinical interventions have been identified based on guidance from the theory-driven case conceptualisation. Regardless of the complexity of the PTSD, there are a few guiding principles which are applicable to all case presentations and should be borne in mind. These are as follows:

1 A good understanding of the theory of PTSD is an essential starting point to working with this disorder.
2 Always assess and formulate in great detail, and identify all beliefs about the self, world, others, the trauma and reactions to psychological upset.
3 Use intrusions and peak moments of distress to access hot cognitions and meaning.
4 Unravel/unpack the meaning of the event(s).
5 Identify the source of the emotional response and key meaning cognition: is it coming from pre-, peri- and/or posttrauma appraisals?
6 Pay particular attention to peritraumatic appraisals that may be represented in SAMs and require updating by use of cognitive restructuring within reliving.
7 Present a good, compelling, theory-based rationale for reliving to the client.
8 Avoid re-traumatisation by checking, prior to embarking on reliving the trauma memories, that the client can access a more balanced meaning for their experience. This may take several months of cognitive therapy or schema-focused cognitive therapy to achieve, and is an essential prerequisite for reliving.
9 It is important to know the evidence base for trauma-focused CBT and, in particular, for reliving. This will harness a sense of confidence in a technique which, all too often, therapists as well as clients wish to avoid.
10 It is invariably impossible to predict the length of time or number of sessions that will be required when working with complex trauma. A plan for the long haul may be prudent, but be realistic, especially if there are problematic negative core beliefs. That said, sometimes seemingly complex cases of PTSD are treated with success within a few sessions.

REFERENCES

American Psychiatric Association (APA) (1980). *Diagnostic and Statistical Manual of Mental Disorders* (3rd edn; *DSM-III*). Washington, DC: APA.
American Psychiatric Association (APA) (2000). *Diagnostic and Statistical Manual of Mental Disorders* (4th edn rev.; *DSM-IV TR*). Washington, DC: APA.

Andrews, B. *et al.* (2000). Predicting PTSD in victims of violent crime: The role of shame, anger and sexual abuse. *Journal of Abnormal Psychology* 109: 40–8.

Beck, A. T. (1963). Thinking and depression: Idiosyncratic content and cognitive distortions. *Archives of General Psychiatry* 9: 324–33.

Beck, A.T. (1967). *Depression: Clinical, Experimental and Theoretical Aspects*. New York: Hoeber.

Blake, D. D. and Sonnenberg, R. T. (1998). Outcome research on behavioural and cognitive-behavioral therapy for trauma survivors. In V. M. Follette, J. Ruzek and F. R. Abueg (eds) *Cognitive Behavioural Therapy for Trauma* (pp. 15–47). New York: Guilford Press.

Blanchard, E. B. *et al.* (1998). Post-traumatic stress disorder and comorbid major depression: Is the correlation an illusion? *Journal of Anxiety Disorders* 12: 21–37.

Brewin, C. R. (1988). *Cognitive Foundations of Clinical Psychology*. Hove, UK: Lawrence Erlbaum Associates, Ltd.

Brewin, C. R. *et al.* (1996). A dual representation theory of posttraumatic stress disorder. *Psychological Review* 103: 670–86.

Butler, G. (1998). Clinical formulation. In A. S. Bellack and M. Herson (eds) *Comprehensive Clinical Psychology, Vol. 6*. Oxford: Pergamon.

Charney, D. *et al.* (1993). Psychobiological mechanisms of posttraumatic stress disorder. *Archives of General Psychiatry* 50: 294–305.

Chemtob, C. M. *et al.* (1988). A cognitive action theory of post-traumatic stress disorder. *Journal of Anxiety Disorders* 2: 253–75.

Chemtob, C. M. *et al.* (1997). Cognitive-behavioral treatment for severe anger in posttraumatic stress disorder. *Journal of Consulting and Clinical Psychology* 65: 184–9.

Christopher, M. (2004). A broader view of trauma: A biopsychological-evolutionary view of the traumatic stress response in the emergence of pathology and/or growth. *Clinical Psychology Review* 24: 75–98.

Dalgleish, T. and Power, M. (2004). Emotion-specific and emotion non-specific components of PTSD: Implications for taxonomy of related psychopathology. *Behaviour, Research and Therapy* 42: 1069–88.

Deering, C. G. *et al.* (1996). Unique patterns of comorbidity in posttraumatic stress disorder from different sources of trauma. *Comprehensive Psychiatry* 5: 336–46.

Ehlers, A. and Clark, D. M. (2000). A cognitive model of posttraumatic stress disorder. *Behaviour Research and Therapy* 38: 319–45.

Ehlers, A. and Steil, R. (1995). Maintenance of intrusive memories in posttraumatic stress disorder: A cognitive approach. *Behavioural and Cognitive Psychotherapy* 23: 217–49.

Foa, E. B. and Kozak, M. J. (1986). Emotional processing of fear: Exposure to corrective information. *Psychological Bulletin* 99: 20–35.

Foa, E. B. and Rothbaum, B. O. (1998). *Treating the Trauma of Rape: Cognitive Behavioural Therapy for PTSD*. New York: Guilford Press.

Foa, E. B. *et al.* (1989). Behavioral/cognitive conceptualisation of post-traumatic stress disorder. *Behavior Therapy* 20: 155–76.

Foa, E. B. *et al.* (1995). The impact of fear activation and anger on the efficacy of treatment for posttraumatic stress disorder. *Behaviour Therapy* 26: 487–99.

Gilbert, P. (1992). *Depression: The Evolution of Powerlessness*. New York: Guilford Press.

Grey, N. *et al.* (2002). Cognitive restructuring within reliving: A treatment for peri-traumatic emotional hotspots in PTSD. *Behavioural and Cognitive Psychotherapy* 30: 37–56.

Holmes, E. and Brewin, C. R. (2003). Psychological theories of PTSD. *Clinical Psychology Review* 23: 23–56.

Holmes, E. A. *et al.* (2005). Intrusive images and 'hotspots' of trauma memories in posttraumatic stress disorder: An exploratory investigation of emotions and cognitive themes. *Journal of Behaviour Therapy and Experimental Psychiatry* 36: 3–17.

Horowitz, M. J. (1986). *Stress Response Syndromes*. Northvale, NJ: Jason Aronson.

Janoff-Bulman, R. (1992). *Shattered Assumptions: Towards a New Psychology of Trauma*. New York: Free Press.

Janoff-Bulman, R. and Frantz, C. M. (1997). The impact of trauma on meaning: From meaningless world to meaningful life. In M. Power and C. R. Brewin (eds) *The Transformation of Meaning in Psychological Therapies: Integrating Theory and Practice*. Chichester, UK: John Wiley and Sons.

Keane, T. M. *et al.* (1985a). A behavioral approach to assessing and treating Vietnam veterans. In C. R. Figley (ed) *Trauma and its Wake: The Study and Treatment of Post-traumatic Stress Disorder*. New York: Brunner/Mazel.

Keane, T. M. *et al.* (1985b). A behavioural formulation of post-traumatic stress disorder in Vietnam veterans. *The Behaviour Therapist* 8: 9–12.

Kennerley, H. (1996). Cognitive therapy of dissociative symptoms associated with trauma. *British Journal of Clinical Psychology* 35: 325–40.

Kubany, E. S. and Manke, F. P. (1995). Cognitive therapy for trauma-related guilt: Conceptual bases and treatment outlines. *Cognitive and Behavioral Practice* 2: 27–61.

Lang, P. J. (1977). Imagery in therapy: An information processing analysis of fear. *Behavior Therapy* 8: 862–86.

Lang, P. J. (1979). A bio-informational theory on emotional imagery. *Psychophysiology* 16: 495–512.

Lee, D. A. (2005). The perfect nurturer: A model to develop a compassionate mind within the context of cognitive therapy. In P. Gilbert (ed) *Compassion: Conceptualisations, Research and Use in Psychotherapy*. London: Brunner-Routledge.

Lee, D. A. and Young, K. (2001). Post-traumatic stress disorder: Diagnostic issues and epidemiology in adult survivors of traumatic events. *International Review of Psychiatry* 13: 150–8.

Lee, D. A. *et al.* (2001). The role of shame and guilt in reactions to traumatic events: A clinical formulation of shame-based and guilt-based PTSD. *British Journal of Medical Psychology* 74: 451–66.

Lerner, M. J. and Miller, D. T. (1978). Just World Research and attribution process: Looking back and ahead. *Psychological Bulletin* 85: 1030–51.

Litz, B. T. and Roemer, L. (1996). Post-traumatic stress disorder: An overview. *Clinical Psychology and Psychotherapy: An International Journal of Theory and Practice* 3: 153–68.

Marks, I. *et al.* (1998). Treatment of post-traumatic stress disorder by exposure and/or cognitive restructuring: A controlled study. *Archives of Psychiatry* 55: 317–25.

Mowrer, O. H. (1960). *Learning Theory and Behaviour*. New York: Wiley.

Padesky, C. A. (1994). Schema change processes in cognitive therapy. *Clinical Psychology and Psychotherapy* 1: 267–78.

Rachman, S. (1980). Emotional processing. *Behaviour, Research and Therapy* 18: 51–60.

Resick, P. A. and Schnicke, M. K. (1992). Cognitive processing therapy for sexual assault victims. *Journal of Consulting and Clinical Psychology* 60: 748–56.

Resick, P. A. and Schnicke, M. K. (1993). *Cognitive Processing for Rape Victims.* Newbury Park, CA: Sage.

Richards, D. A. *et al.* (1994). Post-traumatic stress disorder: Evaluation of a behavioural treatment program. *Journal of Traumatic Stress* 7: 669–80.

Riggs, D. S. *et al.* (1992). Anger and post-traumatic stress disorder in female crime victims. *Journal of Traumatic Stress* 5: 613–25.

Shalev, A. Y. *et al.* (1996). Treatment of posttraumatic stress disorder: A review. *Psychosomatic Medicine* 58: 165–82.

Shapiro, F. (1997). *EMDR: The Breakthrough Therapy for Overcoming Anxiety, Stress and Trauma.* New York: Basic Books.

Terr, L. C. (1991). Childhood traumas: An outline and overview. *American Journal of Psychiatry* 148: 10–20.

van der Kolk, B. A. *et al.* (eds) (1996). *Traumatic Stress: The Effects of Overwhelming Experience on Mind, Body, and Society.* New York: Guilford Press.

Wolpe, J. and Turkat, I. D. (1985). Behavioral formulation of clinical cases. In I. D. Turkat (ed) *Behavioural Case Formulation* (pp. 5–36). New York: Plenum Press.

Yehuda, R. (2001). Biology of posttraumatic stress disorder. *Journal of Clinical Psychiatry* 62: 41–6.

Chapter 8

A cognitive-behavioural case formulation approach to the treatment of schizophrenia

Nicholas Tarrier

INTRODUCTION

Schizophrenia is a debilitating condition that affects 1 in 100. It is traditionally characterised as a loss of contact with reality. The symptoms of psychosis are classified as positive and negative. Positive symptoms include disturbed perception in the form of hallucinations – mainly auditory but sometimes visual, tactile or olfactory – and disorders of thought, including delusions. Negative symptoms include cognitive dysfunction, loss of volition, an inability to enjoy experiences and activities and poor self-care skills. Schizophrenia is frequently associated with impairment of cognition and emotion. Vocational and social functioning are often disrupted and the disorder is associated with considerable social and economic burden to the sufferer, the carers and society as a whole. The mainstay of treatment has been anti-psychotic medication combined with some form of case management delivered by multi-disciplinary mental health services. The outcome is variable in spite of treatment. Typically, the disorder follows an episodic relapsing course with periods of remission, although recovery is often incomplete and residual hallucinations and delusions are common. However, the range of outcomes is broad, with some cases making a complete recovery and others becoming resistant to conventional treatments.

Until recently schizophrenia was thought to be solely biologically determined and impervious to psychological treatment. Traditional forms of psychotherapy appeared to have little or no benefit for those suffering from schizophrenia, and could well be harmful (Mueser and Berenbaum 1990). However, over the last decade or so evidence has accrued that cognitive behaviour therapy (CBT) has considerable utility in treating schizophrenia and psychosis when added to standard psychiatric care (Cormac *et al.* 2004; Pilling *et al.* 2002; Tarrier 2005; Tarrier and Wykes 2004). There has been sufficient evidence for CBT to become a recommended treatment for schizophrenia in the UK, as determined by the National Institute of Clinical Excellence (2003), the government body that recommends which treatments should be used in clinical practice.

THE NATURE OF THE PROBLEM

Someone suffering from schizophrenia will potentially experience distortions in perception and cognition, and related emotional reactions such as anxiety and depression. These experiences or symptoms can significantly impair an individual's ability to function in usual roles and social activity. The sufferer may also be exposed to greater risk of trauma, either through increased victimisation, the traumatic nature of their delusions and psychotic break-down, or through the nature of their contact with mental health services, such as involuntary hospitalisation. Aspects of the disorder and its psycho-logical and social consequences are outlined in Table 8.1. These factors will potentially influence the nature and form of therapy and clinicians need to take these factors into account in their formulation.

Table 8.1 Aspects of the disorder which need to be assessed and possibly taken into consideration in CBT for psychotic patients

Psychological
- interference: disrupted or slowed thought processes
- difficulty discriminating signal from noise
- restricted attention
- hypersensitivity to social stressors and social interactions
- difficulty processing social stimuli and acting appropriately
- social anxiety and avoidance
- flat and restricted affect
- elevated arousal or dysfunctional arousal regulation
- hypersensitivity to stress and life events
- high risk of traumatisation and its consequences, including post-traumatic stress
- high risk of suicide and self-harm
- stigmatisation
- risk of depression and hopelessness
- high risk of substance and alcohol abuse
- onset in late adolescence/early adulthood interfered with normal developmental processes

Psychosocial
- hypersensitive to family environments and social relationships
- risk of perpetrating, or being the victim of, violence
- poor engagement with mental health services
- disruptive and potentially traumatising effect of hospitalisation

Social
- conditions of social deprivation
- poor housing
- downward social drift
- unemployment and difficulty competing in the job market
- restricted social network
- psychiatric career interferes with utilisation of other social resources

The person's perceptions and their emotional reaction to their illness and its consequences are central to the impact on that person's life. This may occur in a number of ways. Interpretation of the subjective experience of unusual perception and cognition may compound and maintain psychopathology in the form of psychotic symptoms (Garety *et al.* 2001; Tarrier 2002a). This may also have a profound effect on the way in which the person perceives him/herself and upon feelings of self-worth. The person's perceptions of the illness and its consequential effect on his/her life can result in feelings of depression, hopelessness and despair, which can be associated with suicidal ideation and behaviour. The risk of suicide in people suffering from schizophrenia is particularly high (Caldwell and Gottesman 1990). Thus, although schizophrenia is characterised by psychotic symptoms of hallucinations and delusions (positive symptoms) and deficits in cognitive and behavioural functioning (negative symptoms), the clinician will need to take into account the profound emotional and traumatic nature of the disorder, the difficulties the sufferer will experience in functioning in their social, educational and vocational roles, and the potential risk of self-harm.

Schizophrenia can differ widely in its clinical presentation, both between individuals and within the same individual at different times. A number of phases of the disorder are recognised during which the intensity of symptoms and disability may vary. These include a prodromal phase that occurs before the development of the illness into psychosis. During the prodromal phase there is an increase in non-psychotic symptoms such as anxiety, irritability, insomnia and mood instability, and in quasi-psychotic symptoms such as delusional mood and magical thinking. This prodrome converts into an acute illness episode during which the positive symptoms become apparent. The acute phase is followed either by remission or by a period of residual symptoms, during which positive symptoms persist but at a reduced intensity compared to the acute episode.

The aims and nature of any CBT intervention will vary depending on the phase of the disorder. In the prodromal phase the aim will be to prevent the development of a psychotic illness or a psychotic episode. In the residual chronic phase, when symptoms are not responding further to medication, the aim will be symptom reduction. In contrast, in the acute phase the aim will be to speed symptom resolution in tandem with medication. In the remission phase, the aim will be to prevent subsequent relapse or deterioration. These differing options and treatment aims are outlined in Table 8.2. Part of the formulation will require an assessment of the illness phase and associated treatment needs.

Table 8.2 Treatment aims and methods in different phases of the schizophrenic illness

Phase	Aim	Treatment Method
Pre-illness prodrome	Prevention of translation into full psychosis	CBT for early signs and prevention of symptom escalation
Acute episode	Speed recovery	CBT and coping training
Partially remitted residual symptoms	Symptom reduction	CBT, coping training, self-esteem enhancement
Remission	Relapse prevention	CBT for staying well
Relapse prodrome	Abort relapse	Early signs identification and relapse prevention

CO-MORBIDITY AND ASSOCIATED CLINICAL CONDITIONS

Further clinical problems associated with schizophrenia can be classified under the heading of co-morbidity, although whether these are separate and distinct disorders rather than part of, or a consequence of, the psychotic illness is unclear. For convenience, suicide risk and self-esteem have also been covered under this heading.

Social anxiety

Social anxiety is a common problem in schizophrenia (Cosoff and Hafner 1998) and itself may also result in further problems: for example, alcohol or substance abuse can be a strategy of self-medication in order to cope with social fears and self-consciousness (Carrigan and Randall 2003); also, the social isolation that comes from social phobia can lead to secondary depression (Stein *et al.* 2001). Individuals suffering with psychosis often have difficulty understanding the social world around them, which can lead to socially awkward behaviour as well as to the misinterpretation of the behaviour of others. Individuals suffering from psychotic disorders might develop social phobia: they are afraid of negative evaluation because of their illness and the stigma it may evoke, or paranoid delusion may take the form of persistent fear of negative evaluation. The cognitive biases that are potentially part of psychosis may also render the individual more vulnerable to developing social phobia (Bogels and Tarrier 2004).

There may be some advantage in treating the co-morbid social phobia. For example, Kingsep *et al.* (2003) showed statistical improvement on social anxiety measures after a cognitive-behaviour group intervention for schizophrenic patients with co-morbid social anxiety. Since patients with schizophrenia and co-morbid social phobia have a higher rate of relapse, it can be speculated that adjunctive treatment of the social phobia might even prevent future relapse. See Chapter 4 for Wells' description of case formulation of social phobia.

Trauma

People suffering from psychosis appear to have a greater exposure to traumatic events. One in six patients suffering from psychosis reported themselves as being the victim of violence in the preceding 12 months (Chapple *et al.* 2004), and life-time rates of childhood physical and sexual abuse far exceed rates in the general community (Greenfield *et al.* 1994; Mueser *et al.* 1998). Elevated rates of PTSD have been noted in populations of the severely mentally ill. Mueser *et al.* (1998) reported a prevalence of 43% in patients with schizophrenia. Other estimates suggest much lower rates in schizophrenia, especially first episodes, compared to major depression (Seedat *et al.* 2003). Neria *et al.* (2002) report co-morbidity of 10% in first-episode schizophrenia. There is evidence that the emergence of psychosis or hospitalisation can be severely traumatic (Frame and Morrison 2001; McGorry *et al.* 1991; Shaw *et al.* 2002). However, there is controversy regarding the accuracy and reliability of trauma reports, and whether the experience of psychosis per se qualifies as a PTSD stressor; there are also difficulties in differentiating phenomenology which make accurate estimates and descriptions of co-morbid PTSD in psychotic patients problematic (Seedat *et al.* 2003). Notwithstanding these problems it is likely that post-traumatic stress reactions will complicate the clinical condition and its treatment. PTSD is associated with elevated risk of self-harm (Tarrier *et al.* 2004) which, when occurring in a person already suffering from schizophrenia, may further increase suicide risk. Little is currently known on how to treat co-morbid PTSD in psychosis or the complex post-traumatic stress response to the psychosis and its consequences, such as involuntary hospitalisation.

Depression

Depression occurs in a large number of patients who suffer from schizophrenia. There are a number of views as to the reason for this: (a) depression may be confused with negative symptoms; (b) depression may be a side-effect of anti-psychotic medication; (c) depression may be an integral part of schizophrenia; or (d) depression may be related to insight and be a secondary response to the illness and its consequences (Gelder *et al.* 2001: 334). In first-episode schizophrenia there is little evidence for a post-psychotic depression and some adjustment to the illness is evident with time (Drake *et al.* 2004). Birchwood *et al.* (2000) reported very high levels of depression – over 60% of their sample of patients with auditory hallucinations. It is suggested that voices act in the same way as external social relationships and the level of distress and depression is related to an appraisal of being subordinate, shamed and inferior to a powerful and dominant other (Birchwood et al. 2004). It is therefore important when assessing patients to identify any depressed mood and understand the potential determinants, which should be accommodated in any treatment plan.

Self-esteem

Low self-esteem is endemic in those suffering persistent mental health problems (Silverstone 1991). It is frequently associated with psychosis, possibly in part due to the disability related to the disorder and the stigma associated with suffering from severe mental illness. Low self-esteem is strongly associated with depression and suicidal ideation and behaviour (Tarrier et al. 2004). Self-esteem is a complex concept and there is evidence that there may be two distinct and independent dimensions: a positive evaluation of the self and a negative evaluation of the self (Barrowclough et al. 2003). Interestingly, there were strong associations between a positive evaluation of the self and negative symptoms of schizophrenia, and between a negative evaluation of the self and positive symptoms of schizophrenia (Barrowclough et al. 2003). These two different aspects of self-esteem may require different treatment approaches, which may have an impact on different symptom clusters. Besides being related to various symptoms low self-esteem is an important de-motivating factor, and potentially compromises initial engagement or maintenance of benefits obtained through treatment.

Suicide risk

It is well known that approximately 1 in 10 patients suffering from schizophrenia will kill themselves and a substantial number will attempt suicide, with suicidal ideation being common in many more. Risk factors for suicide include being young and male, suffering a chronic illness with numerous exacerbations, high levels of symptomatology and functional impairment, experiencing feelings of hopelessness in association with depression, a fear of further mental deterioration, and an excessive dependence on treatment or a loss of faith in treatment (Caldwell and Gottesman 1990). Tarrier et al. (2004) carried out a path analysis of precursors to suicide risk in patients with a less than a three-year history of schizophrenia, and found that the time since the onset of illness independently increased risk. There were also two other paths which acted through hopelessness: one was based on increased social isolation, to which longer illness duration, more positive symptoms, older age and being unemployed contributed; the second path was associated with greater negative views of the self, higher frequency of criticism from relatives and more negative symptoms, to which being male, unmarried and unemployed significantly contributed.

It is important to be aware that suicide attempts are a very real possibility while treating someone suffering from this disorder. It is necessary to assess risk and update this assessment throughout therapy. The presence of suicidal ideation needs to be assessed, as does whether any specific plans have been made or actions have been taken. It is necessary to be aware of potentially risk-elevating factors such as: the erosion of self-esteem; an increased sense of hopelessness and despair, especially related to the patient's perception of their illness and their recovery; disruptive family or social relationships; and any changes in social circumstances or loss of supportive relationships, for example changes in mental health staff or staff holidays or leave. Unfortunately schizophrenic suicides are often impulsive and use lethal methods, such as jumping from heights, immolation or use of firearms. The choice of method and the opportunity to mimic or copy other examples of suicidal behaviour will be important. Furthermore, the occurrence of life events, loss or shameful experiences can lead to despondency. Particular symptoms, such as command hallucinations, may increase risk. Much of the research has investigated the general characteristics of those who commit suicide or self-harm; much less is known about the psychological mechanisms that mediate such behaviour (Bolton *et al.* 2006). The case formulation approach provides a methodology with which the therapist can understand the idiosyncratic pathways to deliberate self-harm, and indicates how risk can be reduced.

REASONS FOR THE DEVELOPMENT OF COGNITIVE-BEHAVIOURAL TREATMENTS

There have been a number of reasons for the increased interest in effective psychological therapies. In spite of improvements in anti-psychotic medication a substantial group of patients, about 40%, show minimal or only partial improvement (Kane 1996). Even with good medication compliance a significant number of patients will relapse. However, medication compliance is often poor, leading to further adverse outcomes (Buchanan 1996). Anti-psychotic medication frequently results in unpleasant and distressing side-effects, especially disorders of movement. Some side-effects can be permanent, such as tardive dyskinesia, and some on rare occasions can be fatal. Furthermore, in recent years there has arisen an increasingly vocal and powerful consumer or user movement in mental health that has sought to increase user choice and preference in treatment for mental disorders. Lastly, there has been much greater emphasis on evidence-based health care and the implementation of treatment approaches that have been shown to work. CBT, with a commitment to evaluation, has demonstrated a significant advantage over other schools of psychotherapy in this regard (Tarrier 2002b).

CBT approaches were initially developed to treat chronic patients who were suffering from chronic and persistent drug-resistant symptoms, and it is with this group of patients that most evaluation has been carried out (Tarrier and Wykes 2004). CBT has also been shown to be applicable to acutely ill patients, typically when they have been hospitalised for an acute psychotic episode (Lewis *et al.* 2002), in relapse prevention (Gumley *et al.* 2003), in the treatment of dual diagnosis (patients suffering from psychosis and alcohol or substance misuse; Barrowclough *et al.* 2001; Haddock *et al.* 2003) and in the prevention of the development of psychosis in vulnerable individuals (Morrison *et al.* 2004)

EVIDENCE FOR COGNITIVE-BEHAVIOURAL TREATMENTS

The evidence base for CBT as a treatment for schizophrenia is now secure, consisting as it does of a considerable number of randomised controlled trials of an increasingly rigorous methodology. Tarrier and Wykes (2004) identified 20 trials investigating CBT in patients with a diagnosis of schizophrenia or schizophrenia spectrum disorder. These studies treated a total of 739 patients with CBT, with a mean of 37 (sd = 48, range = 7–225) treated in each study. Sixteen of these studies were carried out within the UK, with one each from Canada, the Netherlands, Italy and the USA. Sixteen studies involved chronic outpatients, one involved chronic inpatients and three involved patients hospitalised for an acute episode. These studies have a mean effect size[1] of 0.37 (sd = 0.39, median = 0.32) with a range from –0.49 to 0.99. Using Cohen's (1988) convention for categorising effect sizes, 14 (74%) studies achieve at least a small effect size, six (32%) at least a moderate effect size and three (16%) a large effect size. Overall these studies indicate a modest effect size in improving positive symptoms compared to standard psychiatric care (TAU), which is probably not surprising given the nature and severity of the disorder. There is good support for CBT in reducing chronic and persistent residual psychotic symptoms. The evidence for speeding recovery in acute patients and reducing relapse in both acute and chronic patients is less compelling. However, with respect to relapse reduction it appears that there is less success when relapse prevention is part of a larger CBT package, but CBT is significantly effective when the intervention is dedicated solely to keeping well or preventing relapse or rehospitalisation (Tarrier and Wykes 2004). There is encouraging preliminary evidence that modified CBT interventions can result in clinical benefits for dual-diagnosis patients and in preventing psychosis in vulnerable individuals.

A CLINICAL MODEL

CBT for schizophrenia, although following a common theme and set of principles, has developed in a number of centres and been informed by a number of theoretical and conceptual bases (Tarrier 2005). Within centres there have been changes with time as treatments have been refined and faced new clinical challenges. Thus different models have adopted different emphases and clinical tactics. The model described here has been developed by the author but bears many similarities to other models and has benefited from contact and discussion with other clinical researchers in the field. The basic tenet is the recovery model, in which the patient is coping with a persistent illness which may well change many aspects of their lives and the therapist aids the patient in facilitating, as far as possible, the process of recovery.

The clinical model that guides treatment is presented in Figure 8.1. It assumes that the experience of psychotic symptoms, hallucinations and delusions is a dynamic interaction between internal and external factors. Internal factors may be either biological or psychological and can be inherited or acquired. For example, genetic factors may influence the biochemical functioning of the brain and also cognitive capacity. Alternatively, biological and psychological dysfunction may be acquired, for example in the development of maladaptive attitudes and deficits in cognitive flexibility. Such internal factors increase an individual's vulnerability to psychosis and their risk is further increased through exposure to environmental stress, such as certain interpersonal environments or environments that are excessively demanding. The interaction between internal and external factors is important, both in the origins of the disorder and also in maintaining symptoms.

Dysfunction in the processing of information, such as source monitoring in hallucinations and probabilistic reasoning in delusions, in combination with dysfunctions in the arousal system and its regulation, will result in the disturbances of perception and thought that are characteristic of psychosis. The individual is reactive to these experiences and there is a process of primary and secondary appraisal in which the individual attempts to interpret these experiences and give them meaning and then react to their consequences. The immediate reaction to the psychotic experience will be multidimensional and include emotional, behavioural and cognitive elements. Secondary effects such as low mood, anxiety in social situations and the effect of trauma may further compound the situation.

The important aspect of this model is that appraisal and the reaction to the psychotic experience will feed back through a number of possible routes and increase the probability of the psychotic experience being maintained or recurring. For example, the emotional reaction to hearing threatening voices or experiencing strong feelings of paranoia may well be anxiety or anger. Both these emotions include elevated levels of autonomic arousal which, acting either directly through sustained increased levels of arousal or indirectly through further disruption of information processing, will increase the likelihood of psychotic symptoms. Similarly, behavioural responses to psychotic symptoms may increase exposure to environmental stress or increase risk of trauma, which maintains psychotic symptoms. For example,

INTERNAL
FACTORS

EXTERNAL
FACTORS

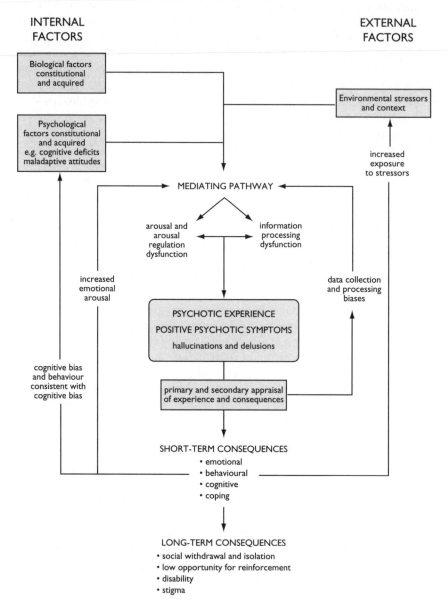

Figure 8.1 A clinical model in the CBT treatment of psychosis.

paranoid thoughts may result in interpersonal conflict or alternatively social avoidance and withdrawal. Both situations are likely to increase the probability of symptoms occurring. Interpersonal conflict is likely to be interpreted as evidence for persecution, whereas withdrawal and isolation will probably result in confirmatory rumination and resentment with a lack of opportunity to disconfirm these paranoid beliefs. The appraisal of the content of voices or delusional thoughts as valid and true may result in behaviour consistent with these beliefs and a confirmatory bias towards collecting and evaluating evidence on which to base judgements of reality.

Psychotic experiences can lead to dysfunctional beliefs which are then acted upon in a way that leads to their confirmation or a failure to disconfirm. This can be termed the experience–belief–action–confirmation cycle or EBAC cycle. It is suggested that such cycles maintain psychotic experience through reinforcement of maladaptive beliefs and behaviour. The generic model outlined in Figure 8.1 provides an overarching picture of how the patient's problems arose and are maintained. Embedded within this model are the micro-elements of specific time-linked events such as the EBAC cycle (see Figure 8.2).

ENGAGEMENT AND ASSESSMENT

Patients suffering from schizophrenia, especially those with paranoid or persecutory delusions, can be extremely difficult to engage. The therapist should initially develop a relationship with the patient and seek to verify that the relationship is secure before commencing on assessment and therapy. To embark upon a too-detailed assessment or on treatment strategies before the patient has understood and accepted the rationale risks the patient disengaging because they find the process too intrusive or without personal relevance. Thus, the early stages of therapy may consist of providing emotional or practical support or learning about the patient and their interests

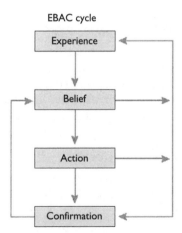

Figure 8.2 The experience–belief–action–confirmation cycle.

so as to develop a therapeutic relationship. Assessment should then proceed in the spirit of collaborative empiricism in an attempt to understand the patient's experience and its determinants and context within the structure of the clinical model described.

A semi-structured interview, the antecedent and coping interview (ACI; Tarrier 2002a), has been developed to form the basis of assessment upon which a formulation of the patient's problems can be made. The ACI asks about the nature of the patient's psychotic experience; the context in which this experience occurs; their reactions in terms of cognition, behaviour and affective and emotional responses, and their interpretation of their experience; the consequences of the illness, with special emphasis on social impact, inability to achieve cherished goals, effect on self-esteem and self-worth, and risk of self-harm; and their ability to cope with their experiences and consequences.

Psychotic symptoms: nature and variation

Each psychotic symptom needs to be elicited. The interviewer needs to enquire about all psychotic experience, for example the types and nature of hallucinations, the types of delusions, and the nature of any interference with thought processes. Once each symptom has been identified the interviewer should elicit the details: frequency, severity or intensity of hallucinations or delusional thought, the physical characteristics of the voices and so on. If the patient hears voices, it is important to know to whom or what they are attributed, their level of power and control and whether they are commanding, positive, negative, supportive, neutral or hostile. Structured assessment instruments such as the PSYRATS (Haddock et al. 1999) can be used to assess symptomatology further.

Emotions that accompany each psychotic symptom

The interviewer should elicit the emotional reaction that accompanies each symptom or psychotic experience. Once the interviewer has elicited the emotional reactions to the symptom in global terms, such as anxiety, anger or distress, they should attempt to break down the emotion in more detail, including cognition, behaviour, physical reaction and affect.

Antecedent stimuli and context

The interviewer is searching for triggers or precipitators which determine the context for the symptoms. Some patients may be very aware of these, others are unaware of any pattern but one does unfold with questioning, and others, even with detailed questioning, are unable to identify any obvious context or pattern to their symptoms. Patients can be asked to monitor their symptoms and keep diaries to establish cues and patterns. The interviewer should ask about each symptom in turn and question whether there are any triggers, whether the symptom occurs in certain circumstances or whether the patients knows a symptom is going to 'come on'. Besides location and circumstances the interviewer should enquire about details such as the time of day and especially any social context. Once the interviewer has asked about potential external stimuli this should be followed up with questions about internal stimuli such as internal feelings or specific thought patterns. The interviewer should also enquire about potential links between internal and external stimuli. For example, being with people may make a patient aware of feeling tense and a throbbing sensation in the head, which makes him have the thought that something has been implanted in his head.

Particular attention should be paid to chains of stimuli and responses, especially where these relate to misidentification or misattribution, such as misattribution of physical sensations or misidentification of noises or olfactory cues. For example, physical sensations of anxiety and stress can be misattributed to the effect of poison being administered by neighbours. In addition, the interviewer should ask about situations which the patient finds stressful, including situations which are characterised by deficits or absence of purposeful behaviour such as periods of inactivity or insomnia.

When the patient is in remission and staying well is the goal, details regarding prodromal symptoms of previous episodes should be investigated. Prodromal symptoms typically include non-specific symptoms, such as anxiety, low mood and insomnia, followed by a feeling of a loss of control and disruption to normal functioning. The interviewer should obtain the chronological progression of symptoms that makes up the individual's prodrome. Scales to tap the specific characteristics of a prodrome are available and can be helpful in this assessment (e.g., Birchwood *et al.* 1989).

Consequences

The interviewer should enquire about the consequences of the symptoms. These can be areas of long-term behavioural change such as severe avoidance, social withdrawal, isolation and loneliness; also, the consequences of persistent symptoms and psychotic disability can be impeded goal achievement, poor employment prospects, restricted social networks and deprivation. Enquiries should also be made about behaviour that protects or encourages particular types of thought or attitudes, such as would support delusional thinking or acting in a way that reinforces negative self-esteem.

Special attention should be given to feelings of depression in combination with hopelessness and the presence of suicidal ideation. These may occur in the context of a failure to be able to achieve previously-held aspirations, hopes and goals, and may be accompanied by a strong sense of loss, low self-worth and inability to break out of a desperate situation. Suicidal thoughts frequently arise as a result of perceiving the illness as a negative situation which is hopeless, from which rescue and escape is perceived as improbable. The interviewer should also be aware of the consequences of trauma and life events – the potentially stigmatising effects of mental illness and the effects on the patient's self-esteem.

There is also the opportunity here to establish reactions to the psychotic experience that may feed back and maintain the psychosis. This line of enquiry is particularly important and can include behaviour change that further exposes the patient to stressful or difficult situations, such as exposure to arguments or hostile social situations, increased inactivity or disengagement, and biased and confirmatory beliefs about their experience. Here it is useful to ask about how they interpret their experience and why it has happened, or what they make of the voices or how they think about themselves, particularly in terms of their own self-worth.

Coping

Having established a comprehensive picture of what the patient experiences and how it affects them, it is now important to find out about how they cope with the situation. What strategies are used to manage their psychotic experiences or the emotional consequences? The therapist should be aware of opportunities to implement positive coping skills which are not utilised: for example, the EBAC cycle may maintain maladaptive beliefs about a psychotic experience but the opportunities to reality-test or disconfirm these beliefs may not be exploited. The therapist should be alerted to any feelings of hopelessness indicated by a failure to use previously successful coping strategies, or a sense of abandoning the effort to cope, as these signs could indicate increased despondency and suicide risk. The therapist should be alerted to such signs of giving up.

It is also useful to evaluate how successful the coping method is. This can be done by ranking the coping strategy on a three-point scale: 0 = no or little use or moderately effective for a very short time; 1 = moderately effective for a reasonable time or very effective for a short time; and 2 = very effective for an extended period of time.

Based upon the information obtained through this interview a formulation can be developed which builds a picture of how the patient's psychosis is being maintained or exacerbated. This formulation is used collaboratively to develop a treatment strategy. It is important to conceptualise the formulation as an individualised assessment from which an individualised strategic plan is developed to bring about the agreed changes to the patient's life.

COGNITIVE-BEHAVIOURAL INTERVENTION

Because of the potential complexity of treating psychosis there is a general progression in the strategic therapeutic process. The therapist needs to be aware of and deal with any potential compromise to engagement throughout treatment. A situation may occur in which the patient is unable to collaborate in identifying problems and proceeding to a formulation because they are too disturbed or the beliefs are too entrenched. In these cases a pragmatic solution is likely to be the most tenable – the therapist agrees to treat the patient's high level of distress or temper their inappropriate behaviour, so that there is some resolution of the problem. Often a decrease in distress and arousal is accompanied by a decrease in symptoms and thus an opportunity to improve engagement and collaboration.

There is a wide range of cognitive-behavioural techniques available to the therapist during the development of an intervention strategy. These involve methods that can bring about benefit through a change in behaviour, and both top-down and bottom-up cognitive processes. It is probable that these intervention strategies are most effective when they are event-specific, that is, when they are linked to an undesirable or problematic experience, such as EBAC cycles. Interventions include: strategies aimed at changing cognitive processes such as attention by means of attention switching or narrowing; strategies to re-direct processing or behaviour through change in meta-cognitive process or self-instruction; and strategies to change interpretation or appraisal through a process of re-evaluation, challenging cognitive content or hypothesis testing through behavioural experiments and reality testing. Because of the frequent occurrence of hyperarousal, patients can be instructed in targeted methods to cope with, and reduce, high levels of arousal.

The identification of EBAC cycles allows the therapist to help the patient to examine their beliefs and behaviour in a strategic manner. They are made aware that inappropriate beliefs are reinforced and confirmed by their own actions, and that this cycle serves to maintain their psychotic experiences. For example, the man who views the other attendees at the day centre as threatening and dangerous and who avoids contact with them does not learn that these people are quite harmless and are in fact friendly. The woman who believes her neighbours are poisoning her with x-rays because she has strange and unpleasant feelings every time she sees them does not learn that this is the result of an incorrect series of beliefs and misattributions. She becomes stressed and anxious in their presence because of past conflicts and misinterprets her physical sensations of anxiety as the consequence of poisonous x-rays. Her perception of their reaction to her past belligerence is misattributed to malevolent intention on their part. Such maintenance cycles are common and the case formulation approach is an ideal method for identifying their occurrence.

Therapists frequently face the choice of whether to try to modify the content of hallucinations or delusions or the attentional processes that these phenomena have captured. In practice, these two therapeutic tactics can work together. Initial modification of attentional processes, through attention switching for example, can decrease the emotional impact of the experience. A similar effect can be produced by attending to the physical characteristics of a hallucination rather than to the voice content. This distancing from the emotional impact allows a tolerance of experience to develop without the necessity to implement escape, avoidance or safety behaviours. This can in turn provide an opening to challenge the truth of the content of the voice or delusional thought, and also provide a sense of control over these experiences. Take, for example, a young man who is experiencing voices that accuse him of having committed a murder and that also say he is Russian. Initially, he can be taught to turn his attention away from the voices in a systematic way to reduce their emotional impact. This technique can be used to elicit a sense of control and to challenge the belief that the voices are all-powerful – a process of reappraisal. He can then evaluate the statement that he is Russian by examining the evidence for and against this statement, and he can be guided to the conclusion that as he is not Russian the voices are incorrect. Later he can challenge the content of the voices that accuse him of murder by investigating the objective evidence that a murder has been committed, rather than concluding that he must have committed a murder because he cannot remember not having done so. Furthermore, the untruthfulness of the voices in saying he is Russian can be used to challenge the veracity of the murder accusation; the voices had been wrong about one issue so they could be wrong about the other. Modification of cognitive process and content provides the therapist with two basic routes to intervention and the flexibility to move from one tactic to the other.

The therapist should aim to treat each symptom and to emphasise constantly which factors have previously maintained the psychotic experience and how changes in interpretation and action have reduced these experiences and their associated distress. The maintenance of treatment benefits is ensured by establishing and sustaining effective coping strategies.

Self-esteem can be a limiting factor, and it may be helpful to develop a number of strategies to enhance the patient's self-esteem. Techniques have been developed to enhance positive aspects of self-esteem (Hall and Tarrier 2003, 2004: Tarrier 2002a). Patients were asked to produce a list of 10 positive qualities or statements (two per session) that they thought pertained to them. They were then asked to rate, on a scale of 0–100 (where 0 = not at all and 100 = absolute conviction), their belief that they actually possessed this quality. Typically the strength of this belief was low. The therapist then went through the list with each patient, and for each positive quality the patient was asked to generate evidence in the form of as many real examples as possible of them actually displaying this quality. Every effort was made to make these autobiographical memories as specific as possible by linking them to time and context and describing them in detail. Patients were asked to rehearse the events mentally so as to strengthen the memory. Once this had been done the patients were asked to re-rate the strength of their belief that they possessed the quality in question. Typically the rating of belief conviction increased. Strong emphasis was placed on the fact that the patients had increased their belief in their positive characteristics and that this was the result of focusing their attention on positive examples. The principle that positive beliefs about themselves varied considerably depending on their focus of attention and elicitation of different types of memory was constantly reinforced. Patients were then set a homework exercise to monitor their behaviour over the following week and to record specific evidence to support the presence of the positive qualities in their actions. At the beginning of the next session these recorded examples were used as feedback to reinforce this process and prompt further examples. Patients were asked again to re-rate their belief, and further change was provided as evidence that positive feelings about themselves were the product of positively focused attention. The advantage of this method is that it focuses on positives, which makes it acceptable to patients (Hall, personal communication).

Social psychology evidence (Crocker and Wolfe 2001) indicates that people evaluate their self-worth based upon the domains in their life which are important to them. It is clinically helpful to ask patients which domains are important and which they consider when making self-evaluative judgements. Thus the methods described above can be embedded within the life domains that are important to each patient.

However, separate methods may be required to counter negative aspects of self-esteem which may well be independent of positive evaluations. Although its appears counterintuitive, there is good evidence that it is possible to hold both positive and negative evaluations about oneself (Barrowclough *et al.* 2003). Methods to reduce negative evaluations are less clear but may involve evaluating the evidence for any extreme negative belief and using social comparisons to evaluate these negative attributes. Patients can be asked to describe all the characteristics of an extreme negative 'archetype' and then compare themselves to this archetype, looking for evidence for and against the accuracy of this comparison. For example, a person who described herself as a bad mother would be asked to define all the negative characteristics of an archetypal bad mother and then compare herself with this archetype, including both favourable and unfavourable evidence, so as to dispute the negative appraisal, which will in all probability be a biased exaggeration.

KEEPING WELL

Lastly, treatment benefits need to be maintained and strategies worked out to deal with any deterioration or potential relapse in the future. Schizophrenia is often a relapsing condition, so this is a very real possibility in many cases. Thus the aim may be to minimise the impact of the relapse rather than expect to avoid it completely. Realistic optimism rather than denial is the best approach. Patients can be taught to identify early signs of relapse through recall of the prodromal signs and symptoms that preceded past episodes (see Birchwood *et al.* 1992). These need to be described in detail and in chronological sequence and to be distinguished from naturally occurring mood fluctuations. One way in which this can be achieved is to ask the patient to keep a diary of their mood fluctuations so that a 'normal pattern' can be established; the prodrome will be a departure from this pattern. Once a picture has been built up of what Birchwood called the patient's 'relapse signature' then an action plan can be formulated for how the patient can deal with these situations should they arise. This may involve various coping techniques and behavioural responses, or seeking help from a forewarned professional who can embark upon a previously agreed intervention plan.

CONCLUSIONS

Schizophrenia is a complex disorder in which different symptomatology, different phases, associated disorders and clinical problems present the therapist with an enormous clinical challenge. There have been considerable advances in the development of CBT in the treatment of schizophrenia, but the considerable variability both between individual patients and within an individual patient at different times requires that treatments need to be individually designed. The case formulation approach is the most likely to achieve this understanding of each patient's circumstances and advance clinical and research endeavours.

NOTE

1   Effect sizes were calculated by subtracting the mean of the control group at posttreatment from that of the CBT group and dividing the result by the standard deviation of the control group.

REFERENCES

Barrowclough, C. *et al.* (2001). Randomised controlled trial of motivational interviewing and cognitive behavioural intervention for schizophrenia patients with associated drug or alcohol misuse. *American Journal of Psychiatry* 158: 1706–13.

Barrowclough, C. *et al.* (2003). Self esteem in schizophrenia: The relationships between self evaluation, family attitudes and symptomatology. *Journal of Abnormal Psychology* 112: 92–7.

Birchwood, M. *et al.* (1989). Predicting relapse in schizophrenia: The development and implementation of an early signs monitoring system using patients and families as observers. *Psychological Medicine* 19: 649–656.

Birchwood, M. *et al.* (1992). Early intervention. In M. Birchwood and N. Tarrier (eds) *Innovations in the Psychological Management of Schizophrenia: Assessment, Treatment and Services.* Chichester, UK: Wiley.

Birchwood, M. *et al.* (2000). The power and omnipotence of voices: Subordination and entrapment by voices and significant others. *Psychological Medicine* 30: 337–44.

Birchwood, M. *et al.* (2004). Interpersonal and role related schema influence the relationship with the dominant 'voice' in schizophrenia: A comparison of three models. *Psychological Medicine* 34: 1571–80.

Bogels, S. and Tarrier, N. (2004). Unexplored issues and future directions in social phobia research. *Clinical Psychology Review* 24: 731–6.

Bolton, C. *et al.* (2006). Developing psychological perspectives of suicidal behaviour and risk in people with a diagnosis of schizophrenia: We know they kill themselves but do we understand why? *Submitted for publication.*

Buchanan, A. (1996). *Compliance with Treatment in Schizophrenia* (Maudsley Monographs No. 37). Hove, UK: Psychological Press.

Caldwell, C. B. and Gottesman, I. I. (1990). Schizophrenics kill themselves too: A review of risk factors for suicide. *Schizophrenia Bulletin* 16: 571–89.

Carrigan, M. H. and Randall, C. L. (2003). Self-medication in social phobia: A review of the alcohol literature. *Addictive Behaviors* 28: 269–84.

Chapple, B. *et al.* (2004). Correlates of victimisation amongst people with psychosis. *Social Psychiatry and Psychiatric Epidemiology* 39: 836–40.

Cohen, J. (1988). *Statistical Power Analysis for the Behavioural Sciences* (rev. edn). New York: Academic Press.

Cormac, I. *et al.* (2004). Cognitive behaviour therapy for schizophrenia (Cochrane Review). In *The Cochrane Library* (Issue 2). Chichester, UK: John Wiley and Sons, Ltd.

Cosoff, S. J. and Hafner, R. J. (1998). The prevalence of comorbid anxiety in schizophrenia, schizoaffective disorder and bipolar disorder. *Australian and New Zealand Journal of Psychiatry* 32: 67–72.

Crocker, J. and Wolfe, C. T. (2001). Contingencies of self-worth. *Psychological Review* 108: 593–623.

Drake, R. J. *et al.* (2004). The evolution of insight, paranoia and depression during early schizophrenia. *Psychological Medicine* 34: 285–92.

Frame, L. and Morrison, A. P. (2001). Causes of posttraumatic disorder in psychotic patients. *Archives of General Psychiatry* 58: 305–6.

Garety, P. A. *et al.* (2001). A cognitive model of the positive symptoms of psychosis. *Psychological Medicine* 31: 189–95.

Gelder, M. *et al.* (2001). *Shorter Oxford Textbook of Psychiatry* (4th edn). Oxford, UK: Oxford University Press.

Greenfield, S. F. *et al.* (1994). Childhood sexual abuse in first episode psychosis. *British Journal of Psychiatry* 164: 831–4.

Gumley, A. *et al.* (2003). A randomised trial of targeted cognitive behavioural therapy in schizophrenia: Effects on relapse at 12 months. *Psychological Medicine* 33: 419–31.

Haddock, G. *et al.* (1999). Scales to measure dimensions of hallucinations and delusions: The Psychotic Symptom Rating Scales (PSYRATS). *Psychological Medicine* 29: 879–90.

Haddock, G. *et al.* (2003). Randomised controlled trial of cognitive-behavior therapy and motivational intervention for schizophrenia and substance use: 18 month, carer and economic outcomes. *British Journal of Psychiatry* 183: 418–26.

Hall, P. H. and Tarrier, N. (2003). The cognitive-behavioural treatment of low self-esteem in psychotic patients: A pilot study. *Behaviour Research and Therapy* 41: 317–32.

Hall, P. L. and Tarrier, N. (2004). The durability of a cognitive behavioural intervention for self-esteem in psychosis: Effects from a pilot study at 12 month follow-up. *Behavioural and Cognitive Psychotherapy* 32: 117–21.

Kane, J. (1996). Treatment resistant schizophrenic patients. *Journal of Clinical Psychiatry* 57 (suppl. 9): 35–40.

Kingsep, P. *et al.* (2003). Cognitive behavioural group treatment for social anxiety in schizophrenia. *Schizophrenia Research* 63: 121–9.

Lewis, S. W. *et al.* (2002). Randomised controlled trial of cognitive-behaviour therapy in early schizophrenia: Acute phase outcomes. *British Journal of Psychiatry* 181 (suppl. 43): 91–7.

McGorry, P. D. *et al.* (1991). Posttraumatic stress disorder following recent-onset psychosis: An unrecognised postpsychotic syndrome. *Journal of Mental Disorders* 179: 253–8.

Morrison, A. P. *et al.* (2004). Cognitive therapy for the prevention of psychosis in people at ultra-high risk: Randomised controlled trial. *British Journal of Psychiatry* 185: 291–7.

Mueser, K. T. and Berenbaum, H. (1990). Psychodynamic treatment of schizophrenia: Is there a future? *Psychological Medicine* 20: 253–62.

Mueser, K. T. *et al.* (1998). Trauma and posttraumatic stress disorder in severe mental illness. *Journal of Consulting and Clinical Psychology* 66: 493–9.

National Institute for Clinical Excellence (2003). *Schizophrenia: Core Interventions in the Treatment and Management of Schizophrenia in Primary and Secondary Care.* London: National Institute for Clinical Excellence.

Neria, Y. *et al.* (2002). Trauma exposure and posttraumatic stress disorder in psychosis: Findings from a first-admission cohort. *Journal of Consulting and Clinical Psychology* 70: 246–51.

Pilling, S. *et al.* (2002). Psychological treatments in schizophrenia: I. Meta-analysis of family interventions and cognitive behaviour therapy. *Psychological Medicine* 32: 763–82.

Seedat, S. *et al.* (2003). Linking posttraumatic stress disorder and psychosis. *Journal of Nervous and Mental Disease* 191: 675–81.

Shaw, K. *et al.* (2002). The aetiology of posttraumatic reactions to psychotic illness. *Journal of Traumatic Stress* 15: 39–47.

Silverstone, P. H. (1991). Low self esteem in different psychiatric conditions. *British Journal of Clinical Psychology* 30: 185–8.

Stein, M. B. *et al.* (2001). Social anxiety disorder and the risk of depression: A prospective community study of adolescents and young adults. *Archives of General Psychiatry* 58: 251–6.

Tarrier, N. (2002a). The use of coping strategies and self-regulation in the treatment of psychosis. In A. Morrison (ed) *A Casebook of Cognitive Therapy for Psychosis.* Cambridge, UK: Cambridge University Press.

Tarrier, N. (2002b). Yes, cognitive behaviour therapy may well be all you need. *British Medical Journal* 324: 291–2.

Tarrier, N. (2005). Cognitive-behaviour therapy for schizophrenia: A review of development, evidence and implementation. *Psychotherapy and Psychosomatics* 74: 136–44.

Tarrier, N. and Wykes, T. (2004). Is there evidence that cognitive behaviour therapy is an effective treatment for schizophrenia: A cautious or cautionary tale? (invited essay). *Behaviour Research and Therapy* 42: 1377–401.

Tarrier, N. *et al.* (2004). Suicide risk in recent onset schizophrenia: The influence of clinical, social, self-esteem and demographic factors. *Social Psychiatry and Psychiatric Epidemiology* 39: 927–37.

Chapter 9

Bipolar disorders

Steven Jones

PREVALENCE AND SEVERITY

Research into the psychology of bipolar disorder has, until recently, been neglected, in spite of it being a severe, chronic psychiatric illness. It is associated with high rates of self-harm and suicide; a recent study of 648 bipolar patients identified 34% as having a history of suicide attempts (Leverich *et al.* 2003). Co-morbid substance abuse (Strakowski *et al.* 2000) and personality disorder (George *et al.* 2003) are also significant features of bipolar presentation; both of these factors are associated with greater morbidity and risk of self-harm (Leverich *et al.* 2003). In contrast to the large number of studies of psychological treatment in schizophrenia (reviewed recently by Pilling *et al.* 2002), such studies in bipolar disorder have been less common.

In addition, it is only in the last 10 years that the importance of psychological, and particularly cognitive behavioural, treatment has been recognised for bipolar disorder. There are probably a number of reasons for this, not least a number of clinical myths concerning this disorder. As Scott has noted, the assumption that bipolar disorder is a genetic/biological illness, with a relatively benign presentation between episodes, had led to medication being seen as the mainstay of treatment (Scott 1995). However, medication is not adequate on its own. A 1990 National Institute of Mental Health (NIMH) report noted that 40% of individuals treated with lithium did not experience a significant improvement in clinical state or relapse risk (Prien and Potter 1990). The same report noted that an individual with a bipolar disorder diagnosis could expect to lose 12 years of normal health and die 9 years younger than average. Other reports have concurred that many bipolar patients continue to relapse despite prophylactic lithium treatment (Burgess *et al.* 2001; Solomon *et al.* 1995). Post and colleagues dramatically illustrated this in their recent study of 258 bipolar patients who completed detailed mood ratings for a year. They spent an average of 44% of the year either depressed or manic. Moreover, 63% of patients in this study had four or more mood episodes per year. These figures were despite 'comprehensive pharmacological treatment' including lithium and newer prophylactic compounds such as lamotrigine (Post *et al.* 2003).

Given that it is a severe, common and under-treated illness, the NIMH report referred to above called for the development of effective psychosocial interventions for the treatment of bipolar disorder (Prien and Potter 1990). Since then there has been rapid development of psychological treatment approaches for this disorder, as will be described later. This chapter will briefly describe the rationale for a psychological approach to bipolar disorder before introducing a clinical heuristic as a context within which to appreciate the clinical examples and case formulations that follow. Key features of the assessment and therapy process with bipolar clients will be described. Potential pitfalls in therapy will be noted and possible solutions identified.

STRESS-VULNERABILITY ISSUES

The stress-vulnerability approach to psychiatric illness assumes that the individual has an inherent vulnerability which is impacted upon by life events and other sources of stress. The extent of the vulnerability and the amount of stress interact to determine whether and when that individual experiences a period of illness. If this approach is to have merit for bipolar disorder it is necessary to demonstrate that non-biological factors have an impact on illness course and onset. Numerous studies have now reported that life events are associated with onset of both manic and depressed episodes (Ambelas 1987; Christensen et al. 2003; Dunner et al. 1979). Studies of family atmosphere have also indicated that relapses of manic and depressive symptoms are associated with high levels of expressed emotion (Butzlaff and Hooley 1998; Rosenfarb et al. 2001). In addition to these psychosocial factors, there is evidence that bipolar episodes are also associated with disruptions of circadian functioning. Thus, sleep disruption has been noted as a factor in mania in particular (Leibenluft et al. 1996; Wehr et al. 1987), and numerous markers of circadian instability have been reported for bipolar patients during episodes (Millar et al. 2004; Teicher 1995; Wolff et al. 1985).

AN INSTABILITY HEURISTIC FOR UNDERSTANDING BIPOLAR DISORDER

Instability has long been proposed as a key feature of bipolar disorder (Goodwin and Jamison 1990). For the purposes of developing psychological treatment approaches, the issue of instability has been integrated into relatively simple vulnerability-stress models such as that presented in Figure 9.1 (Lam et al. 1999). This indicates that social routine, sleep and life events interact with biological vulnerability to cause circadian disruption. These in combination then trigger a prodromal stage. The manner in which the

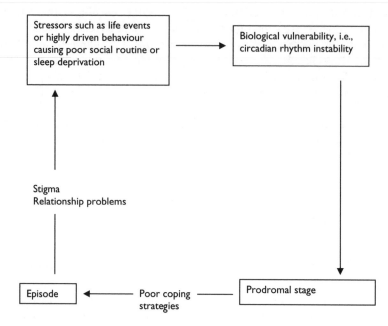

Figure 9.1 Vulnerability-stress model (following Lam *et al.* 1999).

individual deals with this prodromal stage is a key determinant of whether or not an episode develops.

More recently this model has been extended to consider more closely how the disruption of circadian functioning might lead to the observed symptoms of bipolar disorder (Jones 2001). This model builds on the work of Healy and Williams (1989) and integrates circadian approaches with a multilevel model of emotion, based on the SPAARS (schematic propositional associative and analogical representation systems) model (Power and Dalgleish 1997). A particular feature of this approach is that it implies that it may be the individual's interpretation of circadian disruption, as much as the disruption itself, that is crucial in the development of illness episodes. Circadian rhythms are indicated by patterns of behavioural and physiological activity that cycle over an approximately 24-hour light/dark period. Disruption of such rhythms is deemed to occur when these patterns become less strongly entrained to the 24-hour period. When such disturbances of circadian functioning occur the individual will initially tend to experience dysphoria, fatigue and possibly problems with attention and concentration. These are commonly recognised as features of jet-lag following travel across different time zones. When circadian rhythm disruption is more severe the individual can experience feelings of increased arousal, energy and alertness. Under normal circumstances changes of this type would be expected to be self-correcting. However, when the individual tends to make stable internal attributions for the initial physiological changes associated with circadian disruption there is a risk of prodrome exacerbation. Specifically, there will be an increased tendency to engage with the initial changes in mood and behaviour and therefore increase the impact of the initial disruption.

A multilevel model of emotion also encompasses other important clinical features of bipolar disorder. First, it identifies that there is more than one route to mood change. Thus, although cognition plays an important role it is not the sole determinant of mood change. Another important route high- lighted in SPAARS is the associative route to emotion. This associative level of processing is accessed by experience and salience rather than language. As this level is directly related to emotional outputs it is likely to have a powerful effect on emotion. In bipolar disorder this link has been proposed through Post's kindling/sensitisation hypothesis (Post and Weiss 1989; Post *et al.* 1982; Post *et al.* 1986), which argues that later illness episodes are more readily triggered by lower levels of psychosocial disruption, as the individual has already acquired associative links between such events and previous episodes. A multilevel model is also important as it captures the conflicting emotions which are a key feature of bipolar disorder – often the combination of 'feeling' something is right and 'knowing' something is wrong.

A heuristic to summarise the potential relevance of this approach in clinical terms is described in Figure 9.2. This indicates that the ways in which the bipolar patient responds to and interprets instability is crucial. A relation- ship is proposed between this process and a number of psychological and social factors associated with the disorder, all of which are based on available research evidence. The heuristic suggests that sensitivity to circadian disrup- tion is associated with frequent physiological fluctuation, which is in itself associated initially with dysphoric mood. A further proposal is that internal attributions are made for the instability caused by these fluctuations. This could be seen as leaving the bipolar patient in a situation of uncertainty, both with respect to mood and physiology, and hence struggling to evaluate situ- ations objectively. More specifically, the heuristic proposes specific reactions

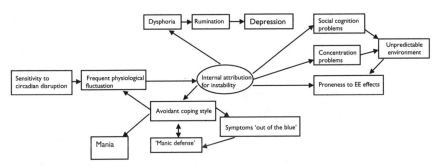

Figure 9.2 An instability heuristic for understanding bipolar disorder.

which have been noted clinically and for which some research evidence exists. Two coping styles are indicated in response to this instability:

1 An avoidant coping style, in which initial changes are ignored or colluded with until mood change is too significant to avoid and most likely to be associated with mania. This is consistent with research on prodromes (Lam and Wong 1997; Lam *et al.* 2001) which reported substantial variability in individuals' responses to early signs of mood change, including responses which could be defined as avoidant, which were associated with poorer outcomes. Furthermore, a study of individuals at risk of bipolar disorder (high scorers on a measure of trait hypomania) reported an increased likelihood of an avoidant approach to mood changes in those at increased risk (Thomas and Bentall 2002). This style is also consistent with research by Bentall and colleagues suggesting that, especially during elevated mood, bipolar patients strive to process information in a manner which protects against low self-esteem (Lyon *et al.* 1999).

2 There is evidence for the contrasting ruminative style in affective disorders in general (Nolen-Hoeksema 1991, 2000) and also in healthy but high risk individuals (Thomas and Bentall 2002) more strongly associated with depression.

The pattern of uncertainty referred to above can be expected to impact on the processing of both social and non-social information. The former is indicated by evidence of social cognition deficits in bipolar individuals (Scott and Pope 2003; Scott *et al.* 2000), while other researchers have identified deficits in information processing (Green *et al.* 1994; Neuchterlein *et al.* 1991; Serper 1993). Instability, dysphoria and social cognition deficits would also be consistent with research findings which indicate vulnerability to family atmosphere, specifically high expressed emotion (Miklowitz *et al.* 1988). This suggests, then, that the bipolar individual is presented with demands associated with an unpredictable environment, an unstable internal environment, fragile self-esteem, ready distraction from focal tasks and vulnerability to exacerbations of early mood change. This indicates the importance of a comprehensive approach to bipolar disorder which seeks to address both instability itself and also responses to this through work on thoughts, assumptions and coping strategies.

HOW DOES TREATING BIPOLAR DISORDER DIFFER FROM OTHER DISORDERS?

For most disorders the rationale for therapy is self-evident to the client. A person who is depressed, anxious or worried will normally request therapeutic help to remove the core symptoms of their conditions which are interfering with their lives. Many bipolar clients will enter therapy when either remitted or mildly depressed. They will often say that they wish to have help with improving their mood and may well also want to avoid having episodes which lead to hospitalisation. However, as Post among others has demonstrated (Post *et al.* 2003), the majority of people with bipolar disorder spend relatively short periods in mania (compared with depression) during their illness course. Thus, many clients wish to address depression with a view to achieving hypomania which does not tip into depression. This is understandable since many clients' experience is of optimism, creativity and often objective improvement in functioning in the initial stages of hypomania, but clients tend to ignore the evidence that such mood states are often associated with an ascent into mania with significant consequences to work, family and social life both at the time and once mood has stabilised. Until this pattern is clear to the individual client it is reasonable to expect ambivalence. A feature of this work, therefore, is ensuring that the rationale for therapy makes sense in terms of the client's own experience and on the basis of a detailed shared account of both the benefits and costs associated with elevated mood.

Another aspect of working with bipolar clients that differentiates it from work with other clients is the explicit focus on stabilising behavioural and social rhythms with a view to reducing circadian disruption. Although circadian functioning may have a role in other disorders this has not been investigated to the same degree as in bipolar disorder. In treating bipolar disorder the development of stable activity and sleep routines is associated with reductions in mood instability and with lowered risk of relapse (Lam *et al.* 2003). Another important difference with bipolar clients is that it is just as important to address positive thoughts as negative thoughts. When mood is becoming elevated the presence of positive thoughts fuels the ascent into a manic state. Often the therapist will work to address such patterns of thinking retrospectively at first. This is normally done when the client's mood is not high. The information agreed on during this work is then applied by therapist and client when mood elevations are detected. Strategies will include the client challenging their own thoughts, and also advance agreements with trusted others (including the therapist or a client's friend or partner) to flag up significant mood change and remind the client of an agreed strategy for mood reduction.

RESEARCH EVIDENCE FOR CBT

The main developments in psychological therapy for bipolar disorder have occurred since 1991 (for a detailed review see Jones 2004). In all the studies reported, psychological interventions have been delivered in conjunction with pharmacotherapy. Initial work focussed on the delivery of psychoeducation to bipolar patients, with a view to increasing knowledge about the illness and enhancing compliance with long-term medication (usually lithium). These studies had mixed results; increases in knowledge were reported in brief open trials (Soares *et al.* 1997) and controlled trials (Harvey and Peet 1991; Peet and Harvey 1991). A recent randomised controlled trial (RCT) of group psychoeducation based on CBT principles found a significant impact on relapse rates and number of episodes in treated patients both during therapy and at two-year follow-up (Colom *et al.* 2003). This psychoeducation study is also unusual in finding objective evidence of increased medication adherence in treated patients at follow-up.

To date, there have been six published reports of studies of individual cognitive behaviour therapy. A single case study described CBT with a rapid cycling bipolar patient, with mood improvements observed during the intervention period (Satterfield 1999). The first randomised controlled trial evaluated the effectiveness of an intervention based on identification of warning signs and development of action plans (Perry *et al.* 1999); this reported significant reductions in manic episodes, maintained at 18-month follow-up. More extensive CBT interventions designed to address both pro-dromal and long-term vulnerability issues in bipolar disorder have been published recently. Lam's group (Lam *et al.* 2000, 2003) found in both a pilot and large-scale RCT that CBT was associated with significantly reduced relapse risk for manic and depressed episodes. Scott and colleagues, using a similar approach, reported improvement mainly in depressive episodes (Scott *et al.* 2001).

THERAPY STRUCTURE

Given the complexity of bipolar disorder, interventions tend to be relatively long, in comparison with unipolar depression or anxiety. It is usually the case that cognitive therapy extends over 16–24 sessions over a period of approximately six months. This duration also offers the clinician the opportunity to help the client apply skills learnt across different mood states. Cognitive therapy is usually offered as an addition to psychopharmacological interventions, but it is not a 'medication compliance' intervention. The importance of developing greater stability in terms of both mood and activity will often be self-evident to the therapist at an early stage in therapy, but this will often not be a view shared by the patient. Therapists need to be aware that their sensible therapeutic suggestions can readily be viewed by clients as seeking merely to reduce their freedom and spontaneity. As indicated below, the time taken to ensure that client and therapist have a shared rationale for change will be crucial for both engagement and effective clinical outcomes.

GENERAL TREATMENT STRATEGY

There are many components to the formulation-driven cognitive behavioural treatment of bipolar disorder. In summarising a general treatment strategy, however, there are essentially four key areas:

1   Psychoeducational model: clients are educated about bipolar illness as a diathesis-stress illness. They are provided with information which indicates the interactions between stress and the onset of episodes and the ways in which cognitive behavioural strategies might be employed to reduce the likelihood of relapse.
2   Cognitive behavioural skills to cope with prodromes: clients learn to monitor and rate their mood to increase their skills in identifying what normal mood fluctuation is. Once a clear understanding of normal variation is obtained the client then works on detecting mood fluctuations which are outside this normal range (clinical mood change). The detection of clinical mood change is crucial for the recognition of prodromes. Clients identify changes in mood and behaviour which represent early warning signs for depression or mania. This will include self-ratings and information from trusted friends or partners. Once such signs are identified the client and therapist develop a programme of strategies to intervene to prevent progression into full clinical episodes.
3   Importance of routine and sleep: as noted already, bipolar episodes are associated with disruptions to sleep and routines in many clients. It is therefore an important aspect of therapy to work with the client to achieve increased stability in both of these areas. Research suggests that CBT does lead to greater stability of sleep and routines through the use of activity schedules and targets and through identifying the relationships between instability and disruptions of mood.
4   Dealing with long-term vulnerabilities: particular themes for bipolar clients include a high need for autonomy and extreme achievement-driven behaviour. This can lead to risk of future relapse through clients overworking, trying to make up for time lost in illness and setting unachievable standards. Later sessions can be used to explore these issues and to test out less rigid beliefs.

The majority of clients will enter therapy in remission or suffering from subsyndromal symptoms. The basic structure above will apply to clients of this type; the evidence base for cognitive therapy has not as yet extended to the treatment of clients who are acutely ill at entry into therapy. However, the instability inherent in bipolar disorder means that most clients will experience significant changes in mood state during intervention. When it is clear that mood is heading towards depression or mania then treatment priorities will be different.

Common features of treating the depressed bipolar client:

1   Activity scheduling to increase range and balance of activities: when mood is low there is, as with unipolar depression, a tendency to withdraw from normal activities. The client will often report that activities require more effort and are less pleasurable than when euthymic. However, it is often possible to illustrate that maintaining activity at a reasonable level leads to better mood than withdrawal. This then serves as a rationale to continue making the effort required to engage in tasks even while they are rated as less pleasurable than normal.

2   Moderation of external stressors: low mood and depression make dealing with planning and decision-making harder. Clients report having less confidence and also that their thinking feels slower and less clear. It is therefore appropriate to plan with clients how to moderate exposure to stressful situations. Thus, while the therapist would commonly encourage a client to continue working (or other normal activities) if possible, it would often be inappropriate to work at normal levels of intensity. Thus the aim is for the client to understand that while working late and making major strategic decisions may not be appropriate at this stage, continuing to engage with routine tasks will still often be possible.

3   Accessing support from social network: mood recovery is often greatly facilitated by the support of friends or family. Where this support is available the client may need to work to overcome initial resistance to engage with others as mood deteriorates. However, it is often possible to illustrate from the individual's own symptom history that maintaining a basic level of social engagement can lead to improvement rather than further decline in mood.

4   Taking an active approach to challenging negative thoughts and assumptions: as mood deteriorates the client will be bombarded by negative thoughts. These may already have been identified but will have greater impact and intensity at this stage. Active work within sessions to challenge these thoughts will be important. It will, in particular, be useful to identify thoughts and beliefs which are likely to interfere with engagement with points 1–3 above, and then address broader issues as mood begins to improve.

Common features of treating the hypomanic client:

1   Reducing the range and intensity of activity: in the early stages of hypomania many clients will want to do more and more. They will find it easier to work longer hours both on work tasks and on other projects or schemes which might inspire them. Putting limits on this can help prevent the initial mood elevation from progressing to mania. However, this is most successful when information has already been identified from the

client's history which they agree shows the importance of avoiding manic relapse (often in terms of previous consequences for themselves or those close to them).

2   Restabilising sleep routines: sleep disturbance is a common early sign of mood change. This can be quite subtle initially, with many clients finding that one or two hours less sleep can be associated with mood changes. Caught early, clients can often restabilise sleep patterns if they see a rationale for prioritising this. In the early stages of mood change the sleep disruption can be associated with thoughts about new projects and impulses to not waste time. Where a pattern of sleep disruption has already been developed it can be useful to discuss whether sleep medication taken when necessary for a brief period might be useful to break the cycle of sleep disturbance.

3   Negotiating agreements to defer impulsive actions with potentially serious consequences: this can be difficult with clients whose mood is already elevated. However, the aim here is to try to encourage the client not to act on major decisions while in an elevated mood state. The rationale for this will be developed through guided discovery based on the client's own history.

4   Challenging positive automatic thoughts and beliefs: the process for challenging positive thoughts is similar to the more familiar work with negative thoughts. The therapist works with the client towards a more balanced appraisal of situations rather than appraisal based on partial biased evidence driven by current mood state.

5   Using social networks to support 'normalising' of behaviour: the identification of trusted partners, carers or clinical professionals who can provide support in restabilising behaviour can be important. There are often individuals who the client will trust to feed back about current mood state and behaviour as the client attempts to address hypomanic symptoms through the approaches outlined above.

ASSESSMENT AND FORMULATION

Given the complexity of bipolar disorder, a number of factors need to be borne in mind during the initial assessment and engagement process. First, the assessment (and subsequent therapy) must be carried out in a spirit of guided discovery. It is also important to collaborate in identifying therapy goals, while also respecting the client's need for autonomy. Beck (1983) proposed that bipolar disorder might be characterised by oscillations between sociotropy and autonomy as people move from depressed to manic states. Clinically, however, the autonomy element appears to predominate in the remitted phase of the illness (Lam *et al.* 1999).

More recent research has also reported that elevated behavioural activation system activity is found in both bipolar individuals and those at high risk (Johnson *et al.* 2000; Meyer *et al.* 1999). These findings concur with clinical observations reported elsewhere (Lam *et al.* 1999) that many bipolar patients presenting for treatment aspire to an autonomous, perfectionistic, striving approach to life. Such individuals therefore need to establish that important issues for therapy come from their own experience and make sense in terms of their own priorities. Clinically, experience indicates that the presence of any sort of didactic approach early in therapy will lead to failure to engage.

A clinical example will illustrate some of the features typical of many individuals with bipolar disorder. Peter is a man with a history of striving, which has met with mixed success. He has ambivalent feelings about attending for psychological therapy and at assessment appeared to have a primarily biological model of his illness.

Peter is a 35-year-old man who has experienced several affective episodes. He was an only child who was aware while growing up of how important it was for him to succeed. Peter recalls worrying from an early age about whether or not he was good enough. He has always had a close but argumentative relationship with his mother. His father has tended to be more distant, but was pleased when Peter did well at school, and later when he took over the family business. Peter worked hard at school and did well. He had trouble concentrating at times, but re-doubled his efforts when he noticed this.

He was expected to go to university, but unexpectedly left home at 18 to travel. Peter explained to the therapist that he had done this because he could not face the strain of further exams, as he could not bear the risk of possible failure. This caused a family rift for several years until he returned to work for the family firm and 'proved' himself again. Peter's mood problems have caused some problems with his work and home life. He has on occasion acted impulsively both financially and in his business relationships. Although the business has survived this, there have been substantial debt problems and periods of high staff turnover.

He first became ill when he was 28 years old, when his mood was significantly elevated. He was living with his wife during this period. They broke up two years ago after a second episode of elevated mood, which was diagnosed as hypomania. Peter now lives at home with his parents. He has a four-year-old son, who he has not seen since the relationship broke down. He speaks occasionally with his ex-wife on the telephone, but they have a poor relationship. He runs his own small business which he developed from his father's firm, which he left five years ago. He works long hours and travels internationally seeking out new clients. He can find this difficult, and is aware that it has a significant impact on his sleep patterns. He is not sure whether this regular travel contributes to some of his periods of illness.

He has in the past used cocaine and alcohol to excess. He claims that this has mainly been due to work stress and he feels under great pressure to grow the business to demonstrate to his family and himself that he is a success. He does also acknowledge that at times he has used drugs to try to bring on a hypomanic state, which he enjoys. He denies having done this in the last six months. In addition to his two periods of mania, Peter has also experienced depression, although he has not been hospitalised as a result of this. Peter understands from his psychiatrist that he needs to remain on lithium for the rest of his life, as he suffers from a chemical imbalance. Peter is therefore unsure about the role of psychological treatment for his condition. He has presented for therapy because his psychiatrist thought it would be a good idea and because he wants to get back in touch with his son.

As Peter was entering into therapy when neither manic nor depressed, the overarching aim of the intervention was relapse prevention. Life chart information indicated that his illness course was characterised by periods of depression with more recent periods of mania and hypomania. These appear to have been closely related to stressful life events. A formulation was developed to illustrate the interactions between events, thoughts, beliefs and episodes to provide a rationale for intervention. The intention was to develop relapse prevention skills through psychoeducation, stabilising of mood and activity, thought challenge and addressing risk factors associated with dysfunctional beliefs. As noted previously, the relative emphasis of the intervention would depend on Peter's mood-state. Should he become more depressed then priority would be given to mood-enhancing approaches (maintaining reinforcing activities, challenging negative thoughts, moderating exposure to stress and maintaining engagement within social network); if there was evidence of elation then conversely priority would be given to mood-stabilising approaches (reducing involvement in stimulating activities, planning in time for non-work tasks, challenging positive thoughts and delaying key financial or business decisions).

To engage him in psychological therapy it was crucial to develop agreed life and symptom histories early on in therapy. These formed the basis of the initial clinical formulation and goal setting. In addition, they provided an opportunity for Peter to make discoveries about the relationships between social and psychological events and episodes of psychological distress.

For many people with bipolar disorder, this early experience in therapy can have profound implications. It will often be the first time that they have managed to develop an integrated chronological account of their experiences. Many patients recall events with regard to illness history in terms of their emotional salience. Although this makes some sense in psychological terms it can often leave the individual with vivid memories of apparently unconnected intense experiences. This process can then serve to reinforce their perception of life as being chaotic and of illness episodes as coming 'out of the blue'.

An initial life chart for Peter is presented in Figure 9.3. This illustrates how mood variability was a characteristic prior to the onset of his bipolar illness.

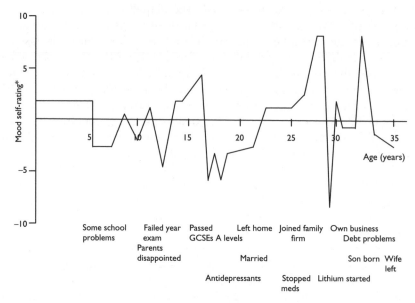

Figure 9.3 Initial life chart for Peter showing self-rated mood over time.

* Values between −5 and +5 are regarded as normal. Higher or lower values than this signify clinical mood disturbance.

It also indicates how mood fluctuation appears to be associated with relationship issues, success and failure experiences, medication and drug use.

Additional formal assessment measures are often helpful:

1   Current mood state measures include:

    a   The Beck Depression Inventory (BDI): a short, self-report measure applicable to adults and adolescents which includes questions on physical, behavioural and cognitive features of depression. Each item is rated for the preceding week and scored on a three-point scale. Score ranges are: 0–9 asymptomatic, 10–18 mild–moderate depression, 19–29 moderate–severe depression and >29 extremely severe depression (Beck and Steer 1987).

    b   The Beck Hopelessness Scale (BHS): this is again a short self-report measure. Beck reported that scores of 9 or above were significantly predictive of eventual suicide in individuals with suicidal ideas followed up over up to 10 years (Beck *et al.* 1985). Score ranges are: 0–3 normal, 4–8 mild, 9–14 moderate and >14 severe (Beck and Steer 1988).

    c   The Internal States Scale (ISS): this uses a visual analogue scale for 16 different items covering perceived conflict, activation, well-being, depression and global bipolar (Bauer *et al.* 1991).

2   The Coping with Prodromes Interview (Lam *et al.* 2001) can provide a helpful initial indication of the individual's approach to mania and depression prodromes. It allows the clinician to capture the individual nature of each person's prodromes. This information is then included in the assessment of prodromal coping as part of the cognitive therapy intervention. It can also be helpful to use a checklist of the sort developed by Smith and Tarrier (1992) to facilitate the identification of prodromal symptoms (see Table 9.1). These are particularly helpful if the client is finding it difficult to identify or articulate the symptoms which they experience.

3   The Dysfunctional Attitudes Scale (Power *et al.* 1994) provides information on sociotropy (dependence on social input) and autonomy (achievement/task focus), which have both been found to be features of many individuals with a bipolar diagnosis.

A small battery of tests can usefully be employed at each therapy session to obtain crucial clinical information in an efficient manner. These measures would normally include the BDI, the BHS and the ISS as a minimum.

Information from symptom and life histories and formal measures will form the basis for working with clients to develop both a goal list and an initial formulation. Many clients will generate a goal list which includes a combination of functional and symptom-related goals. The process of generating the formulation provides the clinician with the opportunity to work with the client to identify relationships between both functional and symptom issues, which leads to enhanced engagement. The formulation is also used to individualise the treatment protocol and to assess the relative importance of the different elements that it might contain. An example of a formulation for an episode of Peter's depressed and agitated mood is presented in Figure 9.4. Here there is a clear relationship between life events and developmental experiences and the formation of assumptions which leave Peter vulnerable to further mood episodes. Both external (friends coming late at night) and internal (sleep loss and desire for spontaneity) triggers then interact with these assumptions. Following both circadian and psychological disruption Peter identified feeling low and agitated, which he then interpreted as being to do with characteristics of himself. This then led to behaviour which colluded with the initial mood change. The end of this cycle will often be triggered by exhaustion, excessive sleep and a sense of failure, which tends to reinforce the original pattern of beliefs. Clearly a formulation of this type allows the individual to begin to see how the proposed elements of a cognitive behavioural intervention can impact on their own specific patterns of thoughts, feelings and behaviours.

Table 9.1 Checklist of possible prodromal symptoms (following Smith and Tarrier 1992)

1   Low in energy/tired[d]
2   Feeling emotionally high[m]
3   Feeling sad[d]
4   Ideas flowing too fast[m]
5   Afraid of going crazy
6   Poor appetite
7   Difficulty concentrating[d]
8   Senses seem sharper[m]
9   More talkative[m]
10 Feeling anxious[d]
11 Low in self-confidence[d]
12 Feeling creative[m]
13 Feeling irritable
14 Stronger interest in sex[m]
15 Feeling very religious[m]
16 Visual hallucinations
17 Worrying a lot
18 Energetic/very active[m]
19 Don't like seeing people[d]
20 Can't seem to get to sleep[m]
21 Spending money more freely[m]
22 Being uncooperative
23 Neglecting hygiene and appearance
24 Feeling in another world[m]
25 Thinking my thoughts are controlled
26 Can't get up in the morning[d]
27 Lots of aches and pains
28 Feeling very guilty[d]
29 Having bizarre thoughts
30 Thinking about death
31 Hearing hallucinations
32 Being uninhibited or outrageous
33 Feeling strong or powerful[m]
34 Low interest in sex[d]
35 Can't face normal tasks[d]
36 Feeling very important[m]
37 Don't need much sleep[m]
38 Nothing seems enjoyable[d]
39 Involved in many projects[m]
40 Thinking of suicide

[m] Endorsed by >70% of Smith and Tarrier (1992) sample as present in mania prodrome.
[d] Endorsed by >70% of Smith and Tarrier (1992) sample as present in the depression prodrome.

KEY FEATURES OF INTERVENTION

As noted above, CBT for bipolar disorder is best delivered on the basis of an individual formulation. However, the research conducted to date has

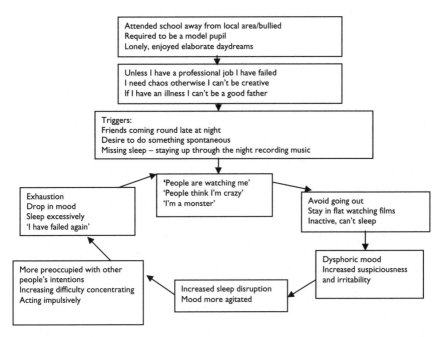

Figure 9.4 Formulation of depressed and agitated mood for Peter.

indicated that a number of features of therapy are likely to be important in reducing instability and relapse risk. These include the following.

Initial sessions

Education/development of therapeutic alliance

This provides the client with an introduction to a diathesis-stress model of bipolar disorder, often of the type outlined above (Lam *et al.* 1999). The role of thoughts and behaviour will be introduced at this stage and referred to throughout the therapy.

Individual symptom history will also be collected during initial sessions and the importance of early signs highlighted with respect to previous episodes. This then forms the basis for work in later sessions on identifying warning signs for relapse prevention. Another important aspect of early sessions is normalisation. Many individuals see themselves as having a fundamental flaw which separates them from 'normal' people. Clearly this can impede therapy and needs to be challenged at an early stage. The process of anchoring episodes in social and psychological contexts can be very important in this process. Additionally, identification of the experiences of others and the prevalence of mood episodes in the general population can also be relevant to this process.

Socialising to therapy/goal setting

As noted above, goals need to be individualised to the client. Peter's primary goals were functional (he wanted to get in touch with his son and to get on with his life) rather than symptom-focussed. They were also very broad and it was initially unclear what his motivation levels for psychological therapy were. Once the life and symptom history information is agreed it is then helpful to try to work with the client to elaborate and clarify their goals for therapy. In Peter's case this involved a collaborative approach to evaluating what contact with his son, over what time-scale, might be realistically achievable. This then led to a discussion of the circumstances which might enhance or impede progress towards this goal. From there it was possible to identify specific steps with respect to this goal. As part of this approach the importance of symptom and relapse management was addressed. Peter saw over time the relationship between mental illness issues and the frustration of his functional goals, which enhanced his engagement in the therapy process. It was also important to refer to his own history to illustrate and assess features of a vulnerability-stress model. This allowed Peter to begin to extend his view of his illness, beyond it being merely a chemical imbalance over which he had no control to something where his own reactions were important in remaining well.

Intermediate sessions

Cognitive techniques are taught, discussed and applied during this stage of therapy.

Understanding the relationship between mood and activity

The completion of mood and activity sheets is a key feature of cognitive therapy with bipolar patients. This will often begin early in therapy and continue throughout the active intervention. Many clients, although clearly very intelligent individuals, will struggle to appreciate the connections between what they do, the experiences they have and their mood. This fits with the heuristic outlined above, in which an internal attribution bias is proposed. If individuals are attributing change to features of themselves, they will not be alert to other possible explanations of mood change. It is therefore important that the therapist employs a repeated approach to guided discovery of mood–activity relationships. Single demonstrations of such patterns will be insufficient. An example is provided in Figure 9.5.

As will be evident, the forms used are adapted from standard activity scheduling forms. They differ in two main respects: first, they make provision for the recording of activity throughout a 24-hour period rather than assuming that people will be active during the day and asleep at night; second, clients record a summary assessment of mood for each day. This is rated on a −10 to +10 scale. On this scale +10 marks the most extreme positive mood ever experienced and −10 the most extreme low mood. A range of −5 to +5 is assumed to indicate the region within which normal fluctuations of mood occur.

The person illustrated here is Bill, who is a 40-year-old artist with a 20-year history of bipolar disorder. He had recently been discharged from hospital after a six-month admission following a period of severe depression. He was preoccupied with the time he had lost in hospital and was very keen to catch up now that he was back in the community. When he brought this record to therapy the following week his mood had decreased back down to +5 from a peak of +9 after exhaustion had led him to spend two days in bed. He was very disturbed about his previous elevated mood and felt that it came 'out of the blue'. By working through the information in his record it was clear that there was pattern of overwork and loss of sleep clearly associated with mood change. Once Bill was able to appreciate this association, he was amenable to discussing how he might aim for targets around sustaining long-term creative output by being alert to overdoing it in the short term. In the absence of such a personally relevant illustration of this relationship, the risk would be that Bill would merely see any such target as being restrictive and inappropriate given the importance of his work.

Challenging positive thoughts

The issue of addressing negative thinking and beliefs has been dealt with extensively elsewhere. Most bipolar individuals, even when euthymic, will present at times with patterns of negative thinking which can be addressed in the normal way, through thought records and evidence gathering. A more complex problem can be that of dealing with positive thoughts.

In the first instance the clinician needs to have a picture of when positive thoughts are associated with mood elevation and when they are merely a function of good mood. This is best done proactively when the client is not in a period of elevated mood. Reviewing periods of mood elevation, it is possible to encourage the client to identify retrospectively the thoughts associated with these periods and to use evidence to challenge them. This process can also be used to work with the client to identify the differences between thoughts during these periods and normally positive thoughts. Hypomanic positive thoughts are usually characterised by their rigidity and lack of relationship to external inputs – the evidence base for such thoughts is usually the individual's feelings rather than concrete outcomes or feedback from others. It is also usual in this process to work out with the client at what level of

WEEKLY ACTIVITY SCHEDULE

Name_____

Mood rating

(−10 to +10)	+5	+6	+8	+7	+9	+8	+9
DATE	M	T	W	Th	F	S	S
6–7am	Asleep	Got up 6.30	Asleep	Asleep	Asleep	Got up 6.30 Coffee	Asleep
7–8am	Got up/coffee	Coffee Start work	Asleep	Coffee then work	Asleep	Argument	Got up 7.30 Coffee
8–9am	Started painting new picture	Organise work for exhibition	Asleep	Call papers re: exhibition	Asleep	Work	Breakfast
9–10am	As above	Work	Asleep	Contact bank re: loan for project	Work	Work	Read papers
10–11am	As above	Work	Work on new project	Work	Work	Work	Work
11–12am	Coffee and sandwich then work	Work	Work	Work	Work	Work	Work
12–1pm	Painting	Work	Work	Work	Work	Work	Housework
1–2pm	Friend rings – short chat then work	Visit gallery re: dates	Work	Coffee	Coffee	Shopping	Housework
2–3pm	Painting	As above	Work	Work	Work	Local pub	Housework
3–4pm	Ring contact re: possible exhibition	Work	Work	Work	Work	Work	Housework
4–5pm	Painting	Work	Work	Work	Work	Work	Made tea
5–6pm	Painting	Work	John visits – seems impressed	Buy materials for work	Work	Work	Dozed

DATE	M	T	W	Th	F	S	S
6–7pm	Jim home	Friend visits – leaves so can work	Cancel mum for Thurs too busy	Miss hospital appt	Pub with Jim	Asleep	Work
7–8pm	Tea then work	Ideas for new project	Work	Argument with Jim	Went home TV	Asleep	Watched TV
8–9pm	Finish picture	As above	Watched TV – more ideas	Walked dogs	Work	Work	Work
9–10pm	Look at recent work	Ring John re: new idea – long chat	As above	Rang Bill then Sam re: ideas	Work	Work	Pub
10–11pm	Ideas for exhibition	List out ideas	Argument with Jim	Work	Argue with Jim	Supper	Pub supper
11–12pm	As above	As above	Email contacts re: project	Work	Internet	Asleep	Argument Bed 11.30
12–1am	As above	Search web for more ideas	Coffee and work	Bed	Internet	Asleep	Awake
1–2am	Bed – thinking	As above	Argument	Awake	Internet	Argument	Asleep
2–3am	As above	As above	Bed	Get up – TV	Bed – Fitful sleep	Fitful sleep	Asleep
3–4am	Asleep	Bed	Awake	Bed	Asleep	Asleep	Asleep
4–5am	Asleep	Asleep	Fitful sleep	Asleep	Asleep	Asleep	Awake
5–6am	Asleep	Asleep	Asleep	Asleep	Awake	Awake	Awake

Figure 9.5 Example activity and mood record for Bill.

mood elevation these thoughts would normally occur. This can then lead to a joint agreement between therapist and client to use challenges developed by the client when and if such thoughts recur. The client can be asked to give advance permission for the therapist or a trusted relative to raise this matter if mood change above the specified threshold occurs. The important issue is that the client's own words with respect to these thoughts are used at that point rather than those of the therapist or worried relatives.

Sometimes positive thoughts and associated mood elevation occur before it has been possible to do this work. In that situation the client will not usually have a repertoire of replies to the thoughts. It can then be helpful to see if it is possible to reach an agreement to defer decision-making. This was initially proposed by Basco and Rush (1996) and has proved to be an effective intervention. When attempting this the clinician needs to avoid directly challenging the positive thoughts, as this will only cause resistance and conflict. Instead it can be helpful to see if the client is able to recall previous periods of similar thoughts and to evaluate the outcomes in those periods. Usually the client will accept that there may have been some previous negative outcomes but will assert that this time it will different. The rationale for deferring decisions is that if they truly believe in this idea it will remain a good idea even if deferred, and that the period of deferment will potentially illustrate to others how well thought through the proposal is. Often deferring decision-making for 48 hours is sufficient for the client not to act, but also leaves it open for the client to proceed if it is still a good idea after that time.

Final sessions

Coping with prodromes

A prodrome has been defined as the interval from first recognition of symptoms to the time of maximum symptom severity (Molnar *et al.* 1988), which in a vulnerability-stress model of bipolar disorder is when an important opportunity for relapse prevention occurs.

Once the client has progressed through the earlier stages of therapy they will have skills in identifying mood fluctuations and relating these to behaviours and thoughts. They will also normally have some experience of the impact that they can have on their mood with changes which they make in thinking or in activity. This is therefore the appropriate stage at which to bring together all this information with the client to identify early warning signs (prodromes) for both mania and depression. Once such warning signs have been identified, the psychologist works with the client to identify adaptive coping approaches to reduce the risk of early mood changes leading to an episode. Research using checklist and interview approaches indicates that it is possible for bipolar clients to identify prodromes (Lam and Wong 1997; Lam *et al.* 2001; Smith and Tarrier 1992). In general individuals tend to find that mania prodromes are easier to identify, as many of the symptoms are clearer changes from 'normal' functioning.

Identifying early, middle and late prodromes

Helping the client to detect prodromes is best done with open-ended questioning to elicit both symptoms and the idiosyncratic responses which the individual associates with mood change. It is helpful to prompt the client to consider mood, behaviour and thoughts when considering signs of mood change. It is also important that such changes are anchored in the social context: issues concerned with social interaction and also the responses of others should be considered. Often the prodromal signs reported will be a combination of changes which the client picks up and those which are reported to them by friends or relatives. Once a list of prodromal signs has been identified then the card sort technique reported by Perry *et al.* (1999) is an efficient method for organising prodromes. Each symptom is written separately on a card. The client then sorts the cards into early and late symptoms, allocating middle stage symptoms by default. Once these stages have been identified the client then estimates the approximate duration of each stage. Once this has been agreed an early warning signs list is drawn up. Figure 9.6 shows Peter's three prodromal stages for a mania prodrome. In his case the entire prodromal period lasts approximately 10 days. The first stage is similar to many mania prodromes in that the 'symptoms' are not in themselves overtly problematic. It is only if the client sees these changes as part of a transition towards mania that their significance becomes apparent. By the second stage more obvious social effects are evident and alcohol use

Stage 1: Early stage (2–3 days from first onset)
Sleep less
Feel quite up and excited
Mum says I'm full of beans
Get more done than usual
Lots of plans for the future

Coping in early stage
Cut down on caffeine
Can still sleep if persist in trying
Consciously decide to slow down and pace self
Moderate exercise
Defer planning
Discuss thoughts and feelings with trusted friend (Bill)

Stage 2: Middle stage (4–5 days from first onset)
Working 12–14 hours a day
People around seem slow and boring
At home don't relax, always busy with jobs
Sleep 2–3 hours
Drink more – bottle of wine each night

Coping in middle stage
Sleep medication
Strategic withdrawal from stimulation
Challenge positive thoughts
Avoid alcohol, don't have in the house

Stage 3: Late stage (swings into full-blown mania within a day or two)
Staying out late at clubs/gambling
Buying things compulsively on credit
Racing thoughts
Can't sleep at all
Can't concentrate at work or home
Sleep less
Feel quite up and excited

Coping in late stage
See psychiatrist
Increase medication
Time off from work
Possible voluntary admission

Figure 9.6 Prodromal signs and coping strategies for Peter.

increases, and by the third stage Peter has lost much control and is on the verge of a full manic episode.

Pairing prodromes with coping skills

Once prodromes have been identified, the next task is to identify what coping approaches might best be applied at each stage. In doing this the therapist will review in some detail the coping approaches which the client has used in the past, as well as the skills developed during therapy. It is often the case that clients have previously addressed some prodromal symptoms, but either have not systematised this response or have failed to employ it because the significance of a particular symptom has been missed. When they are drawn together in this way it becomes more obvious why a coping response might be needed. The therapist and client consider each stage to identify potential coping strategies and to assess their likely effectiveness. This is done with respect to both prior experience and the effectiveness of CBT skills applied during therapy. It can be helpful here to ask the client to review previous prodromes and to visualise how they think particular approaches might have impacted on their symptoms had they applied them.

When considering coping skills and prodromes, a crucial aspect of the rationale is to help the client to maintain choice and control. Many clients will have experienced prodromes leading to episodes in which they have experienced admission to hospital, including involuntary admissions under the Mental Health Act. Even prior to this, many clients will recall having reached a stage when others were making decisions for them. This can be experienced as stressful and upsetting by the client, even if the actions were taken with the best of intentions. When the client understands that early detection of mood changes is associated with having choice and control over what happens, engagement with prodromal work is enhanced. It is important to elicit the client's views on the extent of choice or control that is available to them at each stage of the prodrome. Clients can then see that even when action is taken at the late stage of prodrome identification they can still have more choice and control than if they allow symptoms to take their course. By working through each stage in this manner, clients will be much more willing to see prodromal work as a strategy to help them to get on with their own lives, rather than an attempt to restrict and regiment their behaviour.

Long-term issues

Final sessions should allow time to consider issues that are relevant to many people with a mental health history. Shame and guilt are commonly reported by bipolar patients. This can be related to behaviours engaged in when unwell, such as running up large debts or behaving in a sexually disinhibited manner. It can also be associated with having a label of mental illness and the reactions of others to this. Clinically, I have found that the process of working in a CBT manner with individuals is helpful in addressing some of these issues. It can be helpful to review problem-solving approaches to the different difficulties associated with their own experiences, to see these issues in a balanced way. The important work that Paul Gilbert (2000) has been doing with shame can also be useful with bipolar patients. Stigma is another issue which can be helped by considering mental health problems from a CBT perspective. It cannot of course deal with the stigmatising beliefs of others, but can help individual clients to avoid adding to this problem by stigmatising themselves.

CONCLUSIONS

Bipolar disorder has only recently been studied from a psychological perspective. There is now increasing evidence for the importance of cognitive behavioural therapy in improving functioning and reducing risk of relapse. This chapter has identified a number of key aspects of cognitive therapy as applied to bipolar disorder. The targets of therapy include helping the client to stabilise routines and to deal more adaptively with mood fluctuations, although this is only effective when the client is properly engaged. The likelihood of engagement is increased by taking the time to do a full psychological assessment, which includes developing a shared account of the client's symptom and life history. This information is then configured into a formulation which is used to help guide therapy. Client and therapist work together to establish how making changes consistent with a CBT approach will help achieve important functional and symptom goals. The use of detailed mood and activity records is important in identifying mood variation and its relationship to external events. Identification of prodromes and the development of coping strategies are important aspects of CBT for bipolar disorder and apply to both mania and depression. Successful completion of CBT will include work on longer-term issues which, if left untreated, might leave the client at risk of further relapse.

RECOMMENDED READING

Colom, F. et al. (2003). A randomized trial on the efficacy of group psychoeducation in the prophylaxis of recurrences in bipolar patients whose disease is in remission. Archives of General Psychiatry 60: 402–7.

Jones, S. H. (2004). A review of psychotherapeutic interventions for bipolar disorder. Journal of Affective Disorders 80: 101–14.

Jones, S. H. et al. (2003). Coping with Bipolar Disorder (2nd edn). Oxford, UK: Oneworld.

Lam, D. *et al.* (1999). *Cognitive Therapy for Bipolar Disorder*. Chichester, UK: Wiley.

Lam, D. H. *et al.* (2003). A randomized controlled study of cognitive therapy for relapse prevention for bipolar affective disorder: Outcome of the first year. *Archives of General Psychiatry* 60: 145–52.

Smith, J. A. and Tarrier, N. (1992). Prodromal symptoms in manic depressive psychosis. *Social Psychiatry and Psychiatric Epidemiology* 27: 245–8.

REFERENCES

Ambelas, A. (1987). Life events and mania: A special relationship? *British Journal of Psychiatry* 150: 235–40.

Basco, M. R. and Rush, A. J. (1996). *Cognitive-Behavioral Therapy for Bipolar Disorder*, New York: The Guilford Press.

Bauer, M. S. *et al.* (1991). Independent assessment of manic and depressive symptoms by self-rating: Scale characteristics and implications for the study of mania. *Archives of General Psychiatry* 48: 807–12.

Beck, A. T. (1983). Cognitive therapy of depression: New perspectives. In P. J. Clayton and J. E. Barrett (eds) *Treatment of Depression: Old Controversies and New Approaches*. New York: Raven.

Beck, A. T. and Steer, R. A. (1987). *Beck Depression Inventory*. San Antonio, TX: The Psychological Corporation, Harcourt Brace.

Beck, A. T. and Steer, R. A. (1988). Beck Hopelessness Scale. San Antonio, TX: The Psychological Corporation, Harcourt Brace.

Beck, A. T. *et al.* (1985). Hopelessness and eventual suicide: A 10-year prospective study of patients hospitalized with suicidal ideation. *American Journal of Psychiatry* 142: 559–63.

Burgess, S. *et al.* (2001). Lithium for maintenance treatment of mood disorders. *Cochrane Database of Systematic Reviews* 3: CD003013.

Butzlaff, R. L. and Hooley, J. M. (1998). Expressed emotion and psychiatric relapse: A meta-analysis. *Archives of General Psychiatry* 55: 547–52.

Christensen, E. M. *et al.* (2003). Life events and onset of a new phase in bipolar affective disorder. *Bipolar Disorders* 5: 356–61.

Colom, F. *et al.* (2003). A randomized trial on the efficacy of group psychoeducation in the prophylaxis of recurrences in bipolar patients whose disease is in remission. *Archives of General Psychiatry* 60: 402–7.

Dunner, D. L. *et al.* (1979). Life events at the onset of bipolar affective illness. *American Journal of Psychiatry* 136: 508–11.

George, E. L. *et al.* (2003). The comorbidity of bipolar disorder and axis II personality disorders: Prevalence and clinical correlates. *Bipolar Disorders* 5: 115–22.

Gilbert, P. (2000). Internal 'social' conflict and the role of inner warmth and compassion in cognitive therapy. In P. G. K. C. Bailey (ed) *Genes on the Couch: Explorations in Evolutionary Psychology*. Hove, UK: Brunner-Routledge.

Goodwin, F. K. and Jamison, K. (1990). *Manic-Depressive Illness*. New York: Oxford University Press.

Green, M. F. *et al.* (1994). Backward masking in schizophrenia and mania. I. Specifying a mechanism. *Archives of General Psychiatry* 51: 939–44.

Harvey, N. S. and Peet, M. (1991). Lithium maintenance: 2. Effects of personality and attitude on health information acquisition and compliance. *British Journal of Psychiatry* 158: 200–4.

Healy, D. and Williams, J. M. (1989). Moods, misattributions and mania. An interaction of biological and psychological factors in the pathogenesis of mania. *Psychiatric Developments* 7: 49–70.

Johnson, S. L. *et al.* (2000). Increases in manic symptoms after life events involving goal attainment. *Journal of Abnormal Psychology* 109: 721–7.

Jones, S. H. (2001). Circadian rhythms, multilevel models of emotion and bipolar disorder: An initial step towards integration? *Clinical Psychology Review* 21: 1193–209.

Jones, S. (2004). Psychotherapy of bipolar disorder. *Journal of Affective Disorders* 80: 101–14.

Lam, D. and Wong, G. (1997). Prodromes, coping strategies, insight and social functioning in bipolar affective disorders. *Psychological Medicine* 27: 1091–100.

Lam, D. *et al.* (1999). *Cognitive Therapy for Bipolar Disorder: A Therapist's Guide to Concepts, Methods and Practice*. Chichester, UK: John Wiley and Sons.

Lam, D. *et al.* (2000). Cognitive therapy for bipolar illness: A pilot study of relapse prevention. *Cognitive Therapy and Research* 24: 503–20.

Lam, D. *et al.* (2001). Prodromes, coping strategies and course of illness in bipolar affective disorder: A naturalistic study. *Psychological Medicine* 31: 1397–402.

Lam, D. H. *et al.* (2003). A randomized controlled study of cognitive therapy for relapse prevention for bipolar affective disorder: Outcome of the first year. *Archives of General Psychiatry* 60: 145–52.

Leibenluft, E. *et al.* (1996). Relationship between sleep and mood in patients with rapid-cycling bipolar disorder. *Psychiatry Research* 63: 161–68.

Leverich, G. S. *et al.* (2003). Factors associated with suicide attempts in 648 patients with bipolar disorder in the Stanley Foundation Bipolar Network. *Journal of Clinical Psychiatry* 64: 506–15.

Lyon, H. M. *et al.* (1999). Social cognition and the manic defense: Attributions, selective attention, and self-schema in bipolar affective disorder. *Journal of Abnormal Psychology* 108: 273–82.

Meyer, B. *et al.* (1999). Exploring behavioral activation and inhibition sensitivities among college students at risk for bipolar spectrum symptomatology. *Journal of Psychopathology and Behavioral Assessment* 21: 275–92.

Miklowitz, D. J. *et al.* (1988). Family factors and the course of bipolar affective disorder. *Archives of General Psychiatry* 45: 225–31.

Millar, A. *et al.* (2004). The sleep of remitted bipolar outpatients: A controlled naturalistic study using actigraphy. *Journal of Affective Disorders* 80: 145–53.

Molnar, G. *et al.* (1988). Duration and symptoms of bipolar prodromes. *American Journal of Psychiatry* 145: 1576–8.

Neuchterlein, K. H. *et al.* (1991). Information-processing anomalies in the early course of schizophrenia and bipolar disorder. *Schizophrenia Research* 5: 195–6.

Nolen-Hoeksema, S. (1991). Responses to depression and their effects on the duration of depressed mood. *Journal of Abnormal Psychology* 100: 569–82.

Nolen-Hoeksema, S. (2000). The role of rumination in depressive disorders and mixed anxiety/depressive symptoms. *Journal of Abnormal Psychology* 109: 504–11.

Peet, M. and Harvey, N. S. (1991). Lithium maintenance: 1. A standard education programme for patients. *British Journal of Psychiatry* 158: 197–200.

Perry, A. *et al.* (1999). Randomised controlled trial of efficacy of teaching patients with bipolar disorder to identify early symptoms of relapse and obtain treatment. *British Medical Journal* 318: 149–53.

Pilling, S. *et al.* (2002). Psychological treatments in schizophrenia: I. Meta-analysis of family intervention and cognitive behaviour therapy. *Psychological Medicine* 32: 763–82.

Post, R. M. and Weiss, S. R. (1989). Sensitization, kindling, and anticonvulsants in mania. *Journal of Clinical Psychiatry* 50: 23–30; 45–7.

Post, R. M. *et al.* (1982). Kindling and carbamazepine in affective illness. *Journal of Nervous and Mental Disorders* 170: 717–31.

Post, R. M. *et al.* (1986). Conditioning and sensitisation in the longitudinal course of affective illness. *British Journal of Psychiatry* 149: 191–201.

Post, R. M. *et al.* (2003). Morbidity in 258 bipolar outpatients followed for 1 year with daily prospective ratings on the NIMH life chart method. *Journal of Clinical Psychiatry* 64: 680–90; 738–9.

Power, M. J. and Dalgleish, T. (1997). *Cognition and Emotion: From Order to Disorder*. Hove, UK: Psychology Press.

Power, M. J. *et al.* (1994). The Dysfunctional Attitudes Scale (DAS): A comparison of forms A and B and proposal for a new sub-scaled version. *Journal of Research in Personality* 28: 263–76.

Prien, R. F. and Potter, W. Z. (1990). N.I.M.H. workshop report on treatment of bipolar disorder. *Psychopharmacology Bulletin* 26: 409–27.

Rosenfarb, I. S. *et al.* (2001). Family transactions and relapse in bipolar disorder. *Family Processes* 40: 5–14.

Satterfield, J. M. (1999). Adjunctive cognitive-behavioral therapy for rapid-cycling bipolar disorder: an empirical case study. *Psychiatry* 62: 357–69.

Scott, J. (1995). Psychotherapy for bipolar disorder. *British Journal of Psychiatry* 167: 581–8.

Scott, J. and Pope, M. (2003). Cognitive styles in individuals with bipolar disorders. *Psychological Medicine* 33: 1081–8.

Scott, J. *et al.* (2000). Cognitive vulnerability in patients with bipolar disorder. *Psychological Medicine* 30: 467–72.

Scott, J. *et al.* (2001). A pilot study of cognitive therapy in bipolar disorders. *Psychological Medicine* 31: 459–67.

Serper, M. R. (1993). Visual controlled information processing resources and formal thought disorder in schizophrenia and mania. *Schizophrenia Research* 9: 59–66.

Smith, J. A. and Tarrier, N. (1992). Prodromal symptoms in manic depressive psychosis. *Social Psychiatry and Psychiatric Epidemiology* 27: 245–8.

Soares, J. J. F. *et al.* (1997). Psychoeducation for patients with bipolar disorder: An exploratory study. *Nordic Journal of Psychiatry* 51: 439–46.

Solomon, R. L. *et al.* (1995). Course of illness and maintenance treatments for patients with bipolar disorders. *Journal of Clinical Psychiatry* 56: 5–13.

Strakowski, S. M. *et al.* (2000). The impact of substance abuse on the course of bipolar disorder. *Biological Psychiatry* 48: 477–85.

Teicher, M. H. (1995). Actigraphy and motion analysis: New tools for psychiatry. *Harvard Review of Psychiatry* 3: 18–35.

Thomas, J. and Bentall, R. P. (2002). Hypomanic traits and response styles to depression. *British Journal of Clinical Psychology* 41: 309–13.

Wehr, T. *et al.* (1987). Sleep production as a final common pathway in the genesis of mania. *American Journal of Psychiatry* 144: 201–4.

Wolff, E. A., 3rd *et al.* (1985). Motor activity and affective illness: The relationship of amplitude and temporal distribution to changes in affective state. *Archives of General Psychiatry* 42: 288–94.

Chapter 10

Cognitive formulation in personality disorder

Kate M. Davidson

INTRODUCTION

Cognitive therapists have become adept at treating patients with Axis I disorders and some have taken up the challenge of finding effective cognitive behavioural treatments for patients with personality disorders who do not respond to the classical Beckian type of cognitive model for affective disorders. Several cognitively based approaches to treatment have emerged in the past few years, each with their own emphasis. This chapter will focus on the process of developing a cognitive formulation for borderline personality disorder. Formulation is a key component in treatment of those with personality disorders or difficulties, as it promotes engagement in therapy and guides treatment strategies and interventions.

PERSONALITY DISORDER: BRIEF OVERVIEW

Many people find the term 'personality disorder' and its classification unsatisfactory. It has been thought of as a 'dumping ground' for patients who either do not seem to fit any other diagnostic group or for those who have failed to respond to the treatment offered. As such, patients and clinicians have often objected to the use of the term 'personality disorder', as it appears to be pejorative and used as a label for those who are either unpopular or difficult to treat. One current definition of personality disorder (American Psychiatric Association 1994) suggests that the term is used as a description of those enduring characteristics of a person that impair well-being or social functioning. Psychologists tend to view personality characteristics as part of a continuum of personality functioning, rather than as discrete entities. Individuals vary in the ways in which they view themselves and others, the degree to which they engage in relationships, and the quality of these relationships, and the degree to which they cope with problems. Traits are inferred from specific responses or dispositions, and personality categories are identified when certain traits occur together in samples of many individuals. Clinicians recognise that clinical disorders cannot be isolated from the patient's longstanding style of thinking, feeling, behaving and coping. In other words, the patient's personality style is regarded as important in describing and understanding psychopathology. Personality disorder arises as a complex interaction of biological, familial and social influences, and personality disorder is really a variation or exaggeration of normal personality attributes.

Diagnostic classification systems such as *DSM-III* (American Psychiatric Association 1980) have encouraged clinicians to consider the patient's clinical symptoms and enduring personality patterns alongside each other. *DSM-IV* (American Psychiatric Association 1994) defines personality disorder as enduring patterns of cognition, affectivity, interpersonal behaviour, and impulse control that are culturally deviant, pervasive, and inflexible, and lead to distress or social impairment. Ten types or categories of personality disorder are identified and grouped into three clusters, as illustrated in Figure 10.1.

Our knowledge of what constitutes personality disorder has undergone considerable refinement, as reflected in the changes made in the classification of personality disorder and in the narrowing of the characteristics that are regarded as constituting specific disorders or subtypes. There is also evidence of considerable co-occurrence of clinical syndromes and personality disorders, leading to the conclusion that having a personality disorder increases the risk of having a clinical disorder and vice versa, although patients diagnosed with personality disorder are much more likely to present to services with an Axis I disorder (Dolan-Sewell *et al.* 2001). For example, borderline personality disorder is strongly associated with alcohol abuse and dependence, substance misuse and abuse, and, to a lesser extent, with mood disorders (Oldham *et al.* 1995; Skodol *et al.* 1999). From the clinician's viewpoint, this suggests that patients with personality disorder are likely to be more complex than those with an Axis I disorder alone.

Although useful and probably necessary for the growth of knowledge in this area, the classification system for personality disorder is in itself not sufficient to specify interventions with individual patients. Classification on its own does not provide enough information to aid clinicians in developing individual treatment programmes. This is, in part, due to the uniqueness of each individual resulting from an interaction between biological factors,

Cluster A	Cluster B	Cluster C
Odd and eccentric	*Flamboyant and dramatic*	*Fearful or anxious*
Paranoid	Antisocial	Dependent
Schizoid	Borderline	Obsessive-compulsive
Schizotypal	Narcissistic	Avoidant
	Histrionic	

Figure 10.1 DSM-IV personality disorder clusters.

temperament and genetic constitution, and contextual factors such as experience of family environment and social roles. In order to offer treatment to individuals with personality disorder, we need to reach an understanding of why and how an individual has developed the difficulties he or she experiences and not just what problems they have. Cognitive therapies focus on and attempt to address how patients perceive events in their lives, focus their attention, process information, organise their thoughts and engage with others.

COGNITIVE MODELS OF PERSONALITY DISORDER

There are now several cognitive models of personality disorder and each makes different assumptions about the core psychopathology in personality disorder. As a result, the models have slightly different emphases in terms of therapeutic tasks and strategies. Table 10.1 summarises the main differences.

Dialectical behaviour therapy

Linehan's (1993) dialectical behaviour therapy (DBT) is based on a biosocial theory of borderline personality disorder. The central problem for individuals with borderline personality disorder is seen as deriving from a physiological difficulty in emotional regulation in combination with invalidating social environments, particularly in childhood. The theory suggests that the

Table 10.1 Models of personality disorder and implications for treatment

	Model	Central problem	Main target of treatment	Predominant therapeutic technique
Linehan (1993)	Biosocial	Emotional regulation and invalidating environment	Reduction of self-harm	Behavioural mindfulness training
Young (1990)	Cognitive	Core schemas and associated affect	Change in beliefs	Cognitive
Beck and Freeman (1990)	Cognitive/ evolutionary	Genetically determined personality strategies	Change in behaviour and beliefs	Behavioural and cognitive
Davidson (2000)	Cognitive behavioural	Core beliefs and behavioural strategies	Change in behaviour and beliefs	Behavioural and cognitive

early social experience of individuals with borderline personality disorder has impaired their ability to develop adaptive skills to modulate painful emotions. Suicidal acts and self-mutilation, frequently-observed behaviours in borderline personality disorder, are regarded as attempts to cope with overwhelming emotional states. The primary focus of DBT is to reduce self-harm, not treat personality disorder per se.

The dialectical elements of DBT make it very different from other cognitive therapies. The assumption here is that patients with borderline personality disorder vacillate between contradictory poles or modes without being able to find a dialectical solution – one that could synthesise the contradictions and move them to a more harmonious resolution. For example, a patient could appear apparently competent at one point but behave incompetently and passively at another, or autonomous at one point in time then dependent at another point, and, as a result, not be able to achieve a more balanced synthesis. In DBT, therapists encourage patients to be more accepting of self and yet consider the possibility of change. The idea is that each experience simultaneously contains opposite polarities and the tension between them offers the possibility of change. The therapeutic relationship also plays a central part in DBT, possibly more than in other cognitive therapies. Although cognitive behavioural techniques are used in DBT, they are more recognisably behavioural: skills training, behavioural analysis, contingency management and exposure are examples.

DBT incorporates elements from Eastern philosophical traditions, particularly Buddhism. Mindfulness training, learning to accept reality without judgement, letting go of unhelpful attachments and finding a middle path are all incorporated from Zen principles. Rather than using guided discovery and Socratic questioning to challenge or evaluate beliefs, as in standard cognitive therapy, mindfulness training helps patients to redirect attention away from painful thoughts and emotions and to gain more distance from them.

Young's theory of early maladaptive schemas

Young's theory (Young 1990; Young and Lindemann 1992), although similar to that of Beck *et al.* (1990), places greater emphasis on the development of maladaptive schemas and on affect associated with specific core schemas. Young makes no specific connection between personality disorder categories and schemas. The theory emphasises the connection between early developmental history and the content of the schemas and how these become reinforced. Young (1990) has proposed that schemas are reinforced through three different processes: schema maintenance, schema avoidance and schema compensation.

Schema maintenance is the process by which information or evidence that would disconfirm the schema is resisted through cognitive distortions and by self-defeating behavioural patterns. This type of information processing is thought to be common in clients with personality disorders. It is as if the client cannot take into account new information that would negate what they believe to be true of themselves or others. Information that would appear to be evidence that would directly disconfirm a belief is readily dismissed or discounted and may even appear to be totally ignored. For example, a patient who believes that she is not lovable is unable to recognise when others are being genuinely friendly and warm and rejects signs of friendship, thereby maintaining her belief that nobody could like her.

Schema avoidance occurs when individuals automatically attempt to suppress or avoid triggering schemas associated with intense negative emotions or the unpleasant affect associated with those schemas. Avoidance can operate at three different levels. At the level of cognitive avoidance, clients will not want to speak or think about an event that would bring a schema into sharp focus. At an affective level, avoidance operates by the individual suppressing or dulling down emotions or by carrying out behaviours, such as self-mutilation, that attempt to stop the intolerable or undesirable affect. Lastly, overt behavioural avoidance occurs where situation or events are avoided to prevent rekindling a schema or set of schemas.

Schema compensation involves overcompensating for a negative schema by acting in the direction opposite to the schema's content. The behavioural and cognitive patterns observed are the opposite of those that would be predicted on the basis of the patient's early developmental history. This process can sometimes appear adaptive, as it is a partially successful attempt to challenge early dysfunctional schemas. For example, an individual with a history of early emotional deprivation may develop compensatory strategies such as a high degree of autonomy and beliefs about invulnerability. However, these strategies may create new problems by simply masking the underlying core beliefs, making them difficult to identify and modify.

Young and Brown (1990) have developed a questionnaire to assess the content of schemas. This questionnaire can be useful clinically, helping patients to identify core beliefs about self and others. The schemas assessed include emotional deprivation, abandonment, mistrust and abuse, social isolation, defectiveness and shame, failure, dependence and incompetence, vulnerability to harm and illness, enmeshment, subjugation, self-sacrifice, emotional inhibition, unrelenting standards, entitlement and insufficient control and self-discipline. Where a patient is scoring highly on items that relate to one another is likely to be indicative of the schemas that are central to that individual's view of self or others. This can be utilised with good effect in clinical situations when discussing a clinical formulation and in particular the core beliefs that the patient may hold.

Beck *et al.*'s (1990) cognitive model of personality disorder

Beck *et al.*'s (1990) cognitive model of personality disorder takes a genetic and an evolutionary perspective. In this model, variations in the gene pool have led to some individuals, who could be labelled as having a personality disorder, showing more extreme forms of the personality types or patterns that were once adaptive but are now maladaptive in the contemporary world. Thus, they suggest, prototypical personality patterns or traits are genetically determined strategies favoured by natural selection. Certain behaviours such as help-seeking, attacking or avoidance may have survival value in some situations, but not in others. These personality strategies are overt expressions of deep cognitive schemas or belief structures that have resulted from an interaction of genetics and the environment.

Cognitive theory suggests that individuals with personality disorder hold dysfunctional beliefs and demonstrate maladaptive behavioural strategies that are over-generalised, inflexible, pervasive and resistant to change. Like cognitive therapy for emotional disorders, the cognitive model of personality disorder suggests that biased information processing results from dysfunctional schemas. Unlike Young's (1990) model, Beck *et al.* suggest that each personality disorder is characterised by a distinct cognitive profile, a composite of beliefs, attitudes and affects organised around a general theme of the nature of self and others that dictates a generalised behaviour strategy. An individual with a dependent personality disorder, for example, will have a cognitive schema that demonstrates a concept of others as protective and strong and of self as weak, requiring help and protection. This cognitive schema then directly relates to a behavioural strategy of seeking reassurance and dependence on others.

DIFFERENCES BETWEEN COGNITIVE THERAPY FOR AXIS I AND AXIS II DISORDERS

Key differences in emphasis between standard cognitive therapy and therapy for personality disorders are: (a) the central importance and function of formulation in guiding therapy; (b) the nature of the client–therapist relationship; (c) the emphasis on core beliefs; (d) the importance placed on behavioural change to promote changes in beliefs about self and others; and (e) the need for a longer duration of treatment (Davidson 2000).

There are differences between authors about the degree to which cognitive therapy for personality disorder can change core beliefs or schemas. For example, Young (1999) describes techniques to change early maladaptive schemas and the behavioural strategies that maintain these schemas. Davidson (2000), on the other hand, suggests changing schemas or core beliefs in therapy may be unrealistic given the beliefs' strength of belief and longstanding nature. Instead, the therapist weakens the strength of conviction in schemas or core beliefs by strengthening new, more adaptive beliefs about self and others and by developing more adaptive behavioural strategies. For example, an individual with a diagnosis of antisocial personality disorder might be encouraged to re-evaluate the pros and cons of holding narcissistic beliefs, and helped to develop more flexible and less dysfunctional beliefs. He might also be encouraged to carry out behavioural experiments to test out the benefits and disadvantages of behaving in ways that involve taking into account the needs of others, rather than exploiting other people. These behavioural patterns will have evolutionary survival value, particularly in maintaining relationships where consideration for others, kindness and intimacy are valued, but in antisocial personality disorder these patterns are under-represented.

EVIDENCE FOR CBT IN PERSONALITY DISORDERS

Cognitive behaviour therapy was investigated in a series of cases using single *n* design methodology, and was shown to reduce self-harm in patients with borderline personality disorder and reduce harm to others in patients with antisocial personality disorder (Davidson and Tyrer 1996). Each individual was assessed and a formulation was developed that took into account the development of problems, and beliefs and factors that might account for the maintenance of problems. Although each patient had an individualised formulation, common themes were observed in the two patient groups. Patients with borderline personality disorder typically held self-derogatory beliefs, had self-destructive behavioural patterns, including self-harm, and were poor at self-nurturance. Individuals with antisocial personality disorder, on the other hand, typically held beliefs that they were superior to others and that others were likely to take advantage of them or disparage them, and showed behavioural patterns that were exploitative, hostile or aggressive towards others. Individuals with antisocial personality disorder were likely to misinterpret the behaviour of others as being a 'put-down' and this would lead to an increase in the likelihood of aggression or physical violence to others. In an open trial of patients with borderline personality disorder, CBT was effective in reducing a number of symptoms and problems, such as suicidal ideation and dysfunctional beliefs (Brown *et al.* 2004). However, the least potentially biased evidence for cognitive behaviour therapy in the treatment of personality disorders will come from randomised controlled trials.

Dialectical behaviour therapy

Dialectical behaviour therapy (DBT), an adaptation of cognitive behaviour therapy, has been used with women with borderline personality disorder who repeatedly self-harm (Linehan 1993). DBT is based on a biosocial theory of personality functioning. In those with borderline personality disorder, the primary dysfunction is one of emotional dysregulation that has arisen as a result of biological irregularities in combination with dysfunctional, particularly invalidating, environments in childhood. Linehan and collaborators examined the efficacy of DBT for women with borderline personality disorder who repeatedly self-harm and found it to be superior to 'treatment as usual' in reducing self-harm (Linehan *et al.* 1991, 1994). This finding has been confirmed in an independent Dutch study of 64 women (Verheul *et al.* 2003). In another study of women with borderline personality disorder, DBT was effective in reducing levels of psychological distress during the treatment phase (Koons *et al.* 2001), but no differences were observed in self-harm. The treatment in all studies consisted of group skills training and individual therapy. In a one-year naturalistic follow-up, those women in the original study (Linehan *et al.* 1991) who had received DBT continued to show less parasuicidal behaviour than those who had treatment as usual for the first six months post-therapy, but there was no difference between the groups between 6 and 12 months post-therapy (Linehan *et al.* 1993), suggesting that longer treatment may be required to maintain reduced levels of self-harm.

More recent adaptations of DBT have focused on the treatment of women with borderline personality disorder and substance abuse (Linehan *et al.* 1999). No differences were found in drug use or parasuicidal behaviours between groups receiving treatment as usual and DBT at the end of treatment but, at follow-up, those receiving DBT showed significant gains in a number of important areas such as days abstinent from drugs, parasuicidal behaviour, anger and global and social functioning. When a 12-step drug programme was augmented with validation strategies from DBT and compared with DBT alone, no differences were found between therapies (Linehan *et al.* 2002). This suggests that treatment that focuses on reinforcement and acceptance, without DBT behavioural change strategies, also produces promising results for women with opioid dependence.

Specific techniques

As CBT for personality disorders is an adaptation of CBT for Axis I disorders, and is based on a formulation of an individual's problems, all of the techniques used in standard CBT can be used or adapted to treating individuals with personality disorder. However, individuals with personality disorders have problems that are longstanding and, as a result, treatment takes longer and the changes that patients need to make to improve life in general, and the quality of relationships in particular, need to be practised repeatedly. Specific techniques, such as using a continuum, can be used to monitor and reinforce changes in negative core beliefs. Behavioural experiments are used throughout therapy to assess the experience of behaving in different ways and to evaluate change. Table 10.2 gives examples of some of the techniques used in treating problems using CBT for personality disorders (see Davidson 2000 for further information on using techniques in the treatment of personality disorder).

COGNITIVE THERAPY FORMULATION IN BORDERLINE PERSONALITY DISORDER: MOLLY

Molly (a pseudonym), a 38-year-old woman, was referred for cognitive therapy by a community mental health team. She had been treated by the team for depression and repeated self-harm. The team had known her over a period of five years and had formed the opinion that borderline personality disorder was the most appropriate diagnosis, although she also suffered from episodes of major depression. She had been treated by several members of staff in the team and had seen a series of community psychiatric nurses over the years, although always the same psychiatrist. She had a past history of sexual abuse. In the past year, she had been reviewed regularly by her psychiatrist

Table 10.2 Examples of techniques used in CBT for personality disorders

Technique	Target
Continuum	Monitoring and changing core beliefs
Historical test of schema	Understanding and assessing validity of underlying core beliefs
Notebook to strengthen new ways of thinking	Changing and reinforcing new, more adaptive core beliefs
Notebook to strengthen new ways of behaving	Changing and reinforcing new, more functional behavioural patterns
Involving significant others (behavioural techniques): – behavioural contracting – increasing positive behaviours	Relationship difficulties
Self-monitoring (e.g., weekly diary)	Assessing or changing behavioural patterns (e.g., alcohol use, self-harm)
Graded assignments	Changing behaviours
Stimulus control	Bringing behaviour under environmental control
Assertiveness training	Relationship problems
Social skills and communication training	Social skills deficits or communication problems

and a nurse, had received antidepressant medication and been offered anxiety management training in a group format, but had not attended regularly.

Initial interview: developing a therapeutic alliance

With patients who have complex longstanding problems, the initial interviews are crucial in developing a therapeutic relationship with the patient as well as assessing problems. Although cognitive therapy for patients with personality disorder is structured and time-limited, more sessions are needed to address engagement and change processes. With more complex cases, it is important not to rush the initial stage of engagement, assessment and formulation. Many patients with a diagnosis of personality disorder have experienced years of contact with mental health services and are likely to have seen a large number of health service professionals. There have often been several professionals involved in their care at any one time but, despite this, patients with personality disorder often feel that they have not been listened to, or are regarded as a nuisance by staff as they do not seem to get better. Seeing so many professionals over a period of years can lead to expectations that being referred to yet another professional is a sign of failure on their part and that nobody can really help them. Trusting that someone will listen to their difficulties and take them seriously can be an issue in the initial stages of assessment and therapy, and needs to be taken into consideration.

The purpose of the initial interviews is to be develop as full a psychological understanding of the patient's problems as is possible and to convey this to the patient so that therapy can be focused at the areas of greatest patient need. In other words, formulating is key to assessment and engagement in patients with personality disorder. Taking the time to do this carefully will be essential if the next stages of therapy are to be profitable to the patient.

First session

Molly was a tall thin woman who looked older than her years and was inappropriately dressed for the prevailing temperature. She had short dyed hair and a ring through her nose. She appeared low in mood. Following the initial formalities and introductions, Molly was invited to describe the main difficulties she experienced. Molly described how her self-harm had increased seven months previously. She was now cutting herself several times a week with a razor blade. She had problems in her current relationship of 10 months' standing. This was a lesbian relationship and although Molly's family knew she was lesbian, her partner did not want anyone to know about the relationship. Molly said that she felt bullied by her partner and was not able to assert herself in the relationship, and that she did not like the fact that she and her partner had to be so secretive about it.

Before the beginning of this relationship, Molly had managed to reduce her self-harm, largely because she had felt less depressed, but now she hated herself for cutting and thought that she had let herself down. She said that she was 'pathetic' for having let the cutting increase but that it was the only way she knew how to deal with her feelings of anger and helplessness in the situation with her partner. When asked why she felt angry and helpless she said that she could not cope with their relationship being a secret, and that she had spent her life living with secrets, and could not deal with the emotional distress that this caused. She made several other statements about self-harm that were noted: 'I have to feel pain,' and, 'I know I'm real if I'm hurting.' When asked about the latter statement, Molly said that cutting herself did result in some pain and that, as a child, she had harmed herself as a way of letting the pain out rather than letting it build up inside her. She told the therapist that she had been sexually abused as a child and had been unable to prevent the abuse. Molly described recent disturbing dreams of being abused as a child.

At the end of this first session, there was more information required about Molly's past history and the therapist encouraged Molly to return the following week to continue. Molly had been able to discuss her problems at her own pace and, although a lot of detail was missing, the therapist had not rushed through her personal history.

The therapist's summary focused on Molly's thoughts and feelings about her self-harm: how she had felt more helpless, had increased her self-harm, this had coincided with difficulties with her new partner, and the increase in self-harm had led to a further decrease in her self-esteem as she felt she had let herself down. The therapist identified Molly's self-harm as a long-term strategy of trying to cope with feelings of being entrapped and helpless at having been sexually abused in her childhood. The therapist also noted that her increase in self-harm had coincided with the development of a new relationship that had to be kept secret and that Molly was now experiencing more dreams of being sexually abused.

At the end of this first session, the therapist had a developing hypothesis about the relationship between Molly's self-harm, helplessness and anger at being bullied and having to keep secrets (see Figure 10.2). It appeared that Molly's self-harm was related to past feelings of being entrapped in abusive relationships, and being currently bullied by her partner. Cutting herself appeared to be an attempt to regulate her mood and although this strategy was effective in the short term, it was ineffective in the longer term.

To clarify this preliminary hypothesis, further biographical detail and information about Molly's current problems was needed. In particular, more information was needed to clarify the relationship between past sexual abuse and current difficulties with her partner. For example, as a child, had she been able to confide in someone about the sexual abuse? How had she coped with the abuse? What other problems led Molly to self-harm? Were there other

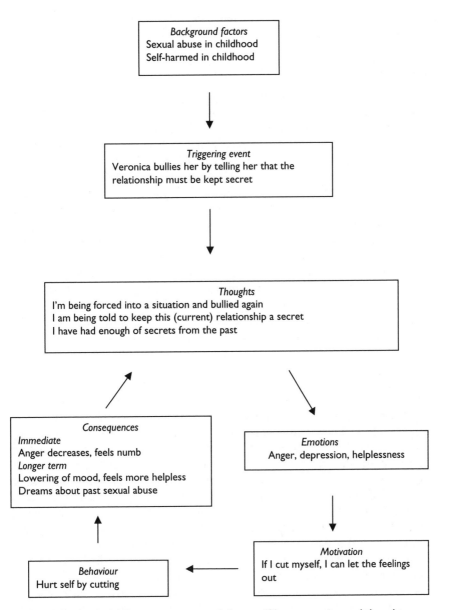

Figure 10.2 Relationship between past sexual abuse, self-harm, emotion and thoughts.

factors contributing to the maintenance of Molly's self-harm and depressive symptoms?

Sessions 2–5

The following week had been particularly difficult for Molly and she had experienced increasingly depressed mood following several arguments with her partner. Molly had cut herself more frequently and some of her older wounds had been re-opened and were infected. She had been dressing these herself and said she knew how to take care of them. She was asked if she felt suicidal but she said she did not, although she had taken an overdose of paracetamol two months before following an argument with her son, Gerard. He had hit her during the argument. When asked about her relationship with Gerard, she described him as being the 'only good thing' about her life so far and said that this was the first time he had been violent towards her. She was now afraid that he might leave her and she thought she could not bear this.

The therapist asked Molly to provide more background information about herself, starting with her childhood, as there were potentially useful links between Molly's view of herself as deserving of pain, sexual abuse and self-harm. Four further sessions were needed to gather this information about her childhood and adolescence and her current problems and fears.

Biographical details

Molly was the youngest of 12 children born in the west of Scotland. She had three surviving older sisters and four older brothers. Two siblings had died in infancy and two had died in childhood. Her mother had died suddenly, aged 55, of cardiac failure and her father had died of cancer aged 50. Her father had sexually abused her from the age of seven. This had stopped when he became ill with cancer when she was about nine years old. From the age of four until eight or nine years old, an uncle also sexually abused her. This had stopped when she threatened to tell someone. In later sessions, it seemed likely that her father had also sexually abused her older sisters. In addition, her eldest brother had sexually abused her on several occasions. She had been unable to complain to anyone about the sexual abuse; she had realised that her sisters may have been abused and it had seemed to her, as a child, that it was her 'turn' as the youngest and that she would have to bear it alone. Whether she had received this idea from her older sisters or mother, either implicitly or explicitly, was not clear. It was, however, evident that sexual abuse was 'normal' though not openly acknowledged within the family.

The family was poor and neither parent was in employment during her childhood. What minimal day-to-day care she received during her childhood had been from some of her older sisters. She had not attended school regularly and had often wandered around the streets aimlessly rather than go home. Nonetheless, Molly thought she had received a better education than her siblings as they had attended school even less than her. Her teachers had given her the impression that the whole family were 'useless' and they had 'given up' on her family by the time she was at school. Some of her brothers had been suspended from school due to unruly behaviour in the classroom and damaging school property.

It was difficult for Molly to articulate how she felt about her childhood, although she could give the basic facts. She would often look rather blank at these times. Nonetheless, it was clear that she had been deeply unhappy as a child and had wanted to escape from her home. She said, 'I wanted out of it,' 'I was put here [in the world] to be abused,' and, 'I can't let go of the past – it is still with me,' suggesting that she continued to experience high levels of distress as a result of her early life and continued to feel a sense of entrapment.

She had no clear memory of when she began cutting herself, although she thought this was around the age of seven or eight. The fact that she cut herself without it being noticed was important to her; she had initially tried to hurt herself by banging her head against a wall when feeling very despondent and frustrated but had stopped this when beaten by her father for hurting herself. Two of her sisters had also self-harmed by cutting. She had observed their scars on several occasions, but they would not talk to her about this. Again there appeared to be a wall of silence surrounding incidents that might indicate severe emotional disturbance. She had learnt to avoid asking questions as a child as her father told her to 'shut up' and her sisters ridiculed her and told her she would learn 'about life' soon enough. Her mother appeared hardly ever to talk to her. One of her older sisters, with whom she had shared a room, had been more supportive towards her during her childhood. The father had also sexually abused this sister, and, although she was unable to talk to Molly about this, she had comforted Molly when she was distressed.

Molly had few relationships outside her home, partly because her attendance at school had been so sporadic. Other children in the neighbourhood were also from large families and poor, and she said that she had not felt herself different from them, except that she did not think that they were sexually abused.

Late adolescence and adulthood

Molly officially left school at 16 with no qualifications. By this time both her parents were dead. She had felt no sense of loss for either parent and, in fact, had been relieved that they were both dead. Neither had taken care of her and she felt no affection for either of them. She had hated her father, and with his death had thought that she was definitely released from sexual abuse.

She had realised she was sexually attracted to women from the age of 13 but had very little knowledge of sexual preferences. She had not been able to talk about this to anyone; neither had she acted on this knowledge. Without the therapist asking, she stated that the sexual abuse had nothing to do with her being sexually attracted to women. Molly had a brief series of sexual encounters with teenagers when she was 16 years old and conceived a child. She was drinking heavily at this time and had been sexually promiscuous and generally reckless with regard to her personal safety as she did not care what happened to her. Without the father's knowledge, Molly had a boy she called Gerard. The relationship with Gerard's father had not lasted more than several weeks after she conceived. She did not want any contact with him and had never pursued him for maintenance of the child. She had brought up the child largely on her own, having been housed by the local authority, though several of her sisters had been supportive, both emotionally and practically. She had experienced very few close lasting relationships but in recent years had met a number of women she liked through a job-finding skills group for women. She had met Veronica through this group and had got to know her relatively well before embarking on a relationship. Molly described wanting to find someone she could be close to but found it hard to trust other people as she usually ended up feeling that she had been rejected or exploited. She had tried to 'build a wall' around herself so that she would not get hurt, but when asked if this was a successful strategy, she acknowledged that she felt desperately alone.

She had worked, on and off, in various hotels and cafes as a waitress or as a domestic cleaner but had never managed to hold down a job for long. She had abused alcohol for several years, particularly when Gerard was young, but had decreased her alcohol intake over five years ago when she was referred to the community mental health team. She now drank very little alcohol. She had taken overdoses of paracetamol on at least seven occasions in the past 10 years, and had self-harmed by cutting since childhood. She also burned herself with cigarettes at times, usually if she had been drinking alcohol. She looked underweight and undernourished and said she was not interested in food. Her sleeping habits were irregular as she sat up late watching television regularly and would cat-nap during the day. She smoked heavily.

Her son, Gerard, was now 22 years old and lived with her in their local tenancy association flat. She had had difficulties with him when he was a younger child, as she had wanted to be affectionate to him but had problems demonstrating this. As Gerard grew, she found it hard to maintain discipline at home but, following some input from a child and family psychiatry department, managed to be reasonably firm with him, thereby improving their relationship. At the time of the referral, Molly described Gerard as having alcohol and drug problems. They had frequent arguments about his drinking and drug abuse and she had asked him not to drink at home. From his late adolescence, Gerard had been verbally abusive towards her and recently he had been physically aggressive towards her. Although she now felt unsafe at home with him, she did not want to put him out 'on the streets'. Despite their current difficulties, Molly was very distressed at the idea that

Gerard did not need her anymore and was afraid of losing her relationship with him.

Building a therapeutic relationship during initial sessions

It was evident from the initial sessions that Molly had difficulties acting assertively in relationships, had difficulty trusting others and appeared to be quite defeated and helpless. Although initially her core beliefs and details about her early life were not fully known, the therapist hypothesised that Molly might not engage in therapy in a collaborative way unless she could be encouraged to trust the therapist, have a sense of control over her problems, and view herself as being able to make changes. The therapist tried to encourage Molly by accepting her as she was and by trying to make sense of her experience through the formulation. She did not judge or label Molly. At no point did the therapist instruct Molly to take action to resolve her problems but rather the therapist listened carefully to what Molly had to say and reflected back the concerns that Molly raised. Molly's strengths as well as difficulties were evident in these initial sessions and these were gently highlighted by the therapist, who enquired how Molly had managed to survive her childhood, given it's awfulness, and how she had coped with earlier problems with Gerard. Molly had many problems but the formulation was helpful in tying these together into a coherent framework, thus making them appear less daunting for Molly.

Following this gathering of biographical material, and having gained an idea of Molly's current life situation and problems, the next stage could begin. A cognitive formulation of her problems was discussed to help understand how these had arisen and were maintained, and to focus on what could be achieved by therapy. Her main current problems were as follows.

Formulation

At the end of the fifth session, the therapist had a clearer idea of the psychological factors in Molly's past that may have contributed to her core beliefs about herself and others and her self-harm behaviours. A brief diagrammatic presentation of the formulation was shared with Molly to help her to understand how her problems could be considered within a cognitive therapy framework (see Figure 10.3).

Main present-day problems

1   Self-harm: her self-harm had increased but she was less concerned about this behaviour per se and more concerned that she felt more hopeless and had let herself down.

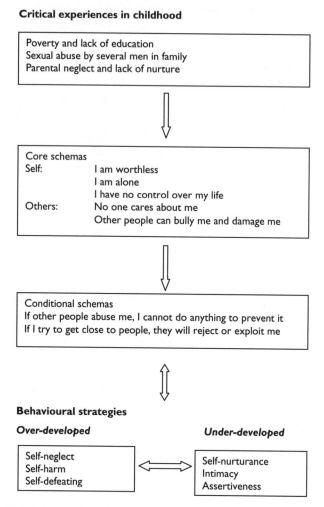

Critical experiences in childhood

Poverty and lack of education
Sexual abuse by several men in family
Parental neglect and lack of nurture

Core schemas
Self: I am worthless
                 I am alone
                 I have no control over my life
Others: No one cares about me
                 Other people can bully me and damage me

Conditional schemas
If other people abuse me, I cannot do anything to prevent it
If I try to get close to people, they will reject or exploit me

Behavioural strategies

Over-developed   *Under-developed*

Self-neglect   Self-nurturance
Self-harm   Intimacy
Self-defeating   Assertiveness

Figure 10.3 Cognitive formulation.

2   Depressive symptoms: again Molly was rather unconcerned about these and saw her lack of appetite, loss of interest in things, helplessness, hopelessness low self-esteem as being 'normal' for her.
3   Relationship with Gerard: she feared losing him but was unable to cope with his current level of drug and alcohol abuse.
4   Relationship with Veronica: Molly felt bullied by Veronica, who insisted that their relationship be kept a secret, and she felt unable to challenge her about this.

These problems can be categorised as being in four main groups (Table 10.3).

Table 10.3 Categories of problems

Problem areas	Description
Intrapersonal	Depressive symptoms: lack of appetite, loss of interest and pleasure, helplessness, hopelessness Beliefs about self
Interpersonal	Relationship with Veronica – cannot assert herself Relationship with Gerard – afraid of asserting herself in case she loses him Beliefs about others
Behavioural	Self-mutilation Risk of overdose
Day-to-day functioning	Lack of structure day to day Poor self-care

Does the formulation fit?

The underlying psychological mechanism accounting for Molly's problems appears, from the cognitive formulation, to be beliefs arising from her childhood experiences and the overdeveloped behavioural strategies that are associated with these. The underlying unconditional and conditional beliefs and behavioural strategies are best viewed as working hypotheses, but can be tested in a number of ways from the data already provided by Molly. Jacqueline Persons (1989) suggests several ways to test whether the formulation fits the proposed underlying mechanism. What do the problems have in common? Is there a central theme running through the problem list that relates to the underlying beliefs? Do Molly's current thoughts and beliefs relate to her past experience?

In Molly's case, it appears that there is a central theme of feeling defeated and entrapped by her current relationships and that this has led to a decrease in her already low self-esteem and an increase in self-harm. Her underlying belief that she cannot do anything to prevent herself from being exploited and abused is activated in her current relationship problems with both Veronica and Gerard. This belief comes from her experiences in childhood, when several male members of her family sexually abused her and she was emotionally and physically neglected. She also believes, on the basis of her past experience, that others will hurt her if she gets close to them. In her childhood she felt defeated, entrapped and unable to do anything about her circumstances. At the time of referral she found herself feeling similarly defeated and unable to assert herself in her current relationships. This, in turn, led her to feel more hopeless and depressed and to increase her self-harm.

In addition, Molly's lack of close and intimate relationships in adulthood makes sense given her childhood experiences of growing up in an exploitative and abusive family with little nurturance. She believes that it is 'dangerous' to get close to others as she will get hurt. Her relationship with Gerard and one of her sisters, however, gave her some experience of being in more satisfactory relationships, albeit neither of these were ideal. Her willingness to establish a relationship with Veronica, at least prior to the argument about having to keep it secret, suggests that Molly is prepared to take some risk in forming relationships although she may have problems trusting others and looking after her needs in relationships. Although Molly stated that her lesbian relationships had 'nothing to do with the abuse', her sexual preference for women did appear to be related to the sexual abuse she had experienced as a child and her subsequent difficulty forming satisfactory and secure sexual relationships with men. She had clearly oscillated between genders for some time before finally making a choice to seek sexual partnerships with women.

Does the formulation make sense to the patient?

The formulation helped to reduce Molly's sense of helplessness regarding the number of problems she experienced, and the link with her childhood experiences also made sense to her.

Prioritising problems and planning interventions

Arriving at and agreeing the formulation was the first priority in therapy. This gave Molly a deeper understanding of her problems and helped her to understand the relationship between her thoughts about herself and others, her emotions and behaviour, all of which engaged her in the process of therapy. Given that Molly's self-esteem had worsened, and feelings of depression and self-harm had increased since the problems had arisen in her relationships with Veronica and Gerard, it appeared that attempting to improve her relationships with them might be a starting point for intervention in therapy. However, Molly's longstanding inability to assert herself when feeling entrapped and overwhelmed in abusive relationships suggested that this might be too difficult a challenge for Molly at the beginning of therapy, and that she would need to be better able to protect herself before standing up for herself. Her relationships with Veronica and Gerard would need further exploration in terms of their benefits and disadvantages. Her overdeveloped behavioural strategies of self-neglect and self-harm further depleted her already low self-esteem and her ability to form more satisfying relationships. If the dominance of these strategies were to be weakened, she needed to develop and strengthen the opposite or reciprocal strategy of self-nurturance. This would aid in her being at less risk of self-harm and parasuicide. The first priority was to improve her ability to look after herself, at both a practical and a psychological level, and to reduce the risk of more serious self-harm.

Other therapeutic intervention points derived from the formulation

The formulation also suggested several other interventions that would be necessary if Molly was to overcome her current problems and develop better long-term coping strategies. Her self-defeating behavioural strategies appeared to be related to her beliefs that she was alone and had no control over her life, particularly in relation to what others might do to her. The early sexual abuse by relatives, including her father, was re-evaluated so that she did not regard herself as being responsible for this as she had had, in reality, little chance of being able to do anything about this as a child. Given that she was now an adult, she was encouraged to re-evaluate her core beliefs about herself and replace them with new, more adaptive beliefs. Behavioural experiments were set up to test out several of her predictions about her lack of control in relationships with others. She tried behaving more assertively in relationships to test out if she could have more control over what happened in relationships. Behaving more assertively did not lead to being rejected or humiliated. Molly chose to think of herself in new terms: 'As an adult, I can have more control over my life,' and, 'I am an OK person.' Note that these new beliefs were not particularly positively phrased – more positive self-statements would have been unbelievable to Molly and would have been rejected out of hand as being unrealistic. Various cognitive techniques, such as the use of a continuum, the historical test of schema and recording ongoing more positive interpersonal experiences, were used to strengthen these more adaptive beliefs and to weaken her old core beliefs. Increasing her ability to nurture herself through greater awareness of her physical and psychological needs, and attending to these rather than ignoring them, she began to even out the troughs and peaks of her moods and reduced her self-harm. She learned to use alternative behavioural strategies when distressed, such as listening to music that soothed her or shouting in the shower instead of at others when too angry to be assertive. Problem-solving and learning assertiveness skills were needed to resolve her specific difficulties with Gerard and Veronica and strengthen her new beliefs. During therapy, she ended her relationship with Veronica successfully, in that they remained in contact.

CONCLUSION

At the end of therapy, it appeared that the formulation guiding therapy had been instructive to both the therapist and to Molly in understanding her problems. It had helped to keep therapy focused and relevant by giving a clear map of the psychological territory as well as helping to prioritise interventions. Reducing suicidal risk in patients who deliberately self-harm is usually given priority in a wide variety of therapies (e.g., Linehan 1993). Molly's formulation also suggested that this should be a top priority. The use of behavioural, as opposed to cognitive, interventions is often a more productive starting point with patients who have more severe personality disorders (Freeman and Jackson 1998). Cognitive therapy, with it's emphasis on structure, openness, collaboration and experimental methods, lends itself well to working with individuals who have complex problems and needs. Cognitive and behavioural interventions are effective in reducing distress and behavioural problems, and improving self-esteem and interpersonal relationships in those with personality disorders, but probably only work if delivered within the framework provided by a formulation.

RECOMMENDED READING

Beck, A. T. *et al.* (2004). *Cognitive Therapy of Personality Disorders* (2nd edn). New York: Guilford Press.

Davidson, K. M. (2000). *Cognitive Therapy for Personality Disorders: A Guide for Clinicians.* London: Arnold (Hodder).

Linehan, M. M. (1993). *Cognitive-Behavioural Treatment of Borderline Personality Disorder.* New York: Guilford Press.

Livesley, W. J. (ed) (2001). *Handbook of Personality Disorders: Theory, Research and Treatment.* New York: Guilford Press.

Persons, J. B. (1989). *Cognitive Therapy in Practice: A Case Formulation Approach.* New York: W. W. Norton.

REFERENCES

American Psychiatric Association. (1980). *Diagnostic and Statistical Manual of Mental Disorders* (3rd edn). Washington, DC: Author.

American Psychiatric Association. (1994). *Diagnostic and Statistical Manual of Mental Disorders* (4th edn). Washington, DC: Author.

Beck, A. T. *et al.* (1990). *Cognitive Therapy of Personality Disorders.* New York: Guilford Press.

Brown, G. K. *et al.* (2004). An open clinical trial of cognitive therapy for borderline personality disorder. *Journal of Personality Disorders* 18: 257–71.

Davidson, K. M. (2000). *Cognitive Therapy for Personality Disorders: A Guide for Clinicians.* London: Arnold (Hodder).

Davidson, K. M. and Tyrer, P. (1996). Cognitive therapy for antisocial and borderline personality disorders: Single case series. *British Journal of Clinical Psychology* 35: 413–29.

Dolan-Sewell, R. T. *et al.* (2001). Co-occurrence with syndrome disorders. In J. Livesley (ed) *Handbook of Personality Disorders: Theory, Research, and Treatment.* New York: Guilford Press.

Freeman, A. and Jackson, J. T. (1998). Cognitive behavioural treatment of personality disorders. In N. Tarrier *et al.* (eds) *Treating Complex Cases* (Wiley Series in Clinical Psychology). Chichester, UK: Wiley.

Koons, C. *et al.* (2001). Efficacy of dialectical behavior therapy in women veterans with borderline personality disorder. *Behavior Therapy* 32: 371–90.

Linehan, M. M. (1993). *Cognitive-Behavioural Treatment of Borderline Personality Disorder*. New York: Guilford Press.

Linehan, M. M. *et al.* (1991). Cognitive behavioural treatment for chronically parasuicidal borderline patients. *Archives of General Psychiatry* 48: 1060–4.

Linehan, M. M. *et al.* (1993). Naturalistic follow-up of a behavioural treatment for chronically parasuicidal borderline patients. *Archives of General Psychiatry* 50: 971–4.

Linehan, M. M. *et al.* (1994). Interpersonal outcome of cognitive behavioral treatment for chronically suicidal borderline patients. *American Journal of Psychiatry* 151: 1771–6.

Linehan, M. M. *et al.* (1999). Dialectical behavior therapy for patients with borderline personality disorder and drug dependence. *American Journal on the Addictions* 8: 279–92.

Linehan, M. M. *et al.* (2002). Dialectical behavior therapy versus comprehensive validation therapy plus 12-step for the treatment of opioid dependent women meeting criteria for borderline personality disorder. *Drug and Alcohol Dependence* 67: 13–26.

Oldham, J. M. *et al.* (1995). Comorbidity of axis I and axis II disorders. *American Journal of Psychiatry* 752: 571–8.

Persons, J. B. (1989). *Cognitive Therapy in Practice: A Case Formulation Approach*. New York: W. W. Norton.

Skodol, A. E. *et al.* (1999). Co-occurrence of mood and personality disorders: A report from the collaborative longitudinal personality disorders study (CLPS). *Depression and Anxiety* 10: 175–82.

Verheul, R. *et al.* (2003). Dialectical behaviour therapy with women with borderline personality disorder: 12-month, randomised clinical trial in the Netherlands. *British Journal of Psychiatry* 182: 135–40.

Young, J. E. (1990). *Cognitive Therapy for Personality Disorders: A Schemas-Focused Approach*. Sarasota, FL: Professional Resource Exchange, Inc.

Young, J. E. (1999). *Cognitive Therapy for Personality Disorders: A Schema-Focused Approach* (3rd edn). Sarasota, FL: Professional Resource Exchange, Inc.

Young, J. E. and Brown, G. (1990). Young Schema Questionnaire. In J. E. Young (ed) *Cognitive Therapy for Personality Disorders: A Schema-Focused Approach*. Professional Resource Exchange, Inc.

Young, J. E. and Lindemann, M. D. (1992). An integrative schema-focused model for personality disorders. *Journal of Cognitive Psychotherapy* 6: 11–23.

Chapter 11

Cognitive-behavioural case formulation in complex eating disorders

Anna Lavender and Ulrike Schmidt

INTRODUCTION AND OVERVIEW

The treatment of people with eating disorders (ED) continues to be a major challenge for clinicians. Patients present with a bewildering array of cognitive, emotional and physical symptoms, resulting from starvation and/or other problematic weight control behaviours (Zipfel *et al.* 2003). Comorbid difficulties are common, including depressive, socially anxious and obsessive-compulsive symptoms, self-harm and other impulsive behaviours, and cluster II or III personality traits or organisation (Bulik 2002; Wilson 2002; Wonderlich 2002). Additionally, these patients may not be motivated to engage in treatment or share others' views about the need to change (Treasure and Schmidt 2001). An individual case formulation approach may offer clinicians an enhanced means of understanding, and guidance in treating, these patients.

This chapter will begin with some thoughts on the classification and nature of eating disorders. We will then move on to an approach to the cognitive-behavioural modelling of eating disorders that may be useful in case formulation with complex patients. We will follow this, using clinical examples, by discussing how this may be applied to the formulation of such cases and used to guide treatment.

Classification

The existing diagnostic structure, both in ICD and DSM, separates eating disorders into the two main categories of anorexia nervosa (AN) and bulimia nervosa (BN), with AN being subdivided into a binge-purge and restricting sub-type and BN being subdivided into a purging and non-purging sub-type. Moreover, binge eating disorder (BED) was included in the appendix to DSM-IV (APA 1994) as a category 'deserving further study'. Recent discussions of the classification and treatment of eating disorders have highlighted the overlap and similarities between diagnostic groups. A 'trans-diagnostic' approach to classification and treatment has been suggested, on the grounds that many eating disorder sufferers do not neatly fit into the existing diagnostic structure and that they move between diagnostic categories (Fairburn and Bohn 2005; Fairburn *et al.* 2003). Against this, there is considerable evidence supporting the notion that restricting anorexia nervosa should be considered a distinct and separate phenotype (Clinton *et al.* 2004; Keel *et al.* 2004; for a review see Collier and Treasure 2004). In our view neither a wholesale 'lumping' approach nor a rigid 'splitting' approach is particularly helpful when thinking about the case formulation of eating disorders. In what follows we will highlight areas of common ground between all types of ED and important differences between anorexic and bulimic disorders.

What is the core psychopathology of eating disorders?

In order to answer this question one needs to look beyond current Western culture. A careful systematic review of historical and non-Western cases suggests that while bulimia nervosa is a Western culture-bound syndrome, anorexia nervosa is not (Keel and Klump 2003). There are well-documented cases of AN dating back to the middle ages. Moreover, there are many contemporary case descriptions of AN from non-Western cultures. What these historical and non-Western cases of AN have in common is that their psychopathology and justification for weight loss is not based on the current slim body ideal and concerns about weight or shape. Rather, these cases complain of 'inappetence' and 'inability to eat' or justify their food restriction in terms of ascetic or religious ideals. Thus, while current diagnostic criteria for AN and BN and a number of CBT models of treatment for ED focus on weight and shape concerns as the central psychopathology of both disorders, we – along with others (Palmer 2003) – see weight and shape-related psychopathology as much more important to bulimic disorders. In contrast, the essence of anorexia nervosa is 'motivated eating restraint'. Weight/shape concerns can be one motivation for such restraint among many others (see below) that are possible (Palmer 2003). This has clear implications for any cognitive-behavioural model of the disorder.

COGNITIVE-BEHAVIOURAL MODELS OF AND THERAPY FOR EATING DISORDERS

Behavioural and cognitive-behavioural models of different degrees of sophistication and specificity for both anorexia nervosa and bulimia nervosa are available (for reviews see Shafran and de Silva 2003; Waller and Kennerley 2003). In bulimia nervosa, cognitive-behaviour therapy based on a specific maintenance model has proved a reasonably effective treatment for many patients, as evidenced by a solid body of research. This is now considered the treatment of choice for the disorder (National Institute for Clinical Excellence 2004). Developed most prominently by Fairburn and colleagues, this treatment and the model supporting it have been well described elsewhere (Fairburn *et al.* 1993), and clinicians wishing to treat patients with uncomplicated BN are advised to consult this work. However, despite the usefulness of this model and treatment, 40–60% of patients with BN, particularly those with the kinds of complexities noted above, remain clinically symptomatic after treatment and drop-out rates, even under optimal conditions in randomised controlled trials, can be high (Agras *et al.* 2000). Fairburn and colleagues are now upgrading their model to target additional maintenance factors such as emotional dysregulation, core low self-esteem and clinical perfectionism with the aim of treating all eating disorders (Fairburn *et al.* 2003). Preliminary results suggest that the revised model may improve outcomes for people with bulimic disorders (BN, BED) and eating disorder not otherwise specified (EDNOS; Fairburn 2004).

For AN the picture is less clear-cut and less positive (for a review see Schmidt and Treasure in press). No single leading cognitive model of anorexia exists and evidence for effective treatments of anorexia, cognitive-behavioural or otherwise, remains slim. This may be partly because of the difficulties of carrying out treatment trials within this group, but is also likely to reflect the inherent complexity and severity of the psychopathology of the disorder, which makes individual case formulation all the more valuable a tool in its treatment. Our colleagues Geoffrey Wolff and Lucy Serpell (1998) have developed a cognitive model of anorexia nervosa that usefully accounts for the development and maintenance of many of its core features. In presenting a model for use in formulating complex cases, we will draw on this account and propose additional maintenance mechanisms that focus specifically on the interpersonal aspects of the disorder (Schmidt and Treasure submitted).

In what follows we will focus on the case formulation of patients with anorexia nervosa and the subgroup of patients with complex bulimia nervosa for whom an alternative approach to standard CBT may be useful. As we go along we will highlight similarities and differences between both.

CHILDHOOD TEMPERAMENT AND EARLY EXPERIENCES

A patient's temperament, physical constitution, early experiences and family environment may be important in understanding her illness. The backgrounds of people with eating disorders have been studied extensively; we will highlight several key themes in these findings that may influence the development and maintenance of the disorder.

One important recent paper reviewed all risk factors for AN and BN studied so far and classified them according to their potency (in terms of effect size) and specificity (Jacobi *et al.* 2004). The only two high potency risk factors for anorexia nervosa were being female and exercising before onset. Early feeding difficulties, picky eating, gastrointestinal problems, problems with sleeping and over-involved, anxious parenting were medium potency risk factors as were childhood perfectionism, obsessive compulsive personality disorder and negative evaluation of self. Preterm birth, perinatal complications and birth trauma were specific risk factors for anorexia nervosa, as was obsessive-compulsive disorder.

Other research findings add to the picture. For example, negative self-evaluation often occurs in relation to others, such as a sister, and jealousy is the predominant emotion aroused (Karwautz *et al.* 2001; Murphy *et al.* 2000). In a proportion of cases sexual experimentation is delayed (Schmidt *et al.* 1995) and sexual development is experienced as negative (Karwautz *et al.* 2001). In approximately 25% of AN cases a life event of a sexual nature (e.g., such as being confronted with premature or forbidden sexuality) is the trigger for the disorder (Schmidt *et al.* 1997a). This can be understood in the context of the high moral standards that are typically part of the obsessive-compulsive personality traits found in anorexia nervosa. Taken together this evidence suggests several developmental trajectories into anorexia nervosa. There may be major continuities in terms of parental preoccupation with a rather small, fragile child, with concerns around feeding, abdominal complaints and physical ill-health being an early theme. Refusing to eat can then become a way of eliciting care or nurturance. A second developmental theme commonly encountered is that of negative self-comparison to others and rigid competitive striving in conjunction with perfectionist standards for the self. Rigid control over food intake can become a way of winning the competition. A third developmental theme is that of sexuality being shameful, with a resultant reluctance to grow up into a woman. These themes are not mutually exclusive and can co-occur.

For bulimia nervosa, being female and dieting were the only high potency risk factors and negative self-evaluation the only medium potency risk factor (Jacobi *et al.* 2004). Pregnancy complications, parental obesity and weight/shape-related criticism were specific risk factors for bulimia nervosa. In addition, just as in other psychiatric disorders such as depression, these patients typically have high levels of other childhood environment risk factors, including parental neglect and abuse (e.g., Schmidt *et al.* 1997b). Taken together this evidence suggests that in terms of a developmental trajectory into BN those predisposed to obesity or plumpness, who experience childhood adversity and develop low self-esteem, may resort to dieting in response to weight/shape-related criticism from their families or others.

CORE BELIEFS: THE SELF, THE WORLD AND OTHERS

Within cognitive conceptualisations of eating disorders, temperamental features and early experiences such as those above are hypothesised to interact to lead to the development of a set of core negative schematic beliefs concerning the self, the world and others. These are not specifically eating disorder-related, but form an underlying system that acts as fertile ground within which an eating disorder may develop.

Core belief content appears to be broadly similar across anorexia and bulimia (Leung *et al.* 1999; Waller *et al.* 2000). However, as core belief formation varies according to an individual's early experiences and temperament, it is important to formulate core beliefs on an individual level and relate these as closely as possible to individual variables. Core beliefs about the self typically involve themes of powerlessness, lack of self-efficacy, defectiveness, failure, worthlessness and lack of identity (Vitousek and Hollon 1990; Woolrich *et al.* 2005). In one study (Woolrich *et al.* 2005) powerlessness/low self-efficacy was the negative self-belief most frequently mentioned by people with AN, the onset of which dated back prior to the development of the eating disorder. Participants with AN reported that restricting their food intake was a deliberate attempt to respond to their sense of powerlessness, and that this reduced the strength of this belief in the short term. Close others may be seen as hostile or unpredictable, or offering only conditional love or care, and the world may be perceived as a chaotic and dangerous place. These beliefs about a powerless self within a hostile environment can lead to the development of an important additional core belief about the extreme vulnerability of the self.

INTERMEDIATE BELIEFS: CONDITIONAL ASSUMPTIONS, RULES AND ATTITUDES

Holding negative schematic beliefs such as these is immensely emotionally distressing. Thus, to avoid their activation and the affect that accompanies them, and to compensate for them by moving as far towards an opposing state as possible, an individual may develop a set of attitudes, conditional assumptions, and 'rules for living' constructed to keep the beliefs at bay.

Intermediate beliefs relate directly to the core beliefs they are developed to compensate for. Thus, for eating-disordered individuals they are often around the need for control to compensate for core beliefs around powerlessness and lack of self-efficacy, and around success, achievement, specialness and lovability in order to compensate for self-beliefs around defectiveness, failure, worthlessness and lack of identity.

A typical example of beliefs at this level may include the attitude, 'It is terrible if anyone realises I am bad and doesn't like me,' the assumption, 'If I please others all the time, people might think I'm OK; if I don't, they will realise I'm bad and reject me,' and the rule, 'I should try to do what others want and expect from me all the time.' As with the core beliefs they are designed to compensate for, these types of intermediate beliefs are not specific to eating-disordered individuals, but form part of the schematic background against which more specific anorexic psychopathology may flourish.

Core beliefs about others and the world may lead to a number of types of intermediate compensatory beliefs. For example, the perception of others as hostile and conditional may give rise to beliefs about the desirability of keeping others at a distance and keeping vulnerable parts of the self 'hidden' or, conversely, the importance of striving to receive adequate care and protection from others. An experience of the world and others as chaotic, unpredictable and overwhelming may lead to compensatory beliefs around the need for orderliness, simplicity and predictability.

An additional intermediate belief domain important for many eating-disordered individuals is around the experience, control and expression of emotions. An individual's early experiences and temperament may mean that she develops attitudes around, for example, the unacceptability of experiencing negative emotions, assumptions about her inability to cope with them and rules about their regulation and expression. These may relate to core beliefs about the vulnerability of the self and the need for protection from others if emotion is expressed, or being overwhelmed by the experience of emotion itself.

TRIGGERS: WHY AN EATING DISORDER SPECIFICALLY?

Within the context of temperamental and experiential vulnerability factors, which lead to the development of a predisposing set of general schematic core and intermediate beliefs, some individuals go on to develop eating disorders. For this group, core beliefs about the self become fused with beliefs about the meaning of weight and/or the control of eating behaviour, such that 'fatness' or lack of control of eating become associated with powerlessness, defectiveness, failure, worthlessness and vulnerability. Conversely, 'thinness' or the control of eating behaviour is associated with reduced powerlessness and raised control, specialness, success and safety – the compensatory opposites. Intermediate beliefs that reflect this fusion also form, so that, for example, a patient might hold beliefs such as, 'If I'm fat I'm a failure,' and 'If I'm able to control my eating, I'm safer.'

This meshing of self- and weight- or eating control-related beliefs and the triggering of an eating disorder may happen for a number of reasons. With anorexia, particularly presentations for which restraint or control of eating per se, rather than a desire for thinness is central, factors such as early-onset obsessive-compulsive personality traits, or a childhood history of feeding difficulties, may be important to take into consideration. With bulimia and presentations of anorexia in which a drive for thinness is central, culturally-based factors that predispose towards the development of links between thinness and self-esteem may be more important. For these individuals, experiences such as being part of a family for whom weight and food have always been contentious issues, or being bullied about being overweight at school may be important. Sometimes it is not possible to identify specific triggers or vulnerability factors; the meshing of beliefs about the self and weight can be a gradual process that becomes progressively self-reinforcing as an eating disorder establishes itself and begins to meet a patient's needs to an increasing degree. This leads us to thinking about the next step in conceptualising eating disorders, which involves identifying how the illness functions for and is maintained within a patient.

WHAT FUNCTIONS DOES THE EATING DISORDER SERVE?

One useful way of thinking about an eating disorder is as a perceived solution that an individual has found to underlying problems that are a product of her experiences and underlying schematic system (Serpell *et al.* 2003, 2004; Vitousek *et al.* 1998). The eating disorder performs important functions as a perceived solution, and it is essential to identify these in formulation. As well as being implicated in the development of an eating disorder, the specific functions it serves will be vital to its maintenance.

We will discuss the potential functions of eating disorders across a spectrum ranging from those most likely to be relevant for restrictive anorexia to those most likely to be relevant for bulimia. We will link these on one level to the specific behaviours and, on another, to the specific core and intermediate beliefs that may be associated with them.

Intrapersonal functions: how an eating disorder works within the self

In studies investigating the functions of anorexia and bulimia, both similarities and differences across disorders have been observed (Serpell and Treasure 2002; Serpell *et al.* 1999). We will integrate these findings with our own ideas and observations about the potential functions of eating disorders for individuals.

Safety

Eating-disordered individuals often have core beliefs concerning the vulnerability of the self within a hostile or chaotic environment. Restriction and rigid control of eating behaviour can give a sufferer a sense of security and protection to help to compensate for this. The clearly defined set of rules that restriction provides can give an individual a sense of consistency and predictability, and the eating disorder can feel like a dependable friend. This function is most common in restrictive anorexia, but may be present in any eating disorder, including bulimia, in which restriction or dietary rules are present.

Control

An individual who perceives herself as powerless or lacking in self-efficacy is likely to have a high need for feeling in control. Rigid control of eating can seem to offer an ideal way to regain control: a patient discovers that, unlike the rest of life, her weight and eating do obey fairly clear-cut rules and the contingencies that govern this are unambiguous and knowable. This can help a patient to feel in control, secure and protected from the arbitrariness of life. There is some overlap here with the safety function.

Achievement and success

The successful control of eating and weight is difficult for many people. It is something that, almost by definition, a person with AN is extremely good at, and a person with BN strives constantly for and may enjoy periodic success at. This success can lead to an enormous sense of achievement and a corresponding increase in confidence, which are particularly sought after and rewarding for an eating-disordered individual in the face of core beliefs relating to worthlessness and failure that mean she is unlikely to feel a sense of achievement in other areas of her life. For bulimic individuals, periods of successful restriction are interspersed with perceived failure experiences when dietary rules are broken, so a person swings between feelings of achievement and activation of her core beliefs around failure.

Specialness and difference

Along with providing a sense of achievement, an eating disorder may also function as a way to help an individual who has a strong perception of herself as useless, or 'a nothing', feel special and more confident. When she evaluates herself in relation to others, she is able to feel set apart from the crowd; her perceived failings do not seem to matter so much because of her difference in this domain. This function is more likely to be relevant in anorexic than bulimic individuals, who are more likely to feel a sense of shame about their eating disorder.

Avoidance

Avoidance of responsibility, maturity and intimacy

As a result of intermediate level beliefs designed to compensate for core beliefs around worthlessness or powerlessness, individuals with eating disorders tend to have high standards for themselves. They demand a great deal of themselves, and can have difficulty saying 'no' to others' demands, so they may take on responsibilities that feel highly demanding for them. Sometimes, particularly in cases of AN, these individuals have taken on very responsible roles, such as caring for other family members, early in life. The experience of a high level of responsibility may fill an individual with anxiety about being able to meet perceived expectations or demands, leading her back to her core beliefs around worthlessness or powerlessness. An eating disorder may act as an effective 'escape route' from this. An illness role, such as may be taken on in anorexia or severe bulimia, may feel like a great relief, a way to retreat from the weight of responsibility she feels. This may be linked with a care-eliciting function, as it can also mean that it becomes others' responsibility to look after her, rather than vice versa.

Anorexia nervosa can also function as a way to avoid the demands of maturity. When the illness develops pre-pubescently, a sufferer may avoid the development of adult physical and sexual characteristics altogether: menses may not begin, and a sufferer retains her childish shape. With post-pubescent onset, an individual loses her menses and can move towards regaining a slim and childish figure. She also avoids the interpersonal aspects of adult sexuality in that she does not have to engage in intimate relationships, and face, as a consequence, the sexual aspects or emotional complexities of these, which she may perceive as threatening.

Related to this, and touched on above, is the potential function of an eating disorder as a way for an individual to distance herself from and avoid others and the rest of life more generally. Particularly with anorexia or severe bulimia, a sufferer may become almost entirely focused on her illness: her cognitive resources are taken up with thinking about food and/or weight and shape, and cognitive functioning may also be impaired due to her starved state. She is emotionally 'cut off', and other domains of her life such as family, friends, work, school and interests fade into the background. In this way, a sufferer can keep herself in a sealed 'bubble', where she may feel safe, secure and protected from a chaotic world she feels unable to cope with.

Emotional avoidance

Individuals with eating disorders often feel enormously threatened by the possibility of experiencing emotions and have a strong drive to avoid or escape from them. Emotions relevant to eating disorders are those typically aroused by threat to rank such as shame, guilt or jealousy (Gilbert 2001). People with eating disorders have been found to be prone to experience shame (for a review see Troop and Connan 2003) and guilt (Burney and Irwin 2000), and those with AN have been found to experience more jealousy than their unaffected sisters (Karwautz *et al.* 2001; Murphy *et al.* 2000).

Restrictive eating behaviour can function as a very effective way to avoid the activation of emotions at a primary level, and bingeing and purging behaviour can function as powerful ways to escape from emotion once it has been activated. In anorexia, an attentional bias towards food and eating-related material means that a great proportion of an individual's processing resources are taken up by thinking about food and resisting her body's drive towards it. This acts to block off thinking about other, potentially more painful, aspects of life and works to 'numb' the patient to emotional experiences associated with these. In bulimia, preoccupation with shape and weight-related material may serve a similar function.

'Beating the system'

In bulimia, a sense of literally being able to 'have your cake and eat it' is a common function of bingeing and purging behaviour. A person's meshed core and weight-related beliefs make thinness seem imperative for her. However, dieting to achieve this leaves her vulnerable to bingeing, which in itself may serve important functions for her. Purging to compensate for bingeing can give an individual who feels powerless and worthless a sense that she can 'beat the system'; while others suffer the consequences (as she sees it) of eating, she has a way around this.

Interpersonal functions: how an eating disorder works in relation to others

Eating disorders can have important interpersonal functions. These are particularly, but not exclusively, relevant for anorexic individuals, principally because anorexia is visible to others while bulimia tends to be hidden by the sufferer. It is worth noting that some of these interpersonal functions may also be very important within therapeutic interactions.

Compliments and care, anger and distance

A person with anorexia stands out from the crowd in a very visible sense. She may initially be complimented on her weight loss and receive admiring comments from others (Branch and Eurman 1980), which is likely to boost her self-esteem and confidence. Gradually, as her weight loss continues, others' admiration turns to worry and she may receive much-craved attention and care from parents, friends, partners, peers and health-care professionals.

Alternatively or in addition to this, others, such as family members and health-care professionals, may become increasingly frustrated and angry as attempts to help are repelled and seem to lead to ever-increasing determination in an individual to stick to her rigid diet and lose more weight (for a review see Schmidt and Treasure in press). For the person with anorexia, who may have pre-existing perceptions of others as threatening and untrustworthy, this can serve the function of increasing her rationale for keeping others at a 'safe' distance and withdrawing further into her illness. Similarly, for an individual who feels powerless in relation to others, anorexia can function as a way to assert control and redress perceived imbalances in power within interpersonal relationships. This is often an important function of the illness within the family and sometimes therapeutic context.

Others may also be kept at a distance when, as sometimes occurs, a person with anorexia seems happier and more full of energy and confidence than ever before. In this situation, the seeming wellness of the individual lulls others into a lack of concern, leaving her to pursue her weight loss goals in relative peace.

Communication

Individuals with eating disorders often have difficulty in communicating their thoughts, emotions and needs to others. This may result from a family environment within which parents had difficulty with communication, or discouraged the expression of emotion. Alternatively, core beliefs around vulnerability may lead a person to develop intermediate beliefs about the dangerousness of expressing themselves. Because of its very visible nature, anorexia can be a powerful tool for communication. It gives a clear signal to others that all is not well, and that the person is not coping effectively with life's demands. This can be an important function of the illness for a patient, as it may feel like her only means of letting others know about her emotional needs.

OTHER MAINTENANCE FACTORS

Meta-cognitive beliefs about eating disorders

Given these potential functions of an eating disorder for a sufferer, it begins to seem unsurprising that for many individuals, particularly those with anorexia, the thought of losing or giving up their eating disorder is a terrifying prospect. Indeed many anorexic patients do not feel as though they 'suffer' at all, and report feeling better and happier than ever (Casper 1998). In the cognitive formulation of this aspect of eating disorders, it is useful to think in terms of meta-cognitive beliefs, or the patient's beliefs about the eating disorder. For some patients, these beliefs are clearly formed and easily accessible, and for others, it may require some work for the patient to be able to identify or disclose them.

These kinds of beliefs relate clearly to the particular functions of the patient's eating disorder. For example, a patient whose eating disorder works for her as a way to achieve and feel special may hold the meta-cognitive belief, 'Without my anorexia I'd be nothing, just a worthless failure.' An individual who depends on her eating disorder to shelter her from her emotional experiences might believe, 'If I didn't have my bulimia, I wouldn't be able to cope with life.' These types of belief are a critical factor in the maintenance of eating disorders, as they mean that the individual may feel very ambivalent about getting 'better', and see good reason for staying as she is. This has important implications for treatment, as it means that patients with strong pro-eating disorder meta-cognitions are likely to feel threatened by the idea of coming for treatment, and are therefore difficult to engage.

Pro-eating disorder meta-cognitions may be more important generally for the maintenance of anorexic than bulimic disorders. Serpell and Treasure (2002) reported fewer pro-eating disorder and more anti-eating disorder meta-cognitions in bulimic than anorexic participants. This is mirrored by cultural phenomena such as the emergence in recent years of a multitude of pro-anorexia but not pro-bulimia websites.

Biological and starvation effects

One prominent biological model of eating disorders hypothesises that during the early stages of an eating disorder, eating little is maintained intra-personally by positive reinforcement from a temporary improvement in mood and well-being (Kaye *et al.* 1999, 2003). This may be moderated by an unknown biological vulnerability. This early stage has been summarised by Casper (1998), who noted that AN patients are initially typically cheerful, content and euphoric with high levels of energy despite a low caloric intake and continued weight loss, suggesting that they feel mentally alert and physically active.

In addition, the physical, cognitive, emotional and social effects of starvation also conspire to maintain eating disorders. Our knowledge about these effects comes from the famous Minnesota starvation experiment conducted in the late 1940s, where healthy normal weight volunteers were made to lose about 15% of their body weight, and then were gradually re-fed (Keys *et al.* 1950). A detailed description of the findings is beyond the scope of the present chapter. People who are starved think constantly about food and eating. They may develop strange rituals around eating, and other obsessive-compulsive symptoms. Mood disturbance and social withdrawal are common. For some the desire for food becomes so overwhelming that they gorge themselves on food, analogous to what happens in bulimia nervosa. With increasing starvation, eating arouses unpleasant physical sensations (such as feeling bloated, nauseous and overfull). Both biological and cognitive factors may play a role in this. For example, delayed gastric emptying increases the sense of fullness and reduces appetite and delayed gut transit times lead to constipation, bloating and discomfort (Treasure and Szmukler 1995). For some the prospect of having to eat may become a threat associated with these aversive consequences. The learnt expectation that certain foods, such as those high in fat, cause particular physical sensations may exacerbate such physical symptoms (Feinle-Bisset *et al.* 2003).

The maintenance of bingeing and purging behaviour

Thus far we have presented an approach to the cognitive modelling of eating disorders that has considered anorexic and bulimic disorders together as far as possible, while highlighting important differences when needed. However, the development and maintenance of bingeing and purging behaviour, occurring in bulimia and binge–purge subtype anorexia, do require a specific account.

It is worth noting that although the model described below, which is an integration of our own ideas with those of other theorists (Cooper *et al.* 2004; Fairburn *et al.* 2003), was developed to account for bingeing and compensatory behaviour, the same constructs may be relevant for individuals who, rather than bingeing on objectively large amounts of food, eat small amounts that nonetheless break their own dietary rules. In this way, the model is adaptable for patients with a variety of different presentations.

The bulimic or binge–purge subtype anorexic individual's concerns about her weight and shape, in conjunction with her underlying schematic system, lead her to believe that thinness is a solution to her problems, and that if she could only attain this, life would be better and she would be happier. In order to reach her goals, she often begins to diet. This is likely to involve restricting her overall food intake, not eating for periods of time and avoiding particular types of foods. Her inflexible and extreme core and intermediate beliefs mean that her dieting is also rigid and extreme. This leads to a number of mechanisms that make her prone to bingeing.

One of the most important of these is hunger, which is an aversive state leading to a strong physiological drive to eat to ameliorate it. Cognitively, she becomes increasingly focused on food and trying not to eat, and more emotionally vulnerable in that she is likely to experience anxiety and a low mood, making it increasingly difficult for her to cope with life's demands.

Within this context, an individual has experiences that act as triggers for bingeing. These may be physiological and related closely to her hunger, and/or they may be more emotionally or interpersonally based, leading, via violation of her intermediate level beliefs, to activation of her negative core beliefs. This leads to automatic thought-level negative appraisals of herself or her situation, which lead in turn to negative affect.

With the experience of negative affect comes the strong desire to escape from it. As with AN, people with BN often have great difficulty tolerating negative emotions and have developed beliefs about the unacceptability of these emotions and their ability to cope with them. At this point, the individual enters into a decision-making process. In their cognitive model of BN, Cooper *et al.* (2004) have developed the useful concept of positive, negative and permission-giving beliefs about eating that come into play at this point. On the one hand, an individual has positive beliefs about how eating will help her, such as, 'I'll feel better if I eat,' or, 'Eating will be a release from feeling like this.' On the other hand, she also has negative beliefs about eating, such as, 'If I eat I'll get fat,' or, 'If I eat I will have failed.' This leaves her caught in the middle between two conflicting sets of beliefs.

This impasse is resolved via permission-giving beliefs, or beliefs that she has no control over her eating, such as, 'I'll start again properly tomorrow,' 'I'll just eat a bit,' or, 'There's no other way I can handle this.' Once she has broken her rigid diet, she may have more of these thoughts, such as, 'I've blown it now, I might as well eat the whole packet,' or 'I have no control over this,' which lead her to carry on eating. Eating may be accompanied by enormous physical release as her hunger is relieved and she allows herself denied food that she has been craving.

Eating also acts to modulate her emotions. During an eating episode, patients often report feeling numb, or alternatively experiencing feelings of contentedness or sometimes euphoria. It is important in formulating BN to establish the specific effect of the eating behaviour on the individual's emotions, as this may be particularly crucial to the maintenance of the disorder.

Once the eating episode has ended, the relief a person feels is often quickly replaced by intensely negative appraisals of her behaviour. She may feel disgusted, disappointed and angry with herself, and be filled with fears about the effects of the eating on her weight. This leads to a second bout of intensely negative affect, which she again feels the need to escape from. This in turn leads to another decision-making process, about what to do to ameliorate this intolerable situation. The most common compensatory behaviour engaged in by people with bulimia is vomiting, and so we will speak in terms of this behaviour, although the same constructs may be applied to other behaviours such as laxative abuse, over-exercise and other ways a patient may try to compensate for eating.

At this point, negative beliefs about her eating behaviour in combination with her negative affect lead to a second set of permission-giving or lack of control beliefs, such as, 'This is the last time,' or, 'I have to get rid of this food or I won't be able to bear it.' The vomiting behaviour follows on from this point and, as with the bingeing, can provide enormous physical relief as well as serving as another powerful modulator of her emotions. Patients may report a sense of calm, cleanliness or numbness after vomiting; as with bingeing, it is important to establish the specific effects of the behaviour on her emotions and then identify the cognitions that accompany or follow them.

After a bingeing and vomiting cycle, an individual may be left with residual feelings of guilt and shame that make her more vulnerable to triggers that initiate the next cycle. Additionally, although bingeing and vomiting provide temporary relief from the cognitions and affect that served as triggers for it, they do not provide any new information or serve to change an individual's situation in any way. If a bingeing and vomiting cycle was triggered by the thought, 'Nobody really likes me,' the behaviour allows the individual to escape from this thought and the affect that accompanies it for a short time, but in the end she is left with the probability that the thought will recur. Her solution works to make her feel better in the short term, and so it is reinforced: the behaviour is likely to recur and the cycle is strengthened and maintained. However, in the longer term, the solution does not address her real problems at a schematic level, although it does inhibit more effective problem-solving strategies. In this way, bingeing and vomiting behaviour is perpetuated and the solution the individual has found for her difficulties serves progressively to increase them.

CLINICAL CASE EXAMPLES

We will move on to two clinical examples to illustrate how the framework we have described may be used to formulate individual cases. Formulations such as those that follow are built up over a number of sessions. We find it useful to discuss with patients the idea that a formulation is always a 'work in progress', which is meant to be useful in therapy to help understand how problems develop and are maintained and to guide therapeutic work like a 'map'; it is not meant to be a definitive explanation or an absolute truth, and will need to be reviewed and revised as understanding increases throughout the therapeutic process.

Sarah: a patient with restricting anorexia nervosa

Sarah was a 20-year-old woman with a six-year history of restricting anorexia. She was referred to the eating disorders service by her GP after her family moved into the area from another part of the country. When she came to the assessment appointment, accompanied by her mother, Sarah presented as neatly dressed, softly spoken and rather withdrawn. She said that she had agreed to the referral to our service from her previous eating disorders service, but felt that she 'hadn't really had much of a choice about it'.

Sarah had a body mass index (BMI) of 15.5 kg/m^2. Her current daily food intake followed a fairly rigid pattern of two small calorie-restricted meals during the day. Additionally, she attended the gym for an hour, five days per week. She said she felt physically quite weak sometimes but otherwise in good health, and reported her mood as being 'fine' although she felt frustrated that she was unable to get on with her life as she wanted at the moment.

Sarah lived at home with her parents and her sister Clare. Sarah's mother had been a solicitor before the birth of her children, and her father was an engineer. Clare (aged 23) had Down's syndrome and a number of associated medical difficulties. Sarah herself had been born prematurely, and had needed to spend a month in hospital before being discharged home. Sarah described her family as generally close and caring, although they did not talk a great deal about their personal feelings, and there had been a lot of arguments over the last few years about her eating and weight. She described her mother as 'a worrier, like me', who had stopped work when Clare and Sarah were young in order to look after them full-time. She said her father was a reserved person, who 'kept to himself'. She said they got along reasonably well, but that he could be quite critical when she did not do as well as he thought she could, and sometimes 'a bit of a bully' as a result of this. Sarah said she loved Clare, but felt that it had been hard growing up having an ill sister, as she had sometimes felt that Clare got all the attention. She added that she felt guilty for feeling like this, as she 'shouldn't think selfish things like that'.

Sarah's eating disorder began to emerge when she was 15. Her weight at this point was in the normal range, and she said she had not particularly thought or worried about her weight or food before this. At this time, in her first year of GCSEs, she described feeling very stressed about her school work; she had always done well at school but was finding the workload for her planned 12 GCSEs difficult to manage. Sarah said she had always been quite shy, but she had two close friends from primary school who she did spend time with. Both of her friends began relationships with boys around this time, and Sarah said she had felt left out and 'different', being the only one without a boyfriend. She said that she did not feel interested in or ready for this kind of relationship at that point, but felt hurt by the increasing distance she felt from her friends. Sarah began to diet and go to the gym, which she described as being because she wanted to be as healthy and fit as possible for her exams.

Sarah had dropped nearly a stone by the beginning of her second GCSE year. Her schoolmates complimented her and admired her self-discipline when they noticed this, and she felt increasingly energetic and positive. Sarah's weight loss continued over the course of the school year; she became increasingly focused on this and her schoolwork, and found that she drifted further away from her friends. Immediately prior to her GCSEs she reached a BMI of 17 kg/m^2. By this time, her parents were becoming extremely concerned; Sarah did not see what the problem was and insisted she had never felt better. However, they eventually persuaded her to go to her GP, at which point she was referred to her community mental health team and then to her local eating disorders service. In the meantime, Sarah continued to work hard for her GCSEs and took these in the summer. She was disappointed by her results and resolved to work harder for her A-levels, for which she enrolled in a sixth-form college.

When Sarah started therapy for her eating disorder, at the start of her A-level course, her weight had fallen to a BMI of 16.5 kg/m^2. She saw a therapist from her local eating disorders service for about six months, and although she did not increase her weight, she did not lose any more. She remained at a stable weight throughout her sixth-form years, and continued to work hard, but became increasingly socially isolated and lost touch with her remaining friends. She sat her A-levels, and although she did not do as well as she had wanted, she got good enough marks to attain a place on a university course in a nearby city.

Sarah began her university course and moved into halls of residence. She felt completely out of place among the other students, and although at times she wanted to join in and make friends as it seemed everyone else was doing, she felt awkward and self-conscious and ended up staying in her room working or exercising. Her weight began to drop. When she came home at Christmas, her parents were very worried, and the holiday passed with many arguments as they tried to persuade Sarah to re-contact her eating disorders service. Sarah was adamant that she was fine, and went back to university with a sense of relief from having escaped from the tense family atmosphere. Her weight continued to drop and she reached a BMI of 15 kg/m^2; in the early summer her university decided that she could not continue with her course until she had managed to sort her eating disorder out. She returned home and re-contacted her local services, who took her on for another course of outpatient therapy. She managed to put on a small amount of weight, but her family moved out of the area after several months, and her care was transferred to our services.

Sarah began working with a therapist within our service and they began to explore the meaning of Sarah's anorexia for her. Over the next few weeks, they developed a cognitive formulation of her eating disorder, and came up with the diagram in Figure 11.1, which they continued to adjust and expand over the course of therapy. They used Sarah's own words as much as possible and emphasised the links between her experiences and beliefs and the functions and maintenance mechanisms relevant for her anorexia.

Karen: a case of complex bulimia

Karen was a 31-year-old woman with an 11-year history of bulimia. She was referred to the eating disorders service by her community mental health team following an overdose which had resulted in her attending her local accident and emergency department. Karen was tearful throughout her assessment appointment, and said she had agreed to the referral because she felt very unhappy and wanted to sort her life out.

Early experiences and predisposing factors:
<ul><li>Preterm birth, tendency to be anxious from early age</li><li>Mum was anxious, always worried about us, protected us, especially Clare</li><li>Clare was often ill and got a lot of attention as a result of this – I felt less important</li><li>Dad was critical of me when I didn't achieve as well as he thought I could</li><li>I never felt I fitted in that well – not one of the popular girls at school, always quite shy</li><li>My family doesn't talk to each other about emotional issues – people keep things to themselves</li></ul>

Core beliefs
<ul><li>I'm weak, powerless and vulnerable</li><li>I'm not good enough, different/defective</li><li>Others are likely to judge and criticise me</li></ul>

Intermediate beliefs: attitudes, rules and assumptions
General:<ul><li>If I let people see I'm weak, or if they realise I'm different and not good enough, I'll be more vulnerable</li><li>I should keep my feelings to myself and others at a distance, so they don't find out I'm not good enough, weak and different</li><li>I should be able to achieve the highest standards; if I don't, it's proof I'm not good enough</li><li>If I work hard and keep focused, I might be able to reach the standards I need to</li></ul>**Anorexia specific:**<ul><li>If I can control my eating, I'm less weak and less vulnerable</li><li>Being able to control my eating means I'm good at something, and different in a good rather than a bad way</li><li>If I can control my eating, I can keep safe, focused and clear</li><li>Keeping focused on my eating means I can keep others at a safe distance</li><li>If I'm ill, it hides the fact that I'm not good enough</li></ul>

Triggers: why anorexia?
<ul><li>Feeling stressed about school work, my friends getting boyfriends, discovered losing weight and going to the gym made me feel better and initially others admired me for it</li></ul>

Functions of my anorexia and my beliefs about it
Intrapersonal (within me):<ul><li>Safety, keeps me in my 'bubble'</li><li>Control: everything is clear and simple</li><li>Achievement: it's something I'm good at</li><li>It makes me 'good' different rather than 'bad' different</li><li>Avoidance: means I don't have to think about or feel bad about other things</li></ul>**Interpersonal (with others):**<ul><li>Avoidance: means I can keep others away, stay in my safe 'bubble'</li><li>Care: although I get annoyed with my parents for interfering, at least they notice me, and because it's an 'illness' it's not so much my fault or because I'm not good enough</li></ul>

Behaviours
<ul><li>Restrict my food, follow my rules exactly</li><li>Keep my emotions to myself, and don't get too near to people</li><li>Try really hard with everything – don't stop until it's perfect</li></ul>

Other factors that maintain my anorexia
Starvation effects:<ul><li>I feel bloated if I eat anything at all</li><li>I feel OK at this weight – it's hard to believe that there's anything really wrong when I feel well</li></ul>

Figure 11.1 Sarah's cognitive behavioural formulation.

Karen estimated that she binged and vomited between two and four times a day. She said that she started each day with a plan to 'be good and keep a grip', and ate several pieces of fruit and crispbread during the morning. However, at lunchtime, if she was at college she tended to go out to several fast food restaurants and binge, after which she would make herself sick. On returning from college she would buy more binge food, which she would eat straight away and then vomit afterwards. Depending on what she was doing for the rest of the evening, she might then go into another binge and vomit cycle later on. On days when she was at home all day, she tended to binge and vomit for most of the afternoon and evening. Karen's current BMI was 25 kg/m^2.

Karen had a history of alcohol difficulties, although she had not had a drink in nearly eight months, after attending a rehabilitation programme. She described how when she was feeling particularly desperate she would cut herself, and that this happened about twice per month at the moment. She was also several thousand pounds in debt, which she attributed largely to her bulimia. In addition to the overdose which had prompted the current referral, she had overdosed on two other occasions. Of all three of these she said that she had not really wanted to die, but to 'get away from everything' during crisis times.

Karen lived alone in a council property. She had begun a full-time course at a local college six months previously. Prior to this, she had been unemployed or in temporary jobs for most of her 20s. She was enjoying her course, but finding it a struggle to get to her lectures and complete assignments as her bulimia took up a lot of her time. She also felt very lacking in confidence about being able to do the course because she believed she was 'too thick'. She felt anxious and sad about this, and was considering giving the course up.

Karen had lived with her parents and her younger brother and sister until she was 18. She described her early life as 'a bit of a nightmare', in that her father, a self-employed plumber, had alcohol problems and was frequently violent towards her mother, herself and her siblings. Karen's parents had separated when she was 16, and she had seen her dad infrequently since then. She said she had a fairly close relationship with her mother, an office administrator, with whom she spoke about once a week, although she did not see much of her siblings. Karen's mother suffered with chronic depression, which had resulted in her hospitalisation twice during Karen's childhood. Karen said that her parents and her siblings were overweight and that they had always been 'a fat family'. She remembered her mother being on 'a constant diet' throughout her childhood.

Karen had not enjoyed school; she had felt bored by her schoolwork and remembered being 'picked on and laughed at' by her peers, which she felt was at least partly due to her weight. During her teens, her BMI had been approximately 28, and she described 'feeling miserable and fat, eating to cheer myself up, then feeling even worse'. When she was 16, she left school and got a job in a local shop. She had begun drinking and spending time with people who she described as 'the wrong crowd, but the only ones who would have me'. She had her first sexual relationship around this time, which she said had been 'pretty casual'. However, she began a relationship with a man and she moved in with him when she was 18; this lasted until she was 20.

Karen was very distraught at the end of this relationship, and took her first overdose soon afterwards. It was at this point that her bulimia began. She started binge eating to comfort herself, and found that vomiting afterwards helped alleviate her guilt and fear about putting on weight and made her feel calmer. In fact, she found that she was able to lose some weight, and she described feeling a sense of elation that she had found a way to 'eat what I want and not be fat'. Karen also began drinking more around this time, and eventually lost her job as a result of this.

Her first contact with services followed, as her GP referred her to her local alcohol team. She was able to control her drinking for some time, but found that both this and her increasingly entrenched bulimia continued to be a struggle for her throughout her 20s. She also began to cut herself occasionally during times of stress. She had intermittent contact with alcohol services, but no specialist eating disorder input throughout this time. Over the next years, she had several short-term involvements with men, but had concluded that she 'couldn't do relationships', as she found that either she got bored and ended them, or she became very dependent and was left by her partners. She had a small group of friends, but did not feel there was anyone she was really close to. This continued to be a point of great distress for her, and she said that one of the worst problems for her was that she was very lonely.

When she was 30, Karen said she had decided to 'take charge' of her life and entered an alcohol rehabilitation programme. She completed this and began her college course shortly afterwards. She started a relationship with a man she met at college, and described how she had been hopeful that 'this time it would be different'. However, he ended the relationship unexpectedly, and this had prompted the overdose that had resulted in her referral to the eating disorders service.

Karen said that she felt very motivated to try to recover from her bulimia. Although she had managed to stop drinking, she felt out of control with her eating. She hoped that if she could make progress with this, it would help her feel more stable and better able to cope with the rest of her life.

Karen began therapy within our service. She expressed interest in trying to make sense of how her diverse difficulties hung together, how they had developed and were maintained. She and her therapist developed a cognitive formulation which they expressed in the diagram in Figure 11.2.

DISCUSSION

We have attempted to outline a framework for the cognitive-behavioural for-mulation of patients presenting with complex eating disorders. Throughout,

Early experiences and predisposing factors
• Family history of alcohol problems, depression and being overweight • Dad was violent, hit and shouted at me, mum and my brother and sister – felt helpless and bad about myself • Picked on at school for being overweight – felt terrible about myself

Core beliefs
• I'm worthless and incompetent • I'm unlovable • I'm vulnerable • Other people and the world are unpredictable, confusing and hostile

Intermediate beliefs: attitudes, rules and assumptions

General:
- There's no point me aiming high with jobs or college, as I'm too worthless and incompetent ever to succeed in anything
- There's no point me trying to make friends or have relationships with people I really like, as I'm too unlovable for these kinds of people to want to be with me
- If I try to do what other people expect and want from me, I might be less unlovable to them, and they might not realise how worthless and incompetent I am, or try to hurt me
- I'm too vulnerable and incompetent to cope with my emotions; if I have difficult emotions, I need to get away from them in any way I can or they'll overwhelm me

Bulimia specific:
- If I was thin, I'd be less worthless, incompetent, unlovable and vulnerable
- My bulimia is a way through which I can at least succeed with something (being thinner), which makes me less incompetent and vulnerable

Triggers: why bulimia?
• Was picked on at school about being overweight; found that bingeing was a good escape from my emotions and vomiting helped me to lose weight and feel calm

Functions of my bulimia and my beliefs about it

Intrapersonal (within me):
- Escape: helps me to cope with my emotions
- Beating the system: I can succeed at something (losing weight) while still being able to eat what I want

Interpersonal (with others):
- Although others don't know about my bulimia, it helps me to get away from the painful feelings I have around my relationships

Behaviours
• Binge and vomit • Drink, harm myself or overdose • Get into relationships with people I don't really care about, or cling and try too hard to please if I do like someone

Other factors that maintain my difficulties
- Using these ways (bulimia, drinking, self-harm) to escape from my emotions gets in the way of me learning how to cope in ways that are more helpful for me
- Trying to diet and not eat all morning makes me more physiologically prone to bingeing because I get so hungry
- I tend to think if I've broken my diet there's no point carrying on with it and that it's further proof I have no control and might as well give in; this makes me more vulnerable to bingeing

Figure 11.2 Karen's cognitive behavioural formulation.

we have sought to emphasise the importance of using these ideas flexibly and adapting them to individual patients. An important aspect of this approach is the need to think more widely than just about the importance of weight and shape concerns. Although these areas are relevant to varying degrees with many eating-disordered patients, for a significant proportion, other issues and factors are equally or even more significant in understanding their eating disorder.

One further aspect deserves mentioning. Patients with complex bulimia nervosa, such as Karen, often present the therapist with lots of material – complicated, dramatic and epic stories. In every session new events will unfold that add further layers of complexity and detail. Yet the week after, these events will be replaced by another event or crisis which is even more urgent and the previous one will have paled into insignificance. Thus it is easy for the therapist to feel overwhelmed by the stories and intense emotions attached to them and derailed by being tempted to follow new leads. A diagrammatic formulation such as the ones shown above helps to focus on themes and issues which are central to all the different stories and problems, and thus helps patient and therapist to stick to task.

In contrast, patients with anorexia nervosa often give away relatively little and their account of themselves may seem somewhat bland and lacking in emotional detail. Thus, the emotional significance of particular events or beliefs can only be inferred or guessed at by the therapist. The 'short-hand' nature of diagrammatic formulations makes it easy to stay somewhat distant from and avoid their emotional impact. We often give patients with AN their case formulation written as a personal letter from the therapist to the patient, in addition to a diagrammatic presentation. Letters more than diagrams speak to the person's emotions. These letters ideally should build on and incorporate what is contained in the diagrammatic presentation. As much as possible the patient's own words and expressions are used. The practice of writing formulation letters derives from cognitive analytical therapy (Ryle 1995), where the patient is typically presented both with a diagrammatic formulation and a formulation letter. In our experience patients value these letters highly; many report feeling very validated by the therapist's effort on their behalf and feeling very understood. We believe that these two very different ways of presenting the patient with their formulation, while involving somewhat more work for the therapist, can usefully complement each other.

REFERENCES

Agras, W. S. *et al.* (2000). A multicenter comparison of cognitive-behavioral therapy and interpersonal psychotherapy for bulimia nervosa. *Archives of General Psychiatry* 57: 459–66.

American Psychiatric Association. (1994). *Diagnostic and Statistical Manual of Mental Disorders* (4th edn). Washington, DC: Author.

Branch, C. and Eurman, L. J. (1980). Social attitudes toward patients with anorexia nervosa. *American Journal of Psychiatry* 137: 631–2.

Bulik, C. M. (2002). Anxiety, depression, and eating disorders. In C. G. Fairburn and K. D. Brownell (eds) *Eating Disorders and Obesity*. New York: Guilford Press.

Burney, J. and Irwin, H. J. (2000). Shame and guilt in women with eating-disorder symptomatology. *Journal of Clinical Psychology* 56: 51–61.

Casper, R. C. (1998). Behavioural activation and lack of concern, core symptoms of anorexia nervosa? *International Journal of Eating Disorders* 24: 381–93.

Clinton, D. *et al.* (2004). Cluster analysis of key diagnostic variables from two independent samples of eating-disorder patients: Evidence for a consistent pattern. *Psychological Medicine* 34: 1035–45.

Collier, D. A. and Treasure, J. L. (2004). The aetiology of eating disorders. *British Journal of Psychiatry* 185: 363–5.

Cooper, M. J. *et al.* (2004). A cognitive model of bulimia nervosa. *British Journal of Clinical Psychology* 43: 1–16.

Fairburn, C. G. (2004). Keynote address at the Meeting of the Academy for Eating Disorders, April 29–May 2, Orlando, FL.

Fairburn, C. G. and Bohn, K. (2005). Eating disorders NOS (EDNOS): An example of the troublesome 'not otherwise specified' (NOS) category in DSM-IV. *Behaviour Research and Therapy* 43: 691–701.

Fairburn, C. G. *et al.* (1993). Cognitive behaviour therapy for binge eating and bulimia. A comprehensive treatment manual. In C. G. Fairburn and G. T. Wilson (eds) *Binge Eating: Nature, Assessment and Treatment*. New York: Guilford Press.

Fairburn, C. G. *et al.* (2003). Cognitive behaviour therapy for eating disorders: A 'transdiagnostic' theory and treatment. *Behaviour Research and Therapy* 41: 509–28.

Feinle-Bisset, C. *et al.* (2003). Role of cognitive factors in symptom induction following high and low fat meals in patients with functional dyspepsia. *Gut* 52: 1414–8.

Gilbert, P. (2001). Evolutionary approaches to psychopathology: The role of natural defences. *Australian and New Zealand Journal of Psychiatry* 35: 17–27.

Jacobi, C. *et al.* (2004). Coming to terms with risk factors for eating disorders: Application of risk terminology and suggestions for a general taxonomy. *Psychological Bulletin* 130: 19–65.

Karwautz, A. *et al.* (2001). Individual-specific risk factors for anorexia nervosa: A pilot study using a discordant sister-pair design. *Psychological Medicine* 31: 317–29.

Kaye, W. *et al.* (1999). New directions in treatment research of anorexia and bulimia nervosa. *Biological Psychiatry* 45: 1285–92.

Kaye, W. H. *et al.* (2003). Anxiolytic effects of acute tryptophan depletion in anorexia nervosa. *International Journal of Eating Disorders* 33: 257–67.

Keel, P. K. and Klump, K. L. (2003). Are eating disorders culture-bound syndromes? Implications for conceptualizing their etiology. *Psychological Bulletin* 129: 747–69.

Keel, P. K. *et al.* (2004). Application of a latent class analysis to empirically define eating disorder phenotypes. *Archives of General Psychiatry* 61: 192–200.

Keys, A. *et al.* (1950). *The Biology of Human Starvation*. Minneapolis, MN: University of Minnesota Press.

Leung, N. *et al.* (1999) Core beliefs in anorexic and bulimic women. *Journal of Nervous and Mental Disorders* 187: 736–41.

Murphy, F. *et al.* (2000). Differential environmental factors in anorexia nervosa: A sibling pair study. *British Journal of Clinical Psychology* 39: 193–203.

National Institute for Clinical Excellence. (2004). *Eating Disorders: Anorexia Nervosa, Bulimia Nervosa and Related Eating Disorders*. London: National Institute for Clinical Excellence.

Palmer, B. (2003). Concepts of eating disorders. In J. Treasure *et al.* (eds) *Handbook of Eating Disorders* (2nd edn). Chichester, UK: John Wiley and Sons.

Ryle, A. (1995). *Cognitive Analytic Therapy: Developments in Theory and Practice*. Chichester, UK: Wiley.

Schmidt, U. and Treasure, J. (in press). Anorexia nervosa: Valued and visible. A cognitive-interpersonal maintenance model and its implications for research and practice. *British Journal of Clinical Psychology*.

Schmidt, U. *et al.* (1995). Puberty, sexual milestones and childhood sexual abuse: How are they related in eating disorder patients? *Psychological Medicine* 25: 413–7.

Schmidt, U. *et al.* (1997a). Is there a specific trauma precipitating anorexia nervosa? *Psychological Medicine* 27: 523–30.

Schmidt, U. *et al.* (1997b). Childhood experiences of care and abuse in eating disorders: Clinical and research implications. *European Review of Eating Disorders* 5: 184–207.

Serpell, L. and Treasure, J. (2002). Bulimia nervosa: Friend or foe? The pros and cons of bulimia nervosa. *International Journal of Eating Disorders* 32: 164–70.

Serpell, L. *et al.* (1999). Anorexia nervosa: Friend or foe? *International Journal of Eating Disorders* 25: 177–86.

Serpell, L. *et al.* (2003). The use of the Pros and Cons of Anorexia Nervosa (P-CAN) scale with children and adolescents. *Journal of Psychosomatic Research* 54: 567–71.

Serpell, L. *et al.* (2004). The development of the P-CAN: A scale to operationalize the pros and cons of AN. *International Journal of Eating Disorders* 36: 416–33.

Shafran, R. and de Silva, P. (2003). Cognitive-behavioural models. In J. Treasure *et al.* (eds) *Handbook of Eating Disorders*. Chichester, UK: Wiley.

Treasure, J. and Schmidt, U. (2001). Ready, willing and able to change: Motivational aspects of the assessment and treatment of eating disorders. *European Eating Disorders Review* 9: 1–15.

Treasure, J. and Szmukler, G. (1995). Medical complications of chronic anorexia nervosa. In G. Szmukler *et al.* (eds) *Handbook of Eating Disorders*. Chichester, UK: John Wiley.

Troop, N.A. and Connan, F. (2003). Shame, social stress, and eating disorders. In G. M. Ruggiero (ed) *Eating Disorders in the Mediterranean Area*. New York: Nova Science Publishers, Inc.

Vitousek, K. B. and Hollon, S. D. (1990). The investigation of schematic content and processing in eating disorders. *Cognitive Therapy and Research* 14: 191–214.

Vitousek, K. *et al.* (1998). Enhancing motivation for change in treatment resistant eating disorders. *Clinical Psychology Review* 18: 391–420.

Waller, G. and Kennerley, H. (2003). Cognitive-behavioural treatments. In J. Treasure *et al.* (eds) *Handbook of Eating Disorders* (2nd edn). Chichester UK: John Wiley and Sons.

Waller, G. *et al.* (2000). Cognitive content among bulimic women: The role of core beliefs. *International Journal of Eating Disorders* 28: 235–41.

Wilson, G. T. (2002). Eating disorders and addiction. In C. G. Fairburn and K. D. Brownell (eds) *Eating Disorders and Obesity*. New York: Guilford Press.

Wolff, G. and Serpell, L. (1998). A cognitive model and treatment strategies for anorexia nervosa. In H. W. Hoek *et al.* (eds) *Neurobiology in the Treatment of Eating
Disorders*. Chichester, UK: John Wiley and Sons.

Wonderlich, S. A. (2002). Personality and eating disorders. In C. G. Fairburn and
K. D. Brownell (eds) *Eating Disorders and Obesity*. New York: Guilford Press.

Woolrich, R. *et al.* (2005). *Negative Self-Beliefs in Anorexia Nervosa: A Detailed
Exploration of Their Content, Origin and Link to Behaviour*. Paper presented at the
Academy of Eating Disorders Meeting, Montreal, April.

Zipfel S. *et al.* (2003). Medical complications in eating disorders and obesity. In
J. Treasure *et al.* (eds) *Handbook of Eating Disorders: Theory, Treatment and
Research* (2nd edn). Chichester, UK: John Wiley and Sons.

Chapter 12

Medically unexplained symptoms

Richard J. Brown

Health care practitioners frequently encounter patients with physical symptoms for which no adequate organic explanation can be found. Patients with such medically unexplained symptoms (MUS) often report high levels of distress, disability and psychiatric morbidity and consume disproportionate amounts of health care resources. Historically, chronic MUS have been regarded as difficult to treat and there have been few effective psychological interventions for these patients. In recent years, however, effective cognitive behavioural interventions for MUS have been developed and the number of patients referred to psychological services with these conditions is increasing. This chapter provides an overview of the cognitive behavioural assessment, formulation and treatment of patients with MUS and summarises the treatment evaluation research in this area.

BACKGROUND

The term 'medically unexplained symptoms' encompasses a heterogeneous group of conditions and presentations characterised by the presence of subjectively compelling (i.e., 'real') physical symptoms[1] that (a) cannot be explained fully by the presence of a general medical condition; (b) are associated with significant distress or functional impairment; and (c) are attributed to a medical cause by the patient. This group includes patients with:

- 'functional somatic syndromes' such as chronic fatigue syndrome (CFS; a.k.a. myalgic encephalomyelitis or ME), irritable bowel syndrome (IBS), fibromyalgia, non-cardiac chest pain, multiple chemical sensitivity, atypical facial pain, Gulf War syndrome etc.
- symptoms of an anxiety or affective disorder that are presented somatically (so-called 'somatised mental disorders')
- preoccupation with the fear of having, or the idea that one has, a serious physical illness (i.e., hypochondriasis) or a deficit in physical appearance (i.e., body dysmorphic disorder)

- somatoform disorders other than hypochondriasis, including a history of multiple unexplained symptoms in different bodily systems (i.e., somatisation disorder; ICD-10; WHO 1992)
- dissociative (conversion) disorders, characterised by unexplained amnesia or other symptoms indicative of, but not explained by, neurological illness (ICD-10; WHO 1992)
- an organic illness associated with greater levels of disability than one would expect given the pathological findings.

There is considerable overlap between these different categories, and mixed presentations are the norm in clinical practice. Many patients with somatoform disorders report both neurological and non-neurological problems, for example, as well as symptoms of an anxiety or affective disturbance that have been catastrophically misinterpreted as evidence of a serious physical illness (Sharpe et al. 1992a). Enquiries about other illness experiences may also uncover previous diagnoses of CFS or IBS, as well as an on-going physical health problem that appears to be causing a disproportionate degree of disability. One of the main strengths of CBT is its capacity to account for all of these different phenomena within a common explanatory framework, while providing for the formulation and treatment of individual clinical cases. In line with this, the current chapter takes a broad CBT approach to this group of conditions (rather than concentrating on specific types of MUS), while emphasising the importance of comprehensive assessment and idiosyncratic formulation in each case.

Many different labels have been applied to this category of complaints, including 'hysterical', 'psychogenic', 'functional', 'nonorganic' and 'psychosomatic'. Each of these labels is either ambiguous or has unfortunate connotations. The terms 'hysteria' and 'hysterical' are particularly offensive to patients and should be avoided at all costs (Stone et al. 2002). For the purposes of this chapter, the terms 'medically unexplained symptoms' and 'medically unexplained illness' will be adopted as theory-neutral labels for the diverse array of symptoms and presentations encountered in this area. In practice, it is both possible and preferable not to use any kind of label (other than 'physical symptoms') for many patients, although some prefer the certainty and apparent authority of a clear diagnostic label (Moss-Morris and Wrapson 2003). In cases where certainty is possible, I tend to favour the term 'somatoform disorder' as it is less equivocal than 'medically unexplained symptoms' and implies that the symptoms in question are understood and fit a recognised pattern. I use the term 'somatisation' to refer to the phenomenon whereby physical symptoms are experienced and/or expressed as a result of psychological processes.

Information concerning the diagnosis, clinical features, epidemiology and theoretical background to MUS can be found in Brown (2004), Brown and

Ron (2002), Brown and Trimble (2000), Kirmayer and Taillefer (1997), Mayou *et al.* (1995) and Wessely *et al.* (1998).

TREATMENT EVALUATION RESEARCH

Although MUS are ubiquitous within health care settings, only a small proportion of patients with these conditions are ever referred to a psychiatrist (Ewald *et al.* 1994; Hamilton *et al.* 1996) and fewer still get to see a psychologist or CBT therapist (Mayou and Sharpe 1997). As a result, research into CBT for MUS is relatively under-developed compared to that for the anxiety and affective disorders. Nevertheless, recent years have seen important advances in the cognitive behavioural formulation and treatment of these conditions. Irrespective of the type of MUS, cognitive behavioural interventions in this area generally include some or all the following elements:

- providing an alternative, non-catastrophic interpretation of symptoms in cognitive behavioural terms
- challenging catastrophic thoughts about symptoms
- modifying dysfunctional beliefs about symptoms through behavioural experiments
- reversing avoidance and other maladaptive coping behaviours
- teaching behavioural coping skills (e.g., relaxation, graded activity, distraction)
- psychoeducation
- problem-solving
- addressing lifestyle and personality factors associated with vulnerability.

Kroenke and Swindle (2000) present a critical review of controlled treatment trials of CBT that have adopted such an approach to unexplained illness. Of the 31 trials reviewed, 25 concerned specific unexplained symptoms (e.g., back pain, chest pain, tinnitus) or functional somatic syndromes (e.g., CFS), three concerned 'unexplained physical symptoms' and three concerned hypochondriasis; control participants were either allocated to a waiting list (14 studies), 'conventional care' (8), an attention placebo (5), daily symptom monitoring (2), 'miscellaneous treatments' (7) or CBT/CT combined with another treatment (5). In 20 of the 31 trials, CBT participants showed significantly greater improvements in their physical symptoms than control participants, with three further studies showing a non-significant trend in this direction; similar effects were found for individual treatments and those administered in a group format. Treatment effects persisted at follow-up in all but one study and evidence of a delayed response to treatment was found in six. Twelve studies (out of 18 examining this) found that CBT participants showed superior effects on various cognitive and behavioural indices, including illness beliefs, hypochondriacal concerns, maladaptive thoughts and perceived control over symptoms. Kroenke and Swindle speculate that changes in these variables might be the source of the observed improvements in physical symptoms, although no evidence pertaining to this is presented. It is noteworthy that only 10 studies (out of 26) found a definite treatment effect for psychological distress, with a probable effect being found in two. Unfortunately, it is impossible to identify the active ingredients of therapy in these studies due to the heterogeneity of the CBT approaches used. Moreover, although treatment dropout rates were generally low in the published reports, the rate of treatment refusals is rarely mentioned, raising questions about the generalisability of the study findings (Kroenke and Swindle 2000).

None of the studies reviewed by Kroenke and Swindle specifically addressed unexplained neurological symptoms (i.e., conversion disorders) and therefore very little is known about the relative efficacy of CBT for these conditions. A recent open trial evaluation of CBT found that this approach was successful in reducing the frequency of seizures in a group of patient diagnosed with non-epileptic attack disorder (Goldstein *et al.* 2004). Controlled evaluations of CBT for unexplained neurological illness are lacking, however. In addition, few studies have considered the efficacy of CBT for patients with multiple unexplained symptoms. In one notable exception, Bleichhardt *et al.* (2004) investigated the efficacy of CBT administered to a large group of inpatients with an average of 10 current unexplained symptoms (mean duration of treatment = 51.9 days). Significant reductions in unexplained symptomatology, medical consultations, depression and anxiety were observed – effects that were not found for a smaller group of waiting list control participants. It remains to be seen whether similar improvements can be obtained when polysymptomatic patients are treated using a less intensive treatment approach in outpatient settings.

In summary, the available research indicates that CBT can be an effective way of understanding and treating many patients with medically unexplained illness. Although this progress is encouraging, CBT for MUS is still in its infancy. Therapeutic effects are often limited, particularly for the emotional symptoms reported by these patients, and a great deal more needs to be done in terms of treatment development and evaluation.

COGNITIVE BEHAVIOURAL FORMULATION OF MUS

One of the main strengths of CBT for MUS is its emphasis on the idea that all illness, whatever its cause, is created and maintained by an interaction between biological, psychological and social processes. This approach side-steps the problems associated with traditional mind–body dualism and the question of whether symptoms are 'physical' or 'psychological', allowing for a blame-free, collaborative approach to symptom assessment and treatment. Taking this view, the purpose of the cognitive behavioural formulation is to understand the range of physiological, emotional, behavioural, cognitive and social processes involved in the creation and maintenance of an individual's symptoms, distress and disability.

Irrespective of the type of MUS in question, most cognitive behavioural models in this area suggest that symptom chronicity results from the persistent misinterpretation of physical sensations as evidence of organic pathology, coupled with the maladaptive forms of coping that develop from this misinterpretation (e.g., Chalder 2001; Salkovskis 1989; Sharpe et al. 1992a; Surawy et al. 1995). According to the model described by Sharpe et al. (1992a; also Salkovskis 1989), the negative affect and emotional arousal resulting from this misinterpretation generate further bodily sensations and increase the perceived salience of somatic sensations by heightening symptom-focused attention. Misinterpretation also triggers coping behaviours that serve to maintain symptoms by: (a) generating further bodily sensations; (b) increasing symptom focus; and (c) encouraging continued misattribution. These behaviours also expose the individual to social factors that have the potential to reinforce symptom focus, illness appraisal and maladaptive coping. Most of the controlled trials in this area are based on this kind of model, which has demonstrated utility.

According to Sharpe et al. (1992a), patients with MUS misinterpret physical sensations arising from various organic sources, including emotional arousal, physiological variation and minor physical pathology. Although this is probably true for many MUS, it is unclear how such physiological processes could be responsible for all unexplained symptoms, particularly the profound alterations in experience seen with symptoms such as unexplained paralysis, pseudo-hallucinations, sensory loss etc. A recent model by Brown (2004) addresses this shortcoming by showing how physical symptoms can arise in the absence of peripheral physiological changes. According to Brown (2004), MUS often arise when the processes underlying the creation of conscious experience and the automatic control of action are over-determined by 'rogue' representations of illness in memory. In this view, the activation levels of these representations can become high enough for the cognitive system to misinterpret these memories of illness as a current illness episode, resulting in a distortion in the conscious body image characterised by a subjectively convincing illness experience. This process is driven by the repeated re-allocation of attentional resources to the rogue representation and perpetuated by the same factors that maintain MUS in the Sharpe et al. (1992a) model (i.e., symptom misinterpretation, body focus, illness cognition and behaviour, negative affect, physiological disturbance, social factors etc.). These psychological processes can also act to maintain symptoms originally produced by demonstrable physical changes, with or without ongoing physical disturbance. Rogue representations can be acquired from several different sources, including exposure to physical sensations and symptoms in the self or others, sociocultural transmission (e.g., via the media) or verbal suggestion (Brown 2004). According to this account, treatment of MUS should focus on reducing the activation of rogue representations in memory by reversing the repetitive allocation of attention to symptoms.

A clinical heuristic for formulating patients with MUS based on the Sharpe *et al.* (1992a) and Brown (2004) models is presented in Figure 12.1. The advantage of this hybrid approach is that it combines the proven clinical efficacy of the model described by Sharpe *et al.* (1992a) with a hypothetical model (Brown 2004) that can account for the development of unexplained symptoms that do not have an obvious physiological basis. The latter also emphasises the importance of the cognitive-attentional processes involved in the creation and maintenance of unexplained symptoms, in addition to the content of the cognitions reported by these patients.

According to this approach, the specific processes involved in the creation and maintenance of chronic unexplained symptoms vary from case to case and from one type of unexplained symptom to another. However, the model assumes that all MUS have certain basic processes in common: chronic MUS arise when the individual gets 'locked' into repeatedly focusing their attention on somatic experiences and interpreting those experiences as evidence of abnormal bodily functioning and/or physical illness (cf. Wells 2000). Catastrophic interpretation of these somatic experiences as evidence of serious pathology, which is central to hypochondriasis, may or may not be present. These somatic experiences may come either from physiological sources (e.g., normal variation, emotional arousal, illness) or psychological sources (i.e., symptom representations in memory) or both. Whether a somatic sensation attracts attention and is misinterpreted as evidence of physical pathology is a function of several factors, including prior beliefs, experiences and predispositions, as well as the cognitive, behavioural, emotional, social and physiological consequences of misinterpretation. These can be loosely categorised as predisposing, precipitating and maintaining factors in the aetiology of MUS. Although there is a growing body of evidence pertaining to these factors, further work needs to be done to establish the reliability and generalisability of the findings in this area and there is a pressing need for further research into the mechanisms of these conditions. Until this is done, the current model must be regarded as a hypothetical account of the creation and maintenance of MUS.

Predisposing factors

Childhood trauma

Patients with MUS often report higher levels of childhood sexual, physical and emotional abuse and a greater lack of parental care than patients with

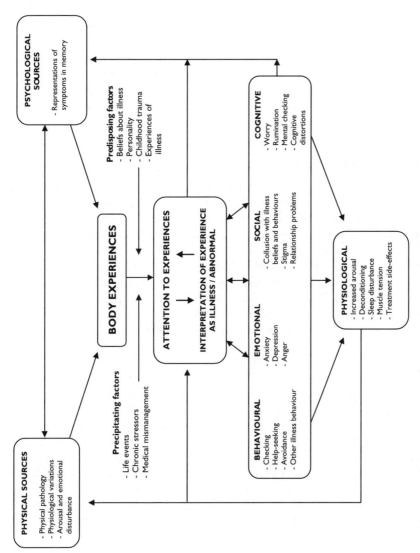

Figure 12.1 Clinical heuristic for formulating patients with MUS (from Brown 2004; Sharpe et al. 1992a).

organic illness (for a review see Brown 2005). Cognitive behavioural models of MUS have rarely considered how such early traumatic events might pre-dispose toward the development of these conditions. One possibility is that individuals who are exposed to early traumatic events develop a tendency to focus their attention on their body as a means of avoiding the unwanted cognitive and emotional processing associated with these experiences (Brown 2004). Another, and perhaps related, possibility is that childhood trauma leads to the use of 'dissociation' (i.e., mental compartmentalisation; see Brown 2005; Holmes *et al.* 2005) as a coping mechanism. It may also be that early trauma creates a vulnerability for psychopathology in general, with the link between MUS and trauma being mediated via increased distress and arousal.

Childhood experience of illness

Patients with unexplained symptoms have often been exposed to high levels of physical illness in themselves and others during childhood (e.g., Craig 2001; Hotopf *et al.* 1999). There is also evidence that reinforcement of child-hood illness behaviour by anxious parents is associated with bodily pre-occupation, anxiety and illness behaviour in adulthood (Kirmayer and Taillefer 1997). In addition to providing a rich source of symptom representa-tions, such early experiences may lead to the development of maladaptive assumptions about health and illness (see below) that, when activated, trigger the misinterpretation of symptoms and drive maladaptive coping behaviours (Sharpe *et al.* 1992a; Warwick and Salkovskis 1990).

Personality

The personality dimension of negative affectivity (NA; a.k.a. 'neuroticism') consistently correlates with subjective symptom reports, as well as illness worry, self-focus, symptom misinterpretation and illness behaviour (Watson and Clark 1984; Watson and Pennebaker 1989). It is therefore likely that NA is an important predisposing factor for MUS in many cases. High levels of introspectiveness (Mechanic 1986), private self-consciousness (Robbins and Kirmayer 1991), absorption (Kirmayer and Taillefer 1997) and hypnotic susceptibility (Roelofs *et al.* 2002) may also confer vulnerability for MUS through their relationship with self-focused attention (Brown 2004).

Precipitating factors

Physical illness

Unexplained symptom onset appears to be associated with a recent history of physical illness for many patients (e.g., Crimlisk *et al.* 1998; Merskey and

Buhrich 1975; Sharpe *et al.* 1992b). Illness episodes associated with medical mismanagement are particularly likely to trigger health anxiety and MUS, or act as a predisposing factor for later problems (Warwick and Salkovskis 1990).

Life events

Many MUS are preceded by adverse and/or stressful life events, such as trauma, relationship difficulties or financial problems (Brown 2005). It is possible that the relationship between MUS and life events is mediated by an increase in anxiety and/or depression associated with those events, or the use of body-focus as a means of avoiding the unwanted cognitive and emotional activity associated with them.

Maintaining factors

Illness beliefs

The misinterpretation of benign physical sensations is thought to be driven by certain beliefs and assumptions about physical health and illness, which act as both predisposing and maintaining factors for these conditions. Patients with unexplained symptoms often believe that they are physically weak individuals who are unable to tolerate strain or exertion (Rief *et al.* 1998) and/or have a particular vulnerability to illness (e.g., 'I am more likely than most people to get an illness,' 'My family is prone to illness'; Silver *et al.* 2004a). Also common are the beliefs that bodily symptoms are necessarily a sign of illness and that health is a state devoid of physical symptoms (Rief *et al.* 1998; e.g., 'Bodily changes are always a sign that something is wrong'; Silver Sanders *et al.* 2004).

Other studies have shown that poor outcomes for MUS tend to be associated with the belief that the condition has a physical rather than a biopsychosocial cause, and that any exacerbation of symptoms is a sign of organic damage (Petrie *et al.* 1995; Wilson *et al.* 1994; cf. Deale *et al.* 1998). Such beliefs are often associated with the idea that activity and exercise should be avoided in order to prevent further physical problems and that rest is the most appropriate course of ameliorative action (Chalder 2001; Sharpe 2001; Surawy *et al.* 1995). In reality, positive outcomes in CFS are associated with a belief shift towards exercise and activity being viewed as helpful rather than hazardous (Deale *et al.* 1998).

Silver Sanders *et al.* (2004) provide an excellent overview of the types of illness beliefs reported by patients with health anxiety. Examples listed by Silver Sanders *et al.* (2004) include beliefs about the importance of maintaining vigilance towards symptoms (e.g., 'If I don't keep a careful watch on my health something terrible will happen,' 'I must keep abreast of all the recent health scares'), the cost of illness or death (e.g., 'If I become ill I will be a burden to my family,' 'If I die I will go to hell'), the danger of anxiety (e.g., 'There is only so much stress that the heart can take,' 'Anxiety can kill') and superstitious/meta-cognitive beliefs about causing or preventing illness (e.g., 'If I let myself think I am healthy, I will tempt fate,' 'If I don't control my thoughts I will go mad').

The cognitive behavioural model of CFS assumes that all-or-nothing beliefs concerning personal standards (e.g., 'Unless I achieve all my career aims I've failed') and psychological strength (e.g., 'I must never admit to difficulties') are predisposing and perpetuating factors for this particular condition (Surawy *et al.* 1995).

Illness behaviours

Illness beliefs are thought to contribute to MUS by perpetuating symptom misinterpretation and by prompting a range of dysfunctional illness behaviours, including avoidance, compensatory behaviour, medical consulting and body checking, which can maintain symptoms through a number of pathways. Many patients with MUS avoid activity and exercise (Chalder 2001; Surawy *et al.* 1995), which can lead to physical de-conditioning and secondary health problems (e.g., contractures) that maintain disease conviction, increase body-focus, produce further bodily sensations and perpetuate the fear of activity. Avoidance also prevents the individual from being exposed to evidence that could disconfirm the belief that they are physically incapable. In contrast, some patients may avoid particular stimuli (e.g., medical information, negative affect) or situations (e.g., a stressful work environment) that are associated with the onset or exacerbation of symptoms. Patients with non-epileptic attacks, for example, often avoid anxiety-provoking situations (e.g., those where the perceived consequences of having an attack are dangerous, embarrassing etc.), thereby increasing the fear associated with those situations and setting up a vicious cycle (Chalder 1996).

Safety and/or compensatory behaviours are commonly observed in patients with MUS. Individuals with chronic pain, for example, often adopt 'defensive' body postures (typically to avoid further pain or to 'protect' their body), which can cause physical damage and additional pain (Main and Spanswick 2000). Physiological side effects may also result from excessive rest, physical interventions and prophylactics (e.g., analgesics, alternative remedies, aspirin etc.), and the use of compensatory aids such as slings, splints, sticks, walking frames and wheelchairs. In addition to their physical impact, such behaviours also act to maintain body-focus and illness beliefs.

Repeated checking of the body for physical signs and symptoms has the effect of maximising the perceived salience of somatic sensations and increases the likelihood that other, previously unnoticed, physical sensations will be identified, thereby 'confirming' the presence of physical illness (Brown

2004; Sharpe *et al.* 1992a). Checking comes in many forms, including visual inspection, physical touching and manipulation of body parts, mirror use, mental scanning of the body, and 'experiments' to test bodily functions (e.g., checking one's pulse, taking deep breaths to test lung function, swallowing to check for lumps in the throat etc). In addition to their cognitive effects, such behaviours can often lead to physical symptoms in their own right; repeatedly touching a tender spot, for example, can produce inflammation and further pain, whereas deep breathing can cause muscular strain and discomfort.

Checking behaviour is regarded as a form of reassurance-seeking that is negatively reinforced by an immediate reduction in anxiety but causes increased anxiety in the longer term (Warwick and Salkovskis 1990). A similar mechanism operates for reassurance- and care-seeking from significant others (including repeated medical consulting and 'doctor-shopping') and seeking reassurance by acquiring medical information from books and the internet, which are often found in medically unexplained illness. These forms of reassurance-seeking also expose the individual to ambiguous (and sometimes incorrect) material concerning health, symptoms, illness and treatment, which increases the likelihood of symptom misinterpretation and abnormal illness behaviour.

Cognitive factors

Many patients with MUS spend a lot of time ruminating and worrying about the causes, implications and treatment of their symptoms and their physical health more generally (Warwick and Salkovskis 1990). Rumination and worry amplify attention to the body and symptoms, increase the likelihood of symptom misinterpretation, feed negative affective states such as anxiety and depression, and reduce the resources available for adaptive behaviour and disconfirmatory processing (Wells 2000). In contrast, a proportion of patients will exhibit a tendency to avoid thinking about their symptoms and health and may deliberately suppress such thoughts (Sharpe 2001), which can produce a paradoxical rebound in worrying thoughts (Wells 1997). Certain cognitive biases and distortions may also act as maintaining factors for MUS. For example, body-focused attention in these patients may be accompanied by a selective attentional bias for information that confirms symptom misinterpretation, while disconfirmatory information and benign interpretations are selectively disattended or minimised (Salkovskis 1989).

Affective factors

The model assumes that negative affect, particularly anxiety and depressed mood, arises when physical sensations are misinterpreted as evidence of organic pathology. In turn, heightened distress and anxiety increase illness worry, rumination, negative self-focus and the likelihood of catastrophic misinterpretation, and prompt dysfunctional illness behaviours such as avoidance and reassurance-seeking. In addition, the physiological symptoms associated with anxiety (e.g., sweating, palpitations, chest pain, dizziness, visual disturbance, muscle tension, shaking, nausea etc.) and depression (e.g., fatigue, muscular pain, headache, sexual dysfunction, loss of appetite etc.) provide additional evidence for a catastrophic illness model and fuel body-focused attention.

Social factors

Once the individual pursues reassurance, assessment and treatment for their condition, they may be exposed to a range of social forces that can maintain symptomatology. Significant others may collude with maladaptive illness beliefs and dysfunctional coping strategies such as safety/compensatory behaviour and reassurance/care-seeking, or disagree with the patient's beliefs and actions, leading to conflict and distress. Stigma about emotional distress and psychological illness within the interpersonal environment may also reinforce a physical interpretation of symptoms and undermine attempts at reattribution.

Contact with medical professionals may be particularly important in maintaining MUS. It is common for doctors to collude with patients' illness models (Salmon et al. 1999), to order inappropriate investigations or treatments, to provide ambiguous or contradictory information (e.g., 'I'm sure that there is nothing wrong, but I'll order another test, just to make sure'; Sharpe et al. 1992a), and to endorse inappropriate illness cognitions (e.g., 'Keep an eye on it') and behaviour (e.g., 'Go home and rest'; Sharpe et al. 1992a). Doctors may also lack the training necessary to convey a psychological understanding of symptoms and are often perceived as suggesting that the problems are feigned or 'all in the mind', leading to deterioration of the doctor–patient relationship and a further loss of faith in the health care system.

Physiological factors

In addition to the physical changes associated with emotional arousal and dysfunctional illness behaviour, there are other physiological factors, such as sleep disturbance, medication use, organic illness and reduced serotonergic precursor production (Rief et al. 2004), that can maintain disproportionate levels of disability and distress either directly or through their effects on the attentional, cognitive, behavioural and emotional processes outlined above.

ASSESSMENT

The assessment should be conducted with a view to: (a) establishing whether the necessary steps have been taken to exclude physical disease; (b) engaging patients in the therapeutic process; and (c) obtaining enough information to provide a positive cognitive behavioural formulation of the presenting symptoms (cf. Sharpe *et al.* 1992a). The latter also entails a detailed understanding of the client's medical and psychological state, including the presence of co-morbid physical and psychiatric conditions.

Assessment of symptoms and medical history

Establishing whether physical explanations for symptoms have been excluded is essential and requires close liaison with the referring physician. Ideally, all of the necessary investigations will have been conducted prior to the initial assessment and an unequivocal diagnosis made. If possible, both the patient and their GP should be asked to postpone further investigations until the end of treatment (Sharpe *et al.* 1992a). Where co-morbid physical disease is present but is insufficient to account for the symptoms and their associated disability, the therapist should obtain information about the disease and its medical management (Sharpe *et al.* 1992a) and liaise with the relevant physicians as appropriate.

Asking clients to provide a full account of their past and current medical history and a list of all existing symptoms generates important information while assisting in the engagement process (Wessely *et al.* 1998). Asking the client to recall previous experiences of illness provides information about likely predisposing, precipitating and maintaining factors for their current condition. In addition, it gives an indication of whether the client has a long history of multiple unexplained symptoms (as in somatisation disorder), which is likely to require a different approach to that used for more limited episodes of unexplained illness (Sharpe *et al.* 1992a). It is important to bear in mind that some patients with unexplained symptoms do not provide reliable information about past symptoms and diagnoses (Schrag *et al.* 2004; Simon and Gureje 1999). As such, it is useful to compare any medical information volunteered by the patient with that obtained (with the patient's consent) from the GP and their records.

A useful tool in this context is the Screening for Somatoform Symptoms-7 scale (SOMS-7; Rief and Hiller 2003), a self-report instrument with good psychometric properties that provides information about the baseline presence and severity data of 53 somatic symptoms. Scales for specific symptoms can also be used (e.g., the McGill Pain Questionnaire, Melzack 1987; the Fatigue Severity Scale, Krupp *et al.* 1989; for a review of different fatigue scales, see Dittner *et al.* 2004), which may help obtain clear operational definitions of ambiguous terms such as 'pain' and 'fatigue'. The SCL-90

(Derogatis *et al.* 1974) has a somatisation sub-scale that is commonly used in research in this area, although this probably captures the somatic components of depression and anxiety rather than MUS per se.

A list of current and previous medications and other treatments should also be obtained, as well as some idea of caffeine intake, diet and sleep pattern.

Engaging patients with MUS

By definition, patients with MUS emphasise the physical aspects of their problems and many are therefore confused or worried about psychological referral. Some patients are overtly or covertly hostile to the process, feeling as though the referring physician has dismissed their problems as 'made up' or 'all in the mind'. For these reasons, engagement is a particularly crucial part of working with MUS and therapists should expect to spend more time on this aspect of therapy than usual. Engagement is thought to be easier if clients can be seen in a physical health setting (e.g., GP's surgery or general hospital clinic) or in joint consultation with the referrer (Sharpe *et al.* 1992a), as this implies on-going medical management of their symptoms. Such an approach is not always possible, however.

At the outset, clients should be encouraged to discuss their views about the referral, with a view to identifying any misconceptions and validating any concerns (Sharpe *et al.* 1992a). Clients should be reassured that the referral does not imply that they are 'mad' or that their symptoms are not real. It is essential that the therapist takes any physical symptoms seriously and acknowledges the client's suffering. If at all possible, the issue of symptom causation should be avoided during the early stages and no attempt should be made to contradict the patient's existing viewpoint (Chalder 2001); if necessary, the therapist can shift the focus of discussion from the causes of symptoms to symptom management (Chalder 2001), perhaps with reference to the utility of CBT as a way of coping with both physical and psychological problems. Clients should be given plenty of opportunity to discuss their symptoms and disease concerns; psychological symptoms and issues should only be addressed after this has been done. Opportunities for breaks should be provided. Careful attention should be paid to in-session behaviour and, in particular, how the client responds to any discussion of psychological factors. Any indication of hostility in this regard suggests that the early sessions should focus on establishing an alliance rather than treatment itself; this could involve discussing the advantages and disadvantages of change (Chalder 2001) or possibly motivational interviewing techniques (Miller and Rollnick 2002). When the discussion does turn to psychological issues, it is important to emphasise that the client is not to blame for their symptoms (Sharpe *et al.* 1992a). Scripts detailing how the assessment of patients with MUS (and/or other somatic symptoms) can be introduced and facilitated are provided by Salkovskis (1989).

Providing an alternative explanation for symptoms in the form of a positive cognitive behavioural formulation and 'socialising' the client to that model is also an important part of the engagement process. The issue of socialisation will be considered in more detail below.

Cognitive behavioural assessment

The basic principles of cognitive behavioural assessment (e.g., Kirk 1989; Wells 1997) generally apply in this context. Thus, patients should be asked to provide an account of a recent exacerbation of symptoms with a view to identifying relevant thoughts, behaviours and feelings before, during and after the episode (i.e., A–B–C analysis). Asking about occasions where symptom relief was experienced can also be informative, as can questions seeking to identify patterns in symptom occurrence.

Identifying illness beliefs and assumptions

Relevant illness beliefs will often become apparent as the patient describes their symptoms and relates their medical history, or completes symptom diaries for homework. Asking patients about illness experiences in their family may also provide useful information in this respect. A number of specific questions can also be asked to elicit illness beliefs (from Salkovskis 1989; Sharpe *et al.* 1992a):

- When you experience [symptom], what goes through your mind?
- What went through your mind when you noticed that your [symptom] was worse?
- What do you think is the cause of your problems?
- When your symptoms are at their worse, what do you think is the worse thing that could happen?
- What is your worst fear about your symptoms?

Illness beliefs are often indicated by the kind of negative automatic thoughts (NATs) experienced by the patient, which typically vary according to the type of symptom present (as in panic disorder). Chest pain and palpitations are often associated with NATs about heart disease, for example, whereas head-aches may be associated with NATs about brain tumours or a stroke (for other examples see Sharpe *et al.* 1992a; Wells 1997). NATs can also occur in the form of intrusive visual images associated with specific illness concerns (Salkovskis 1989).

It is often difficult to identify illness beliefs, particularly in chronic cases or those where the patient is reluctant to contradict the referring physician. In other cases, illness beliefs are masked by avoidance and illness behaviours; these can be tackled by asking, 'If you had been prevented from doing [x] to manage your symptoms, what is the worst thing that could have happened?' (Sharpe *et al.* 1992a), which also provides information about the perceived benefit of specific illness behaviours.

Several scales for identifying illness beliefs are available. The Cognitions About Body and Health questionnaire (CABAH; Rief *et al.* 1998) can be used to assess assumptions commonly found in patients with MUS, including the beliefs that physical symptoms are normally a sign of illness and that the individual is weak and unable to tolerate activity. The Illness Perceptions Questionnaire, Revised (IPQ-R; Moss-Morris *et al.* 2002) is a general measure of illness attribution that assesses the perceived timeline, cause, cure and consequences of an individual's illness (unexplained or otherwise), as well as the identity of the illness in relation to 14 common somatic symptoms. A specific version of the IPQ-R has been developed for patients with chronic fatigue. Belief ratings concerning the presence of some specific illnesses can be obtained using the Health Anxiety Scale (HAS; Wells 1997).

Illness behaviour

Activity diaries can be particularly useful for identifying patterns of avoidance and inappropriate illness behaviours such as excessive rest. Asking patients to describe what they can and can't do as a result of their symptoms also yields information about avoidance and provides an indication of their over-all level of disability. Patients can be asked, 'If you didn't have [symptom], what would be different about your life? What would you be able to do/no longer have to do/do differently?' This approach may also yield information about coping and compensatory behaviours, which can be augmented by asking the patient what they do in order to cope with their symptoms and what specific interventions and treatments they are using. Possible questions include: 'Are there any things you try to do when the problem is there?' (Salkovskis 1989) and 'When your symptoms are bothering you, are there things that you do to make yourself feel better?' More detailed enquiries may be required to identify specific illness behaviours such as body checking and reassurance-seeking; these may also be revealed as part of the client's in-session behaviour. Information about avoidance, checking and reassurance-seeking can also be obtained using the HAS (Wells 1997). Discussion with the client's GP can provide important information about their help-seeking and medical consulting behaviour over and above that provided by the client.

Information about pre-morbid behaviour and levels of activity should also be obtained, with a view to establishing possible relationships with the development of symptoms (e.g., over-work as a predisposing factor for the development of CFS; Surawy *et al.* 1995).

Mood and affect

Eliciting information about emotional symptoms is essential, but is often difficult with this patient group and should be approached with caution in the first instance. A useful approach is to begin by discussing the client's physical symptoms and then asking them about the effect of their symptoms on their mental state as a natural bridge into this area (Sharpe *et al.* 1992a). Affect associated with symptoms can also be assessed using diary measures. Information from partners and significant others can also help build up a picture of the patient's psychological state (Sharpe *et al.* 1992a). The client's previous psychiatric history should be enquired about.

Certain standardised measures of anxiety and depression, such as the Beck Depression Inventory (Beck *et al.* 1961) and Beck Anxiety Inventory (Beck *et al.* 1988), are of limited use with this patient group as they rely heavily on physical symptom reports. The Hospital Anxiety and Depression Scale (Zigmond and Snaith 1983), in contrast, does not rely on such reports and is therefore a more appropriate measure of emotional disturbance in this context (Salkovskis 1989). Questions concerning specific symptoms of depression, including interest, pleasure, guilt and suicidal thoughts, should be asked (Sharpe *et al.* 1992a) and treatment of mood disturbance planned appropriately. The possibility of alternative or co-morbid psychiatric disorders must also be considered. Although MUS treatment is not contraindicated by moderate anxiety and/or depression (cf. Sharpe *et al.* 1992a), treatment for certain problems, such as suicidality, severe depression, eating disorders with physical health complications and psychosis, should be prioritised.

MUS patients should also be assessed for health anxiety using a standardised instrument such as the Health Anxiety Inventory (HAI; Salkovskis *et al.* 2002) or the Health Anxiety Questionnaire (Lucock and Morley 1996). A single-item measure of health anxiety-related distress is also included in the HAS (Wells 1997).

Other cognitive factors

Patients can be asked how much time they spend thinking and worrying about their symptoms or asked to complete experience sampling diaries (e.g., recording their thoughts when the clock strikes the hour; Salkovskis 1989) if the issue needs to be approached more indirectly. Worry and rumination may also manifest themselves directly during the consultation. If there is a suspicion that worry is an important component of the presenting problem, non-specific measures such as the Penn State Worry Questionnaire (PSWQ; Meyer *et al.* 1990) can be considered. Patients should also be asked whether they attempt to suppress thoughts about their symptoms and illness, or engage in other strategies to avoid thinking about these issues.

Social and contextual factors

Patients should be asked about their family situation and the reactions of relevant others to their symptoms, with a view to establishing: (a) whether family members are reinforcing inappropriate illness beliefs and behaviours; (b) whether symptoms have led to, or were preceded by, relationship problems and interpersonal conflict; and (c) whether local stigma about psychological illness is undermining more appropriate symptom appraisals. Interviewing family members can be particularly illuminating in these respects. Indeed, the role of family factors in symptom maintenance may be directly apparent during such joint consultations. It is also important, although potentially problematic, to obtain information about physician factors (e.g., collusion with inappropriate illness model, ordering inappropriate tests and treatments) that might be contributing to the maintenance of symptoms.

Information about legal and financial matters pertaining to symptoms (e.g., litigation claims, disability payments) should be enquired about, as should the patient's current employment situation and their long-term plans for work (Chalder 2001).

Other historical factors

In addition to the details of previous symptoms and illness experiences, it is important to obtain historical information about possible predisposing and precipitating factors, including early traumatic experiences and recent life events.

TREATMENT

The approach to treatment follows basic cognitive behavioural principles such as agenda setting, guided discovery and collaborative empiricism. The specific intervention strategies used depend on the nature of the presenting problems and the results of the assessment.

Socialisation

Socialising patients to the cognitive behavioural model and providing a therapeutic rationale are fundamental aspects of both engagement and treatment. Presenting a simple formulation based on a generic three-systems model (i.e., cognitive, physiological and behavioural; Lang 1978) is appropriate at this stage, as a complete cognitive behavioural formulation (such as that described above) can be confusing and/or disengaging at the start of treatment (Chalder 2001); more complex formulations can be developed with the client later in therapy. The basic formulation provides a tactful way of presenting the idea that physical symptoms can be maintained or made worse by certain behaviours and patterns of thinking. This can be facilitated by emphasising that the patient's thoughts and actions are understandable responses to their physical symptoms and that acute and chronic symptoms may require different coping strategies (Chalder 2001).

Simple experiments can be used to demonstrate the role of selective and self-focused attention in the patient's experience of physical sensations and symptoms (e.g., Wells 1997). Thus, the patient's attention can be directed to the feelings in their fingertips, the tightness of their shoes or the feel of the chair underneath them, before asking them whether they had been aware of those sensations prior to having focused on them. Examples where the severity of the patient's symptoms varied according to how busy they were, what they were thinking about or the occurrence of distracting events in the environment (e.g., telephone calls) can also be enquired about and capitalised upon.

Socialisation may be aided by examples of the close link between psychological and physical processes and the fallacy of mind–body dualism (cf. Chalder 2001). Most people are familiar, for example, with the fact that nervousness is often experienced as 'butterflies' in the stomach, that headaches may follow a stressful day at work, and that people can feel sick when they see something disgusting or frightening in a horror film. Similarly, people are generally aware that a woman's mood can vary according to her menstrual cycle and that ingesting alcohol can lead to changes in thought, mood and action. Other useful examples include the placebo effect, 'battlefield analgesia' (where wounded soldiers can be unaware of their injuries until they escape from danger) and various hypnotic phenomena, such as hypnotic analgesia, paralysis, sensory loss and the like. Patients can also be informed that people with physical illnesses (e.g., cancer) may be more or less disabled depending on their mood and mental set. Symptom diaries can be useful for illustrating specific links between psychological factors and the patient's own physical symptoms. Eliciting examples where the patient's symptoms responded positively (at least in the short term) to reassurance can also help reinforce a psychological account of their problems (Wells 1997).

Where appropriate, patients can be provided with information about the nature of anxiety and depression, particularly the physiological components of these conditions and how these may overlap with the patient's symptoms. Information booklets (e.g., Brown et al. 2002) and other forms of psychoeducation about medically unexplained illness itself (e.g., Goldstein et al. 2004 for information about dissociative seizures) can also be helpful for some patients. One particularly important piece of information concerns the effect of unnecessary rest on physical health, which provides the rationale for the graded activity component of treatment (Chalder 2001: 306).

It is not necessary for patients to abandon a physical interpretation of their unexplained symptoms in order for them to engage in CBT. Salkovskis (1989), for example, recommends that patients simply commit themselves to testing the effectiveness of the cognitive approach for four months, with the proviso that a physical perspective would be reconsidered at the end of that period if the patient had tried everything agreed with their therapist and still not improved.

Goal setting

As with all CBT, explicit and realistic goals should be negotiated with the client before treatment begins. Symptom reduction will often be identified as a goal, although reductions in the disability and stress/emotional disturbance associated with symptoms are also appropriate targets for intervention and may be more realistic in some cases. The therapist may also have implicit goals for treatment, such as reductions in unnecessary health care expenditure and abnormal illness behaviour, which may become explicit as treatment progresses. A contract for a specific number of sessions should be negotiated in relation to the goals and reviewed as appropriate. Most authorities counsel against making symptom 'cure' an explicit goal and suggest warning patients that progress can be extremely slow. Indeed, both patients and therapists should be aware that symptoms are unlikely to have remitted completely by the end of therapy. In severe cases with a long history of multiple unexplained symptoms, the goal of treatment may be 'damage limitation' (e.g., reduce disability, rationalise medical care, obtain help for relatives) rather than cure (Sharpe *et al.* 1992a). The most severely disabled patients may need in-patient treatment (Sharpe *et al.* 1992a).

Chalder (2001) identifies a number of early sub-goals for therapy, including: (a) a consistent approach to activity, which is likely to produce an early experience of success and requires little psychological understanding; (b) reductions in reassurance-seeking and the repeated discussion of symptoms, both of which can interfere with therapy; (c) engaging a family member as a co-therapist, with a view to minimising negative reinforcement of inappropriate illness behaviour; and (d) establishing a good sleep routine.

It remains controversial whether it is necessary for patients to relinquish an organic interpretation of symptoms in order to make gains (e.g., Chalder 2001; Deale *et al.* 1998). It may be enough, for example, for the patient to change the way in which they cope with their physical symptoms (Chalder 2001). In cases where there are hypochondriacal concerns, however, it is necessary to help the patient identify a more benign interpretation of their symptoms; whether this interpretation is physical or psychological is probably less important than its effect on the patient's mood and behaviour.

Behavioural interventions

Behavioural interventions, such as graded activity, are an essential part of the treatment process for many patients, particularly those for whom excessive rest or avoidance of activity have been identified as important maintaining factors.

Graded activity scheduling involves helping the client to develop a consistent approach to activity with small graded increments over time. The activity schedule should be developed by identifying the discrepancy between current and desired activity levels, which allows a series of sub-goals to be agreed. The client can then practise the relevant behaviour until the first sub-goal is achieved and the next sub-goal can be attempted (Sharpe *et al.* 1992a); it is important that each sub-goal is within the patient's tolerance level before it is attempted (Chalder 2001). Patients should be warned that each increase in activity will lead to a temporary increase in symptoms, but that this will pass as they regain fitness. Clients must also be advised not to 'overdo it' on good days by engaging in sudden or large increases in activity, as these are likely to cause a major exacerbation of symptoms and further avoidance (Sharpe *et al.* 1992a). Graded activity scheduling can often be used in conjunction with other behavioural interventions including occupational therapy and physiotherapy. Further details of graded activity scheduling in the treatment of MUS are provided in Chalder (2001).

Behavioural techniques for improving sleep hygiene and establishing a good sleep routine are described elsewhere (e.g., Chalder 2001).

Cognitive interventions

Behaviour change is often hindered by beliefs concerning the potential dangers of exercise and activity, necessitating the combined use of cognitive and behavioural interventions. Behavioural experiments can be particularly useful for challenging the belief that illness behaviours, such as reassurance-seeking, avoidance, checking and safety/compensatory behaviour, are protecting the patient from harm (for useful guides to possible behavioural experiments see Silver *et al.* 2004a, 2004b). Patients should be encouraged to test predictions about different illness behaviours by varying the frequency of the behaviour in question and assessing the impact of this on their physical symptoms and mood. In cases where on-going medical investigations cannot be avoided, tests can be set up as behavioural experiments to assess the impact of reassurance on symptom severity and frequency (Salkovskis 1989; Wells 1997); a more appropriate plan for medical consulting can then be devised (Wells 1997).

Clients can also be encouraged to increase and decrease their levels of worry and rumination to assess their effect on symptom maintenance. Worry postponement with controlled worry periods can be effective at reducing worry frequency and intensity (Salkovskis 1989), particularly when patients are encouraged to adopt a detached stance in relation to their worrying thoughts (Wells 1997). A useful tool in this context is the 'trains of thought' metaphor, where clients are encouraged to view their mind as a train station and their worrying thoughts as trains that they can either 'board' or 'watch as they pass through'. Strategies such as this can have the additional benefit of challenging negative meta-beliefs concerning the uncontrollability and dangerousness of worry (Wells 1997). Worry and rumination can also be reduced using Wells' (1990) attention training treatment, which may have the additional advantage of reducing the activation of any rogue representations associated with the presenting symptoms (Brown 2004). For this reason, attention training may be particularly useful for symptoms where obvious pathophysiological mechanisms cannot be identified (Brown 2004).

Successful experiments concerning illness behaviour may also help undermine the patient's disease conviction, which can be weakened further by other behavioural experiments designed to challenge illness beliefs directly. Concerns about heart function, for example, can be assessed by encouraging the patient to engage in strenuous physical exercise during the therapy session, whereas survey techniques can be used to test beliefs concerning the abnormality of symptoms (Wells 1997). Other factors, such as caffeine intake, diet and stress levels, can also be manipulated to obtain support for a more benign interpretation of symptoms. Symptom provocation tests can be used to demonstrate how unpleasant symptoms can develop following minor physical changes, such as over-breathing.

Illness conviction can also be addressed using standard cognitive restructuring techniques, such as reviewing evidence for and against negative thoughts/symptom interpretations and generating more balanced alternatives (Chalder 2001; Salkovskis 1989; Wells 1997). In order to do this, the therapist needs to understand the likely physiological and psychological mechanisms associated with different MUS (e.g., Brown 2004; Sharpe et al. 1992a), so that these can be offered as alternative explanations. Other potentially useful verbal reattribution strategies include cost–benefit analysis for repeated reassurance-seeking, pie charts and the 'inverted pyramid' technique (Wells 1997).

Other aspects of treatment

Previous studies of CBT for MUS have often involved training participants in the use of relaxation procedures to help them cope with their symptoms. Such exercises are also useful for challenging catastrophic thoughts about the causes of symptoms (e.g., 'What does the fact that relaxation helps you tell you about the cause of your chest pain?'; van Peski-Oosterbaan et al. 1999). Other patients may benefit from assertiveness training (Chalder 2001).

In some cases, patients should be assisted to problem-solve interpersonal, financial, occupational and other practical difficulties as they arise during treatment (Sharpe 1997). In particular, the issue of disability payments and other benefits may need to be tackled. The question of how the patient can explain any improvement in their symptoms to others without losing face also needs to be considered (Chalder 2001).

Medication regimes need to be rationalised in collaboration with other health care professionals (e.g., liaison psychiatrist, GP). In general, however, the number of professionals involved in treatment should be minimised as far as possible.

Finally, some patients with MUS will realise that they are suffering from wider psychological problems during treatment and a shift in therapy focus may need to be negotiated.

Ending therapy

The patient should be encouraged to take more and more responsibility for their treatment as therapy progresses in preparation for the end of the therapy contract. A therapy blueprint should be generated by the patient at this time and goals relating to the patient's remaining problems should be negotiated. The patient should be reminded that minor setbacks are likely and a plan for how to cope when this happens should be discussed (Chalder 2001).

CASE EXAMPLE: SANDRA

Sandra was a 41-year-old single mother presenting with an 18-year history of headaches, tiredness, pins and needles in her fingers, poor concentration, forgetfulness, dizziness, shaking and frequent episodes of 'detachment', which she described as feeling 'like I'm getting lost in myself . . . everything seems weird and distant and not quite right'. Sandra's symptoms had come and gone over the last 18 years, but had been particularly bad in the last two years since the death of her mother, who had died suddenly of a brain haemorrhage; her younger brother had died 18 months before that of 'mental health problems'. Sandra had originally been diagnosed with epilepsy and had been taking anti-convulsant medication since that time; she had also been signed off from work and had not worked regularly for 15 years. She was referred for psychological therapy after a thorough neurological re-assessment, prompted by the increase in her symptoms, had ruled out epilepsy and other neurological problems. Despite this, the neurologist kept Sandra on her anti-convulsants as he thought it 'might worry her' to come off them.

Sandra described feeling embarrassed about the referral for psychological therapy and was concerned that the therapist would perceive her as 'weak'. However, she described being 'open to the experience' of cognitive behaviour therapy as 'nothing else had helped'. Psychological assessment revealed that Sandra experienced frequent feelings of nervousness and tension associated with episodes of worry about various topics, including her health, her family, work, money and terrorism. Diaries revealed that most of Sandra's physical symptoms, particularly her episodes of detachment, tended to be at their worst during a worry episode. When she noticed her symptoms, Sandra would become concerned that she was putting 'pressure' on her brain by worrying and that this might cause a blood vessel to burst. When her worry was at its peak, Sandra would start to think that she was 'about to go mad, just like my brother'. In order to prevent these catastrophes from happening, Sandra would try to control her worrying thoughts or distract herself from them. Sandra noted that she and her brother had 'always been worriers', having 'inherited it' from their mother.

Sandra also described episodes of sadness, despondency, tearfulness and social withdrawal, as well as problems falling and staying asleep. In order to cope with her sleep problems, Sandra had taken to staying up late until she was absolutely exhausted and expected to fall asleep quickly. She would then have to get up after only a few hours' sleep to take her daughter to school and she would be so tired during the day that she would end up sleeping for an hour in her armchair. She described a previous episode of depression after her divorce from her first husband, which was treated successfully using anti-depressant medication.

Sandra had a relatively normal pattern of help-seeking behaviour and rarely sought reassurance for her problems. When asked what she thought was causing her symptoms, Sandra said, 'I thought I had epilepsy but Dr X said that I might not.'

Formulation

The pattern of Sandra's pins and needles, dizziness, shaking and episodes of detachment, coupled with their emotional and cognitive concomitants, indicated that these symptoms were probably the physiological components of an anxiety state. Sandra's symptoms of detachment were therefore formulated as episodes of anxiety-related depersonalisation rather than dissociative seizures. Her tiredness, headaches, poor concentration and forgetfulness were formulated as possible side-effects of her anti-convulsant medication and/or physiological symptoms associated with her low mood and disturbed sleep. From a psychiatric perspective, Sandra's chronic anxiety symptoms and her tendency to worry about a range of topics, including the dangers of worry, indicated that her main problem was likely to be generalised anxiety disorder (Wells 1997), with a co-morbid affective disturbance. The timing of the increase in Sandra's emotional and physical symptoms suggested that they had been precipitated by the deaths of her brother and mother. Sandra's previous history of worry and depression indicated that she was vulnerable to the development of emotional disturbance in the face of such stressors.

The formulation suggested that Sandra's view of herself as an 'ill' person with neurological vulnerability resulted largely from the inappropriate diagnosis of epilepsy that she had been given many years before. Sandra's perceived vulnerability was subsequently heightened by her mother's unexpected brain haemorrhage, which Sandra thought had been caused by her mother's tendency to worry – a tendency that she herself had inherited. As a result, Sandra had started to attend closely to her bodily experiences and any sensations that might indicate further neurological problems. The inevitable increase in her physical anxiety symptoms appeared to confirm Sandra's belief that her neurological health was deteriorating, while the escalation in her worry reinforced the idea that she was bringing this deterioration on herself. Although she had later been relieved to discover that she did not have epilepsy, she perceived the neurologist's continuing prescription of anti-convulsants as evidence that she remained vulnerable to neurological illness.

The increase in Sandra's worry had also activated meta-cognitions suggesting that she might drive herself mad with worry, which seemed to have developed following the death of her brother after he had 'gone crazy with worry', leading to a further escalation in her anxiety. It was hypothesised that Sandra's attempts to cope with this by suppressing her worrying thoughts led to a paradoxical increase in her worries and physical anxiety symptoms, apparently confirming her belief that her worrying was out of control and was damaging her.

The formulation suggested that Sandra's affective disturbance probably originated in the death of her brother and mother and had been maintained by the perceived deterioration in her physical health and the maladaptive way that she coped with her sleep disturbance. See Figure 12.2.

Treatment

For what seemed like a complex case, Sandra's treatment turned out to be relatively straightforward, particularly as she already identified her worry as a significant problem. At the outset, Sandra's neurologist was contacted and he confirmed that Sandra was no more vulnerable to neurological illness than anyone else her age and that she did not require anti-convulsant medication. This was discussed with Sandra and she agreed to come off her anti-convulsants under the supervision of her GP. Sandra's sleep problems were then addressed using a standard approach involving reducing her caffeine and the development of better sleep hygiene.

The psychological intervention initially consisted of presenting Sandra with a simple cognitive behavioural formulation of her problems and psycho-education about anxiety and depression, with emphasis on their physiological components. Sandra was socialised to the model by demonstrating the effect of simple attention manipulations on physical sensations and by completing a diary charting the relationship between her symptoms and her

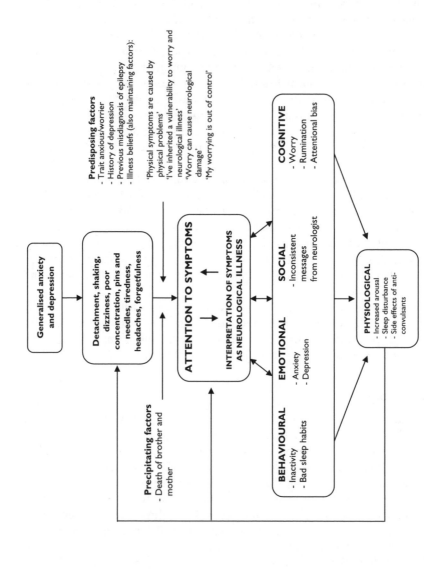

Figure 12.2 Formulation for Sandra.

worry episodes. Several sessions then focused on tackling Sandra's tendency to worry and her maladaptive beliefs associated with this. Behavioural experiments were conducted in which Sandra first increased and then decreased her efforts at worry control, the latter facilitated by the use of worry postponement and a detached approach to worrying thoughts. Sandra was also encouraged to test the belief that she could go mad with worry by pushing her worrying to the limits. In addition, Sandra was asked to evaluate her main piece of evidence for this belief by considering whether there were other explanations for her brother's death. Psychoeducation and verbal reattribution were also used to dismantle her beliefs about the physical dangers of worry. On occasions when Sandra raised concerns about specific physical symptoms, she was encouraged to consider the evidence for and against different interpretations of her problems; other verbal reattribution techniques were also used, including pie charts and the inverted pyramid. In addition, a survey experiment was conducted to test Sandra's belief that physical symptoms were an abnormal occurrence.

At the end of a nine-session therapy contract, Sandra was sleeping better and her anti-convulsant medication was being reduced. She no longer believed that she had neurological problems, her episodes of detachment were much less frequent and she was less concerned by her other physical symptoms. She still worried somewhat, but was not concerned about going mad with worry and was often able to let her worries go.

NOTE

1   The presence of compelling symptoms differentiates MUS from factitious and malingered physical illnesses, both of which are characterised by physical symptom reports in the absence of a genuine symptom experience.

REFERENCES

Beck, A. T. *et al.* (1961). An inventory for measuring depression. *Archives of General Psychiatry* 4: 561–71.

Beck, A. T. *et al.* (1988). An inventory for measuring clinical anxiety: Psychometric properties. *Journal of Consulting and Clinical Psychology* 56: 893–7.

Bleichhardt, G. *et al.* (2004). Cognitive-behavioural therapy for patients with multiple somatoform symptoms – a randomised controlled trial in tertiary care. *Journal of Psychosomatic Research* 56: 449–54.

Brown, R. J. (2004). The psychological mechanisms of medically unexplained symptoms: An integrative conceptual model. *Psychological Bulletin* 130: 793–812.

Brown, R. J. (2005). Dissociation and conversion in psychogenic illness. In M. Hallett *et al.* (eds) *Psychogenic Movement Disorders: Psychobiology and Treatment of a Functional Disorder*. Philadelphia: Lippincott, Williams and Wilkins.

Brown, R. J. and Ron, M. A. (2002). Conversion and somatoform disorders. In V. S. Ramachandran (ed) *Encyclopedia of the Human Brain, Vol. 2.* San Diego, CA: Academic Press.

Brown, R. J. and Trimble, M. R. (2000). Dissociative psychopathology, non-epileptic seizures and neurology. *Journal of Neurology, Neurosurgery and Psychiatry* 69: 285–91.

Brown, R. J. *et al.* (2002). *A Patient's Guide to Somatisation* [information booklet]. Guildford, UK: Clarius Press Ltd.

Chalder, T. (1996). Non-epileptic attacks: A cognitive behavioural approach in a single case with a four year follow-up. *Clinical Psychology and Psychotherapy* 3: 291–7.

Chalder, T. (2001). Cognitive behavioural therapy as a treatment for conversion disorders. In P. W. Halligan *et al.* (eds) *Contemporary Approaches to the Study of Hysteria: Clinical and Theoretical Perspectives.* Oxford, UK: Oxford University Press.

Craig, T. K. J. (2001). Life events: Meanings and precursors. In P. W. Halligan *et al.* (eds) *Contemporary Approaches to the Study of Hysteria: Clinical and Theoretical Perspectives.* Oxford, UK: Oxford University Press.

Crimlisk, H. L. *et al.* (1998). Slater revisited: 6 year follow up of patients with medically unexplained motor symptoms. *British Medical Journal* 316: 582–6.

Deale A. *et al.* (1998). Illness beliefs and treatment outcome in chronic fatigue syndrome. *Journal of Psychosomatic Research* 45: 77–83.

Derogatis, L. R. *et al.* (1974). The Hopkins Symptom Checklist (HSCL): A self-report symptom inventory. *Behavioral Science* 19: 1–15.

Dittner, A. J. *et al.* (2004). The assessment of fatigue: A practical guide for clinicians and researchers. *Journal of Psychosomatic Research* 56: 157–70.

Ewald, H. *et al.* (1994). Somatization in patients newly admitted to a neurological department. *Acta Psychiatrica Scandinavica* 89: 174–9.

Goldstein, L. H. *et al.* (2004). An evaluation of cognitive behavioral therapy as a treatment for dissociative seizures. *Cognitive and Behavioural Neurology* 17: 41–9.

Hamilton, J. *et al.* (1996). Anxiety, depression and management of medically unexplained symptoms in medical clinics. *Journal of the Royal College of Physicians of London* 30: 18–20.

Holmes, E. *et al.* (2005). Are there two qualitatively distinct forms of dissociation? A review and some clinical implications. *Clinical Psychology Review* 25: 1–23.

Hotopf, M. *et al.* (1999). Childhood risk factors for adults with medically unexplained symptoms: Results from a national birth cohort study. *American Journal of Psychiatry* 156: 1796–800.

Kirk, J. (1989). Cognitive-behavioural assessment. In K. Hawton *et al.* (eds) *Cognitive Behaviour Therapy for Psychiatric Problems: A Practical Guide.* Oxford, UK: Oxford University Press.

Kirmayer, L. J. and Taillefer, S. (1997). Somatoform disorders. In S. M. Turner and M. Hersen (eds) *Adult Psychopathology and Diagnosis* (3rd edn). New York: Wiley.

Kroenke, K. and Swindle, R. (2000). Cognitive-behavioral therapy for somatization and symptom syndromes: A critical review of controlled clinical trials. *Psychotherapy and Psychosomatics* 69: 205–15.

Krupp, L. B. *et al.* (1989). The fatigue severity scale: Application to patients with multiple sclerosis and systemic lupus erythematosus. *Archives of Neurology* 46: 1121–3.

Lang, P. J. (1978). Anxiety: Toward a psychophysiological definition. In H. S. Akishal and W. L. Webb (eds) *Psychiatric Diagnosis: Exploration of Biological Predictors.* New York: Spectrum.

Lucock, M. P. and Morley, S. (1996). The Health Anxiety Questionnaire. *British Journal of Health Psychology* 1: 137–50.

Main, C. J. and Spanswick, C. C. (eds) (2000). *Pain Management: An Interdisciplinary Approach.* Edinburgh, UK: Churchill Livingstone.

Mayou, R. and Sharpe, M. (1997). Treating medically unexplained physical symptoms. *British Medical Journal* 315: 561–2.

Mayou, R. *et al.* (1995). *The Treatment of Functional Somatic Symptoms.* Oxford, UK: Oxford University Press.

Mechanic, D. (1986). Illness behaviour: An overview. In S. McHugh and T. M. Vallis (eds) *Illness Behaviour: A Multidisciplinary Model.* New York: Plenum Press.

Melzack, R. (1987). The short-form McGill Pain Questionnaire. *Pain* 30: 191–7.

Merskey, H. and Buhrich, N. A. (1975). Hysteria and organic brain disease. *British Journal of Medical Psychology* 48: 359–66.

Meyer, T. J. *et al.* (1990). Development and validation of the Penn State Worry Questionnaire. *Behaviour Research and Therapy* 28: 487–95.

Miller, W. R. and Rollnick, S. (2002). *Motivational Interviewing: Preparing People for Change* (2nd edn). New York: Guilford Press.

Moss-Morris, R. and Wrapson, W. (2003). Representational beliefs about functional somatic syndromes. In L. D. Cameron and H. Leventhal (eds) *The Self-Regulation of Health and Illness Behaviour.* New York: Routledge.

Moss-Morris, R. *et al.* (2002). The revised illness perception questionnaire (IPQ-R). *Psychology and Health* 17: 1–16.

Petrie, K. *et al.* (1995). The impact of catastrophic beliefs on functioning in chronic fatigue syndrome. *Journal of Psychosomatic Research* 39: 31–7.

Rief, W. and Hiller, W. (2003). A new approach to the assessment of the treatment effects of somatoform disorders. *Psychosomatics* 44: 492–8.

Rief, W. *et al.* (1998). Cognitive aspects of hypochondriasis and somatization syndrome. *Journal of Abnormal Psychology* 107: 587–95.

Rief, W. *et al.* (2004). Psychobiological aspects of somatoform disorders: Contributions of monoaminergic transmitter systems. *Neuropsychobiology* 49: 24–9.

Robbins, J. M. and Kirmayer, L. J. (1991). Cognitive and social factors in somatization. In L. J. Kirmayer and J. M. Robbins (eds) *Current Concepts of Somatization: Research and Clinical Perspectives.* Washington, DC: American Psychiatric Press.

Roelofs, K. *et al.* (2002). Hypnotic susceptibility in patients with conversion disorder. *Journal of Abnormal Psychology* 111: 390–5.

Salkovskis, P. M. (1989). Somatic problems. In K. Hawton *et al.* (eds) *Cognitive Behaviour Therapy for Psychiatric Problems: A Practical Guide.* Oxford, UK: Oxford University Press.

Salkovskis, P. M. *et al.* (2002). The Health Anxiety Inventory: Development and validation of scales for the measurement of health anxiety and hypochondriasis. *Psychological Medicine* 32: 843–53.

Salmon, P. *et al.* (1999). Patients' perceptions of medical explanations for somatisation disorders: Qualitative analysis. *British Medical Journal* 318: 372–6.

Schrag, A. *et al.* (2004). The reliability of self-reported diagnoses in patients with somatoform disorder. *Journal of Neurology, Neurosurgery and Psychiatry* 75: 608–11.

Sharpe, M. (1997). Cognitive behaviour therapy for functional somatic complaints. *Psychosomatics* 38: 356–62.

Sharpe, T. J. (2001). Chronic pain: A reformulation of the cognitive-behavioural model. *Behaviour Research and Therapy* 39: 787–800.

Sharpe, M. *et al.* (1992). Follow up of patients presenting with fatigue to an infectious diseases clinic. *British Medical Journal* 305: 147–52.

Sharpe, M. *et al.* (1992). The psychological treatment of patients with functional somatic symptoms: A practical guide. *Journal of Psychosomatic Research* 36: 515–29.

Silver, A. *et al.* (2004a). Health anxiety. In J. Bennett-Levy *et al.* (eds) *Oxford Guide to Behavioural Experiments in Cognitive Therapy*. Oxford, UK: Oxford University Press.

Silver, A. *et al.* (2004b). Physical illness and disability. In J. Bennett-Levy *et al.* (eds) *Oxford Guide to Behavioural Experiments in Cognitive Therapy*. Oxford, UK: Oxford University Press.

Simon, G. E. and Gureje, O. (1999). Stability of somatization disorder and somatization symptoms among primary care patients. *Archives of General Psychiatry* 56: 90–5.

Stone, J. *et al.* (2002). What should we say to patients with symptoms unexplained by disease? The 'number needed to offend'. *British Medical Journal* 325: 1449–50.

Surawy, C. *et al.* (1995). Chronic fatigue syndrome: A cognitive approach. *Behaviour Research and Therapy* 33: 535–44.

van Peski-Oosterbaan, A. S. *et al.* (1999). Cognitive-behavioral therapy for noncardiac chest pain: A randomized trial. *American Journal of Medicine* 106: 424–9.

Warwick, H. M. and Salkovskis, P. M. (1990). Hypochondriasis. *Behaviour Research and Therapy* 28: 105–17.

Watson, D. and Clark, L. A. (1984). Negative affectivity: The disposition to experience aversive emotional states. *Psychological Bulletin* 96: 465–90.

Watson, D. and Pennebaker, J. W. (1989). Health complaints, stress and distress: Exploring the role of negative affectivity. *Psychological Review* 96: 234–54.

Wells, A. (1990). Panic disorder in association with relaxation-induced anxiety: An attentional training approach to treatment. *Behavior Therapy* 21: 273–80.

Wells, A. (1997). *Cognitive Therapy of Anxiety Disorders*. Chichester, UK: Wiley.

Wells, A. (2000). *Emotional Disorders and Metacognition*. Chichester, UK: Wiley.

Wessely, S. *et al.* (1998). *Chronic Fatigue and Its Syndromes*. Oxford, UK: Oxford University Press.

Wilson, A. *et al.* (1994). Longitudinal study of outcome of chronic fatigue syndrome. *British Medical Journal* 308: 756–9.

World Health Organisation. (1992). *The ICD-10 Classification of Mental and Behavioural Disorders: Clinical Descriptions and Diagnostic Guidelines*. Geneva, Switzerland: Author.

Zigmond, A. S. and Snaith, R. P. (1983). The hospital anxiety and depression scale. *Acta Psychiatrica Scandinavica* 67: 361–70.

Chapter 13

What about patients who can't sleep?

Case formulation for insomnia

Allison G. Harvey

> Just as night follows day, so does sleep disturbance follow psychological disturbance.
>
> (Spielman and Glovinsky 1997: 133)

The aim of this chapter is to outline an approach to formulating and treating insomnia, especially insomnia that is comorbid with another disorder. Every clinician knows that insomnia can occur as the sole presenting problem or as a condition that is comorbid with another psychiatric or medical disorder. In the complex comorbid cases, conceiving of insomnia as merely epiphenomenal to the comorbid disorder is unwise for two reasons. First, the evidence indicates that insomnia serves as a risk factor for, and can be causal in, the development and/or maintenance of the comorbid disorder (for reviews see Harvey 2001; McCrae and Lichstein 2001). Second, substantial evidence is accruing to suggest that insomnia that is comorbid with another psychiatric or medical disorder does not necessarily remit with the treatment of the so-called 'primary' disorder (Smith *et al.* 2005). Four brief case descriptions are presented in Table 13.1 to illustrate these points.

THEORETICAL BASIS FOR CASE FORMULATION

The cognitive model of insomnia that forms the basis for the case conceptualisation discussed in this chapter draws heavily from, and owes much to, cognitive models of other psychological disorders (e.g., Beck 1976; Clark 1999), as well as previous theoretical work highlighting the importance of cognitive processes to insomnia (e.g., Borkovec 1982; Espie 2002; Lundh 1998; Morin 1993; Perlis *et al.* 1997). According to the conceptualisation put forward in the model (Harvey 2002), insomnia is maintained by a cascade of cognitive processes that operate at night and during the day. The five key cognitive processes that comprise the cascade are: (a) worry (accompanied by arousal and distress); (b) selective attention and monitoring; (c) misperception

Table 13.1 Examples of insomnia that is comorbid with another psychological disorder or medical problem

---

Insomnia that is comorbid with another psychological disorder

Bipolar disorder

Lisa had just dropped out of her third year as an undergraduate at the local university because of episodes of mania and depression. Lisa experienced insomnia when she was between episodes and it got much worse approximately two weeks prior to a relapse. Accordingly, Lisa has come to fear bad sleep because it tends to herald in a relapse. Because Lisa was aware of the damage each episode caused in her life, and that sleep disturbance was an early warning signal of an impending episode, she was very worried about her sleep. She no longer had a social life in the evening, in an attempt to ensure a good night of sleep. She would nap during the day to try to ensure she was getting enough sleep. Some days she wouldn't get out of bed at all. Lisa believed she should aim to get over nine hours of sleep a day to avoid episodes of mania and depression and if she didn't get nine hours she would become worried and preoccupied with her sleep.

Posttraumatic stress disorder

Simon had posttraumatic stress disorder following a car accident in which the driver of the other car was killed. One year after the accident Simon came for treatment. Simon had two main concerns. First, he was troubled by horrible vivid and lifelike flashbacks of the accident. Second, he was afraid to go to sleep because most nights he experienced nightmares that related to the accident. Because he was sleeping so badly he was unable to cope at work during the day and so Simon was also afraid of losing his job.

Insomnia that is comorbid with a medical problem

Bladder problem

Gemma's sleep difficulties led her to resign her job as a bank manager three months prior to coming for treatment. Gemma thought that her sleep difficulties were due to a urinary tract disorder (which she had been told was called 'irritable bladder'). This problem caused her to get up between five and eight times each night to go to the bathroom. After getting back into bed she found it hard to get to sleep and would worry about the consequences of the disturbed sleep on her health and her ability to cope the next day. She had had two surgeries in an attempt to correct the bladder problem. These had not helped. Although Gemma felt that this medical problem was the major contributor to her insomnia she came for treatment because she was so worried about her sleep.

Chronic pain

Paul had chronic lower back pain. This made it difficult for him to sleep. Because he couldn't sleep he felt tired and unmotivated during the day and really did not feel up to being active. Because he wasn't active he was losing more and more muscle tone, which meant he experienced even more pain when he occasionally tried to be active during the day. Another consequence of not being active during the day was that he would nap. This combination of inactivity during the day and napping meant that he was not sufficiently tired at night. Bob was angry and worried about the impact of his insomnia and pain on his future and on his relationship with his wife.

---

of sleep and daytime deficits; (d) dysfunctional beliefs; and (e) counter-productive safety behaviours.

Before describing the model in more detail there are two important points to note. First, the cognitive processes proposed to operate at night are conceived of as applying equally to patients who: (a) have difficulty getting to sleep at the beginning of the night; (b) have difficulty getting back to sleep after waking during the night; and (c) wake too early in the morning. Second, the maintaining processes described can 'kick in' at any point in the model, and as a consequence of either a daytime or a nighttime experience.

The night

The five cognitive processes, and the way they interrelate (as graphically depicted in Figure 13.1), will now be described as they apply to the night.

Worry

It is well documented that people with insomnia lie in bed worrying about a range of topics including not being able to get to sleep. The cognitive model suggests that worry activates the sympathetic nervous system (the so-called 'fight or flight response'), thereby triggering physiological arousal and distress. This combination of worry, arousal and distress plunges the individual into an anxiety state – a state that is antithetical to falling asleep and staying asleep.

Selective attention and monitoring

The experimental literature in cognitive psychology indicates that, when one is anxious, the range of stimuli in the environment that are attended to narrows (Easterbrook 1959) and attention is preferentially directed toward potential threats (Dalgleish and Watts 1990). Hence, the model suggests that the anxious state leads people with insomnia to narrow their attention and selectively attend to or monitor for sleep-related threats that might be internal stimuli (e.g., bodily sensations) and/or external stimuli (e.g., the environment for noise that might prevent sleep onset). This selective attention and monitoring is automatic in the sense that it consumes minimal attentional resources and can happen without conscious decision-making (Kahneman 1973). As monitoring for threat increases the chance of detecting random and meaningless cues that can then be misinterpreted (Clark 1999), and the aroused state means that there is likely to be an abundance of body sensations present to be detected, monitoring is likely to provide further cause for worry. Hence, a vicious cycle is established, as indicated in Figure 13.1 by the feedback arrow from 'selective attention and monitoring' to 'worry'.

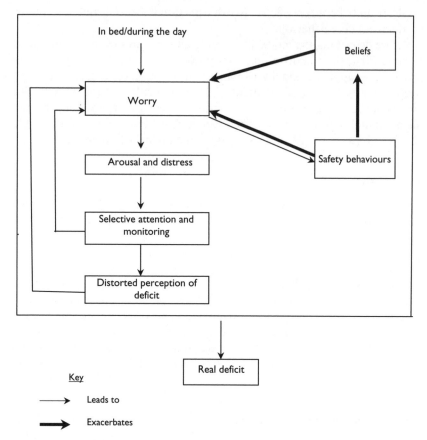

Figure 13.1 A cognitive model of the maintenance of insomnia: the cascade of processes depicted is proposed to apply to both the day and the night (reprinted from Harvey, A. G. (2002). A cognitive model of insomnia. *Behaviour Research and Therapy* 40: 869–93. Copyright © 2002 with permission from Elsevier).

Misperception

Many people with insomnia inadvertently overestimate how long it takes them to fall asleep and underestimate how long they sleep in total (e.g., Bonnet 1990). Thus it is suggested that insomnia is like most other psychological disorders in being characterised by 'distortions in reality' (Beck 1976: 218). To give some examples of misperception in other psychological disorders: people with anorexia nervosa think they are overweight when actually they are underweight, and people with panic disorder think they are having a heart attack when actually they are experiencing symptoms of anxiety. In a similar way, perhaps processes are operating that somehow trick patients with insomnia into overestimating the extent to which their sleep is inadequate.

However, a tendency to misperceive sleep does not preclude the presence of a real sleep deficit (the section below titled 'A real sleep deficit' will elaborate on this point).

The three mechanisms by which patients may get tricked into overestimating the extent of their deficit in sleep are suggested to be: (a) worry; (b) selective attention and monitoring; and (c) anxiety (the combination of worry, arousal and distress). The rationale for the first prediction – that worry serves to trigger misperception of sleep – is drawn from the robust finding in the time perception literature that time seems longer when the number of units of information processed per unit of time increases (Thomas and Cantor 1975). On this basis, it has been proposed that worry while trying to get to sleep may function to distort the perception of how long it is taking to get to sleep (Borkovec 1982). Evidence is accruing to support this first prediction (e.g., Tang and Harvey 2004a). The rationale for the second prediction – that selective attention and monitoring contribute to misperception of sleep – is based on the proposition that monitoring for sleep-related threat increases the chance of detecting random and meaningless cues that would otherwise pass unnoticed. When patients with insomnia detect these cues, they mis-interpret them as indicative of threat (Clark 1999) which, in turn, contributes to misperception of sleep and/or daytime functioning. To give an example, 'innocuous cues (e.g., a momentary lapse in memory, trouble concentrating when reading morning email) are interpreted as "signs" of inadequate per-formance resulting from a lack of sleep, the myriad of possible influences on feelings and levels of alertness are discounted' (Harvey 2002: 883). A third possibility, somewhat related to the second, is that insomnia is characterised by ex-consequentia reasoning or emotional reasoning (Arntz *et al.* 1995). That is, patients with insomnia draw faulty conclusions about a situation because they base their judgment on how they feel. In other words, danger is inferred from subjective feelings. For example, when a patient with insomnia notices feeling tired during the daytime they tend to use this subjective feeling to conclude that they must not have slept well during the previous night (when the feeling may have arisen from lots of different sources such as being bored or needing to eat).

It should be noted that if an individual perceives they have not slept adequately a further cause for worry is established (see the feedback arrow from 'misperception of deficit' to 'worry' in Figure 13.1). Further, if an individual wakes up in the morning believing they have had inadequate sleep, this is likely to contribute to the cascade of daytime cognitive processes, as will be discussed below.

Unhelpful beliefs about sleep and safety behaviours

Finally, it is proposed that there are two additional exacerbating processes. First, unhelpful beliefs about sleep are likely to fuel worry (Morin 1993).

For example, if you believe you need more than eight hours of unbroken sleep each and every night to function adequately during the day it is likely that you will worry about your daytime functioning (because most people find that getting eight hours of unbroken sleep is impossible to achieve). Second, in an attempt to cope with the escalating anxiety caused by the processes described, people with insomnia often make use of safety behaviours (Salkovskis 1991), such as drinking alcohol to reduce anxiety and promote sleep onset. A safety behaviour is an overt or covert action that is adopted to avoid feared outcomes. The problem is that these behaviours prevent the person experiencing disconfirmation of their unrealistic beliefs, and may make the feared outcome more likely to occur (Salkovskis 1991). The drinking alcohol example is a classic safety behaviour in that although it may promote initial sleep onset, it results in more awakenings and more disturbed sleep during the night (Roehrs and Roth 2001). That is, drinking alcohol before bedtime makes the feared outcome (poor quality sleep) more likely to occur.

The day

A novel aspect of the cognitive model is that the processes operating at night are considered to be equally important to the processes that operate during the day. Indeed, parallel processes to those described for the night are proposed to operate also during the day (as depicted in Figure 13.1). Specifically, on waking, people with insomnia often worry that they haven't obtained sufficient sleep. This worry, in turn, triggers arousal and distress, selective attention and monitoring for sleep-related threats, misperception and the use of counterproductive safety behaviors.

Each of these processes serves to maintain the insomnia: worry, arousal, and distress are likely to interfere with satisfying and effective daytime performance; selective attention and monitoring are likely to increase the detection of ambiguous cues (e.g., feelings of tiredness) that are then misinterpreted ('I mustn't have slept enough'), leading to misperception of daytime deficits. Further, the use of safety behaviours can contribute to distress and worsening of sleep, as well as preventing disconfirmation of unhelpful beliefs. For example, cancelling appointments at work (the safety behaviour) will prevent disconfirmation of the belief, 'If I feel tired at work the best way to cope is to cancel my appointments,' and will have unfortunate consequences such as getting behind at work, which is likely to increase anxiety further.

A real sleep deficit

As depicted at the bottom of Figure 13.1, it is suggested that these processes culminate in a real sleep deficit. Three points are relevant here. First, when a patient suffers from a real sleep deficit it is conceived to be the product of escalating anxiety which is not conducive to sleep onset (Espie 2002) or to effective daytime performance (Eysenck 1982). Second, misperception of sleep and a real sleep deficit can co-exist. It is not uncommon for a patient with insomnia to report sleeping only two hours a night. However, after completing an objective assessment of sleep over multiple nights (described by the patient as 'typical'), it could be discovered that they are actually sleeping four hours. In this example, the client is misperceiving their sleep *and* suffering from a serious real sleep deficit. Third, the occasional clients who think they have a real sleep deficit but don't (known as sleep state misperception) are at grave risk of getting trapped into becoming progressively more absorbed by, and anxious about, their sleep problem. The unfortunate consequence of this is that they are at high risk of developing a real sleep deficit.

EMPIRICAL STATUS OF THERAPY AND THE COGNITIVE MODEL

Cognitive behaviour therapy for insomnia (CBT-I) is an effective treatment, as indicated by two meta-analyses (Morin *et al.* 1994; Murtagh and Greenwood 1995) and a review conducted by the Standards of Practice Committee of the American Academy of Sleep Medicine (Morin *et al.* 1999). However, it is not the approach discussed here as CBT-I is a protocol-driven treatment that does not emphasise the importance of the therapist and the patient working as a team as they seek to develop, together, an 'ever-evolving formulation' of the difficulties faced by the patient (Beck 1995: 5). The individualised case formulation-driven treatment approach described below is based on the cognitive model just described and was developed for two reasons. First, while CBT-I is effective there is room for improvement, as indicated by the significant proportion (19–26%) of patients who do not improve following CBT-I and by the average overall improvement among those who respond to treatment being only 50–60% (Morin *et al.* 1994; Murtagh and Greenwood 1995). Although this degree of change is statistically significant it is not enough to move the average patient convincingly into a state where we would call them, and they would call themselves, good sleepers. Second, the individualised case formulation-driven approach described here has not yet been evaluated in the context of insomnia but, as evident from the other chapters in this book, has resulted in highly effective treatments for a range of psychological disorders. However, there is empirical evidence for many of the predictions made by the cognitive model (see Harvey 2005 for review), which is the basis for the formulation and treatment approaches that will now be described.

INITIAL CASE FORMULATION FOR INSOMNIA (1–2 SESSIONS)

Following several other successful cognitive therapy treatments (e.g., Clark *et al.* 1994; Ehlers *et al.* 2003), this approach begins by deriving a version of the cognitive model that is personalised for the patient. We derive two models, one for the night and one for the day. The decision about which of the models to derive first is made after checking with the patient whether they have most difficulty with/are most distressed by the night or the day. During the development of these personalised cognitive models we aim to build up a picture of how the daytime and nighttime processes identified are linked to, and feed into, each other. Each model is based on a detailed discussion of a recent specific night of poor sleep (which forms the basis for the nighttime model) and a recent specific day characterised by daytime tiredness and/or other problems associated with sleep (which forms the basis for the daytime model). Note that only part of the model will be derived in the initial case formulation stage; we do not introduce the role of dysfunctional beliefs and misperception of sleep and daytime performance until later sessions. The impact of these two is more effectively demonstrated by experience. Figure 13.2 presents one example of a nighttime model derived with one insomnia patient. As is evident, this is a very simplified version of the cognitive model presented in Figure 13.1 (the format is based on Morrison 2001).

Table 13.2 presents some questions we find helpful for elucidating each of the potential maintaining processes. It is often difficult to identify the maintaining processes because they manifest in different ways, and to different degrees, for each client. But with careful questioning we have found most of the processes to be present in most of the cases we have treated, including the complex comorbid cases.

So, during this initial case formulation phase we aim to complete an individualised formulation of the patient's difficulties; this is not a time to intervene, instead it is a time to be curious and develop, in close collaboration with the client, an understanding of how their difficulties are maintained. After drawing out the two personalised cognitive models we take the opportunity to introduce the basic tenets of the therapy: that thoughts lead to powerful emotions and unhelpful behaviours and that both make it difficult to get back to sleep. It is important to link the presentation of these ideas directly back to the two personalised cognitive models that have just been derived. The ideas are grasped more fully if linked to the patient's own experience. Finally, the patient and the therapist then brainstorm ways in which they can intervene in the vicious cycles described within the two personalised cognitive models. This phase forms the basis for and provides the rationale for the subsequent intervention. It also provides the patient with hope that improvement is realistic by changing one or more of the core parts of the vicious cycles.

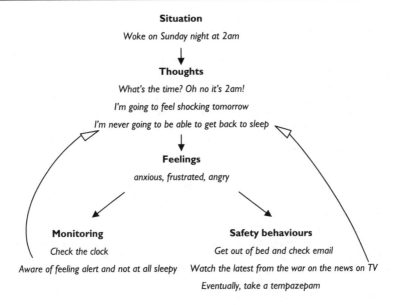

Situation

Woke on Sunday night at 2am

Thoughts

What's the time? Oh no it's 2am!

I'm going to feel shocking tomorrow

I'm never going to be able to get back to sleep

Feelings

anxious, frustrated, angry

Monitoring   **Safety behaviours**

Check the clock   *Get out of bed and check email*

Aware of feeling alert and not at all sleepy   *Watch the latest from the war on the news on TV*

Eventually, take a tempazepam

Outcome: *Couldn't get back to sleep and taking temazepam so late made me feel terrible in the morning*

Figure 13.2 An example of a personalised version of the cognitive model for the night (reprinted with permission from Harvey, A. G. (2005). Toward a cognitive theory and therapy for chronic insomnia. *Journal of Cognitive Psychotherapy* 19: 41–59, Springer Publishing Company, Inc., New York 10012).

TREATMENT PLAN: A PROCESS-FOCUSED TREATMENT

The treatment plan arises directly from the initial case formulation. The plan involves reversing each of the processes that were identified during the initial case formulation phase as maintaining the sleep disturbance. However, it is important to emphasise the 'initialness' of the case formulation because, as the treatment progresses, this initial formulation is honed and developed and the two additional maintaining processes – misperception of sleep and unhelpful beliefs about sleep – are introduced. So while case formulation provides the initial map for treatment it is also an ongoing part of the treatment.

The use of tailored behavioural experiments is core to the treatment phase. Because verbal techniques such as directly questioning the logical basis of thoughts and beliefs are typically not enough, behavioural experiments are used. Behavioural experiments are:

Table 13.2 Examples of useful questions for the initial case formulation

Worry
During the night/the day . . . What went through your mind/what were you thinking before getting into bed/on waking, as you got into bed/as you got ready for the day, and as you noticed you weren't getting to sleep/weren't performing well? What ran through your mind then? Did you ruminate/become preoccupied/seem to get things stuck in your mind? What sort of things did you say to yourself in your head? What triggered this kind of thinking? Did you have any pictures or images come to mind? What differences did you notice in your thinking patterns when you were having a bad day in comparison to when you are having a better day?

Feelings
How did thinking X make you feel? When you were afraid that X would happen, what did you notice happening in your body? What sensations did you experience?

Selective attention and monitoring
How did you determine or measure how close to falling asleep you were/what the time was/that you were feeling so tired? How did you monitor/measure that the insomnia was back? What were you paying most attention to/listening to/looking at/noticing/focusing on in this situation? How did you divide your attention? Did you concentrate your attention on anything in particular? Were you paying attention to your thoughts, your feelings or the situation? What was happening just before you paid attention to this? How do you decide what you are going to pay attention to?

Safety behaviour
When you felt X, what did you do to try to cope or feel better? Are there things that you did just in case something happens? What activities, situations or people did you avoid? Are there any strategies you use to try and avoid ruminating/dwelling on things?

Drawing out the consequences
From the 'monitoring' box: What were the consequences of paying attention to this? Does watching out for fatigue and tension have any consequences for your day?
From the 'feelings' box: Were there any consequences of these emotions for how the rest of your day went/for getting back to sleep?
From the 'safety behaviours' box: Were there any consequences of these behaviours for how the rest of your day went/for getting back to sleep? What would happen if you stopped doing this? How much does the avoidance stop you doing what you want? What are the short-term effects of trying to cope this way? What effect does it have on you in the longer term? Have you ever done something different? What happened then? What helped you to do something different?
From the 'thoughts' box: What effect did thinking X have on your mood or your actions? Were there any consequences of thinking this way for how the rest of your day went/for getting back to sleep?'

Adapted with permission from Harvey, A.G., Watkins, E., Mansell, W. & Shafran, R. (2004). *Cognitive Behavioural Processes Across Psychological Disorders: A Transdiagnostic Approach to Research and Treatment.* Oxford, UK: Oxford University Press.

planned experiential activities, based on experimentation or observation, which are undertaken by patients in or between . . . therapy sessions. Their design is derived directly from a cognitive formulation of the

problem, and their primary purpose is to obtain new information which
... [includes] contributing to the development and verification of the
cognitive formulation.

(Bennett-Levy et al. 2004: 8)

Some examples of the behavioural experiments we find to be particularly
useful for insomnia are described below (for others see Ree and Harvey
2004).

When devising a treatment plan, the order in which the various maintaining processes identified in the initial case formulation are typically introduced
is as presented below. This order seems to maximise engagement with the
treatment and promote rapid change. Having said that, it is important to be
sensitive to the many differences between patients in terms of which processes
are most important for maintaining their distress, and to address those processes at an earlier stage of treatment. Sometimes one or two of the processes
are not so relevant to a particular patient or some processes fall away when
other processes are successfully treated. So there is room for considerable
creativity and flexibility. Note also that the treatment approaches described
below are often interwoven with each other, partly because the processes are
interrelated, and also because it is often wise to provide an intervention at the
very moment when a patient raises the issue, which might be midway through
a discussion on another topic. For example, as soon as a patient mentions
that they manage unwanted thoughts while trying to get to sleep by trying to
suppress them or by 'blanking the mind' we immediately do a thought suppression behavioural experiment (described below).

In the section that follows a brief description of how the treatment for
each of the core maintaining processes can unfold is provided. For a fuller
description of the treatment see Harvey (2005).

Misperception

It does not change beliefs about sleep simply to tell a patient, 'You probably
get more sleep than you think you do,' and 'It is hard to estimate sleep.'
However, it is incredibly powerful to set up experiences that show the difficulty
perceiving sleep or that allow the patient to experience the difficulty perceiving
sleep. Hence, the intervention includes the use of behavioural experiments
(Ree and Harvey 2004; Tang and Harvey 2004b) as well as the therapist
watching out for natural opportunities to explore this topic. An example of a
natural opportunity that arose in a recent session was when a patient said:

> Something weird happened last night. I honestly thought I'd hardly slept
> at all but when I told my wife over breakfast this morning she laughed
> loudly and then said that I was fast asleep, and breathing heavily, all
> night – she knew because she wasn't feeling well so she was awake a

lot. You know, I believe her because she's very supportive of me and wouldn't say I was asleep if I wasn't.

This was a perfect time for the therapist to raise the possibility that there is a distinction between how much sleep you feel you get and how much you actually get. We also emphasise that sleep is incredibly difficult to perceive reliably because sleep onset is defined by the absence of memories.

Worry

We begin the intervention for worry by defining negative automatic thoughts (NATs) and then teaching the patient to monitor for, catch and evaluate their negative automatic thoughts, using the method described by Beck (1995). In this exercise we ask the patient to pick sleep-related negative automatic thoughts as examples to work on, although we suggest to the patient that it is a helpful procedure for worrisome thoughts relating to any topic. Themes that emerge from the patient observing and recording their negative automatic thoughts are then used to detect unhelpful beliefs that serve to maintain insomnia. These can be tested with behavioural experiments.

The above procedure is rarely sufficient for managing worry so several other approaches are required, three of which will now be described.

1   Ask what the patient does to manage unwanted worrisome thought. Typically they will report that they try to stop worrying by 'blanking my mind' or 'trying to stop all thought'. If so it is helpful to conduct a behavioural experiment within the session to demonstrate the adverse consequences of thought suppression. This involves conducting Wegner's (1989) white bear experiment, as a behavioural experiment, within the session. The patient is asked to close their eyes and try to suppress all of their thoughts relating to white bears (the therapist does this too). After a couple of minutes stop and share how successful your suppression attempts were (or more typically, were not!). This provides a springboard to discuss alternative thought management strategies like letting the thoughts come (i.e., the opposite of suppression) or gently directing attention to interesting and engaging imagery. Then, for homework during the subsequent week, we will set up one or more behavioural experiments, trying various alternative thought control strategies.

2   On the basis of a recent paper by Watkins and Baracia (2002), we stay on the lookout for patients asking themselves 'why' questions (e.g., 'Why am I not sleepy?' 'Why are my thoughts racing?' 'Why do I always feel so sleepy?'). These often become evident either during the initial case formulation when the thoughts the patient is having are elicited or when the content of worry episodes are described. 'Why' questions rarely have definite answers and so asking them tends to lead to more distress. For

example, if a person were to ask 'Why can't I control my sleep?' chances are that he/she would not find a simple, definite answer, and would end up feeling as if there was no solution to the problem, heightening anxiety and distress. In these cases we set up behavioural experiments so that the patient can discover whether asking 'why' questions is helpful or unhelpful in terms of generating solutions and in terms of emotional consequences.

3   It is also important to be on the lookout for positive beliefs about worrying in bed (Harvey 2003). The importance of positive beliefs about worry is drawn from the generalised anxiety disorder literature which suggests that pathological worry may be, at least partly, maintained because the individual believes that worry will lead to positive consequences (see Wells 1995). An example of the positive beliefs held by patients with insomnia is: worrying while trying to get to sleep helps me get things sorted out in my mind and is a way to distract myself from worrying about even more emotional things, things that I don't want to think about. If we discover that patients hold these beliefs we use Socratic questioning and behavioural experiments to examine and test their validity.

Selective attention and monitoring

Within-session behavioural experiments are used to introduce the concept of monitoring and to raise the patient's awareness of what is often an automatic process (we liken it to a virus checker on a computer that checks for threats to the smooth running of the computer but which we're often not aware of operating in the background). Then we use a combination of 'monitoring for monitoring' (a diary for recording monitoring and its consequences) and behavioural experiments to discover the extent to which there are adverse consequences associated with monitoring and to work out how to reduce or stop monitoring.

Safety behaviours

Although safety behaviours will have been identified and dealt with in the treatment components already described, it is important to identify remaining safety behaviours and use behavioural experiments to establish whether the safety behaviour is helpful or unhelpful (see Ree and Harvey 2004 for examples). Examples of safety behaviours often used during the day include those that exacerbate sleepiness (e.g., avoiding difficult chores/tasks and only doing the mundane ones), make the day unpleasant or boring (e.g., cancelling appointments, meetings, obligations or social activities) or increase preoccupation with sleep (e.g., spending excessive amounts of time considering ways to improve sleep). Examples of safety behaviours often used during the night include those that interfere with the sleep cycle (e.g., sleeping in after a poor night's sleep or napping), interfere directly with sleep (e.g., drinking alcohol before bed) or that paradoxically fuel pre-sleep cognitive activity (e.g., via thought suppression).

Unhelpful beliefs about sleep

We use the Dysfunctional Beliefs about Sleep Scale (DBAS; Morin 1993) and themes that emerge from the work on negative automatic thoughts to identify remaining unhelpful beliefs (some of which will have already been tackled in earlier treatment sessions). These beliefs are tested with behavioural experiments (see Ree and Harvey 2004 for examples).

Our 'fear of poor sleep' behavioural experiment seems to be one of the most important. This experiment is done towards the end of treatment when the patient feels they have developed an ability to manage the daytime consequences of a poor night.[1] This experiment involves actually creating one 'poor night' of sleep (e.g., choosing to sleep for 6.5 hours even though the patient thinks he/she needs eight hours). The point is that by this stage of treatment this behavioural experiment has been done by accident on several occasions (i.e., those sessions when a patient has come in and said, 'You know I only slept six hours last night and I actually feel OK today'). However, these experiences still haven't always fundamentally changed the belief, 'I need eight hours of sleep to cope,' and may even have been dismissed as a fluke or attributed to some other occurrence (e.g., 'I coped because I drank a lot of coffee'). So by actually choosing to sleep less, for just one night, the possibility of dismissing the information is eliminated and a core belief is challenged. Before attempting this experiment it is important to decide whether the patient wishes to go to bed later or to set the alarm earlier or some combination of both. We then plan fun activities to do during this time to keep awake and to make the experiment a memorable experience. Those who choose to wake earlier in the morning might decide to have a leisurely breakfast in bed or take more time reading the morning newspaper. Of course, we take care not to choose a night prior to a day when the patient is driving or would be at risk if they were tired. With a careful rationale, planning and support (e.g., phone calls and/or emails), most patients will give this experiment a try and benefit enormously.

Linking the night and the day

Toward the end of treatment we often find it is necessary to more explicitly tie together the discoveries made during therapy for managing the nighttime and daytime processes that were identified in the initial formulation and others that emerged throughout the treatment. This is important because up until this point the treatment has tended to focus on teaching one skill at a time; there needs to be time to practise explicitly combining them. The 'fear of poor sleep' experiment, just described, is a very useful way to achieve this goal as it involves combining all the skills during the day to combat the effects, on the day, of the poor night of sleep.

Relapse prevention

In the final phase of treatment, session time is devoted to consolidating treatment gains and to relapse prevention. Together, the patient and therapist complete a detailed written summary of the discoveries made throughout the treatment to reinforce what has been learned. They also set goals to ensure continued progress.

TRANSDIAGNOSTIC AND PROCESS-FOCUSED TREATMENTS FOR COMORBID CASES

One important issue that remains to be addressed is: When insomnia is comorbid with another disorder, which should I treat first? Given the results of the National Comorbidity Study (Kessler *et al.* 1994), showing that comorbidity is the norm rather than the exception, this question is relevant. I have two suggestions. One is to start by treating the problem which is most distressing to the client. The second is to focus on the maintaining processes. The basis of this suggestion is the striking nature of the similarities in the processes that maintain a broad range of psychological disorders. In this chapter, the processes that have been discussed are thought processes (worry), attentional processes (monitoring), unhelpful beliefs and the use of safety behaviours. These processes also feature in most other chapters in this book. If the various psychological disorders share common maintaining processes it may be possible to develop a 'transdiagnostic' treatment. The term 'transdiagnostic processes' refers to the processes that are in common across the disorders. So a transdiagnostic treatment would be one in which the maintaining processes that are common to the comorbid disorders are the target of the intervention, rather than the specific diagnostic categories for which the client meets criteria. The presence of transdiagnostic processes provides a potential account of the high levels of comorbidity we observe in clinical practice and may provide a way forward for treating comorbid cases (Harvey *et al.* 2004).

CONCLUSION

The case formulation-driven approach described in this chapter begins by devoting one to two sessions to working closely with the client to develop a picture of the processes that maintain their sleep disturbance. This is done by reviewing a specific recent episode of insomnia, with the aim of deriving a detailed understanding of the cognitive and behavioural processes that maintain the sleep disturbance. Five processes are proposed to be important maintainers of insomnia, even insomnia that is comorbid with another psychological disorder. They are: worry, selective attention and monitoring, misperception of sleep and daytime deficits, unhelpful beliefs about sleep, and counterproductive safety behaviours. The understanding that results from this initial case formulation not only gives the patient hope that change is possible but it provides a map that guides the treatment. The aim of the treatment is to reverse all five maintaining processes during both the day and during the night. It is proposed that this approach can be used for cases where insomnia is the sole presenting problem and for complex comorbid cases. Table 13.3 gives some examples of the latter.

Table 13.3 Brief discussion of treatment outcome for the patients described in Table 13.1

Insomnia that is comorbid with another psychological disorder

Bipolar disorder
Lisa: In conjunction with mood stabilising medication, Lisa found that the worry intervention effectively reduced her worry and anxiety about sleep. This made sleep onset more achievable. Interventions for the daytime increased Lisa's activity level, which had the 'knock-on' effect of her feeling more sleepy at bedtime. It also resulted in Lisa re-initiating friendships she had let slip and she felt better about herself. Lisa's beliefs about sleep were examined using behavioural experiments (especially the 'fear of poor sleep' experiment) in which she probed her real sleep need and found that eight hours of sleep was ideal but that she could cope fine (and didn't relapse) if she only got six hours. This discovery led to a more relaxed, less effortful approach to sleep.

Posttraumatic stress disorder
Simon: A combination of exposure therapy for the contents of the flashbacks and the nightmares and the sleep-focused intervention described here was effective. The aspects of the sleep intervention that were particularly helpful were: the intervention for monitoring to reduce Simon's hypervigilance and anxiety while trying to get to sleep, the worry intervention to reduce Simon's worry about sleep loss and the impact of sleep loss on his employment prospects, and the misperception intervention because it turned out that Simon was getting more sleep than he had thought.

Insomnia that is comorbid with a medical problem

Bladder problem
Gemma: To Gemma's (and the therapist's) surprise, by the end of the treatment targeting psychological maintaining processes (especially monitoring for needing to go to the bathroom while trying to get to sleep), Gemma was getting up to visit the bathroom no more than once each night and she had changed her view about what was causing the insomnia and what was causing the 'urinary tract disorder'; she viewed both as being caused by worry and monitoring, and the resultant anxiety.

Chronic pain
Paul: In conjunction with physiotherapy, the sleep-focused intervention described in this chapter was given. The back pain continued to interfere with Paul's sleep, but the sleep disturbance was markedly reduced. The interventions that proved to be particularly helpful included: the intervention for worry which served to moderate Paul's strong emotional reactions (the anger and frustration were making it even harder for him to get to sleep), the interventions for the daytime because they supported the physiotherapist's attempts to encourage Paul to be more active during the daytime (an 'energy generating' behavioural experiment was particularly helpful), and the intervention for monitoring for pain sensations and for daytime tiredness.

NOTE

1 Methods used to manage the daytime consequences of poor sleep include 'energy generating' behavioural experiments and conducting surveys of friends and family to discover that some daytime tiredness, particularly in the post-lunch dip period, is experienced by everyone, even people who are good sleepers (for further description see Ree and Harvey 2004).

ACKNOWLEDGEMENTS

This research was supported by the Wellcome Trust (grant no. 065913). I gratefully acknowledge the staff and graduate students at the Oxford Centre for Insomnia Research and Treatment for their important contributions to the development and ongoing testing of the treatment approach described here. In particular, thanks to Melissa Ree, Ann Sharpley, Nicole Tang, Lindsay Browning, Christina Neitzert Semler, Alison Bugg, Katriina Burnet and Kathleen Stinson. I would also like to acknowledge the important contributions of David M. Clark and Ann Hackmann.

RECOMMENDED READING

Harvey, A. G. (2002). A cognitive model of insomnia. *Behaviour Research and Therapy* 40: 869–93.

Harvey, A. G. (2005). Toward a cognitive theory and therapy for chronic insomnia. *Journal of Cognitive Psychotherapy* 19: 41–59.

Morin, C. M. and Espie, C. A. (2003). *Insomnia: A Clinical Guide to Assessment and Treatment*. New York: Plenum Publishers.

Morin, C. M. *et al.* (1999). Nonpharmacologic treatment of chronic insomnia: An American Academy of Sleep Medicine review. *Sleep* 22: 1134–56.

Ree, M. J. and Harvey, A. G. (2004). Behavioural experiments in chronic insomnia. In J. Bennett-Levy *et al.* (eds) *Oxford Guide to Behavioural Experiments in Cognitive Therapy*. Oxford, UK: Oxford University Press.

REFERENCES

Arntz, A. *et al.* (1995). 'If I feel anxious there must be danger': Ex-consequentia reasoning in inferring danger in anxiety disorder. *Behaviour Research and Therapy* 33: 917–25.

Beck, A. T. (1976). *Cognitive Therapy and the Emotional Disorders.* New York: International Universities Press.

Beck, J. (1995). *Cognitive Therapy: Basics and Beyond.* New York: Guilford Press.

Bennett-Levy, J. *et al.* (2004). *Oxford Guide to Behavioural Experiments in Cognitive Therapy.* Oxford, UK: Oxford University Press.

Bonnet, M. H. (1990). The perception of sleep onset in insomniacs and normal sleepers. In R. R. Bootzin *et al.* (eds) *Sleep and Cognition.* Washington, DC: American Psychological Association.

Borkovec, T. D. (1982). Insomnia. *Journal of Consulting and Clinical Psychology* 50: 880–95.

Clark, D. M. (1999). Anxiety disorders: Why they persist and how to treat them. *Behaviour Research and Therapy* 37: S5–27.

Clark, D. M. *et al.* (1994). A comparison of cognitive therapy, applied relaxation and imipramine in the treatment of panic disorder. *British Journal of Psychiatry* 164: 759–69.

Dalgleish, T. and Watts, F. N. (1990). Biases of attention and memory in disorders of anxiety and depression. *Clinical Psychology Review* 10: 589–604.

Easterbrook, J. A. (1959). The effect of emotion on cue utilization and the organization of behavior. *Psychological Review* 66: 183–201.

Ehlers, A. *et al.* (2003). A randomized controlled trial of cognitive therapy, a self-help booklet, and repeated assessments as early interventions for posttraumatic stress disorder. *Archives of General Psychiatry* 60: 1024–32.

Espie, C. A. (2002). Insomnia: Conceptual issues in the development, persistence, and treatment of sleep disorder in adults. *Annual Review of Psychology* 53: 215–43.

Eysenck, M. W. (1982). *Attention and Arousal.* New York: Springer-Verlag.

Harvey, A. G. (2001). Insomnia: Symptom or diagnosis? *Clinical Psychology Review* 21: 1037–59.

Harvey, A. G. (2002). A cognitive model of insomnia. *Behaviour Research and Therapy* 40: 869–93.

Harvey, A. G. (2003). Beliefs about the utility of pre-sleep worry: An investigation of insomniacs and good sleepers. *Cognitive Research and Therapy* 27: 403–14.

Harvey, A. G. (2005). Toward a cognitive theory and therapy for chronic insomnia. *Journal of Cognitive Psychotherapy* 19: 41–59.

Harvey, A. G. *et al.* (2004). *Cognitive Behavioural Processes Across Psychological Disorders: A Transdiagnostic Approach to Research and Treatment.* Oxford, UK: Oxford University Press.

Kahneman, D. (1973). *Attention and Effort.* Englewood Cliffs, NJ: Prentice Hall.

Kessler R. C. *et al.* (1994). Lifetime and 12-month prevalence of DSM-III-R psychiatric disorders in the United States. *Archives of General Psychiatry* 51: 8–19.

Lundh, L. G. (1998). Cognitive-behavioural analysis and treatment of insomnia. *Scandinavian Journal of Behaviour Therapy* 27: 10–29.

McCrae, C. S. and Lichstein, K. L. (2001). Secondary insomnia: A heuristic model and behavioral approaches to assessment, treatment, and prevention. *Applied and Preventive Psychology* 10: 107–23.

Morin, C. M. (1993). *Insomnia: Psychological Assessment and Management*. New York: Guildford Press.

Morin, C. M. and Espie, C. A. (2003). *Insomnia: A Clinical Guide to Assessment and Treatment*. New York: Plenum Publishers.

Morin, C. M. *et al.* (1994). Nonpharmacological interventions for insomnia: A meta-analysis of treatment efficacy. *American Journal of Psychiatry* 151: 1172–80.

Morin, C. M. *et al.* (1999). Nonpharmacologic treatment of chronic insomnia: An American Academy of Sleep Medicine Review. *Sleep* 22: 1134–56.

Morrison, A. P. (2001). The interpretation of intrusions in psychosis: An integrative cognitive approach to hallucinations and delusions. *Behavioural and Cognitive Psychotherapy* 29: 257–76.

Murtagh, D. R. and Greenwood, K. M. (1995). Identifying effective psychological treatments for insomnia: A meta-analysis. *Journal of Consulting and Clinical Psychology* 63: 79–89.

Perlis, M. L. *et al.* (1997). Psychophysiological insomnia: The behavioural model and a neurocognitive perspective. *Journal of Sleep Research* 6: 179–88.

Ree, M. J. and Harvey, A. G. (2004). Behavioural experiments in chronic insomnia. In J. Bennett-Levy *et al.* (eds) *Oxford Guide to Behavioural Experiments in Cognitive Therapy*. Oxford, UK: Oxford University Press.

Roehrs, T. and Roth, T. (2001). Sleep, sleepiness and alcohol use. *Alcohol Research and Health* 25: 101–9.

Salkovskis, P. M. (1991). The importance of behaviour in the maintenance of anxiety and panic: A cognitive account. *Behavioural Psychotherapy* 19: 6–19.

Smith, M. T. *et al.* (2005). The psychological treatment of chronic insomnia occuring within the context of medical and psychiatric disorders. *Clinical Psychology Review* 25: 559–92.

Spielman, A. J. and Glovinsky, P. B. (1997). The diagnostic interview and differential diagnosis for complaints of insomnia. In M. R. Pressman and W. C. Orr (eds) *Understanding Sleep: The Evaluation and Treatment of Sleep Disorders*. Washington, DC: American Psychological Association.

Tang, N. K. Y. and Harvey, A. G. (2004a). Effects of cognitive arousal and physiological arousal on sleep perception. *Sleep* 27: 69–78.

Tang, N. K. Y. and Harvey, A. G. (2004b). Correcting distorted perception of sleep in insomnia: A novel behavioural experiment? *Behaviour Research and Therapy* 42: 27–39.

Thomas, E. A. C. and Cantor, N. E. (1975). On the duality of simultaneous time and size perception. *Perceptual Psychophysics* 18: 44–8.

Watkins, E. and Baracia, S. (2002). Rumination and social problem-solving in depression. *Behaviour Research and Therapy* 40: 1179–89.

Wegner, D. M. (1989). *White Bears and Other Unwanted Thoughts: Suppression, Obsession and the Psychology of Mental Control*. New York: Viking.

Wells, A. (1995). Meta-cognition and worry: A cognitive model of generalised anxiety disorder. *Behavioural and Cognitive Psychotherapy* 23: 301–20.

Chapter 14

Self-harm

Gary L. Sidley

INTRODUCTION

For the purposes of this chapter, self-harm refers to expressions of personal distress that involve intentional and directly self-injurious acts that are not lethal. Such a definition excludes habitual and more culturally acceptable behaviours (for example smoking, alcohol abuse or excessive dieting), where physical or psychological damage may occur over a longer time-scale and is typically not the primary intention.

Self-harm constitutes a widespread problem for clinical services, the true prevalence of which is difficult to gauge. Official figures from the Registrar-General suggest an annual incidence for England and Wales of around 160,000. However, such estimates are likely to be significant underestimates as they rely heavily upon admissions to district general hospitals and, by so doing, tend to disproportionately focus on people who have taken deliberate drug overdoses (Horrocks *et al.* 2003). The national interview survey of Melzer *et al.* (2002) found that between 4.6% and 6.6% of British people have self-harmed and this is more likely to reflect the actual size of the problem.

The evidence for clinical interventions that are generally effective in reducing subsequent self-harm is extremely limited (National Collaborating Centre for Mental Health 2004). Following a brief review of the relevant outcome literature, this chapter will examine a potentially central reason for poor treatment response, namely the heterogeneous nature of self-harm. Self-harm is not a unitary disorder, and may be underpinned by a number of dimensions. As such, a psychosocial intervention that reduces self-harm in some people may be completely ineffective with a different sub-group. There-fore, an individualised case formulation approach is ideal for working with clients who self-harm, as illustrated in the final section of this chapter by a detailed example of a clinical case.

INTERVENTIONS TO REDUCE SELF-HARM

There is some limited empirical evidence to suggest that cognitive-behavioural interventions can have a significant impact upon subsequent self-harm behaviour in specific clinical groups who are at high risk of repetition. Salkovskis *et al.* (1990) found that five one-hour sessions of problem-solving delayed further post-treatment self-harm in comparison to a 'treatment as usual' control group. A longer and more intensive cognitive-behavioural intervention, dialectical behaviour therapy (DBT), was provided by Linehan (1993; Linehan *et al.* 1991) to females with borderline personality disorder. A combination of weekly group and individual sessions, spanning 12 months and incorporating a range of techniques within a context of respectful acceptance of the way things are for the patient, was successful in reducing both the frequency and severity of self-harm in comparison to 'standard aftercare'. Furthermore, a recent study has demonstrated the effectiveness of DBT for women with borderline personality disorder within an inpatient setting (Bohus *et al.* 2004).

Despite these isolated examples of clinical interventions positively influencing subsequent self-harm, evaluations employing larger and more heterogeneous groups of adult participants have led to negative conclusions. Thus, a meta-analysis of brief problem-solving therapies found no significant difference (only a trend) between those participants receiving the active treatment and the control groups with regard to reduced risk of self-harm repetition (Townsend *et al.* 2001). Similarly, following earlier optimism around the potential efficacy of a combination of brief cognitive behaviour therapy and bibliotherapy (Evans *et al.* 1999), a large, multi-centre randomised trial concluded that such an intervention was no more effective than 'treatment as usual' in reducing rates of self-harm repetition (Tyrer *et al.* 2004). Informed by negative findings such as these, a recent comprehensive review of the self-harm literature concluded that there was 'insufficient evidence to support any recommendation for interventions specifically designed for people who self-harm' (National Collaborating Centre for Mental Health 2004: 177).

However, two main considerations caution against premature pessimism concerning whether clinical intervention can benefit people who self-harm. First, although no positive impact upon the likelihood that self-harm will be repeated has been consistently demonstrated, other desirable and meaningful clinical outcomes have been achieved in response to cognitive-behavioural interventions. For example, the meta-analysis of problem-solving interventions (Townsend *et al.* 2001) found significant improvements for the treatment group with regard to levels of both depression and hopelessness. Likewise, the evaluation of manual assisted cognitive therapy (Tyrer *et al.* 2004) found that although the active treatment achieved no significant decrease in the percentage of people who repeated self-harm, the overall frequency of self-harm episodes was significantly reduced in the cognitive therapy group in comparison to treatment as usual. Furthermore, this study also reported a differential response to the treatment package in favour of those people who did not present with borderline personality disorder. Therefore, although it is unsurprising that self-harm repetition rates have typically been used as the main outcome measure, particularly given that about one in six people who attend accident and emergency departments following self-harm will repeat in the subsequent 12-month period (Owens *et al.* 2002), such a focus may be inappropriately narrow and result in the neglect of other meaningful clinical outcomes.

The second and more crucial consideration to counter pessimism about therapeutic ineffectiveness with large groups of people who self-harm relates to the observation that self-harm is not a unitary disorder. A deliberately self-injurious act can be the end-product of the interaction of a wide range of aetiological and maintaining factors. As such, the ineffectiveness of 'one size for all' interventions should come as no surprise. The literature to support the premise that self-harm is characterised by a range of underlying dimensions will now be briefly reviewed.

THE MULTI-DIMENSIONAL NATURE OF SELF-HARM

There have been many attempts over the last 50 years to isolate different categories of suicidal behaviour (for reviews see Arensman and Kerkhof 1996; Ellis 1988). Theoretical categorisations have emerged from a combination of sociological theories and clinical experiences, and some of these studies have addressed self-harm (Devries 1968; Neuringer 1962; Pokorny 1974). More recently, Lester (1990) suggested five categories of self-injurious behaviour based upon whether the self-harm was foreseen or desired, namely: failed suicide, in which the person intended to die but failed due to incompetent planning or unexpected intervention; deliberate self-harm, in which there is a wish to harm or punish oneself but not sufficiently to die; sub-intentioned self-harm, in which the person has some ulterior motive such as to communicate or change the behaviour of others; counterproductive self-harm, in which the person is unaware of how much self-harm is being inflicted; and pseudo self-harm, characterised by mild gestures of minimal self-harm.

An empirical study by Colson (1973) classified 79 graduate students with a history of suicidal behaviour or ideation into four groups based on the reasons given for wanting to die, namely: interpersonal loss/loneliness, health problems, fear of failure/concern for the future and wish to hurt/manipulate.

Larger studies using the statistical technique of cluster analysis (Henderson *et al.* 1977; Kurz *et al.* 1987; Paykel and Rassaby 1978) have all proposed three sub-groups of self-harm behaviour, two of which sound similar. All three studies described what approximates to a depressed/high risk of suicide group and a group characterised by many previous attempts/low risk/high hostility. Rassaby (1978) and Kurz *et al.* (1987) both highlight interpersonal motivations in the third group, whereas the third category in the Henderson *et al.* (1977) system could not be characterised by any of the variables examined. These three large-scale, psychiatrically-orientated studies therefore suggest sub-groupings distinguished by high levels of depression, high anger and a desire to use self-harm as a means of communication.

Other empirical research has given prominence to the intentions for the self-harm expressed retrospectively by the patients shortly after a deliberate drug overdose (Bancroft *et al.* 1977, 1979; Williams 1986). Interestingly, the most frequently endorsed reason for the overdose was not a desire to die but, rather, 'The situation was so unbearable that I had to do something and didn't know what else to do,' this being ratified by 56% and 67% of subjects in the Bancroft *et al.* (1979) and Williams (1986) studies respectively. Approximately 50% also endorsed, 'I wanted to get relief from a terrible state of mind,' and, 'I wanted to escape for a while from an impossible situation.' The responses to these three statements taken as a whole are consistent with motives of problem-solving and mood regulation. Interpersonal communication appeared to underpin the motives of 'I wanted to show how much I loved someone,' and 'I wanted to make people understand how desperate I was feeling,' these reasons being supported by about one-quarter of respondents.

Collective consideration of the empirical research and theorising based on clinical experience suggests a number of dimensions that may potentially underpin self-harm (see Table 14.1 for summary). Hopelessness – essentially a lack of positive anticipation about the future – has been shown to be predictive of both non-fatal self-harm and completed suicide (Beck *et al.* 1989; Fawcett *et al.* 1990; Petrie *et al.* 1988). Furthermore, problem-solving deficits, a plausible pre-cursor of hopelessness, have been consistently demonstrated in patients who self-harm (Linehan *et al.* 1987; McLeavey *et al.* 1987; Orbach *et al.* 1990; Rotherham-Borus *et al.* 1990; Schotte and Clum 1987). Additional support for hopelessness as an important dimension of self-harm derives from the frequent endorsement of intentions suggestive of the perceived insolubility of life problems in the studies of Bancroft *et al.* (1979) and Williams (1986) discussed above. Finally, the sub-group associated with fear of failure/concern for the future proposed by Colson (1973) also appears consistent with a hopelessness dimension.

Given that a negative view of self is a defining cognitive characteristic of depressed people (Beck 1976; Beck *et al.* 1979), the repeated identification of a depressed sub-group in the cluster analytical studies of Henderson *et al.* (1977), Paykel and Rassaby (1978) and Kurz *et al.* (1987) is consistent with a self-punishment component to self-harm. The 'deliberate self-harm' category of Lester (1990) also seems to correspond to this self-punitive dimension.

Whereas the above two self-harm dimensions of hopelessness and self-punishment are associated at their extremes with potentially fatal self-injurious acts, the remaining three dimensions are more likely to lead to

Table 14.1 Summary of self-harm dimensions, the underlying motivational theme, and typical negative automatic thoughts present prior to the self-harm

Dimension	Primary motivation	Typical negative automatic thoughts
Hopelessness	To escape from what is perceived to be an impossible situation	'Nothing can help me with my problems' 'My life is crap and always will be'
Self-punishment	To punish self for being a bad person	'I am evil' 'I deserve to die'
Mood regulation	To alleviate an intense, negative emotion	'I can't stand this feeling any longer' 'My agitation is unbearable'
Communication	To convey information to others	'No one understands how desperate I'm feeling' 'People don't realise how much I am hurting'
Effecting change in others	To make other people behave differently	'Help me' 'She shouldn't treat me this way'

milder forms of self-harm, albeit behaviours that are still associated with significant distress. Support for a mood regulation function has been reported above in the form of a 'relief from an intolerable state of mind' response as a reason for taking a drug overdose. Further evidence comes from a study by Favazza and Conterio (1989), who found that questionnaire responses from over 200 'habitual self-mutilators' indicated that the majority of them (65% and 58% respectively) felt more relaxed and less depressed after deliberate self-harm. Similarly, Wilkins and Cold (1991) investigated 74 remand prisoners with self-injurious behaviours and found that 81% of this prison population experienced positive effects on their dysphoria after self-mutilation, whereas reductions in tension and irritability were reported for 73% and 66% respectively. In addition, MacLeod *et al.* (1992) propose that parasuicide can have a powerful effect on mood via prolonged sleep, distraction from emotional stimuli, or some direct biological effect on the emotional system.

Evidence for a communication dimension to self-harm is provided by the identification of an interpersonally motivated sub-group in the studies by Paykel and Rassaby (1978) and Kurz *et al.* (1987). Furthermore, interpersonal communication also appeared to underpin the motives 'I wanted to show how much I loved someone,' and 'I wanted to make people understand how desperate I was feeling,' these reasons being supported by about one-quarter of respondents in the Bancroft *et al.* (1979) and Williams (1986) studies.

Finally, a dimension relating to effecting a change in others fits with one of the sub-groups identified by Colson (1973), namely 'a wish to hurt/manipulate'. Some further support for this dimension derives from the Bancroft *et al.* (1979) study of people who had taken drug overdoses; for more than half the participants the motivation behind the overdose was judged by psychiatrists as being 'to influence others' (although interestingly the service users themselves endorsed this reason much less frequently).

THE VALUE OF INDIVIDUAL CASE FORMULATION

A case formulation can be defined as an individually tailored, theoretical framework that attempts to explain the development and/or maintenance of a person's presenting problems. As self-harm is not a unitary disorder, but the behavioural end-product of one or more motivational dimensions, case formulation is an ideal tool for the development of an individualised guide that determines the priorities and sequencing of intervention strategies. Indeed, considering the heterogeneity of the self-harm population, together with the ineffectiveness of general treatment approaches, it is reasonable to propose that all therapeutic effort with a person who self-harms should be informed by a formulation that provides an explanatory framework for the person's expressed problems (which may or may not incorporate direct reference to the self-harm behaviour).

As proposed by Tarrier and Calam (2002), the formulation exercise should initially focus on explaining the maintenance of the presenting problems. Given that self-harm is a multi-faceted phenomenon, the development of case formulations for this group of service users has to be achieved without the benefit of disorder-specific models. As such, the maintenance of self-harm behaviour can be helpfully conceptualised by reference to a generic framework, such as Greenberger and Padesky's (1995) widely employed five-system model. Using this framework, detailed exploration of recent, specific self-harm episodes allows the therapist and service user to draw out the escalating interactions between situations (environmental triggers, reactions of others), thoughts (interpretations, beliefs), moods (emotions experienced), physical reactions (physiological responses) and behaviour (what the person did). In order to elucidate the temporal relationships between these five elements, meticulous questioning is required to analyse the prelude to, and aftermath of, the self-harm event frame by frame. For example, gauging the intensity of a specific emotion (on a 0–100 scale) immediately before, during and after self-mutilation can be informative.

The 'situations' component of the five-systems model is often a particularly important part of a maintenance formulation for people who self-harm, incorporating not only environmental triggers for the self-harm behaviour itself but also the reactions of others to it. Indeed, negative reactions to self-harm from professional staff are not uncommon, being particularly severe towards those people who harm themselves repeatedly (Alston and Robinson 1992; Bailey 1994; Pallikkathayil and Morgan 1988). As such, these unhelpful service responses can be an important element of the maintenance formulation.

Examples of maintenance formulations are shown in Figures 14.1, 14.2 and 14.3, illustrating the primary self-harm dimensions of mood regulation, communication and self-punishment respectively. These representations demonstrate that the same self-harm behaviour (for example cutting one's arms) can potentially be maintained by very different psychological mechanisms, each with varying implications for therapeutic intervention. Thus, whereas teaching anger management skills may potentially reduce the likelihood of future self-harm in the mood regulation example (Figure 14.1), such an intervention would be relatively ineffectual in cases where there is a primary self-punitive or communication dimension (Figures 14.2 and 14.3).

Although maintenance formulations are typically of most immediate relevance in identifying interventions that are likely to reduce self-harm behaviour, collaborative conceptualisation of aetiology can also be very

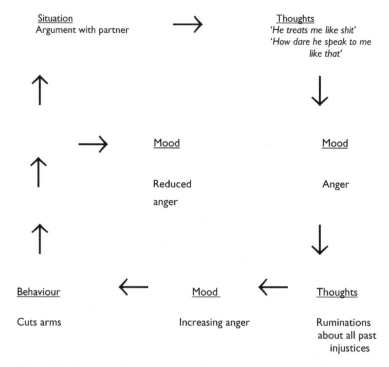

Figure 14.1 Example of a maintenance formulation illustrating the mood regulation dimension of self-harm.

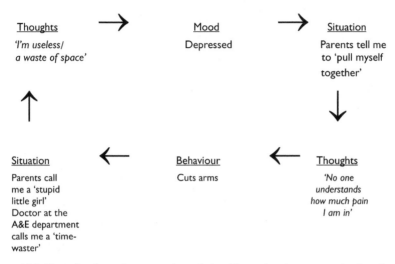

Figure 14.2 Example of a maintenance formulation illustrating the communication dimension of self-harm.

informative, particularly for the more complex presentations. Exploration of how a person acquired a vulnerability to self-harm can be formulated in cognitive terms by using the framework described in Beck's classic developmental model of depression (Beck *et al.* 1979). Such a framework suggests that experiences in childhood and early adulthood result in the emergence and strengthening of negative core beliefs and associated conditional assumptions that collectively constitute heightened vulnerability to subsequent emotional and behavioural problems. When triggered by a critical incident these cognitive structures become activated, producing a stream of negative automatic thoughts that then fuel the maintenance of distressing moods and problematic behaviours. Utilising this kind of developmental formulation with a person who self-harms not only guides clinical intervention but can in itself be therapeutic – a means of conveying a compassionate understanding of the current difficulties and thereby countering self-blame and the negative attitudes of others.

CASE ILLUSTRATION

A real case will now be described in detail to illustrate the utility of both maintenance and developmental formulations in guiding therapeutic intervention for a person who repeatedly self-harms (the name and some details have been changed to ensure anonymity).

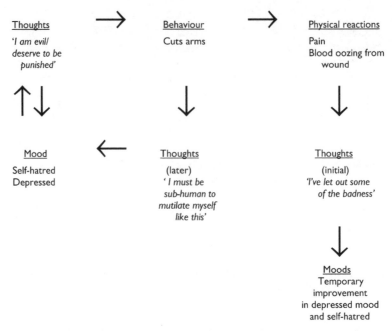

Figure 14.3 Example of maintenance formulation illustrating the self-punishment dimension of self-harm.

Jane, 28 years of age, was referred by a consultant psychiatrist for psychological therapy following a deliberate drug overdose and inpatient admission.

Sessions 1–4

Jane initially presented in a jolly and gregarious manner, smiling frequently. She was very well groomed and somewhat flirtatious. Jane described her presenting problems as 'sometimes going off at the deep end' when she would become angry and violent towards her ex-partner following his access visit to their three-year-old son. Other angry outbursts would typically occur during social evenings when, usually after consuming large amounts of alcohol, she would interpret other people's comments as being critical of her ('taking the piss'), resulting in immediate violence and aggression. With a lot of prompting, she identified her priority problems as drinking too much and angry outbursts.

Despite having a 10-year history of episodic self-cutting, together with three previous large drug overdoses (one within the previous two months), Jane did not at this stage wish to work on these behaviours. Indeed, she did not spontaneously speak about the self-harm and when she was asked about it she played down its significance, referring to it as 'silly'. However, towards the end of a couple of these early sessions Jane became visibly distressed when talking about how a previous partner had left her, going on to state, 'They always do when they get to know me.' These in-session expressions of emotion did not last long; Jane quickly regained her composure and continued to talk about her life in a jovial manner. During this early part of therapy, Jane shared very little about her past, apart from cheerfully informing me that her stepfather was 'not a nice man' in contrast to her natural father (who left the family home when Jane was seven years old) who she described as 'a terrific guy'.

Consistent with Jane's expressed current problems, behavioural targets to reduce her alcohol consumption were agreed, and homework mainly comprised completing the first three columns of a thought record (situations/thoughts/moods) as soon as possible after a significant increase in anger.

At this early stage in therapy there was a sense of having a very limited understanding of Jane's difficulties. As Jane had not identified the self-harm as a problem to work on, its development and maintenance had not at this time been explored in any detail. In retrospect, the limited information available at this stage could have been suggestive of the self-harm behaviour serving a communication function, given the recurrent angry episodes.

Subsequently, Jane did not arrive for the fifth session. It was later discovered that she had been re-admitted to an acute inpatient ward following further self-mutilation and suicidal ideation. Jane declined further psychological therapy while in hospital, but opted to re-start shortly after her discharge four weeks later.

Sessions 6 and 7

Jane presented for these sessions in a cheerful manner, as before, saying that she just gets 'a bit crazy' at times and needs help to control her emotions. However, on these occasions she described further problems of intense and recurring feelings of 'self-hatred' and 'despair'. During this part of therapy it seemed as if Jane was trying hard to be more open about her difficulties. She said that there were things in her past and present life that she probably should disclose but could not at present because she felt so ashamed. Also, she expressed concern that her feelings associated with these events would be overwhelming and lead to irresistible urges to self-destruct.

Discussion took place regarding how the sessions could be made to feel safer for her. First, it was agreed we both try to be open and honest with each other. It was suggested that people often find it difficult to trust others (including therapists) when important people in the past had let them down or treated them badly. Second, it was decided that Jane would be in complete control with regard to deciding what she disclosed. Third, it was agreed that Jane could have a 'time-out' if she felt overwhelmed in the session. She agreed to stay with painful feelings for as long as she could but if it became too much she would say 'too risky' and we would immediately move away from the topic under scrutiny, and try to return to it at a later time if she felt able to do so. Collectively, these therapy ground-rules allowed Jane to largely abandon her 'happy-go-lucky' facade and thereby enabled faster access to the real clinical issues that were contributing to her distress.

Sessions 8–12

Detailed exploration of recent, specific experiences of despair and self-hatred revealed that they were typically an immediate precursor of self-harm (the sequence usually being anger → despair → self-harm). Careful questioning about thoughts that were present when experiencing these intense negative emotions identified 'No-one will ever love me,' 'I'll always be alone,' and 'I deserve to be punished.' Downward arrowing of these negative automatic thoughts led to the detection of 'I am unlikeable,' and 'I am unlovable,' accompanied by a marked in-session increase in her level of distress, suggesting core belief status. A tentative maintenance formulation for her despair and self-hatred was collaboratively drawn out at this stage, illustrating how reflecting on earlier incidents such as criticism evoked negative thoughts (for example, 'I am unlikeable' and 'I deserve to be punished'), which in turn increased these distressing emotions as well as initiating self-cutting. Frame by frame analysis of the intensity of affect showed that cutting produced a modest, temporary reduction in her feelings of emptiness. However, Jane also revealed that some time after self-harming she would always negatively evaluate the behaviour as indicative of her being 'defective' or 'deformed', thereby further strengthening her unlikeable belief and fuelling additional feelings of despair and self-hatred. This maintenance formulation seemed to make a lot of sense to Jane, and it was at this stage that she recognised her self-harm behaviour as having a detrimental impact on her overall well-being.

During this phase of therapy, Jane also revealed further information about her past experiences and current behaviour. Her stepfather had major alcohol problems and was frequently violent, sometimes sadistically so, towards both Jane and her mother. Punches and kicks were commonplace, together with several instances of more pre-meditated physical abuse (for example, stubbing lit cigarettes out on Jane's arms because he 'felt like it'). In addition, both mother and stepfather were relentlessly critical of Jane; as the oldest child, they believed she should be responsible for the behaviour of her three younger siblings. Furthermore, because of the violence and general chaos within the household, Jane was too ashamed to bring any peers from school around to her house and generally had very few friends.

A particularly powerful negative experience for Jane occurred when she was 10 years old. Her natural father, apparently aware of the abusive home environment, returned and reached agreement with mother that the three younger siblings should go and live with him. Jane was left behind as she was, in the view of her natural father, old enough to take care of herself.

Jane also provided further details about her current behaviour. She described typically putting on an act of being 'the life and soul of the party' when socialising, despite feeling depressed and worthless. The frequency of self-mutilation was much higher than initially disclosed, usually being about three to four times per week. Also, Jane referred to a number of other habitual self-abusive behaviours including sexual promiscuity and starving herself of food, in addition to the previously disclosed alcohol binges. She also at this point expanded her problem list to include recurrent flashbacks to both her stepfather's acts of cruelty and to the day her natural father returned to remove her younger siblings from the house.

Armed with all this additional information, much of the in-session time at this stage of therapy was devoted to the tentative and collaborative development of a comprehensive case formulation (as shown in Figure 14.4). Homework tasks typically comprised further reflection around specific aspects of the formulation, together with thought records of recent episodes of despair and self-hatred (the latter being used both to substantiate or refute aspects of the formulation and to challenge negative automatic thoughts such as 'No-one will ever love me' as a coping strategy for reducing emotional distress). Although completion of the thought records often produced some modest reduction in mood intensity, the most helpful intervention at this point appeared to be the formulation itself. Thus, Jane embraced (at times accompanied by marked increases in levels of affect during the session) the central self-punishment theme underpinning her current problems and recognised the main therapeutic challenge for her as being self-acceptance or, in her own words, 'learning to like myself'. She seemed able to accept, at least as a possibility, the compassionate explanation of her difficulties afforded by the formulation as an alternative to her long-standing view that all her problems were due to her being inherently unlikeable and thereby deserving of punishment. Encouragingly, during this period of formulation development, several changes occurred, namely: Jane totally abandoned her in-session 'happy-go-lucky' manner (although she continued to put on this front in her day-to-day life); she significantly reduced her alcohol intake and ate more regular meals; and there was a moderate reduction in the frequency of her self-cutting. She did, however, continue to experience strong suicidal urges, although managing to contain these feelings without the need for further inpatient admission.

Sessions 12–20

During this period of therapy it was agreed with Jane to shift the emphasis onto her enduring belief about being unlikeable along with her personal rules that followed logically from this global and negative view of herself.

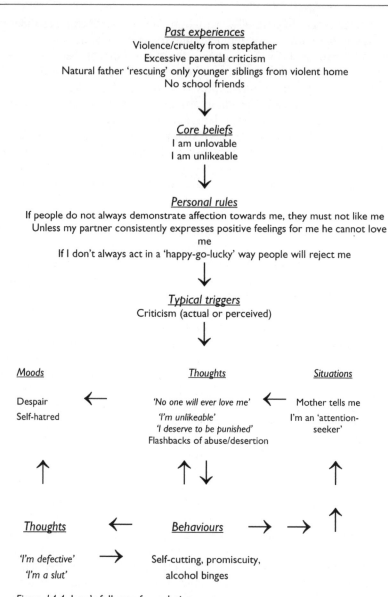

Figure 14.4 Jane's full case formulation.

There were two main thrusts to this part of the intervention. First, more adaptive alternatives to Jane's personal rules were generated and tested in real-life situations. Most usefully, instead of, 'If I don't always act in a happy-go-lucky way people will reject me,' Jane was able to develop, 'Most people will accept me if I just be myself.' By operating in this alternative mode while in social situations for increasing amounts of time, Jane began to discover that virtually everyone did accept her without the veneer of joviality – a couple of closer acquaintances even commenting that she was more comfortable to be with than before. (However, one male associate and previous fellow drug-user did comment that she was becoming a bore!) Importantly, signs of affection and positive regard could now be attributed to her real self rather than the role she had previously played, thus enabling the loosening of beliefs about not being likeable.

Second, cognitive interventions targeting 'I am unlikeable' were used to reduce Jane's conviction in this core belief, the one that (according to our formulation) was fuelling much of her self-harming behaviour and problematic moods. The methods employed were similar to those outlined by Greenberger and Padesky (1995). Thus, Jane completed daily positive data logs to record any snippets of evidence, no matter how small, that were consistent with an alternative core belief, namely 'I am likeable.' In addition, detailed historical reviews of previous chronological segments of Jane's life were undertaken to identify any events or occurrences that fit the theme of being likeable. A grandmother who had treated Jane (her first grandchild) as special during her infant school years was a rich source of such evidence. Continua criteria were also employed, whereby Jane identified operational components that contributed, in her view, to any person's likeability (for example, asking about other people's interests, being able to laugh at oneself) and then rated herself on each of them. She was surprised to discover that, on average, she scored 85% on these likeability criteria.

Sessions 20–30

Consistent utilisation of the above-mentioned approaches resulted in Jane's conviction in the belief 'I am likeable' increasing from 0% at the start of therapy to 45% by session 20. Although achieving further reductions in the rate of self-harm, and less frequent episodes of despair and self-hatred, Jane continued to report occasions when she felt very near to suicide. Although knowing intellectually at these times that she probably was likeable, she felt anything but. She also continued to be troubled by flashbacks to the physical abuse and a recurring memory of her father leaving with her siblings. It was hypothesised that the engine for these residual problems continued to be the core themes of unlikeable/unlovable. Given the persistent re-experiencing symptoms, together with the need for a more emotionally relevant shift in core belief conviction, the imagery re-scripting and reprocessing approach of Smucker and Dancu (1999) was employed. Although originally developed and evaluated with adult survivors of childhood sexual abuse, it seemed reasonable to assume it would be equally relevant to those having suffered early trauma of any type. In brief, this therapeutic approach involved three components: imaginal re-exposure to an accurate recollection of the traumatic event; imagining an adult form of the child victim (Jane) intervening and rescuing the child from the traumatic event; and imagining how the adult would attempt to comfort the child victim in the immediate aftermath of the traumatic event. Repeated in-session and between-session practice of imagery re-scripting and re-processing was accompanied by an almost total elimination of the flashbacks. Most encouraging, however, was Jane's sharp increase of conviction in her 'I am likeable/loveable' belief, which by the end of treatment was reported as being 100%. Jane reported that the third strand of the treatment had been particularly beneficial, the articulation of what her adult self would say to comfort her child victim self apparently acting as a powerful challenge to her inherent self-blame and self-hatred associated with the abuse from her stepfather and perceived desertion by her natural father.

Follow-up

At 12 months after the end of treatment, Jane reported no further episodes of despair, self-loathing or strong suicidal feelings. There had been one instance of superficial self-cutting, immediately following a major argument with her current partner. The physical damage inflicted did not require medical attention. Importantly, Jane stated that this isolated episode of self-harm 'felt different' from previous ones, not being accompanied by extreme negative feelings of self-hatred, being short-lived and not spiralling into stronger self-destructive urges. Furthermore, Jane had returned to full-time employment, was involved in a relatively stable relationship, and she continued to refrain from self-punishing behaviours such as promiscuity, food starvation and alcohol binges.

CONCLUDING COMMENTS

The main argument throughout this chapter has been that the heterogeneous psychological difficulties of people displaying self-harm behaviour necessitate an individually tailored, case formulation approach in order to meet the needs of this client group. The (unusually) effective intervention with Jane, described above, is consistent with this premise that idiosyncratic conceptualisations explaining problem development and maintenance will, if meaningful and relevant to the service user, enhance the therapeutic value of psychological treatment.

Clearly, it is inappropriate to generalise from a single case study to the self-harm population as a whole, and controlled investigations comparing formulation-based approaches with standardised, manual-driven approaches are urgently required. The relative ineffectiveness of standardised treatment approaches might increase the feasibility of such studies in that, if formulation-based approaches were superior, the effect size would be expected to be relatively large and therefore the number of participants for a sufficiently powered study would not be prohibitive (Tarrier and Calam 2002). Such comparative studies should use a wide range of outcome measures rather than being primarily restricted to self-harm repetition, for (as in the case of Jane) people who deliberately self-injure often do not identify self-harm reduction as a priority goal. Also, given the high levels of dissatisfaction with services reported by people who self-harm, the acceptability of the intervention package would be one important outcome measure.

RECOMMENDED READING

Hawton, K. and van Heeringen, K. (eds) (2000). *The International Handbook of Suicide and Attempted Suicide*. Chichester, UK: Wiley.

Hjelmeland, H. *et al.* (2002). Why people engage in parasuicide: A cross-cultural study of intentions. *Suicide and Life-Threatening Behaviour*, 32: 380–93.

Walsh, B. W. and Rosen, P. M. (1988). *Self-Mutilation: Theory, Research and Treatment*. New York: Guilford Press.

REFERENCES

Alston, M. H. and Robinson, B. H. (1992). Nurses' attitudes toward suicide. *Omega* 25: 205–15.

Arensman, E. and Kerkhof, J. F. (1996). Classification of attempted suicide: A review of empirical studies. *Suicide and Life Threatening Behaviour* 26: 46–67.

Bailey, S. (1994). Critical care nurses' and doctors' attitudes to parasuicide patients. *Australian Journal of Advanced Nursing* 11(3): 11–17.

Bancroft, J. *et al.* (1977). People who deliberately poison themselves: Their problems and their contacts with helping agencies. *Psychological Medicine* 7: 289–303.

Bancroft, J. *et al.* (1979). The reasons people give for taking overdoses: A further enquiry. *British Journal of Medical Psychology* 52: 353–65.

Beck, A. T. (1976). *Cognitive Therapy and Emotional Disorders*. New York: International Universities Press.

Beck, A. T. *et al.* (1979). *Cognitive Therapy of Depression*. New York: Guilford Press.

Beck, A. T. *et al.* (1989). Prediction of eventual suicide in psychiatric in-patients by clinical ratings of hopelessness. *Journal of Consulting and Clinical Psychology* 42: 861–5.

Bohus, M. *et al.* (2004). Effectiveness of inpatient dialectical behaviour therapy for borderline personality disorder: A controlled trial. *Behaviour Research and Therapy* 42: 487–99.

Colson, C. (1973). An objective analytical approach to the classification of suicidal phenomena. *Acta Psychiatrica Scandinavica* 49: 105–13.

Devries, A. G. (1968). Definition of suicidal behaviours. *Psychological Reports* 22: 1093–8.

Ellis, T. E. (1988). Classification of suicidal behaviour: A review and step toward integration. *Suicide and Life Threatening Behaviour* 18: 358–71.

Evans, K. *et al.* (1999). Manual-assisted cognitive-behaviour therapy (MACT): A randomised controlled trial of a brief intervention with bibliotherapy in the treatment of recurrent deliberate self-harm. *Psychological Medicine* 29: 19–25.

Favazza, A. R. and Conterio, K. (1989). Female habitual self-mutilators. *Acta Psychiatry Scandinavia* 79: 283–9.

Fawcett, J. *et al.* (1990). Time-related predictors of suicide in major affective disorder. *American Journal of Psychiatry* 147: 1189–94.

Greenberger, D. and Padesky, C. A. (1995). *Mind over Mood: A Cognitive Therapy Treatment Manual for Clients*. New York: Guilford Press.

Henderson, A. *et al.* (1977). A typology of parasuicide. *British Journal of Psychiatry* 131: 631–41.

Horrocks, J. *et al.* (2003). Self-injury attendances in the accident and emergency department. *British Journal of Psychiatry* 183: 34–9.

Kurz, A. *et al.* (1987). Classification of parasuicide by cluster analysis: Types of suicidal behaviour, therapeutic and prognostic implications. *British Journal of Psychiatry* 150: 520–5.

Lester, D. (1990). A classification of acts of attempted suicide. *Perceptual and Motor Skills* 70: 1245–6.

Linehan, M. M. (1993). *Cognitive-Behavioural Treatment of Borderline Personality Disorder*. New York: Guilford Press.

Linehan, M. M. *et al.* (1987). Interpersonal problem-solving and parasuicide. *Cognitive Therapy and Research* 11: 1–12.

Linehan, M. M. *et al.* (1991). Cognitive-behavioural treatment of chronically parasuicidal borderline patients. *Archives of General Psychiatry* 48: 1060–4.

MacLeod, A. K. *et al.* (1992). New developments in the understanding and treatment of suicidal behaviour. *Behavioural Psychotherapy* 20: 193–218.

McLeavey, B. C. *et al.* (1987). Interpersonal problem-solving deficits in self-poisoning patients. *Suicide and Life Threatening Behaviour* 17: 33–49.

Melzer, H. *et al.* (2002). *Non-Fatal Suicidal Behaviour Among Adults Aged 16–74 in Great Britain*. London: The Stationery Office.

National Collaborating Centre for Mental Health. (2004) *Self-Harm: Short-Term Physical and Psychological Management and Secondary Prevention of Intentional Self-Harm in Primary and Secondary Care*. London: National Institute for Clinical Excellence.

Neuringer, C. (1962). Methodological problems in suicide research. *Journal of Consulting Psychology* 26: 273–8.

Orbach, I. *et al.* (1990). Styles of problem-solving in suicidal individuals. *Suicide and Life Threatening Behaviour* 20: 56–64.

Owers, D. *et al.* (2002). Fatal and non-fatal repetition of self-harm. *British Journal of Psychiatry* 181: 193–9.

Pallikkathayil, R. N. and Morgan, S. A. (1988). Emergency department nurses' encounters with suicide attempters: A qualitative investigation. *Scholarly Inquiry for Nursing Practice: An International Journal* 2: 237–53.

Paykel, E. and Rassaby, E. (1978). Classification of suicide attempters by cluster analysis. *British Journal of Psychiatry* 133: 45–52.

Petrie, K. *et al.* (1988). Psychological predictors of future suicidal behaviour in hospitalized suicide attempters. *British Journal of Clinical Psychology* 27: 247–58.

Pokorny, A. D. (1974). A scheme for classifying suicidal behaviours. In A. Beck *et al.* (eds) *The Prediction of Suicide*. Philadelphia: Charles Press.

Rotherham-Borus, M. J. *et al.* (1990). Cognitive style and pleasant activities among female adolescent suicide attempters. *Journal of Consulting and Clinical Psychology* 58: 554–61.

Salkovskis, P. M. *et al.* (1990). Cognitive-behavioural problem solving in the treatment of patients who repeatedly attempt suicide. *British Journal of Psychiatry* 157: 871–6.

Schotte, D. E. and Clum, G. A. (1987). Problem solving skills in suicidal psychiatric patients. *Journal of Consulting and Clinical Psychology* 55: 49–54.

Smucker, M. R. and Dancu, C. V. (1999). *Cognitive-Behavioral Treatment for Adult Survivors of Childhood Trauma: Imagery Rescripting and Reprocessing*. New Jersey: Jason Aronson Inc.

Tarrier, N. and Calam, R. (2002). New developments in cognitive-behavioural case formulation. Epidemiological, systemic and social context: An integrative approach. *Behavioural and Cognitive Psychotherapy* 30: 311–28.

Townsend, E. *et al.* (2001). The efficacy of problem-solving treatments after deliberate self-harm: Meta-analysis of randomised controlled trials with respect to depression, hopelessness and improvement in problems. *Psychological Medicine* 31: 979–88.

Tyrer, P. *et al.* (2004). Differential effects of manual assisted cognitive behaviour therapy in the treatment of recurrent deliberate self-harm and personality disturbance: The POPACT study. *Journal of Personality Disorder* 18: 102–16.

Wilkins, J. and Cold, J. W. (1991). Self-mutilation in female remanded prisoners I: An indicator of severe pathology. *Criminal Behaviour and Mental Health* 1: 247–67.

Williams, J. M. G. (1986). Differences in reasons for taking overdoses in high and low hopelessness groups. *British Journal of Medical Psychology* 59: 369–77.

Chapter 15

Working with asylum seekers

Jake Bowley

INTRODUCTION

This chapter aims to examine issues relating to working with asylum seekers using cognitive behavioural therapy (CBT). It addresses engagement, assessment, case formulation and intervention, and hopes to raise awareness of the need to offer psychological interventions to this client population and to identify the advantages of using CBT and individual case formulation.

Classing asylum seekers together as a group is in some ways misleading, indeed it is hard to find a more heterogeneous population, but this chapter hopes to provide cognitive therapists with an understanding of the complexities frequently involved in conceptualising and working with asylum seekers and to suggest that frameworks addressing recovery and adjustment processes offer a valuable conceptual framework to support individual formulations and interventions.

ASYLUM SEEKERS IN THE UNITED KINGDOM

The process of seeking asylum in the United Kingdom (UK) receives much media attention and it is undoubtedly a major contextual factor in working with asylum seekers. Because of the type of media coverage, the complexity of the system, and as there have been many recent changes, a brief overview of the UK context is given here. Because of the rapid rate of change, readers may want to access more detailed and updated information such as can be found on the Refugee Action or Refugee Council internet sites.

Asylum seekers' legal context

The UK has had an international obligation to offer a safe haven to refugees who come to this country since it signed the United Nations Convention On The Rights Of Refugees in 1951. A refugee is a person who –

owing to a well-founded fear of being persecuted for reasons of race, religion, nationality, membership of a particular social group, or political opinion, is outside the country of his nationality, and is unable to or, owing to such fear, is unwilling to avail himself of the protection of that country.

(United Nations 1951: 16)

When an individual claims asylum in the UK, immigration staff initially interview them to assess their claim. The majority are refused at this point because they are deemed to have unsatisfactorily supported their claim for refugee status.

Most applicants then enter a process that allows their claim to be more intensively examined and judged independently. This involves claimants obtaining legal support and developing a case. During this process claimants are called 'asylum seekers' and are dispersed to live across the UK.

Asylum seekers' initial legal appeal is in front of an independent adjudicator. The decision of this adjudicator is then open to appeal from both the Home Office and the asylum seeker; these appeals are heard in front of a panel of adjudicators who in most cases give a final judgement.

The application process involves gathering evidence, such as obtaining medical documentation of torture, and often takes a year between application and an adjudicator hearing, and a further 18 months for a second adjudication panel hearing.

When an application is accepted and asylum seekers are accepted as refugees they are entitled to the same social and economic rights as UK citizens. They have, for example, full access to medical treatment, education, housing and employment. Failed applicants (whose legal right to appeal has been exhausted) are deemed to be in the country illegally, and they await deportation, are placed in detention or become homeless.

Outline of dispersal process

While their applications are being processed the National Asylum Seeker Service (NASS) disperses asylum seekers across the UK to many major towns and cities. The rationale for dispersal is that distributing asylum seekers around the UK reduces the disproportionate pressure on services and populations in the areas where asylum seekers traditionally choose to live. This has meant that many areas and services unused to multi-cultural populations have had to adapt to new demands.

Local councils or large private landlord companies provide asylum seekers with predetermined accommodation that is usually shared. This housing is often in deprived areas, where statutory services are already pressured, and where there are higher than average crime rates and poor local facilities.

Asylum seekers are often disoriented and exhausted by their journey, and dispersal is often a quick process, so they can arrive in the regions within weeks of their arrival in the UK. The reception they receive varies, but can be limited to a brief orientation meeting with support staff, help with signing on with a local GP and directions on where to receive benefits.

Asylum seekers are then not allowed to work and have to manage on 70% of income support (£39 a week for an individual) to pay for utilities, food, clothing and transport. An Oxfam report highlighted the fact that many asylum seekers cannot afford to feed and clothe themselves adequately and that they in effect live below the poverty line (Oxfam and Refugee Council 2002).

Asylum seekers have the right to access all parts of the National Health Service; however, there is considerable evidence that they, like many minority groups, are often both unaware of and unable to gain access to existing services (National Institute for Mental Health in England 2003).

Asylum seeker demographics

Over the past decade an average of 60,000 people a year have applied for refugee status in the UK – around 2% of the world's refugees, and 10% of Europe's. Approximately three quarters of the refugees who reach the UK are male, and most of these are aged 18–34. There are, though, many families who also seek refuge in the UK and in 2002 they brought with them 18,950 dependants, 80% of whom were children. Significant numbers of children also arrive unaccompanied in the UK each year. In 2002 there were over 6,000 aged under 17 (Home Office 2002a).

People flee their own countries mainly to reach a place of safety (Home Office 2002b) from conflicts and repressive regimes in their places of origin. In 2002 asylum seekers in the UK came from Africa (35%), Asia (25%), the Middle East (22%) and Europe (16%).

Refugees flee to the UK for a number of reasons including the presence of family and friends, having a shared language and the existence of a perceived affinity, but often they have no actual control over their destination and merely follow agents' directions. The UK is, however, not seen as an 'easy target' and most asylum seekers are unaware of the benefit systems or work prospects in the UK or across Europe (Home Office, 2002b).

Asylum seekers come from widely ranging backgrounds, from highly educated politically active dissidents to uneducated agricultural workers, and their levels of English can be equally diverse. Their experiences of health and statutory services can range from services comparable to or better than the UK, to none at all.

Asylum seeker wellbeing

The majority of asylum seekers arriving in the UK are physically healthy (British Medical Association 2002), and are usually relieved and optimistic at having managed to get to what many think of as a safe and democratic country.

Psychological distress is, though, almost ubiquitous, and adult rates of 'psychological disorders' such as depression, anxiety and post-traumatic stress disorder (PTSD) are much higher than in the general UK population (e.g., Lavik *et al.* 1996; Tribe 1999; Turner and Gorst-Unsworth 1990; Van der Veer 1998). Studies have also found that refugee children have up to three times the rate of significant psychological problems when compared to the general UK child population (Fazel and Stein 2003).

This is perhaps not surprising given the considerable losses and changes that asylum seekers have experienced in fleeing their home countries. It is also common for asylum seekers to have experienced traumas such as detention, beatings, torture, rape, and sexual assault, or being forced to witness the torture and murder of others. Other persecutions can include long-term political repression, the deprivation of human rights and repeated harassment (Summerfield 1996).

There is evidence that asylum seekers' mental and physical wellbeing can deteriorate over the extended asylum application process (BMA 2002) and this may reflect factors inherent in the asylum process, such as poor accommodation, lack of personal control, financial hardships, the inability to work, social isolation based on language, general uncertainty and ongoing legal problems (Lavik *et al.* 1996).

One further important factor in asylum seeker wellbeing in the UK is the high level of threat and antipathy from the local population. Racism is a common experience for asylum seekers, and the British media have been criticised for the 'climate of verification of asylum seekers that has taken hold in the UK' (UNHCR 2001).

One particular protective factor for asylum seekers' wellbeing has been found to be social support, to the extent that a lack of support is more predictive of problems than pre-existing trauma (Gorst-Unsworth and Goldenberg 1998). In the context of dispersal this could mean that asylum seekers placed in new areas with no existing populations might have higher rates of psychological problems.

Therapy services therefore might be assumed to be providing interventions to refugees and asylum seekers, and this has both been strongly argued for (Mahtani 2003) and commented on as part of the *Mental Health National Service Framework* (Department of Health 2000). In general, however, access to these services can be difficult for asylum seekers and often they do not receive support.

EVIDENCE FOR THERAPEUTIC INTERVENTIONS

Despite the body of literature showing the increased psychological difficulties associated with being an asylum seeker, there has been relatively little investigation into the efficacy of psychological interventions with this population.

This reflects many factors, but for therapists asked to work with asylum seekers, the absence of such evidence can lead to anxiety about both the appropriateness and effectiveness of interventions.

What literature there is has not focused on asylum seekers but instead has examined interventions for refugees, for whom the threat of repatriation has been removed. These studies have also mainly examined treatments for PTSD, and in general have been found to lack the required sophistication or consistent methodology to evaluate their efficacy (Başoğlu 1993).

Studies assessing CBT with torture victims suffering PTSD have looked at the application of both behavioural exposure and cognitive approaches (Başoğlu 1992; Başoğlu et al. 2004; Paunovic and Öst 2001). They are mainly case studies and small controlled studies but they have demonstrated therapeutic effectiveness, and hence the potential value of current CBT trauma therapies. Two other published studies have focused on developing coping skills strategies in refugees suffering with PTSD (Snodgrass et al. 1993) and adopting a narrative exposure approach (Neuner et al. 2002) with similarly positive yet not definitive results.

A separate approach specifically developed in work with survivors of torture and political persecution is testimony psychotherapy (Cienfuegos and Monelli 1983). Developed in Chile in part as a political response to the atrocities of the then military dictatorship, in this approach survivors and 'therapist' form a working alliance in order to document the survivor's story, producing an accurate written testimony of the experiences of the individual. This approach has a number of features similar to cognitive-behavioural interventions for trauma. The drawing up of a complete and precise testimony contains clear elements of exposure, while the emphasis on 'politicising' the act and experience of torture offers survivors a framework in which to reappraise their experiences, with strong resemblances to the examination of trauma-related meanings and appraisals in CBT.

Testimony has been found to have therapeutic effects in both pilot and case studies (Agger and Jensen 1990; Lustig et al. 2004; Neuner et al. 2002; Weine et al. 1998) and in one empirical study (Cienfuegos and Monelli 1983), although there are currently no published controlled studies.

The evidence for interventions with asylum seekers is therefore limited, and restricted mainly to PTSD, yet therapists are faced with asylum seeker clients who can present with high levels of distress that cross many disorder categories. Therapists must then turn to the strong and growing body of evidence for the efficacy of cognitive therapy across many disorders (for a review see Roth and Fonagy 2001), and apply themselves to the task of matching the therapy to their client.

LIMITATIONS IN APPLYING COGNITIVE MODELS TO ASYLUM SEEKERS

The fact that published accounts of work with asylum seekers focus mainly on relatively straightforward interventions based on cognitive behavioural models of PTSD is not particularly useful for therapists working with asylum seekers who present with difficulties of such complexity.

Hence, therapists are presented with the difficulty of adapting the theoretical underpinnings of CBT, with both its general cognitive understanding and focused models of specific disorders, to clients with complex comorbid problems in difficult ongoing circumstances.

One example of this is applying the treatment models of PTSD. The most recent cognitive models make the assumption that both the intrusive phenomena and distorted appraisals of risk and danger are a result of insufficiently processed sensory memories (Ehlers and Clark 2000). To asylum seekers, however, who remain at very real risk of being returned to the dangers from which they fled, intrusive and anxious appraisals may reflect an entirely appropriate anxiety response. Asylum seekers are still at risk and their trauma is ongoing; the specific treatment models of PTSD do not encompass this.

In the same way, depression and more general anxiety can be seen not as mental disorders but as clear sequalea of the ongoing environmental stressors they encounter. The cognitive biases seen in generalised anxiety, where the self is seen as vulnerable, the world as dangerous and the future unpredictable (Blackburn and Davidson 1990) do not seen so biased when seen in an asylum seeker's experience or context. This 'realistic' distress is highly contagious and can impact on therapists quite readily, especially if they have beliefs about their role as trying to cure their client's problems.

So to reduce an individual's problem to a formulation guided by a simple disorder model runs the risk of 'treating an illness which the refugee does not have' (Eisenbruch 1991: 25). And, further, the very meanings such models attach to 'symptoms' are based on a view that they are a disordered process, which can be very different from both the client and therapist view.

CBT does not consist of such rigid models, and although they are often the starting point for a therapist's understanding and possible intervention, CBT has the ability instead to explore a client's reality and develop a shared formulation comprising of shared meanings and understandings.

WAYS OF FORMULATING WITH ASYLUM SEEKERS

When formulating with asylum-seeking clients it can be difficult if not impossible to transpose straightforward disorder-specific models, due to the complexity and high number of client problems and their contexts of ongoing uncertainty, threat and powerlessness. Clients could often be formulated, for example, as simultaneously depressed, anxious, traumatised and grieving, resulting in formulations that could easily become incredibly complex and unusable for therapist and client alike.

Two approaches that can be helpful to guide clinicians' ongoing formulations of asylum seekers' experiences are Stirling Moorey's approach to working with adjustment (Moorey 1996) and the staged or phased approach to working with trauma outlined by Judith Herman (1997).

Adjustment formulations

Working with people in adverse life circumstances such as serious or terminal illness has many similarities to working with asylum seekers. Their situations are both extremely difficult, and their feelings of helplessness and powerlessness may reflect real difficulties in many areas of their lives. Stirling Moorey has written about the role of cognitive therapy with individuals suffering cancer whose situations are objectively difficult, and whose anxiety or depression can be seen as a rational responses to an appalling situation (Moorey 1996: 450). He has argued that when 'bad things happen to rational people', formulating their difficulties as one of 'adjustment' is a productive and effective approach.

Theorists have explored the process of adjustment from many different approaches (e.g., Herman 1997; Horowitz 1986; Kubler-Ross 1969) yet the nature of adjustment has not yet and may not be exactly defined, covering as it can the processes of grief, trauma and/or coping with life changes. There is though a general agreement that adjustment involves 'the processing of the cognitive and emotional significance of adverse life events' (Moorey 1996: 755)

Cognitive explanations of this 'emotional processing' (Rachman 1980) have mainly focused on clients with PTSD, where the processing is seen as being what happens when clients recover, and there are increasingly specific and useful models of the cognitive substrates of this process (e.g., Ehlers and Clark 2000). It is important, however, to acknowledge that this process is not limited to PTSD but can apply equally to clients adjusting to major aversive life changes.

With asylum seekers, approaching work with the task or process of adjustment in mind can help manage and draw together formulations. It allows client and therapist to accept the distress and emotions experienced and to explore them rather than see them as symptoms of disorder.

Cognitive therapy can then play a role in working with adjustment, helping clients to recognise and accept their immediate thoughts, appraisals and feelings and then develop appropriate coping strategies, and also helping them to seek a deeper understanding of their experiences and identify what cognitive distortions or coping strategies may be maintaining distress and blocking adjustment (Moorey 1996).

This exploration of the personal meanings attributed to a situation or feeling, no matter how realistic, can highlight idiosyncratic distortions and assumptions that can be examined using standard cognitive techniques. Despite the degree of adversity and apparent helplessness clients experience, the 'underlying theoretical rationale that an individual's affect and behavior are largely determined by the way in which [they structure] the world' (Beck 1979) still holds true.

Recovery models

Many asylum seekers have histories of traumatic experiences and a useful approach to aid developing formulations is Judith Herman's description of trauma recovery. She has described a conceptual framework that can act to guide psychotherapy with the common patterns of distress associated with atrocities whether they be domestic violence, physical or sexual assault or even political terror.

This approach is not alone in positing stages of healing and it bears similarities to Keane and colleagues' 'phase oriented' cognitive approach (Keane *et al.* 1994; Kimble *et al.* 1998).

Herman identifies three stages:

- safety, where the restoration of control and establishment of safety are key
- reconstruction, where traumas are explored and transformed
- reconnection, involving developing activity and relationships.

She relates these tasks to an ongoing process of healing and recovery (perhaps closely comparable to an adjustment process). They are seen as concepts that can be used to impose simplicity on the complex recovery process rather than entities in themselves.

She argues that establishing safety and control is always the first task of recovery as well as being a guiding principle. This sense of control and safety covers all features of an individual's experience, from physical and emotional health to self-destructive or risky behaviours, and outward into environmental, financial and social situations. A key feature of this stage of the process is supporting and developing the individual's autonomy, so often removed in both victims of trauma and asylum seekers.

In the second stage the transforming process of reconstruction, comparable to therapeutic interventions for PTSD, is seen as part of an ongoing remembrance and mourning in which retelling the trauma and especially facilitating emotional expression are means by which individuals regain control of their experiences, and in doing so ameliorate the intrusive and uncontrollable nature of associated distress.

Finally, individuals work towards reconnecting with wider social and interpersonal worlds. Taking control of one's life and actions, and then developing a future, are all part of the final and ultimately ongoing process of recovery.

PRACTICE

Working with interpreters

A sizeable proportion of asylum seekers will need to use interpreters for therapy to occur. This can often be as novel an experience for the therapist as working with an asylum seeker, and can raise further anxieties associated with the work.

There is a systemic need for both therapy services and training courses to increase focus around this issue, but often it remains the therapist's role to obtain the appropriate knowledge and skills. Working with interpreters is an extra complexity, especially as often both therapist and interpreter are unaccustomed to working with each other in therapy.

It is beyond the scope of this chapter to summarise how best to work therapeutically with an interpreter. However, the recent book *Working With Interpreters In Mental Health* is an ideal primer for therapist and service alike (Tribe and Ravel 2003).

Key issues when working with asylum seekers and interpreters are those associated with confidentiality and trust. Asylum seekers can often appear to have few concerns about the trustworthiness or professionalism of therapists but can be very concerned about the interpreter. At one extreme, political, religious and ethnic differences can mean that interpreters from the same country as a client may be viewed as being part of the oppressive or persecutory groups they are trying to flee. More commonly, and especially in small refugee communities, interpreters can be well known by clients, their relatives and even their community, having obvious implications in ensuring trust and confidentiality (Tribe and Ravel 2003).

A further issue when working with asylum seekers and interpreters, as with any different ethnic group, is the issue of mental health concepts and categorisation. Often terms and models do not have equivalents in different cultures, and working with an interpreter to decipher and work with these differences is especially important. The issue of working across cultures is too complex and important to address superficially in this chapter, but the fundamental CBT practices of working in collaboration with client concerns and developing shared understandings and formulations are, I suggest, a firm foundation on which to approach cross-cultural work.

Engagement

As mentioned before, the issue of trust is of particular importance in working with asylum seekers and therapists need to address it at the outset. Establishing your helping role and explaining confidentiality is of key importance, especially when working with interpreters, as their commitment to confidentiality needs to be explicitly discussed. Informing clients that you are not connected to the Home Office can be useful and many therapists choose to make their commitment to human rights explicit.

As with all clients, explaining the reason and rationale for the appointment and therapy is extremely important, especially since clients may not have any awareness of the profession of 'therapy', and may have very idiosyncratic views as to the reason for the session. Explaining the limits of the therapeutic role can also be useful: our helping role does not involve prescribing medication, and we have little involvement in processes such as benefits and accommodation.

Allowing time for both the development of trust and the establishment of a working alliance is vital, and the important message of concern for the client's safety and autonomy needs to be constantly reiterated. Clients need to know that they do not have to meet, that they do not have to talk and that you are aware how difficult talking and trusting can be.

This engagement process can be seen as part of Herman's safety stage, establishing safety in the relationship and with the goals of the relationship. For some clients the idea of therapy may be threatening, especially with its association with ill health or weakness, and being able to give positive normalising rationales for your role can be invaluable.

Assessment

Asylum seekers often present with many difficulties and this can present a challenge to therapists needing to assess and formulate quickly. It is important not to rush through engagement or to determine model-driven formulations, but instead to follow the initial case formulation task of collaboratively developing a problem list (Persons 1989). This process can also be seen as part of Herman's initial safety stage.

Often the most pressing concerns are not immediately psychological, but instead are problems for example with medication, other health concerns, accommodation, racism or legal difficulties. These can seem overwhelming in number and complexity, and working together to develop a problem list can be a valuable strategy in developing a shared and controllable understanding of the difficulties faced by your client. Assessment of asylum seekers' current situation needs to include their legal situation, as their stage in the dispersal process can have a marked impact on possible interventions.

Although the focus of cognitive therapy is appropriately on the psychological factors associated with a client's difficulties, with asylum seekers active and practical assistance is often also warranted. This can challenge a therapist's boundaries but, practically, there are very rarely alternative sources of support, the interventions required are often short term and highly effective in developing engagement, and the option of doing nothing can seem therefore impossible.

The assessment of wellbeing is similar to standard non-refugee populations, but the intensity of distress and the sense of crisis asylum seekers often present with can make it less straightforward. Although fears and anxieties are often clear they can often have an intensity that can appear delusional yet remain consistent with an individual's experience.

Asylum seekers often report suicidal ideation and therapists need to be prepared to assess risk. It is especially common for asylum seekers to say, 'I'll kill myself rather than be sent back,' and there are cases where individuals have committed suicide rather than be returned. If an individual's legal claims have expired then this may be an imminent concern.

In assessing ideation, it is not uncommon for clients to non-disclose due to personal religious reasons or the cultural unacceptability of suicide. Presenting a normalising rationale and challenging personal responsibility for such intrusive thoughts can be helpful, especially as feelings of guilt around such experiences may be impacting greatly.

An important feature of assessing symptomatology is to elicit the meaning of those symptoms. Assumptions of pathology may not apply and clients may see problems as culturally normal. Similarly, clients may view experiences common in the West as aversive. Especially in victims of political violence, remembering can be seen as a powerful act of self-integrity and forgetting seen as the perpetrator winning. Prior expectations of torture have been found to be a protective factor for post-traumatic symptomatology in torture victims (Başoğlu et al. 1997), and often working with clients involves exploring the wider political meaning of their experiences.

Assessing different socio-cultural interpretations of wellbeing can also be useful, not only in eliciting beliefs about the cause and nature of problems, but in socialising clients to the CBT model. Asking clients about the traditional or local name of a problem, of its signs and of its causes and how would it be prevented can all help in the engagement process and in the development of the shared goal of working together.

When working with asylum seekers, it is important to be sensitive when assessing their history, especially when their coping strategies focus on avoidance. It can be very easy as part of the assessment process to elicit memories, thoughts and feelings that clients have been suppressing or which can lead to high unmanageable levels of affect. It is important to identify the degree to which they have talked about their experiences, their strategies for managing affect and even their view of the result of talking about things. Often clients may have a view that talking about it may make things immediately better, when in practice an increase in negative affect may result. If unprepared for this, clients may opt out of therapy, feeling overwhelmed and afraid.

Gaining an understanding of a client's history can initially seem a difficult task as often they have long and complicated life histories. It can be helpful to conceptualise client's histories as having three stages:

- pre exile: childhood, and the time leading up to fleeing the country
- flight: experiences of fleeing to the UK, arrival, and asylum application
- exile: experiences in the UK including dispersal.

It can be useful to gain an understanding of clients' countries of origin, and information is easily available on the internet at sites such as Amnesty International, which can provide brief but detailed summaries of most relevant countries. This can also be useful in identifying languages and religious contexts.

Developing and sharing formulations

Assessing and formulating are not separate processes, and through identifying the client's concerns and understanding, and providing a rationale for support and joint working, many of the safety and trust issues key to the first recovery stage can be developed.

Early presentation of a general normalising recovery formulation with explicit trust and safety requirements can be helpful in supporting clients in the early stages of work, and this can be particularly useful to help prevent some clients going into early detailed descriptions of trauma that may lead to excessive distress.

Supporting clients' basic health and safety, assisting with environmental problems and engaging effective social support all help establish safety and trust. Explicitly giving control to clients is vital, as is clear discussion of the difficulties, risks and challenges associated with therapy.

Establishing safety and control can be difficult with asylum seekers, who face the threat of repatriation and whose lives are controlled by powerful legal, financial and social constraints. Restoring control is clearly a goal of developing shared formulation and in normalising and accepting symptoms.

Working from an adjustment model, in some cases distress may be seen as an appropriate part of the individual's normal emotional processing and not in need of support or therapy. Clients are often referred or come for help because of the sense that they shouldn't be in distress. In these cases a normalising rationale can alter appraisals, reduce anxieties and allow individuals to continue on the process of recovery without formal assistance.

Assessment and formulation can then be seen as part of the safety stage of Herman's conceptualisation, with the goals of normalising reactions, validating experiences and developing a respectful therapeutic relationship.

For some, however, where the level of distress or the existence of maladaptive beliefs or coping strategies prevent recovery, cognitive formulations, psychoeducation and interventions aimed at symptom management strategies can be very useful. For those clients whose problems closely match specific models of psychological disorder (e.g., panic) sharing the formulations of these problems is entirely appropriate. Socialising to a cognitive model may, but not necessarily, require extra effort.

Interventions

Using Herman's concept of a process of recovery, therapists can order their interventions around the three phases: safety, transformation and reconnection. At the Traumatic Stress Clinic in London a three-phase model of interventions is currently being used and developed (Robertson 2003; Young and Grey submitted). Although in practice clients' needs are not static they can be formulated as moving between these stages and interventions can then act at different levels on various problems over time.

Initial phased interventions focus on developing safety, control and trust, and could include the ideas already mentioned in the processes of engagement and assessment as well as the following strategies and techniques:

- strategies aimed at helping clients reduce their levels of isolation
- providing non-pathological education regarding common reactions
- providing normalising formulations and explanations for reactions
- work aimed at managing hopelessness and suicide risk
- helping clients manage sleep difficulties
- helping clients develop anxiety management and coping strategies
- making assertive referrals to other health and support services
- helping clients develop strategies to manage intrusive problems such as nightmares or dissociative episodes
- providing supportive therapy
- helping clients manage interpersonal difficulties such as estrangement and detachment
- validating clients' experiences
- providing practical support in dealing with issues such as housing and asylum status.

The decision on which intervention approaches to use should reflect the formulation; however, the current legal situation, the level of English language or interpreter skills can mean that simple behavioural approaches are often the initial choice.

With asylum seekers these interventions can often have a marked effect on levels of distress and feelings of self-control. Due to the uncertainty of appealing for refugee status, many asylum seekers feel unable to continue with therapy beyond this stage. Clients often have a clear awareness of their limits and can return for more specific therapy after gaining refugee status or having just become more established.

When working with asylum seekers whose appeal process has been exhausted and who are awaiting deportation, therapists need to assess carefully the impact of working past this level, as it might be unlikely to benefit the client and might instead be likely to cause harm.

Phase two interventions correspond to Herman's stage of reconstruction of experiences. These centre on the transformation of clients' experiences, and in practice these can often closely match the active therapeutic components of cognitive therapy for disorders such as PTSD and depression, and for the emotional problems of guilt and shame. This is especially true if clients' difficulties appear discrete and reflect specific traumas or losses. Often, however, clients may have had a lifetime of trauma and in these cases the adoption of specific interventions can be augmented by consideration of the human rights testimony approach that reinforces the important notion of bearing witness to clients' experiences.

Themes that can emerge in this phase include:

- bearing witness, validating and holding the client's experience
- helping clients develop a coherent and detailed narrative of their experiences
- helping clients explore and develop the personal meaning of these events
- exploring and reframing feelings of shame and guilt
- confronting extreme levels of affect including despair and anger
- reviewing life before trauma and exile, and developing a sense of continuity
- supporting clients in mourning their multiple losses
- exploring the shattered beliefs and assumptions of ruptured belief systems
- focused therapeutic work aimed at altering traumatic memories.

With asylum seekers, the degree to which this process can bring about observable reductions in distress is variable. Many are able to move forward despite the anxieties associated with not being assured of refuge, and this can be a powerful experience for client and therapist alike, but therapists must always be aware of and therefore assure their clients of the 'rational' nature of their distress and the need to some extent to accept the adversity of their current situation.

Phase three interventions, mirroring Herman's reconnection stage, focus on moving from the past into an active present and future.

Here the focus of work is on supporting clients to engage with the world. Therapists can aim to support this by:

- encouraging clients to resume everyday activities
- helping clients establish new relationships or re-establish old relationships and family bonds
- helping clients rebuild a new life in a new country, developing goals and aspirations
- helping clients rebuild beliefs, and religious and political convictions.

With asylum seekers this is particularly difficult, as they are unable to work, usually financially restricted, and often through dispersal isolated from communities and friends. Education and volunteering are two areas, however, that are open to asylum seekers. Learning English can be a powerful, though challenging task, while many find the act of helping others an immensely powerful emotional support. Linking with colleges and voluntary agencies can be a major role of therapy in this stage.

As in stage two, however, for many asylum seekers the goals of reconnection can be extremely difficult given the temporary nature of their accommodation and social networks. In this context the development of relationships, including in therapy, can be seen as something else to lose and care needs to be taken in exploring such steps.

Ending therapy

Ending therapy can be a particularly difficult process for therapist and client alike. Most statutory services are unable to offer ongoing support, so therapy can end while an individual remains in an uncertain situation, often still experiencing symptoms.

The decision to end therapy should be arrived at collaboratively and with clear rationales. Reasons can include that basic coping strategy work has been completed, or that further work is contraindicated or not required.

Given that asylum seekers have experienced multitudes of losses and unplanned and unwanted endings, it is important that the therapeutic ending be as different an experience as possible. In this way the ending can be seen as a further therapeutic intervention in itself. Endings need to be talked about from the start of therapy, and clearly, as part of the contracting process, but maintaining a shared awareness of the stage of therapy can be especially important. What constitutes a positive ending will differ between clients, but exploring this, raising awareness of difficulties this may raise and asking clients to design their own ending strategy can promote ending as a powerful intervention in itself.

Self-care

Working therapeutically with asylum seekers can significantly impact on therapists, and self-care can be especially important. The act of listening alone to people's experiences of persecution, horror, injustice and suffering has been shown to have a impact on both mental and physiological health, but the role of therapist is particularly prone to negative effects (Pennebaker 1990).

Terms such as 'vicarious traumatisation' (McCann and Pearlman 1990) and 'burnout' (Maslach 1982) have been used to describe this impact, and it is a real factor in work with asylum seekers. This is particularly so for a number of factors. Asylum seekers are almost always coping with high levels of adversity, they often present with extreme emotional intensity and histories of horrific 'inhuman' experiences, while their situations can often appear hopeless. This is especially so if therapists have entered work with a notion of cure – with a belief that ameliorating distress is a given. Although a lot of change is possible in work with asylum seekers, an adjustment or recovery process philosophy possibly offers more protection for both client and therapist.

Working with asylum seekers can challenge therapists' sense of competence and skill. Professional boundaries can be tested and the political nature of the work can impact on a therapist's sense of justice and faith.

The issue of self-care can be addressed in part at an organisational level, through supervision and caseload management, but it also needs to be taken as a personal responsibility. There is no easy solution to managing this work, and therapists need to monitor and be self-aware of the impact it has on them.

CONCLUSION

Working with asylum seekers presents cognitive therapists with many challenges, yet the collaborative goal-focused approach, with its use of individual, shared formulations and tailored interventions, means that it is highly suitable for this client group and the problems they often experience. This chapter suggests that working both with a heuristic of general adjustment and 'coping with adversity' and using a staged recovery model approach to trauma in a general sense, cognitive therapists can develop formulations that can effectively guide their interventions and support both their clients and themselves.

RECOMMENDED READING

Herman, J. L. (1997). *Trauma and Recovery: From Domestic Abuse to Political Terror.* London: Pandora.

Tribe, R. and Ravel, H. (2003). *Working with Interpreters in Mental Health*. Hove, UK: Brunner-Routledge.

RECOMMENDED WEBSITES

http://www.harpweb.org.uk
http://www.amnesty.org
http://www.torturecare.org.uk
http://www.refugeecouncil.org.uk
http://www.refugee-action.org.uk

REFERENCES

Agger, I. and Jensen, S. B. (1990). Testimony as ritual and evidence in psychotherapy for political refugees. *Journal of Traumatic Stress* 3: 115–30.

Başoğlu, M. (1992). *Torture and its Consequences: Current Treatment Approaches*. Cambridge, UK: Cambridge University Press.

Başoğlu, M. (1993). Prevention of torture and care of survivors: An integrated approach. *Journal of the American Medical Association* 270: 606–11.

Başoğlu, M. *et al.* (1997). Psychological preparedness for trauma as a protective factor in survivors of torture. *Psychological Medicine* 27: 1421–33.

Başoğlu, M. *et al.* (2004). Cognitive-behavioral treatment of tortured asylum seekers: A case study. *Journal of Anxiety Disorders* 18: 357–69.

Beck, A. T. (1979). *Cognitive Therapy For Depression*. New York: Guilford Press.

Blackburn, I. M. and Davidson, K. M. (1990). *Cognitive Therapy for Depression and Anxiety: A Practitioner's Guide*. Oxford, UK: Blackwell.

British Medical Association. (2002). *Asylum Seekers: Meeting their Healthcare Needs*. London: BMA Publications.

Cienfuegos, A. J. and Monelli, C. (1983). The testimony of political repression as a therapeutic instrument. *American Journal of Orthopsychiatry* 53: 43–51.

Department of Health. (2000). *National Service Framework for Mental Health: Modern Standards and Service Models*. London: Department of Health.

Ehlers, A. and Clark, D. M. (2000). A cognitive model of posttraumatic stress disorder. *Behavioural Research and Therapy* 38: 319–45.

Eisenbruch, M. (1991). From post traumatic stress disorder to cultural bereavement: Diagnosis of south east Asian refugees. *Social Science and Medicine* 30: 637–80.

European Monitoring Centre on Racism and Xenophobia. (2002). *Racism And Cultural Diversity*. Vienna: European Research Centre on Migration and Ethnic Relations.

Fazel, M. and Stein, A. (2003). Mental health of refugee children: Comparative study. *British Medical Journal* 327: 134.

Gorst-Unsworth, C. and Goldenberg, E. (1998). Psychological sequelae of torture and organised violence suffered by refugees from Iraq. *British Journal of Psychiatry* 172: 90–4.

Herman, J. L. (1997). *Trauma and Recovery: From Domestic Abuse to Political Terror*. London: Pandora.

Home Office. (2002a). *Home Office Statistical Bulletin: Asylum Statistics*. London: Research Development and Statistics Directorate.

Home Office. (2002b). *Understanding the Decision Making of Asylum Seekers*. London: Communications Development Unit.

Horowitz, M. J. (1986). *Stress Response Syndromes*. Northvale, NJ: Jason Aronson.

Keane, T. M. *et al.* (1994). Post-traumatic stress disorder. In M. Hersen and R. T. Ammerman (eds) *Handbook of Prescriptive Treatments for Adults*. New York: Plenum.

Kimble, M. O. (1998). Cognitive behavioural treatment for complicated cases of post-traumatic stress disorder. In N. Tarrier *et al.* (eds) *Treating Complex Cases: The Cognitive Behavioural Treatment Approach*. Chichester, UK: Wiley.

Kubler-Ross, E. (1969). *On Death and Dying*. New York: Macmillan.

Lavik, N. J. *et al.* (1996). Mental disorder among refugees and the impact of persecution and exile: Some findings from an outpatient population. *British Journal of Psychiatry* 169: 726–32.

Lustig, S. L. *et al.* (2004). Testimonial psychotherapy for adolescent refugees: A case series. *Transcultural Psychiatry* 41: 31–45.

Mahtani, A. (2003). The right of refugee clients to an appropriate and ethical psychological service. *The International Journal of Human Rights* 7: 40–57.

Maslach, C. (1982). *Burnout: The cost of Caring*. New York: Prentice Hall.

McCann, I. L. and Pearlman, L. A. (1990). *Psychological Trauma and the Adult Survivor: Theory, Therapy and Transformation*. New York: Brunner/Mazel.

Moorey, S. (1996). When bad things happen to rational people: Cognitive therapy in adverse life conditions. In P. M. Salkovskis (ed) *Frontiers of Cognitive Therapy*. New York: Guilford Press.

National Institute for Mental Health in England. (2003). *Inside Outside: Improving Mental Health Services for Black and Minority Ethnic Communities in England*. Leeds, UK: Department of Health.

Neuner, F. *et al.* (2002). A narrative exposure treatment as intervention in a refugee camp: A case report. *Behavioural and Cognitive Psychotherapy* 30: 205–9.

Oxfam and the Refugee Council. (2002). *Poverty and Asylum in the UK*. London: Refugee Council.

Paunovic, N. and Öst, L.-G. (2001). Cognitive-behavior therapy vs. exposure therapy in the treatment of PTSD in refugees. *Behaviour Research and Therapy* 39: 1183–97.

Pennebaker, J. W. (1990). *Opening Up: The Healing Power of Expressing Emotions*. London, UK: Guilford Press.

Persons, J. B. (1989). *Cognitive Therapy in Practice: A Case Formulation Approach*. London: W. W. Norton and Company.

Rachman, S. (1980). Emotional processing. *Behaviour Research and Therapy* 18: 51–60.

Robertson, M. (2003). *The Traumatic Stress Clinic's Phased Model of Intervention*. Paper presented at the Mental Health Needs of Refugees Conference, London, UK.

Roth, A. and Fonagy, P. (2001). *What Works for Whom?: A Critical Review of Psychotherapy Research*. New York: Guilford Press.

Snodgrass, L. L. *et al.* (1993). Vietnamese refugees with PTSD symptomatology: Intervention via a coping skills model. *Journal of Traumatic Stress* 6: 569–75.

Summerfield, D. (1996). *The Impact of War and Atrocity on Civilian Populations: Basic Principles of NGO Interventions and a Critique of Psycho-social Trauma Projects.* London: Relief and Rehabilitation Network Overseas Development Institute.

Tribe, R. (1999). Therapeutic work with refugees living in exile: Observations on clinical practice. *Counselling Psychology Quarterly* 12: 233–43.

Tribe, R. and Ravel, H. (2003). *Working with Interpreters in Mental Health.* Hove, UK: Brunner-Routledge.

Turner, S. and Gorst-Unsworth, C. (1990). Psychological sequelae of torture: A descriptive model. *British Journal of Psychiatry* 157: 475–80.

United Nations. (1951). *Convention Relating to the Status of Refugees.* Geneva: Office of the United Nations High Commissioner for Refugees.

United Nations High Commission for Human Rights. (2001). Press briefing given by Spokesman Kris Janowski on August 10 at the Palais des Nations, Geneva.

Van der Veer, G. (1998). *Counselling and Therapy with Refugees and Victims of Trauma: Psychological Problems of Victims of War, Torture and Repression* (2nd edn). Chichester, UK: Wiley.

Weine, S. M. *et al.* (1998). Testimony psychotherapy in Bosnian refugees: A pilot study. *American Journal of Psychiatry* 155: 1720–6.

Young, K. and Grey, N. (submitted). Cognitive behavioural assessment and treatment of psychological difficulties in traumatized refugees and asylum seekers.

Chapter 16

Conceptualising and formulating cognitive therapy supervision

Peter V. Armstrong and Mark H. Freeston

Supervision is widely believed to be essential to the development and maintenance of skills in cognitive behavioural therapies (CBTs). It is a requirement for most training courses and is a component of the training standards for accreditation as a cognitive behavioural therapist with the British Association of Cognitive and Behavioural Psychotherapy (BABCP 2000) and the European Association of Behavioural and Cognitive Therapy (EABCT 2001), although surprisingly supervision is only 'strongly recommended' as part of training for accreditation with the Academy of Cognitive Therapy (ACT 2005). Anecdotally, supervision is reported to be a key element in developing skill and there is some evidence to support this (Ashworth *et al.* 1999).

It is somewhat of a paradox that, given the value placed upon and the time invested in supervision, such a highly valued and sought-after activity is underpinned by such a sparse literature. There is a small number of useful accounts that surprisingly date from almost 20 years after the development of the therapy (e.g., Beal and DiGiuseppe 1998; Liese and Beck 1997; Padesky 1996; Perris 1994). The evidence base for efficacy is very limited (for a review see Milne and James 2000) and the key study to date in fact only addresses very brief training and supervision rather than the longer periods that are often practised (Sholomskas *et al.* 2005). In terms of conceptual knowledge of the supervision of cognitive therapy (CT), there are a few accounts, mostly making some parallels to therapy (e.g., Greenwald and Young 1998; Newman 1998; Padesky 1996; Safran and Muran 2001; Sloan *et al.* 2000). Empirical support for existing and emerging conceptual models is almost totally absent but a degree of mapping has started (e.g., Freeston *et al.* 2002; Milne *et al.* 2003; O'Carroll 2002; Thwaites 2004; Townend 2002; Twaddle *et al.* 2003; Waite and Gordon 2003). Critically, there are a number of tools emerging that are specific to cognitive therapy supervision which can support a more systematic approach to supervision (e.g., Armstrong and Freeston 2003; James *et al.* 2004a; Lewis 2005; Townend 2004). The evidence base in supervision for CT supervision is contrasted with the status of cognitive therapy in Table 16.1.

The second part of Table 16.1 contrasts how people become cognitive

Table 16.1 Cognitive therapy and supervision

Dimension	Cognitive therapy	CT supervision
The evidence base		
Explicit procedural knowledge	Extensive shared CT case lore, extensive writings	A few written sources
Evidence base for efficacy of procedures	Extensive shared CT case lore and extensive scientific data	Very limited, mostly, with a few exceptions, extrapolated from elsewhere
Explicit conceptual knowledge	Extensive written sources specific to CT	Very few written sources specific to CT
Evidence base for conceptual knowledge	Extensive and increasing	Very limited and emerging
Available tools and measures	Numerous	Scarce and emerging
Developing skills		
Formal dissemination methods	Multiple means, well structured	Limited means, relatively little structure
Own experience of activity	Few therapists have experienced CT as patient	Many supervisors have previously experienced CT supervision as supervisee
Attainment of competence	Well-structured training and supervision	Experience of receiving supervision; rare training, rarer supervision
Demonstration of competence	Competence can be established through criteria and measures; measurement of client outcomes	Competence normally assumed, based on experience as therapist and experience of receiving supervision
Decision criteria	Established criteria and intuition	Almost entirely intuitive
Skills develop through	Ongoing CPD, practice and supervision	Ongoing practice; CPD and supervision of supervision is rare

therapists with how they become supervisors. Although there are now a number of accredited courses in CBT supervision in the UK, examination of course outlines would suggest that most are drawing heavily on non-CT sources as well as the few CT sources named above. While there are many features that are shared or can usefully be imported from other supervision models, the therapies themselves may be cast within different epistemologies and are procedurally different. The number of shorter workshops is increasing but they are still infrequent when compared to workshops based on cognitive therapy. One key difference is that almost all supervisors have experience of supervision of their CT practice, but few, at least within the UK, have experience of receiving CT, although there is a growing trend to self-practice in training (e.g., Bennett-Levy *et al.* 2003). Cognitive therapists have typically become supervisors by nomination, by self or by others, often following supervision of their own therapy by an expert. In many ways, cognitive therapy spans both scientist-practitioner and psychotherapy models and, indeed, the former is central to the therapy's identity. It could be argued that CT supervision currently operates largely within a psychotherapy model, which presents a series of interesting challenges to cognitive therapy and its development both in its epistemology and its implications for building capacity (Freeston *et al.* 2004).

So how, then, do people know how to supervise? In the absence of extensive explicit knowledge and evidence of supervision, people borrow explicitly or implicitly from other models of supervision that they may have experienced in or in which they have received training. They also draw on their own experience as a cognitive therapy supervisee, on their common sense, and on features of cognitive therapy. Many of the features of cognitive therapy are indeed appropriate because it is a therapeutic approach that requires a sound alliance, and is collaborative, goal-oriented, time-limited, structured, and seeks to develop skills and autonomy (Beck 1995). It is interesting to note that it is perhaps Beck's first principle, that of an evolving formulation, that is most difficult to apply to supervision.

However, there is a fundamental difference between therapy and supervision and here the useful parallel can break down. There is an assumption in therapy that one person, the client (or more if a couple, a family, or a group), is either experiencing distress or is having difficulty functioning in one or more areas of life and that the other, the therapist, is sufficiently competent and in sufficient physical and psychological health to provide help to the client in a safe manner. In supervision, however, there is an assumption that although there may be differences in knowledge, skills, and experience, both are in sufficient physical and psychological health at the outset to occupy professional roles safely as therapists, supervisee, and supervisor. In most cases supervision does work: two (or more) functional and committed people working jointly and effectively toward some (shared) goals. Indeed, most therapists accredited with BABCP who responded to a survey on supervision reported a high degree of satisfaction with their supervision arrangements (Townend *et al.* 2002). On the other hand, during workshops that we have conducted over the last three years with over 150 people, the vast majority report experiences of supervision, either as supervisor or supervisee, where the process or outcome has not been satisfactory. Importing models from therapy into supervision in an overly literal manner therefore runs the risk of importing a style of thought which implicitly or explicitly implies that there are pathological processes in the behaviours of supervisee or supervisor. This risk is probably highest when the parties engaged in supervision find themselves in difficulties or in conflict and affect is therefore running high.

This absence of an explicit coherent conceptual framework that would allow an understanding of supervision processes has meant that much of our best experience of supervision is reliant upon the intuitive skills and knowledge of supervisors. However high its quality, the skill and knowledge is difficult to replicate, and therefore is difficult to use in the training of new supervisors. Similarly, where supervision goes wrong, or is of a low standard, there is little to guide attempts to improve the situation. The absence of a framework to serve as the basis for formulating such blocks to supervisory progress, or coherently describing deficits, can impair the ability of those who find themselves in such situations to repair damage or consistently raise standards.

OVERVIEW OF CONCEPTUAL FRAMEWORK

It is against this background, and recognising the wealth of intuitive skill and knowledge held within the community of cognitive therapy supervisors, that the authors and their collaborators have developed a conceptual framework for cognitive therapy supervision (Freeston *et al.* 2003). Through a series of workshops at the Newcastle Cognitive and Behavioural Therapies Centre, we have drawn upon the experience of both supervisees and supervisors to describe the range of factors necessary to the establishment, review, and within-session management of effective supervision and thus develop a conceptual framework of CBT supervision.[1] The framework also draws on a number of acknowledged and unacknowledged sources that the supervisors were individually or collectively using to guide their practice. In this way, many elements of the framework have no claim to originality. However, we do believe that the framework as a whole offers a degree of originality and utility.

This framework differs from more familiar 'central heating' or 'plumbing' models containing boxes and arrows for two main reasons. First, while there was broad agreement on the features contained within the framework, there was less agreement on links and the directions of arrows. Individual cases could be usefully formulated from this framework but, as one would expect, the relevant boxes and arrows were idiosyncratic to each case. Second, this model is in development. We believe that consistent linkages will be found with empirical investigation. Through both informal use in supervisory practice and early attempts at a more formal investigation, we are starting to observe patterns that may in the future lead to greater specification of consistent patterns of linkage.

The framework will be illustrated by a formulation of a case example. By way of brief introduction, the framework identifies four interacting levels and then specifies the characteristic features of each level.

The top level, learning process, framed within a model of experiential learning (Kolb 1984), concerns itself with the stages through which activities in supervision proceed in order to achieve new knowledge, skill, or application of these with a specific patient. It may be thought of as: 'What do we need to do to ensure that consistently effective learning takes place?'

The next level down, dynamic focus, tracks the minute-to-minute focus across a range of topics in the course of any supervisory dialogue or activity. While much supervision time is rightly focused on case conceptualisation, technique, and the therapeutic relationship, it is acknowledged that the context, the therapist/supervisee, or the supervision process itself may need to be addressed to enable experiential learning to take place. It may be thought of as: 'What might we need to focus on in-session to ensure that the supervisory process moves forward and learning does not get blocked?'

The third level down, parameters, outlines the characteristics of a specific supervisory project or of a specific supervision session, and includes structure, required outputs, the material brought to supervision, the evolving relationship between supervisee and supervisor, and the range of roles and functions. These parameters become set to a greater or lesser degree and will determine the shape of supervision. The setting of the parameters would happen by default as supervision progresses, but many are best set explicitly through contracting, negotiation, feedback, and review. They may be thought of as: 'What needs to be agreed?'

The bottom level, primary inputs, includes the context in which supervision occurs and what is brought to supervision by the supervisor and the supervisee. The client's impact upon supervision is recognised, as is the filtering effect of the selection and representation of therapy by the therapist. These are the raw materials from which supervision emerges. Although primary inputs necessarily evolve as supervision progresses, there are some aspects that are highly stable (e.g., gender, profession, etc.) and other aspects that are highly variable (e.g., therapist reaction to specific characteristics of a single patient in a particular session). Primary inputs may be thought of as: 'Who brings what to supervision?'

Experience to date working with this framework is that the effectiveness of supervision will be less than optimal when there is a lack of explicit agreement at one or more levels. Although the lack of explicit agreement may be initially innocuous, and in many cases of little impact or indeed self-repairing, there may be other cases where an increasing drift over time and unhelpful (rather than pathological) patterns are established. In minor cases, supervision is less effective than it could be. In other cases, the supervisory relationship may deteriorate and head towards a point where either there is partial withdrawal (supervisor and/or supervisee invest less) or, in the most serious cases, rupture occurs.

Within this framework, explicit agreement is, we believe, fundamental to supervision if the outcomes and process are to be satisfactory to all involved. Lack of explicit agreement occurs in several forms. Lack of clarity on detail within broad areas of agreement is probably the most common. Assumed agreement when in fact somewhat but not irreconcilably different positions are held is probably almost as common. Unexpressed disagreement can occur when there is a lack of mechanisms that could potentially allow agreement to be reached on important areas. Unawareness, through mutual blind spots, of areas that need agreement and tacit agreements on 'no-go' areas both prevent any agreement being reached. Finally, and we believe this is infrequent, genuine explicit disagreement may occur. If there is no agreement about how the disagreement is to be managed, termination is probably indicated before rupture occurs. The following case shows how lack of explicit agreements can cause ineffective supervision and the deterioration of a supervisory relationship.

THE CASE[2]

John is a trainee on a cognitive therapy (CT) diploma course. It is early in the second term and the date is rapidly approaching when he must submit videotape for formal evaluation. His second training case involves a young woman (Mary) with social anxiety characterised by a high degree of in-situation avoidance and camouflaging behaviour. John's pragmatic stance and professional background, reinforced by working in a primary care setting with a 6–10 session mandate, encourages him to want to 'get on with things'. He has assessed his client and is confident not only of his diagnosis but also of the client's suitability for a cognitive-behavioural approach. He has become frustrated in supervision because he wants practical guidance about the treatment of a client with social anxiety. Jane is an experienced and reflective cognitive therapist from a profession that values skill in formulation. She is concerned because she sees that her supervisee lacks a conceptual model of social anxiety upon which to build his formulation and hence guide his interventions. Several unsatisfactory supervision sessions ensue in which the supervisor attempts to guide the supervisee towards a deeper grasp of the model and the supervisee struggles to convey to his supervisor the need to 'get something done' with this client in the next session. He refers frequently to his service setting and the pressures on him to reduce the number of sessions and discharge rapidly. As this situation 'hardens', John begins to doubt the abilities on which he had previously based his confidence. He does not wish to have his confidence further undermined so he neglects to bring along a videotape which he expected would have generated more fruitless discussion about either his style or how to formulate Mary's difficulties in social situations.

Although John is generally sure of himself in many areas and comes across as confident, he is also anxious about his prospects of passing the course. His anxiety is maximised in the consultation room because his attention is taken away from his client towards the video, which he sees as recording his every mistake. He wants his supervisor to provide guidance that will address his anxiety by prescribing the actions necessary for him to pass the course. In essence, John's awareness is dominated by his training course requirements and specifically the need to demonstrate a range of complex behaviours to a high standard in one 55-minute session. During the first few weeks of supervision, he was satisfied with Jane's style and focus on conceptualisation and formulation. However, as the deadline approaches and his anxiety increases, he is less sure that Jane is the right supervisor for him; he is thinking about whether a change would be a good thing. John's anxiety and frustration can be seen in such thoughts such as, 'What if I fail?' and, 'She doesn't understand the pressure I'm under.'

By way of contrast, Jane's focus remains upon developing the formulation that will guide the intervention. She is also trying to ensure that John maximises his learning about formulation-based approaches while on the course. Jane strongly believes that formulation-based approaches are difficult to develop without good supervision. She also believes that these skills are the key to becoming an effective and flexible therapist, especially with some of the more challenging cases found in a primary care setting that will be referred to John as the recognised cognitive therapist in his team. Jane is increasingly disappointed that although John has good natural therapy skills and that although she had originally been impressed with his curiosity, openness, and willingness to learn, he recently seems to be heading towards a very procedural style of therapy. Of even more concern to her, the interpersonal side of his therapy is suffering. He appears to be increasingly directive and trying to 'talk his client into' what she sees as poorly thought-out exposure-like exercises that are at variance with the teaching he has received on the course. Jane's concern and disappointment can be seen in such thoughts as, 'He's getting worse, not better,' and 'He's not making the most of what I have to offer.'

Conceptualising what is happening

Learning process

One core assumption of the framework proposed is that CT supervision is primarily a forum for supervisee learning, without losing sight of the necessity of ensuring safe practice. According to the level of development of the supervisee, the learning may be more or less advanced, but the model asserts that all therapists remain learners and that supervision is a key component of their on-going learning. What is blocking learning in the case described? Kolb (1984) proposes a four-phase model of experiential learning, whereby concrete experience is subject to reflective observation, which in turn facilitates the development of conceptualisation of the experience subject to reflection, which provides the basis for experimentation or planning, in which the conceptualisation will be tested out in the next phase of concrete experience (see Figure 16.1).

In this case, in past sessions the concrete experience was the clinical encounter with the client, brought into the supervision room via videotape. Both parties are agreed on this procedure and John has been bringing tapes to supervision on a regular basis. Both Jane and John expected to then spend time reflecting on the important features of the encounter. But then their inclinations began to diverge. John has a sense of urgency that takes his attention rapidly to planning, when he anxiously considers what he should be doing next. Jane wishes to dwell on an interim stage of conceptualising before planning, which she believes will enhance both this client's treatment and John's training. As a result the learning cycle cannot be completed and fed successfully back into treatment. The block to learning can therefore be understood as a divergence in learning processes between supervisor and supervisee.

At this first level, therefore, it is proposed that blocks to learning can be understood in terms of over-matches, whereby both parties agree on the process but still miss essential components of the cycle, leading to incomplete learning (for example, two 'doers' or two 'thinkers' together). The alternative, as in the case of John and Jane, is an unhelpful mismatch. But what other factors will facilitate or inhibit learning?

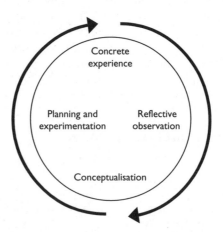

Figure 16.1 Learning process based on the Kolb cycle (1984).

Note: The progression between the different activities does not, in our experience, follow the orderly sequence suggested here. It may, for example, move from conceptualisation to planning and back again several times before moving on to concrete experience.

Dynamic focus

Learning is not an abstract process of entirely self-contained cycles; it must be about something. The Newcastle framework proposes that the natural focus of learning in any given CT supervision session rotates between six different but interacting areas (see Figure 16.2). Three represent the key features of the clinical contact (therapeutic task, therapeutic relationship, and safety[3]) and three represent factors that interact with that contact (supervisee, contextual factors affecting therapy and supervision) or pertain to the supervision process itself.

In order for learning to take place that is sufficiently coherent, complete, and comprehensive, it is proposed that there needs to be a fluid, constructive shift in the focus of the supervision session, such that this focus will accurately address areas of need, and will dwell long enough upon those points of need to permit movement through the necessary phases of learning. In the case of Jane and John the block to learning can be further understood as deriving from a less than optimal distribution of focus.

Within the overall area of the therapeutic task, there is a wrenching of focus back and forward from case formulation ('What do you think is happening when Mary [the client] does . . .?') to planning interventions in a procedural way ('What do I do? How do I do that?') and back again. As a result, there is insufficient time or attention paid to either that would permit the necessary cycle of learning to come to completion. If the learning cycle were completed, John would have a clear sense of what to do next (even if he did not have an exact plan of how), guided by a clear understanding of a model-based individual formulation.

Jane has, on occasion, varied her strategy and directed John's attention to his increasingly didactic and directive interpersonal style as seen on tapes and asked him about the possible impact on the therapeutic relationship: 'What may Mary be thinking and feeling about therapy and your work together

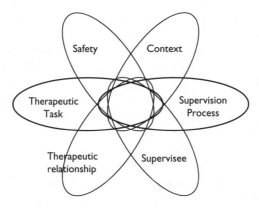

Figure 16.2 The dynamic focus of supervision.

after that last five minutes that we have just watched?' However, each time John has returned to the theme of 'getting things done' (i.e., the therapeutic task of planning the intervention) by arguing, 'If I can just get her to do something different here, she will see that we are making progress and that therapy is working!' Once again there is a wrenching between two points of focus with incomplete learning occurring on either. So, there is a far from smooth transition between the different points of focus in these sessions.

In addition, there are a number of other potential points of focus that have not been addressed in recent weeks in any meaningful way. These include the context, or more accurately the contexts. Therapy is occurring within an evaluatory setting for John because of the course requirements. The supervision is also occurring in a context of training, where the course has a strong identity and commitment to formulation-driven therapy that Jane shares. Neither of these issues has been addressed, and in fact John has raised instead his service context to support the need to get things done quickly. Although it may be true, it is a bit of a red herring in this situation. John, as supervisee, is feeling anxious, pressured, and unsupported; this has not been expressed, at least not to Jane in supervision. The supervisory relationship, that had started so promisingly, is rapidly deteriorating. Thus the process of supervision itself is starting to become 'the elephant in the sitting room' although neither has broached the subject. The problem then is not the time spent on therapeutic tasks but the lack of constructive shared focus on tasks and an inability to touch briefly on other areas when necessary. But what are the factors that are affecting the problems with focus?

Parameters

As is the case with therapy, the focus of a session of supervision cannot be assumed to look after itself. Several factors need to be in place that will enable dynamic yet constructive movement between the points of focus described within this framework. A further level is therefore proposed describing these factors. It is suggested that they can be understood within two time-frames: that of the individual session, and that of the overall course of supervision.

First, in order to determine what foci should be addressed, John and Jane need to know what they need to achieve (see Figure 16.3). Focus would then be guided by the goal, or required output, of the session and of the course of supervision. But in our case example, Jane and John have problems already at this level in that their respective goals are clearly disparate. John's goals relate to skill acquisition and passing an essential course component; Jane's relate to formulation, its impact upon treatment, and the importance of developing this skill during training. While there need not necessarily be conflict between these required outputs, the absence of explicit recognition of them has resulted in conflict.

Next, this lack of clarity regarding goals has limited the material brought

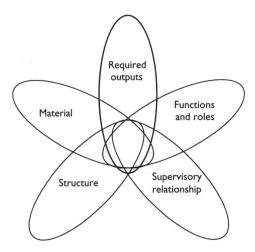

Figure 16.3 Parameters of supervision.

to this particular session and is not offering general guidance session-on-session as to the type of material to be brought. In this instance, the material appears to relate to the therapeutic task of formulation and plans that may flow from it. But since John's goals relate to his own skills and his anxieties about them, these are part of the key material that needs to be brought, in order to facilitate focus upon these vitally important supervisee factors. As soon as supervision has to deal with multiple issues (i.e., learning different complex skills and managing anxiety), the need for clear structures becomes apparent. Within the time-frame of a single supervision session, structure relates to agendas, prioritisation, allocation of time, and consideration of homework. Across the longer time-frame, structure relates to overarching goals, contracts, record keeping, and review.

Further, there is a restriction regarding the respective roles and functions occupied by supervisor and supervisee. John is keenly aware of his role as a trainee and as a novice. This is an anxiety-provoking role for him, and he implicitly requires and expects Jane to occupy the reciprocal roles of a trainer of necessary techniques and of someone who 'contains' his anxiety. Jane, however, primarily sees John in his role as a practitioner and as a seeker of formulatory skills. She sees herself in the joint roles of guarantor of standards of treatment and educator in particular areas of knowledge. She may well be willing to take on other roles, but may not be aware that this is what is required. As with their disparate goals, there is no inherent conflict between these various roles, but absence of clear acknowledgement of the roles that each expects of the other has resulted in conflict.

Finally, it can be presumed that the supervisory relationship between John and Jane is suffering. But it may also be that there was a failure to understand the kind of relationship into which they were entering at the outset of supervision. What were their expectations? Is there a mechanism within their supervisory relationship that will allow them to address the deterioration in it?

Clarity of parameters, therefore, appears essential to the establishment and maintenance of functional supervision. But, just as focus will not look after itself, parameters cannot be established without proper attention to the primary inputs of the supervision.

Primary inputs

Supervision will only occur when certain people come together in certain contexts, and what those people bring to the supervision will determine the parameters that should be set, and the realistic limits of what can be obtained from their meeting. As with parameters, it is proposed in this model that these inputs can be understood within shorter and longer time-frames. Shorter-term inputs relate to individual sessions, or parts of sessions; longer-term inputs relate to factors that will be slower to change, or may be stable 'givens' that will not change at all, or at least not in the context of a course of supervision. These inputs are summarised in Figure 16.4.

First, supervision is always of someone or some people. What the supervisee brings in the short term will be particular therapeutic problems or questions, a specific puzzle with a particular therapy session, a particular feeling state on a particular day, or a highly focused time-limited need. In the case under consideration, John brings his anxiety about his training, and his felt need for a quick fix in order to be able to submit a 'pass'-level tape. His attention within the session is therefore repeatedly drawn away from Jane's questions and directions towards his own preoccupation with the next deadline for tape submission. In the longer time-frame, slow-change factors include overall level of skill and experience, theoretical orientation, or personal values, and 'givens' are factors such as gender, personality, cultural background, and

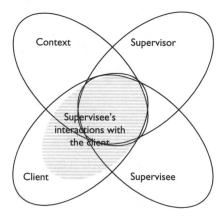

Figure 16.4 Primary inputs to supervision.

profession. Many of these can be expressed in familiar terms as attitudes, assumptions, or beliefs without casting them in pathological light. It may also be useful to think of some of these as schema if this term is defined in a way that emphasises both process and content and does not assume a dysfunctional or pathological entity (e.g., James *et al.* 2004b). John as a self-avowed pragmatist consistently tends to look for practically applicable answers to specific problems. As a nurse, he was never convinced from his basic training onwards by the nursing models to which he has been exposed, and he has developed a more general reluctance to give large amounts of attention to other conceptual models, preferring to engage in attention to technique.

The encounter is only seen as supervision if there is also a supervisor who will bring a range of personal inputs that cover broadly the same ground as the supervisee's inputs. Jane is a busy psychologist who spends much of her time in personally unrewarding management meetings when she would rather be 'getting on with what she does best'. The morning spent supervising CT trainees is an oasis in her week, when she feels that her skills are being used best. As a result, she relaxes, slows down, and wants to give full attention to the needs of her supervisees. She is unsettled as she notices the frustration she feels when supervising John, as she has such difficulty in slowing him down to her own pace of sufficient conceptual activity eventually leading to reasoned and targeted action. This also fits with some of the preconceptions she has developed about other professions that she sees as less sophisticated than her own, and she begins to feel alienated from John. This in turn yields a conflict within herself, as she has a strong sense of self-as-helper, and she begins to doubt her own skills as a supervisor as she sees John struggling to progress as she would wish him and had expected him to.

It is perhaps at this level that issues of mismatch and overmatch are most profoundly encountered. Do Jane and John bring a complementary difference of characteristics that will produce a harmonic interaction such that the supervisee is enriched by the experience? Or are they so closely matched that little is added to the supervisee's knowledge, skills, or perspectives by accessing this supervision? Or are they so radically mismatched that there is recurrent or persistent discord in this supervision, or simply no real meeting between supervisor and supervisee? At least two possible conclusions can be drawn in their case. The pessimistic one is that John's pragmatism and Jane's conceptual leanings are so at odds that they cannot form a good learning partnership. The more optimistic reading is close to precisely the opposite: both can benefit from the strengths of the other. John provides Jane with a learning challenge to her clinical and supervisory skill: elegant conceptualisations greatly enhance therapy, but how can a primary care worker arrive at, and apply, a conceptualisation quickly enough (and of sufficient quality) in the time constraints? Jane offers John the opportunity to extend his practical skills with theoretical perspectives that will better direct rather than detract from his brief interventions.

Of course, supervision is only supervision (as opposed to personal therapy or clinical teaching) if it relates to clinical practice, so the third essential input is that provided by the client. As with supervisee and supervisor, these client inputs can be understood in the short term as states, and in the longer term as traits, although 'traits' in this sense is not meant to refer only to personality characteristics, but to such factors as the nature of the presenting problem, previous experience of treatment, etc. An important proposal of this model is that the client is rarely if ever present within the supervision in an unmediated fashion, but mediated via the supervisee's interaction with the client. This recognition is crucial in relation to how primary inputs relate to parameters, especially with respect to the material brought to supervision. Is clinical material brought via case notes, via verbal report, or via audio- or videotape? And how will the medium via which the clinical encounter is brought affect the goals that can be set within the supervision?

The most obvious problem in John and Jane's most recent session is that the client, Mary, has not been brought in the same way as she has been brought to previous sessions. In his anxiety, John brings a brief verbal report of the session and a recognisable and moderately case-specific formulation which, he informs Jane, was developed between himself and Mary during the last session. Jane is not now in a position to judge accurately the degree to which this is actually the case. She is unable to critique the strengths and weaknesses of this session or the formulation. In order to manage perceived criticism, John has brought something designed more to impress his supervisor than to progress Mary's treatment. His own goals are impeded, and the possible constructive meeting of his and Jane's different strengths is lost. If, on the other hand, his session with Mary contained a good example of economic use of formulation in the context of tight time constraints, his and Jane's failure to make clear the different emphases within their practice has obstructed an opportunity for reinforcement and anxiety reduction.

Last, these three essential inputs do not meet in a vacuum, but are brought together in the context that has given rise to the supervision. An essential feature of the case under consideration is the training course that has led this supervisee to bring this client to the attention of this supervisor. This context has also played a key role in generating the anxiety that is a central piece of material that needs to be brought to this supervision session, determining goals, focus, and learning. The final piece of the jigsaw is therefore the way in which parameters can only be fully and collaboratively set by reference to a clear understanding of who is bringing what to the supervision.

Case summary

A full account of the features leading to the block in learning and subsequent deterioration of the supervisory relationship is given in Table 16.2. The key processes at each level are detailed below on p. 364.

Table 16.2 Summary of important features of the case as conceptualised within the framework

Experiential learning	
Concrete experience	Generally unproblematic
Reflective observation	Generally unproblematic
Conceptualisation	Jane's priority and strength, apparently unappreciated by John
Experimentation or planning	John's priority and need, apparently unsupported by Jane
Dynamic focus	
Therapeutic task	Jane and John are wrenching between two aspects of task, namely case formulation and specific techniques
Therapeutic relationship	Jane occasionally wrenches attention here, John wrenches back to specific techniques
Safety	Not an issue in this case
Supervisee	John's anxiety and sense of being under pressure are not expressed or attended to
Contextual factors	Contextual factors are present (see below) but have not been explicitly mentioned in recent weeks
Supervision process	The 'elephant in the living room': both are skirting around a deteriorating supervisory relationship, neither is addressing it; currently a 'no go' area
Parameters	
Required output	John needs to pass on the submitted tape by containing his anxiety and learning specific intervention techniques; Jane requires John to develop conceptual skills and maintain a standard of competence
Material brought	John brings sections of tapes that are more or less suitable for developing conceptualisation skills; John's anxiety and need to develop confidence in specific skills are not explicitly brought
Structure	In the short term, the agenda is consistently missing key items; in the long term the supervisory contract is limited, goals are not clearly specified, a mechanism to address supervision process is not in place, no recent review
Roles and functions	John requires a technical skills trainer and someone to contain his anxiety, while Jane provides a guarantor of standards and a developer of specific therapeutic skill (formulation); Jane expects John to be a competent practitioner, and a seeker of formulation skills while John is starting to fall below a competent practitioner level and is seeking procedural expertise

Continued overleaf

Table 16.2 (Continued)

Parameters	
Supervisory relationship	Started well, has fallen short of expectations, has recently deteriorated, but no current means of addressing it

Primary inputs	
Supervisee	John is generally confident, specifically anxious about passing course, and naturally 'a doer' by personality, profession, and professional setting
Supervisor	Jane is professionally and personally a conceptualiser, and committed to the type of training associated with the course
Context	John's therapy session is in a context of academic evaluation; Jane's supervision session is in the context of a training course with a particular identity and emphasis on formulation-driven therapy
Client	Socially anxious, engaged in therapy, shows a degree of complexity that is within John's scope
Supervisee's interaction with client	Initially unproblematic; John is increasingly didactic and trying to 'talk client into' doing exposure-like tasks; client is reluctant (does not understand rationale?)

1   In the learning process, Jane's and John's instincts typically take them to different points in the Kolbian cycle, thereby inhibiting adequate attention to each other's strengths and 'blind spots'.
2   Conflicting points of dynamic focus between supervisor and supervisee lead to 'wrenching' that denies both John and Jane adequate time to work steadily through stages of learning and adversely affects the collaborative set of the supervision partnership. The breadth of focus is too narrow and fails to address John's concerns, the impact of contextual factors on supervision, and the deteriorating supervisory relationship.
3   The problems with focus interact with the parameters in two ways. Considering the initial contract, the difficulty can be understood as deriving from both parties' failure to agree clear parameters with respect to required outputs (confidence, skill acquisition, and conceptual integration), material brought (the client's problems, the theory underpinning intervention, and, as required, John's feelings in the context of this course), and complementary roles within the session. Once the 'wrenching' has set in, however, other parameters are affected with negative impacts upon structure (e.g., the time given to each topic) and upon the supervisory relationship between John and Jane. In this most recent session, the material brought (a formulation in isolation) and manner in which it has been presented (no tape) have been significantly affected.

4   This failure to set the parameters correctly is further understood by hypothesising a lack of attention given to the primary inputs during contract setting and review. Neither Jane nor John appear to have given adequate thought to the anxiety and frustration often experienced in the training context in which this supervision is taking place, leading to a lack of understanding of the current state and needs of the supervisee. Neither appears to have considered as thoroughly as they might the differences that their professions and personal clinical styles within those professions may contribute to the situation (see Table 16.2).

MOVING FORWARD: UNBLOCKING THE LEARNING PROCESS

If Jane and John are to repair this problem, they need to stand back from their current wrestling match and reconsider explicitly where their attention needs to be focused. Simple lack of clarity about the required outputs of a session can lead both parties to assume agreement where none exists. In all probability they would both agree that they have a shared overarching goal of John learning and passing the course; they have not agreed on what is required for this to happen. Without clarity about the outputs they do not know where to focus their attention.

Consider the start of the next supervision session in this case. Imagine that this is perhaps a regular review session, so both parties are prepared to consider what is working and what is not. Or perhaps the situation has reached a point where John, referring back to his professional code, decides that he should inform Jane that he is considering approaching the course directors about a change of supervisor. Or perhaps Jane has access to that relative luxury, supervision of her supervision. Reflection and review in that forum has suggested she and John sit back from the wrestling match. Whatever may have triggered an enhanced awareness of needing to address the situation, where do they start?

Experience to date of working with this model suggests commencing with discussion of goals (required outputs). Fortuitously, and consistent with the useful parallel with cognitive therapy, Jane and John start here. They recognise John's need to pass the course, and to apply CT in a scaled-but-not-watered-down fashion in his regular workplace. They are then required to attend to what each brings professionally and by way of personal disposition in order to decide whether or not they constitute a potentially congruent harmonic pairing (primary inputs). They briefly consider that one constructive outcome might be the termination of this supervision project so that better matched partners can be identified. However, referring back to their initial impressions and optimism at the start of supervision, they recognise their different leanings and how their different strengths and relative weaknesses are complementary. John and Jane then explicitly agree that each will look out for and clearly signal the operation of their own and each other's 'blind spots'. Such an agreement would constitute a clear feature of the updated (and more explicit) contract with respect to roles and functions. They both agree that they will explicitly review the evolving supervisory relationship on a regular basis – it is no longer a 'no-go' area.

An evolving contract such as this would then enable both parties to be clearer in their agendas on a session-by-session basis. What are we trying to achieve today? In order to achieve that, where does our focus need to be? How shall we use the time available? What material needs to be brought and how? Structure then supports appropriate focus and learning. Such clarity of agenda-setting requires those involved to consider explicitly what learning steps need to be taken. Here the 'you-look-out-for-my-blind-spots-and-I'll-look-out-for-yours' agreement comes strongly into play. John and Jane will need to spend a little more time negotiating realistic agendas, balancing the need to cover all the areas as the dynamic focus shifts against the adequacy of time given to any one area of focus so that substantive learning may occur.

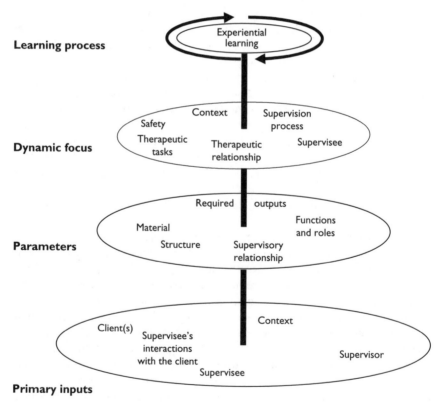

Figure 16.5 Newcastle conceptual framework for cognitive therapy supervision.

It is likely that this supervision project can now continue in an effective way. By maintaining and updating their understanding of how their supervision is progressing through regular feedback and review, Jane and John can avoid further difficulties or at least deal with them in a timelier manner. Perhaps as little as 20 minutes of review in the critical session just described and then a few well-spent minutes in each of the subsequent sessions may be sufficient to turn a supervision project that was heading for an unsatisfactory conclusion to one that has the potential to fulfil its original promise.

One further theoretical point entirely coherent with this account is that whereas the Kolbian cycle accounts for the acquisition of learning in particular instances, it does not describe the process of learning over time (i.e., the development of new knowledge and skill above the existing baseline). Vygotsky (1978), by way of contrast, provides a dynamic understanding of this process whereby the learner is enabled to operate at a level above current competence because of the scaffolding provided by an educational context. In this case, the newly complementary roles and the ability to shift focus appropriately provide the scaffolding within which John can develop both increased confidence in his techniques and fuller conceptualisations than his current level of skill and knowledge allow (see also James *et al.* 2004c).

DISCUSSION

Readers will observe that these are the kind of steps that characterise good supervision in everyday practice already. They may enquire whether the model adds anything to current understanding. This would be entirely congruent with the authors' position, which is to encourage the systematic enactment of what has previously been delivered intuitively, or on an ad hoc basis, and has varied in quality from supervision to supervision. A number of issues that flow from the framework presented here require brief discussion.

If the assumption of necessary minimal competence (of therapist or supervisor) cannot be met, training rather than supervision of practice is indicated. Likewise, if the assumption of sufficient psychological and physical health cannot be made at the outset, supervision should not start. If this assumption changes at any point an immediate review is needed. If it is the supervisor who is unfit, supervision should normally be suspended or transferred to another supervisor. If it is the supervisee, three options exist. First, supervision (and work with clients) could be suspended while help is sought. Second, supervision could be continued while psychological help is pursued elsewhere, an option only possible if the supervisee's psychological status permits him or her to continue to perform their work with clients safely. The supervision then remains focused on client needs; the therapy for the supervisee can focus on his or her needs. Third, perhaps supervisee issues could be adequately addressed in supervision without losing sight of the client's needs and maintaining standards of work with the client. In this case John's competence is not seriously called into account but his performance anxiety needs to be considered carefully. It is not generalised and only applies to taping this client in this situation for a specific purpose. It is likely that Jane and John can address his in-session anxiety adequately as part of supervision while maintaining sufficient attention to the therapy with Mary. It is unlikely, in this case, that personal therapy is required.

It is probable that Jane and John paid insufficient attention to contracting. Time spent contracting, whether this uses an off-the-shelf and sufficiently detailed pro-forma (see Armstrong and Freeston 2003; Townend 2004) or is done in sufficient detail from first principles, results in a set of parameters that would support the supervision project throughout its course. Experience to date in working with this model suggests that vagueness in the initial contract is one of the most common sources of difficulty. This vagueness is often caused by a reluctance to 'waste' time in thorough negotiation when there is a pressing sense of the need to get on with the business of supervision – an understandable urge when supervision is so often a rare resource. The essential point to be made here is that the supervision contract goes well beyond defensive or defensible practice, and beyond organisational and financial requirements. It is most importantly a parameter-setting device or aid that provides a bridge between primary inputs and necessary learning by explicitly setting parameters and ensuring that seamless and fluid movement between the various points of dynamic focus can and will happen.

Jane and John's difficulties may also, to some extent, be due to the course directors who thought that Jane's conceptual emphasis and John's pragmatism would combine well and help 'stretch' John to his advantage and to a level that they believed was within his scope. They may also have assumed that Jane and John would have discovered and explicitly discussed their differences. If the course directors had found an appropriate mechanism to contribute their views to the contracting process, the difficulties may have been avoided. Their contribution to these events is understandable. From this framework, it can be argued that there is nothing to be gained in bringing people together who are so close in approach that there is no 'value added'. Moreover, shared blind spots could lead to enlarging the existing deficits in a supervisee's repertoire. On the other hand, if the participants are too different there may be a fatal disparity of approaches. This framework suggest that a critical step before agreeing on a supervision project is to consider what experience, ability, and characteristics the supervisee and the supervisor bring. Likewise, what is the context and which particular clients or populations are being brought to the supervision and how? Consideration of such factors may go beyond those directly involved in supervision and concern managers, educational advisors, and course directors, who must make decisions about resource allocation in line with their responsibilities.

Newcomers to this framework remark on its complexity and we do not disagree. Experience to date suggests that the application of the model to real difficulties within particular supervision projects yields a much greater clarity than does either attempting to think one's way out of those difficulties without any conceptual framework, or attempting to come to grips with the model in purely abstract terms. We do not propose that the whole of this framework is needed to understand any given difficulty or success in supervision, as, in given instances, these might be adequately described by reference to only one or two of its levels. Further, it is sometimes difficult to apply the model to supervisory difficulties in which one is currently involved. For example, to achieve the level of agreement achieved by John and Jane obviously required a high degree of psychological functioning, self-reflection, and professionalism on both their parts. If the level of affect had been too high, such a discussion may have been impossible without the prior or concurrent intervention of a third party. Our initial experiential findings of working with the model (which, of course, now require more systematic research) point firmly to the need for the supervision of supervision in order to provide a forum for supervisors systematically to review, conceptualise, and plan their supervisory practice. This appears to be a need most acutely felt in supervisors at the beginning of their practice, but clinicians retain learning needs whatever their seniority and experience.

NOTES

1   The authors gratefully acknowledge the contribution of numerous colleagues, especially those in the north east of England, who have contributed to the development of the ideas expressed in this chapter, particularly Ivy Blackburn, Vivien Twaddle, and Ian James. We also express our appreciation to colleagues from throughout the UK and those from Norway, Iceland, and Switzerland who have participated in workshops in which we have been involved or with whom we have held stimulating discussions and whose thoughtful reflection on their own experiences or understanding of theoretical issues has contributed to our current understanding of the supervision process.
2   This case is a composite of a number of different supervisor–supervisee pairings of which the authors either have direct knowledge or have become aware through their roles as course directors, trainers, or supervisors of supervision. We believe that what the case may lack in veracity, it gains in its demonstration of key features. The case is based on no single individual or supervisory pair and any likeness is unintentional.
3   The authors regard safety as a matter of sufficient importance to warrant highlighting within the model, although in purely conceptual terms this relates to a particular subset of therapeutic tasks.

REFERENCES

Academy of Cognitive Therapy. (2005). *Candidate Handbook*. Retrieved May 3, 2005, from http://www.academyofct.org/documents

Armstrong, P. and Freeston, M. H. (2003). *Agreement Between Supervisor and Supervisee*. Unpublished document available from the Newcastle Cognitive and Behavioural Therapies Centre, UK.

Ashworth, P. *et al.* (1999). What becomes of cognitive therapy trainees? A survey of trainees' opinions and current clinical practice after postgraduate cognitive therapy training. *Behavioural and Cognitive Psychotherapy* 27: 267–77.

Beal, D. and DiGiuseppe, R. (1998). Training supervisors in rational emotive behavior therapy. *Journal of Cognitive Psychotherapy* 12: 127–37.

Beck, J. (1995). *Cognitive Therapy: Basics and Beyond*. New York: Guilford Press.

Bennett-Levy, J. *et al.* (2003). Cognitive therapy from the inside: Enhancing therapist skills through practising what we preach. *Behavioural and Cognitive Psychotherapy* 31: 143–58.

British Association for Behavioural Cognitive Psychotherapies. (2000). *Minimum Training Standards for the Practice of CBT*. Retrieved April 14, 2005, from http://www.babcp.org.uk

European Association for Behavioural Cognitive Therapies. (2001). *EACBT Standards for the Training and Cognitive Behavioural Therapies*. Retrieved April 14, 2005 from http://www.eabct.com/training.htm

Freeston, M. H. *et al.* (2002, July). What can supervisees tell us about supervision? Mapping feedback onto concepts and using concepts to elicit feedback. In M. H. Freeston (chair) *Towards an Evidence Base: New Research into Clinical Supervision in CBT*. Symposium presented at the 30th Annual Conference of the British Association of Behavioural and Cognitive Psychotherapies, Warwick, UK.

Freeston, M. H. *et al.* (2003). *Supervision: Integrating Practical Skills with a Conceptual Framework*. Unpublished document available from the Newcastle Cognitive and Behavioural Therapies Centre, UK.

Freeston, M. H. *et al.* (2004, September). From anointment to training: becoming a supervisor. In J. Bennet-Levy (chair) *From CBT Training to Supervision – and Back Again*. Symposium presented at the 34th Annual Conference of the European Association of Behavioural and Cognitive Therapies, Manchester, UK.

Greenwald, M. and Young, J. (1998). Schema-focused therapy: An integrative approach to psychotherapy supervision. *Journal of Cognitive Psychotherapy* 12: 109–26.

James, I. A. *et al.* (2004a). *Supervision Training and Assessment Rating Scale for Cognitive Therapy (STARS-CT)*. Unpublished instrument available from the Newcastle Cognitive and Behavioural Therapies Centre, UK.

James, I. A. *et al.* (2004b). Schemas revisited. *Clinical Psychology and Psychotherapy* 11: 369–77.

James, I. A. *et al.* (2004c). A post-hoc analysis of emotions in supervision: A new methodology for examining process features. *Behavioural and Cognitive Psychotherapy* 32: 507–13.

Kolb, D. (1984). *Experiential Learning*. Englewood Cliffs, NJ: Prentice-Hall.

Lewis, K. (2005). *The Supervision of Cognitive Behavioural Psychotherapists*. Supplement to *BABCP Magazine* 33(2).

Liese, B. S. and Beck, J. S. (1997). Cognitive therapy supervision. In C. E. J. Watkins (ed) *Handbook of Psychotherapy Supervision*. New York: John Wiley and Sons, Inc.

Milne, D. and James, I. (2000). A systematic review of effective cognitive-behavioral supervision. *British Journal of Clinical Psychology* 39: 111–27.

Milne, D. L. *et al.* (2003). Transferring skills from supervision to therapy: A qualitative and quantitative N=1 analysis. *Behavioural and Cognitive Psychotherapy* 31: 193–202.

Newman, C. F. (1998). Therapeutic and supervisory relationships in cognitive-behavioral therapies: Similarities and differences. *Journal of Cognitive Psychotherapy* 12: 95–108.

O'Carroll, P. J. (2002, July). Post-accredited cognitive-behavioural therapy supervision and training: The weakest link. In M. H. Freeston (chair) *Towards an Evidence Base: New Research into Clinical Supervision in CBT*. Symposium presented at the 30th Annual Conference of the British Association of Behavioural and Cognitive Psychotherapies, Warwick, UK.

Padesky, C. A. (1996). Developing cognitive therapist competency: Teaching and supervision models. In P. M. Salkovskis (ed) *Frontiers of Cognitive Therapy*. New York: Guilford Press.

Perris, C. (1994). Supervising cognitive psychotherapy and training supervisors. *Journal of Cognitive Psychotherapy* 8: 83–103.

Safran, J. D. and Muran, J. C. (2001). A relational approach to training and supervision in cognitive psychotherapy. *Journal of Cognitive Psychotherapy* 15: 3–15.

Sholomskas, D. E. *et al.* (2005). We don't train in vain: A dissemination trial of three strategies of training clinicians in cognitive-behavioral therapy. *Journal of Consulting and Clinical Psychology* 73: 106–15.

Sloan, G. *et al.* (2000). Cognitive therapy supervision as a framework for clinical supervision in nursing: Using structure to guide discovery. *Journal of Advanced Nursing* 32: 515–24.

Thwaites, R. (2004, September). Measuring idiographic perceptions of CBT competence: A case study observing the impacts of supervision and CBT postgraduate training. In J. Bennet-Levy (chair) *From CBT Training to Supervision – and Back Again*. Symposium presented at the 34th Annual Conference of the European Association of Behavioural and Cognitive Therapies, Manchester, UK.

Townend, M. (2002, July). Clinical supervision in CBT – do we have a model? In M. H. Freeston (chair) *Towards an Evidence Base: New Research into Clinical Supervision in CBT*. Symposium presented at the 30th Annual Conference of the British Association of Behavioural and Cognitive Psychotherapies, Warwick, UK.

Townend, M. (2004). *Supervision Contracts in Cognitive Behavioural Psychotherapy*. Supervision supplement to *BABCP Magazine* 32(3).

Townend, M. *et al.* (2002). Clinical supervision in practice: A survey of UK cognitive behavioural psychotherapists accredited by the BABCP. *Behavioural and Cognitive Psychotherapy* 30: 485–500.

Twaddle, V. *et al.* (2003, July). What can supervisors tell us about supervision? Mapping supervisor attributes to a conceptual model. In J. Bennett-Levy (chair) *In Models of Training and Supervision*. Open paper session presented at the 31st Annual Conference of the British Association of Behavioural and Cognitive Psychotherapies, York, UK.

Vygotsky, L. S. (1978). *Mind in Society: The Development of Higher Psychological Processes*. Cambridge, MA: MIT Press.

Waite, S. and Gordon, K. (2003, July). A naturalistic study of cognitive therapy supervision activity. In J. Bennett-Levy (chair) *In Models of Training and Supervision*. Open paper session presented at the 31st Annual Conference of the British Association of Behavioural and Cognitive Psychotherapies, York, UK.

Index

Page numbers in **bold** indicate tables. Page numbers in *italic* indicate figures.
Page numbers for main entries that have subheadings refer to general aspects of that topic.